The Making of Jane Austen

The MAKING of JANE AUSTEN

Devoney Looser

With a New Afterword

Johns Hopkins University Press
Baltimore

© 2017 Johns Hopkins University Press
All rights reserved. Published 2017
Printed in the United States of America on acid-free paper

Johns Hopkins Paperback edition, 2019
2   4   6   8   9   7   5   3   1

Johns Hopkins University Press
2715 North Charles Street
Baltimore, Maryland 21218-4363
www.press.jhu.edu

*The Library of Congress has cataloged the hardcover
edition of this book as follows:*

Names: Looser, Devoney, 1967– author.
Title: The making of Jane Austen / Devoney Looser.
Description: Baltimore, Maryland : Johns Hopkins University Press, 2017. |
Includes bibliographical references and index.
Identifiers: LCCN 2016041514| ISBN 9781421422824 (hardcover) |
ISBN 9781421422831 (electronic) | ISBN 1421422824 (hardcover)
Subjects: LCSH: Austen, Jane, 1775–1817—Influence. | Austen, Jane,
1775–1817—Appreciation—History. | Austen, Jane,
1775–1817—Adaptations—History and criticism. | Austen, Jane,
1775–1817—Criticism and interpretation—History. | English
literature—Social aspects. | BISAC: LITERARY CRITICISM / European /
English, Irish, Scottish, Welsh. | SOCIAL SCIENCE / Popular Culture.
Classification: LCC PR4038.I52 L66 2017 | DDC 823/.7—dc23
LC record available at https://lccn.loc.gov/2016041514

A catalog record for this book is available from the British Library.

ISBN-13: 978-1-4214-2899-4
ISBN-10: 1-4214-2899-7

Unless otherwise noted, illustrations are from the author's private collection.
Additional images described in the book are available
at makingjaneausten.com.

*Special discounts are available for bulk purchases of this book.
For more information, please contact Special Sales
at 410-516-6936 or specialsales@press.jhu.edu.*

Johns Hopkins University Press uses environmentally friendly book
materials, including recycled text paper that is composed of at least
30 percent post-consumer waste, whenever possible.

To my tween sons, Carl and Lowell Justice:
You asked me if Jane Austen belongs among the top 100
authors of all time. When I assured you that she does, you
replied, "What is she then, like, 99?"

CONTENTS

The Making of Jane Austen

Introduction

Jane Austen Matters

She was not born, but rather became, Jane Austen.

On one hand, this is a ludicrous statement. Jane Austen was an actual historical person. She came into the world on December 16, 1775. She wrote six full-length novels. She died, age forty-one, on July 18, 1817. These details are not in dispute by anybody, nor should they be.

But it was only after she died—and in some cases long after she died—that her life and its story gained its public dimensions. Adjectives were attached to her name. They included glowing words and phrases, such as great novelist or greatest novelist. Shakespeare of the novel. Devoted daughter, sister, aunt. Universal. Satirist. Genius. Gentlewoman. Celebrated. Less glowing words and phrases emerged, too: Minor novelist. Lady novelist. Without passion. Narrow. Uneventful. Apolitical. Vulgar. Elitist. Old Maid. Some phrases go both ways, like chick lit, feminine, and feminist. It's at the moment when we acknowledge the formative power of these phrases on past readers, viewers, and critics—and on us today—that Jane Austen, actual historical person, becomes the Jane Austen of prayer candles, learned tomes, and salt and pepper shakers.

Simone de Beauvoir famously wrote, "On ne naît pas femme: on le devient" (One is not born, but rather becomes, a woman). De Beauvoir revolutionized understandings of gender identity and performance.[1] Her statement also reminds us that famous women authors are manufactured creations who had an especially challenging time of it. The invention of Jane Austen has been, and continues to be, a fraught public process—in her case, a bizarre, unprecedented, social, literary, and historical extravaganza. Austen's celebrity has a fantastically shambolic past, its depths only partly and very misleadingly plumbed.[2] Many say she's a great English novelist. Some claim she's the greatest novelist writing in English. Others speak of her as a great woman writer or a pioneer or a role model. We're often probed to agree or disagree with these assessments. It might be more fruitful to ask ourselves how and by whom these questions were framed and posed in first place. Some ask, "Why Jane Austen?" We might just as easily ask, "Whose Jane Austen?"

She has been so much to so many for so long that in some circles she can pass for "Jane," going by one name and requiring no introduction. She's emerged as our go-to classic novelist, whether for smart romance, campy fun, or serious life lessons. She's referenced by politicians, actors, critics, teachers, artists, fellow writers—by almost every category of people who speak and work in public. These people, whether or not they believed they were being true to her, have repurposed her words and images. Even de Beauvoir herself participated. In *The Second Sex* (1949) she mentions Austen as a cultural-victim-woman-author who supposedly had to hide herself in order to write (124). It's a caricature that de Beauvoir had every reason to believe and repeat as accurate in the 1940s. It was a circulating myth that suited the case she was making. Many myths have come and gone in the years since Austen's death. Tracking their fashionability and staying power has taken on greater importance as her popularity has soared in our own time.

There's little to be gained, except perhaps false comfort, in approaching Jane Austen's posthumous road to fame as a straight-line history. It's not an account best laid out with a single overarching argument. The bona fide story of the making of Jane Austen has neither a comic novel's rising action, climax, and happy ending nor a tragedy's disturbing, mass killing-off. Worthier histories of the making of Jane Austen must take on strands, offshoots, and contradictions. In this book, I set out to describe particularly important stories of her making as they unfolded in culturally significant zones. Each chapter digs into images, texts, people, and institutions of Austen, describing contributions, debates, and patterns over time and seeking places that we haven't yet scrutinized or scrutinized enough. The story of the making of Jane Austen ought to weigh more heavily on matters such as book illustration, dramatization, early film, and uses by politicians, activists, and teachers, rather than on the musings of literary critics ensconced in academic communities.

Despite a massive amount of scholarship and commentary on Austen, we've only just begun to offer better histories of her legacy, especially for anything pop culture–related that happened prior to 1995. We like to talk about Austen's film adaptations of the past decades above all else, but we often describe them as if they arose only out of the original novels and their own present. That's simply not the case. As the chapters of this book show, their characterizations and visual patterns are almost always indebted to earlier films, dramatizations, and even book illustrations. We imagine that fictionalized biopics like *Becoming Jane* (2007) and *Miss Austen Regrets* (2008) are something newfangled, yet a play copyrighted in 1919 and performed in New York in 1932, *Dear Jane*, sounds many of the same notes. It also has a fascinating queer history to its credit, as we'll see in chapter 6.

Many believe our own era deserves credit for discovering Austen's potential as an inspiration for what we call girl-power feminism. We're wrong. We'll see in chapter 4 how countless *Pride and Prejudice*-inspired amateur theatricals of the 1890s taught women not only elocution and acting but led them to ventriloquize Austen's most fervent domestic protest speeches. Their Austen was an author invested in female independence, self-determination, and forceful public oration. Still, the amateur dramatizations did not offer an uncontested view of Austen. School textbooks of the same era described her as a placid and pious woman who lived a life of quiet retirement, as we'll see in chapter 11. Late nineteenth-century students of acting and public speaking and students of English literature were getting Austens that were entirely at odds.

It sounds impossible, but Jane Austen has been and remains a figure at the vanguard of reinforcing tradition *and* promoting social change. In early 1900s London, when elite men were drinking, singing, and calling Austen an apolitical author in their private men's clubs (chapter 8), suffragists were marching through the streets outside with her name emblazoned on a banner (chapter 9). One marcher—the first to play Jane Austen on stage, the first to codirect a Jane Austen dramatization for the legitimate stage, and the first professional actor to play Elizabeth Bennet—even participated in a suffragist protest that threw rocks at the clubmen's windows, in order to gain attention and provoke arrest. Each group saw its image of Austen as the right one, although these versions of the author couldn't have been more different. For more than a century, Austen has been an inspiration, role model, and mascot for groups that have otherwise had little in common. In some situations, and at some moments, Austen has been presented as gloriously conservative. At others, she's described as unflinchingly progressive. No wonder it's exceptionally difficult to tell the history of her image, reputation, and legacy with any nuance.

Whatever we make of her, Austen comes to us now as a household name, with greater recognition than any other author writing in England not named William Shakespeare.[3] She also has the most creative, active, visible followers, unless you count all of the world's Renaissance Faires as Shakespearean fan sites. (Let's agree to leave J. K. Rowling's Harry Potter novels out of the running for the designation "classic" for a generation or two.) Unlike celebrities of her day and afterward who were deeply involved in the creation, repetition, and extension of their public images, Austen—the actual person—had very little to do with hers. Her anonymously published novels were at first considered merely very good examples of their then-little-respected genre. She was revealed as their author the year after she died, in her brother Henry Austen's hagiographic preface to *Northanger Abbey* and *Persuasion* (1818).

Her literary reputation, then, was created almost entirely posthumously, first by her siblings, familial descendants, and a few reviewers, involving what we'd now call celebrity endorsements, logrolling quotes, trash talk, commercial efforts, and enthusiast activities. Austen's legendary status was also driven forward in part by being mentioned, discussed, beloved, and detested by luminaries of the nineteenth and early twentieth centuries, whose words, once made public, were repeated ad nauseam. Their assessments were often reported reductively or crudely: Sir Walter Scott (loved, jealously), Charlotte Brontë (hated, jealously), Thomas Babington Macaulay (loved, excessively), Mark Twain (hated, unclear), Henry James (loved, unclear), Rudyard Kipling (loved, cheekily), Virginia Woolf (loved, condescendingly), and Winston Churchill (loved, narrowly). The Famous noticing her at all has served as evidence of Austen's importance, longevity, and centrality. But "we" cannot just look at "them" from the outside. In a sense, all of us who talk about or repurpose her become a part of her legacy. Saying this isn't meant to give those of us who describe or use her too much power. It's to suggest that we do indeed have power—over *her* even—just as our invoking her gives her a kind of power over *us*.

Jane Austen has taken many shapes and forms, as we'll see over the course of this book. One near constant is that her imagined intimacy with audiences has been described as of the coziest, quotidian, familial kind.[4] Some of us describe her as if we know her personally. Some talk about her characters as if they are real people or compare people in our lives to those in her novels. She's certainly not the only author for whom these practices exist. It's just that Janeites have taken this kind of thing to another level. We've created an industry out of visiting her places and then staunchly defended or laughed at ourselves for doing it. Or both at once. What is Shannon Hale's clever novel (later made into a film) *Austenland* (2007) about, if not the hilarious yet serious ways that some of us want long-dead authors like Austen to fulfill present needs and desires? How did Jane Austen, and we, get here? The following chapters set out to answer that question with newly identified patterns of representation, stories of pioneering individuals, and hard evidence.

One place it all started was with a powerful moniker. In the first decades of Austen's wide celebrity, some conceived of her not just as "Jane" but as a close relative. No nickname became more influential in the making of her reputation than that of Aunt Jane. There were other nicknames, too, such as dear Jane and St. Jane, but one of the author's first and furthest-reaching pet names turned her into an aunt. Scott had been the Wizard of the North, and Shakespeare the Bard of Avon, but Austen would end up on the receiving end of a name far more intimate and domestic, less tied to any particular geographical place.[5] The label Aunt Jane suited what were then the most repeated stories of her life and the most valued qualities of her fiction—their reassuring moral safety, their genius with precious little details, and their unobtrusive charm.

The safe, beloved auntie myth was formed in part by twisting Austen's own words. She wrote a private letter to her nephew, comparing her own writing to a "little bit (two Inches wide) of Ivory on which I work with so fine a Brush, as produces little effect after much labour."[6] It was a tongue-in-cheek line—evidenced by the fact that it's communicated in the course of telling a joke about theft, of all things! But Austen's "bit of ivory" quip, "famous, if not mindlessly overused,"[7] has been intoned and recycled with the utmost seriousness, inviting readers to envision her as a miniature, modest, familial author, working on a small piece of ivory to create a portable portrait. These were just the sort of objects an unobjectionable aunt might be assumed to deal in, in literary technique and in life. Where Austen's public image was concerned, the idea of a harmless genius aunt who was comfortable in her own two inches of the world came to be writ astonishingly large. One late twentieth-century critic refers to Austen as "the most active and successful aunt in our literary history," a claim that ought to be seen as more problematic than praiseful.[8]

In the late nineteenth century, aunt was but one Austen nickname. Her other monikers invoked literary status and authorship, for example, the

Shakespeare of Prose.[9] It's important to note that she wasn't the first woman author who'd been called a Shakespeare of something. Bestselling Gothic novelist Ann Radcliffe (1764–1823) was known to some as the Shakespeare of Romance Writers (Frye 319). One-time celebrity poet and dramatist Joanna Baillie (1762–1851) occasionally went by The Female Shakespeare or Shakespeare in Petticoats (318). (Baillie's nickname was a tradition said to begin with Scott.[10]) George Eliot was for a time also in the running for the title female Shakespeare.[11] As this nickname-jockeying was happening, some Victorians were loudly denouncing the notion that any woman could be the Shakespeare or the female Shakespeare of anything.[12] It didn't help that the two most famous British male eighteenth-century novelists, Samuel Richardson (1689–1761) and Henry Fielding (1707–54), each held a longstanding claim to the honor of the sobriquet Shakespeare of Novelists.[13] Some commentators tried to give Austen a link to Shakespeare's greatness in a way that doubly (and literally) belittled her, calling her "a female Shakespeare in miniature" or "a little female Shakespeare."[14] But nothing gained more traction in the formation of her early public image as a celebrity author than Aunt Jane.

Previous critics have described the emergence and repetition of Aunt Jane as a sign that her collateral descendants wanted to prop up her polite, conservative reputation. For a time, it worked. Austen descendants steered the conversation in safer, milder directions. But the label Aunt Jane would eventually spin out of familial control. By the early twentieth century, Aunt Jane would prove more than an inconsequential echo of reputation-protective or name-dropping descendants. It would become a politicized riff. Some today may be tempted to ridicule anyone in the past who referred to Austen as Aunt Jane, seeing that choice as unserious or as insufficiently scholarly. We ought to check that impulse. Nothing makes that clearer than a look behind the circumstances of the production of the groundbreaking book, *Jane Austen: Her Homes and Her Friends* (1902), by the sisters Constance Hill (1844–1929) and Ellen G. (Gertrude) Hill (1841–1928).

The larger story of how Aunt Jane came about over the course of the nineteenth century is one now well told. After Austen died in 1817, the management of her writings and the curation of her public image fell at first to her surviving siblings. Two were especially influential: Henry Austen (1771–1850), her soldier-turned-failed-banker-turned-clergyman brother, and Cassandra Austen (1773–1845), her only sister, closest confidante, and literary-artistic collaborator. By the mid-nineteenth century, as Austen's reach began to extend further into the reading public, all of the Austen siblings followed their sister to the grave. Their surviving children, her nieces and great-nieces and, especially, her nephews and great-nephews, would try to shepherd her legacy from there forward, but they had to rely on publishers, critics, and illustrators, too. These people and organizations had their own agendas.

Austen descendants published two landmark books that tried to set the tone, if not the stage, for her late nineteenth-century reception and gradually growing fame. First was the biography, the *Memoir of Jane Austen* (1870), by her nephew James Edward Austen-Leigh (1798–1874). Second was the first edition of the *Letters of Jane Austen* (1884), collected and introduced by her great-nephew, Edward, Lord Brabourne (1829–93).[15] These men, naturally enough, referred to Austen as Aunt Jane. She *was* their Aunt Jane. Calling her Aunt in print not only advertised their intimacy; it underwrote their right to speak about her life and writings. The effects of this naming would become more profound. The phrase Aunt Jane was quoted approvingly over decades of subsequent Austen criticism and biographies. Dubbing the Aunt Jane years as the origin of the "Jane Austen myth," Emily Auerbach argues that we're "still feeling the effects" of it.[16] The notion of Austen's safe innocuousness may have been quick to mutate, but it was slow to die.

These first two family-authored works promoted their author-ancestor as a very particular kind of aunt—the cheerful, pious, domestic, polite, maiden aunt. She was, as readers were assured at every turn, the opposite of the sour, jealous, busybody old maid. Victorian single women had come in for special cultural vitriol, referred to not only as spinsters but as surplus or redundant women. J. E. Austen-Leigh describes Aunt Jane's life as one "singularly barren . . . of events," not an innocent word choice (1). He takes great pains to make Aunt Jane out to be a friendly, prim gentlewoman. A few lines sum up his agenda: " 'Aunt Jane' was the delight of all her nephews and nieces. We did not think of her as being clever, still less as being famous; but we valued her as one always kind, sympathizing, and amusing" (3–4). It's adorable that Aunt Jane wrote those clever, famous novels, Austen-Leigh suggests, but what you really need to know about her is that she was a nice lady.

This was pigeonholing her, plain and simple. We can see this by comparing Austen-Leigh's typecasting to one used in a work of fiction from earlier in the period, *The Maiden Aunt* (1849), a novel by Menella Bute Smedley (1820–1877). Its practically-perfect-in-every-way protagonist is described as "one of a class, which, fortunately for mankind, is neither small, nor rare. She was a Maiden Aunt, and she possessed that cheerful unselfishness, that indefatigable activity in the service of others, those warm, ready, and expansive affections, which we are enabled, by happy experience, to pronounce the appropriate characteristics of her genus."[17] It gets deeper. The phrase Aunt Jane wasn't coined by Austen-Leigh. Many adults would have encountered Aunt Jane in their childhood reading as a fictional teacher in *Aunt Jane's Grammar* (1850), by Elizabeth Warren, or as the teacher-poet in *Aunt Jane's Verses for Children* (1851, 1855).[18] In those works, the figure of Aunt Jane was an educated, educating gentlewoman, serious and pious, morally uplifting—good with and good for children.[19]

Setting up the charged conflicts about Austen's feminism or lack thereof, there were some then who bristled at the Aunt Jane image. These readers questioned whether the delightful auntie stereotype accurately captured the more critical, acerbic-witted author also on display in her fiction. Among the skeptical was novelist and critic Margaret Oliphant (1828–97), who questioned Austen-Leigh's apotheosis of his aunt. Not entirely approving of Austen herself, Oliphant suggests that Austen-Leigh doesn't give enough credence to the "fine vein of feminine cynicism which pervades his aunt's mind" as seen through her frequently not sweet, nor always good-natured, fiction.[20] However, the response of critic Richard Simpson (1820–76) was more typical. He argues in an unsigned review that the public ought to "borrow" from Austen-Leigh the "title" and "recognise her officially as 'dear Aunt Jane.'"[21] His call was certainly answered. But as Aunt Jane was recycled beyond the family circle, the phrase came to carry more complicated meanings. Taking up the nickname, writers reformed it for their own purposes, using it to describe something other than a domestic, unambitious, cheerful figure.

This brings us back to Constance and Ellen Hill, among the most powerful revisers of the name Aunt Jane. Their best-selling book, *Jane Austen: Her Homes and Her Friends* (1902), offers a merry concatenation of details and stories, as many have ably noted. Constance wrote and Ellen illustrated the work.[22] Their book describes real places, using Austen's own writings. It quotes liberally from other sources, especially from Austen-Leigh's *Memoir* and Brabourne's Austen *Letters*. The Hills even consulted Austen's unpublished writings in manuscript that were then in family hands, a labor that Kathryn Sutherland declares of "lasting value."[23] But *Jane Austen: Her Homes and Her Friends'* main contribution is describing the sisters' own journey—an "Austen pilgrimage," following the author's "gentle steps" through life.[24] The Hill sisters claimed they traveled to every place associated with the novelist.

The Austen places they visited were then virtually unmarked with imprints of the author. The Hills take readers on an adventure envisioned not only as a trip with a purpose but as pseudo–time travel. As Constance Hill puts it, "We would now request our readers, in imagination, to put back the finger of Time for more than a hundred years and to step with us into Miss Austen's presence" (viii). It's a book full of perhapses, would-have-beens, and fantasy, in a narrative that hovers between travelogue, biography, memoir, and work of fiction. The eager protagonists set out with an educational purpose—to learn all that could be learned in what they curiously called, in both a chapter title and an illustration of a fictional road sign, "Austen-Land."[25] The Hills' Austen-Land made history. It brought readers to a figurative crossroads to meet Aunt Jane and laid the groundwork for actual signs and plaques.[26]

For a time, the Hills' book was considered the most important Austen title after the *Memoir* and the *Letters*.[27] It also shifted the meaning of Aunt Jane as a family author. The Hills' book was a commercial success, going into two further editions.[28] It prompted companion volumes, documenting the lives and sites of other female author contemporaries.[29] The Hills' book made visiting dead literary foremothers (or foreaunts) in the pages of books into a cheap, educational family vacation. Yet a closer look demonstrates that Austen descendants' much-vaunted image of the safe, domestic, miniaturized Aunt Jane is profoundly decentered in the Hills' appropriation. It's a decentering that can be traced back to the book's conception.

Constance and Ellen's author-artist partnership echoes that of Jane and Cassandra Austen.[30] But the Hills cast *themselves* as a new, improved kind of family member, proponents of an Austen-for-all-of-us. Their book refers to Aunt Jane on nearly every other page.[31] It renders "Aunt Jane" in quotes, as if putting the phrase in someone else's mouth, but its repetition shapes the narrative. Noting that Austen's fame was slow growing and her first devotees few, Hill concludes, "Now her works are enjoyed by thousands of readers who owe to her some of the happiest hours of their lives" (262). This is a monumental claim and phrasing: Austen's work for thousands, who owed her for her labor, and which produced happiness. The Hills move Aunt Jane, the author, beyond the safe modesty of Austen-Leigh's Aunt Jane. Acknowledging her "racy humour," the Hills' Aunt Jane retains her cheerful, charitable aunt-like veneer (vi). But in their formulation, Austen's reputation gains a public service dimension. Her novels are reimagined as acts of charity that improved the lives of many. The last lines of the Hills' book echo Simpson:

"We should like to close this account of Jane Austen with the words of another critic," asking readers, Shouldn't we "recognise her officially as 'dear Aunt Jane'?" (268).[32]

This Aunt Jane is designedly not from someone else's family. She's a people's aunt, a public figure, and an agent of change. She's the aunt who gives happiness to thousands. In creating that image, the Hill sisters rewrote themselves into Austen's family history/story, a bold act that came not just from a wild, presumptive imagination but from a family history of social reform, economic privilege, and literary standing. The Hills describe themselves as a central part of Austen's family legacy so that you, too, dear imaginary-niece-or-nephew reader, could picture her as your aunt. This rhetorical sleight of hand might even be understood as an act of literary altruism. Few could afford to go on an Austen pilgrimage. The Hills' comfortable circumstances made their venture possible, as spinsters of independent means.[33] Their charitable literary labor in *Jane Austen: Her Homes and Her Friends*, like Austen's novels, provides thousands of less fortunate readers with a few happy hours.

Jane Austen: Her Homes and Her Friends wears its politics very lightly, but the Hill sisters were carrying on a family tradition of advocating for women. Their mother worked with male and female criminals, refugees, and schools for the poor. She read books advocating for women's rights, teaching her daughters that women were held "in a restraint and a subjection that was most unjust."[34] It's a line that ought to have us rereading with fresh eyes the claim in *Jane Austen: Her Homes and Her Friends* that Austen must be beloved by men and women with an "equal interest" and discussed on "equal terms" (vii). The Hill sisters also had the example of their own writer-activist maiden aunts and their women's literature-minded uncles.[35] The Hills' repurposing of "Aunt Jane" ought not to be belittled as an exercise in echoing its previous presentations of her as an inoffensive author for all. Constance and Ellen Hill turned what had been an anodyne act of naming into a charitable family project verging on literary activism.

⸜

The Making of Jane Austen begins with the premise that Austen's posthumous journey to becoming an icon looks very different when we take the back roads. It looks different when it's not narrated by protective collateral descendants or prevailing cultural gatekeepers, by relatives or literati. We get a different history of Austen—author, woman, and works—from perspectives of literary populism, moments of commercial opportunism, or political and cultural clashes. All of these standpoints mattered to Austen's making. Sanctioned intellectuals and illustrious authors, even at moments when they might rightly be credited with Austen-inspired discoveries and innovations, have had an awful lot of now-uncredited help. This book is committed to reorienting our accounts of Jane Austen's afterlife, steering us away from a hyperfocus on the words and ideas of the elite caretakers of her image or on breezy accounts that mention only the biggest names. Little-studied book illustrations, artists, dramatizations, actors, early films, teachers, and textbooks, as well as the uses of Austen's name, image, and writings in political speech and activism, were critical to building and expanding her literary status. Too often these kinds of things have been dismissed as cultural detritus. The most snobbish and closed minded of our learned experts have a bad habit of telling us that Austen herself would have been disgusted by such lightweight trash put forward in her name.

That's their Austen. It's not my Austen. But it's also not the point. Whoever we say Austen is, or whatever we suspect she would or wouldn't have liked, we're writing inferior literary and cultural histories if we leave out the incredible range of people, practices, texts, and images that contributed to her complicated and unlikely trek to becoming an icon. We need more histories that put in conversation a greater number of the people who had a role in making Jane Austen into *Jane! Austen!* Many well-rounded, egalitarian accounts describe how Jane Austen became first a good enough, then a great, and now one of our greatest novelists. (You can find these books and essays described in the further reading appendix and in each chapter's copious notes.) These studies have sought to include more kinds of evidence and to widen our sense of Austen's afterlife. After Jane Austen's post-1990s cinema superstardom, many asked, "Why Austen? Why now?" One way to answer is by turning to the history of her afterlife, taking seriously the notion that past is prologue.

The century and a half of Jane Austen's legacy on which this book focuses was crucial to the formation of her never-fixed image. From her novels' republication in 1833 to the bicentenary of her birth in 1975, this middle period laid the groundwork and set out the terms of debate for the Jane Austen who would become ours.[36] Highbrow, middlebrow, and lowbrow culture makers, whether working together or at cross-purposes, collectively changed Austen's persona from that of a marketable author of sensational domesticity to an apolitical Christian-spinster moralist to an inspirer of women's suffrage protesters to a flirtatious gender-role-bending demure rebel to the hyper-heterosexual creator of the sexiest fictional man alive. Perhaps Austen was "really" all of these. Who can say—and with what authority?

Many have tried to have their say. This book shares their stories, especially the previously little-known or unknown individuals who were innovators in fashioning Austen's mutable reputation in their own day and the impact they made. They include Austen's previously unidentified first English illustrator, the eccentric, heart-rending artist Ferdinand Pickering, whose artistic career tanked against a backdrop of bullying, bigamy, and an attempted matricide. Austen's little-known first dramatist, Rosina Filippi, was also a colorful, daring director-actress, whose efforts led thousands of young women to ventriloquize Elizabeth Bennet's most audacious lines in front of drawing-room audiences. The first actresses to play sisters Jane and Cassandra Austen on the professional stage, director-visionary Eva Le Gallienne and stunning starlet Josephine Hutchinson, turn out to have been a real-life romantic couple whose queerness prompted snarky comments from reviewers. The student-author of the first Jane Austen dissertation, George Pellew, was believed by his Harvard professor-mentor to have come back from the dead. Jane Austen shaped their lives (and afterlives), but their efforts shaped her reputation in return. In the course of offering their remarkable stories, I make sense of larger-scale patterns for visualization and dramatization, for teaching and political preaching, as these forms and media radically changed Austen's image and our sense of how she matters.

The story of Jane Austen's rise to fame can certainly be told small, with the words of a select, privileged few. But it can and should also go big, offering us a reflection not only of Austen but of ourselves reflected through her, as her fiction and her image spoke to the many. That her stories and characters have been rediscovered with each new generation suggests their amazing adaptability, if not universality. *The Making of Jane Austen* tells tales of fame and infamy, art and schlock, poverty and wealth, in order to grasp her mutable legacy and cultural influence over time. It charts old and new fashions, things that change and those that endure, setting out on an expedition to redraw Austen-Land on a few more maps, across time as well as oceans.

PART ONE

JANE AUSTEN, ILLUSTRATED

[Jane Austen's] tide has risen high on the opposite shore, risen rather higher, I think, than the high-water mark . . . The critical spirit . . . is not responsible . . . Responsible, rather, is the body of publishers, editors, illustrators, producers of the pleasant twaddle of magazines; who have found their "dear," our dear, everybody's dear, Jane so infinitely to their material purpose, so amenable to pretty reproduction in every variety of what is called tasteful, and in what seemingly proves to be saleable form.
—Henry James, "The Lesson of Balzac" (1905)

Miss Austen has suffered more than most authors at the hands of her illustrators.
—H. C. Beeching, *Pages from a Private Diary* (1898)

WE'VE ALL SEEN IT at least once. A purist complains that Jane Austen's fiction is being cheapened or even destroyed by film and television adaptations, vlogs, and memes, or by zombies, paper dolls, and porn. (Just Google "ruined *Pride and Prejudice*.") A century and more ago, similarly disposed readers lamented that Austen was being done in by book illustration. Before there were large numbers of three-dimensional actors populating our Jane Austen imaginations, there were hundreds of two-dimensional illustrations that functioned in strikingly similar ways. Novelist Henry James is the most famous among the early pop-culture Austen haters, although he was not the first to express this opinion. In his 1905 lament (excerpted in the epigraph above), James condemns the cultural saturation and commercialization of all things Austen. His sarcasm might read now as amusing witticism or trenchant insight, especially if you ignore his self-serving exoneration of critics, relieving them of all blame for the "twaddle." But what's most important to notice in his rant is the degree to which he homes in on illustrations of all kinds. James particularly singles out Austen's "illustrators," and their "pretty reproduction" in "saleable form," poking fun at their supposedly "tasteful" images, as well as the flawed perceptions of the consumers willing to appreciate them. Don't believe the unsophisticated hype, James seems to say.

Did Jane Austen really suffer more than most authors at the hands of her nineteenth-century illustrators? It's difficult to prove either way, but it seems unlikely. What is demonstrably clear is that Austen's illustrators had a profound impact on her afterlife. They shaped her public image, imprinting messages and impressions that readers took away after first and repeated viewings. Those who came, saw, and were most troubled by these illustrations seem to have worried that the images would keep readers from other, "better," although less memorable messages and impressions of Austen. In that sense, at least, Henry James was absolutely right to be worried.

Many Austen illustrators came to have a far more profound—or at least a more wide-ranging—impact on audiences than did most critics, even if the best-known Austen critics did enjoy greater name recognition. Illustrations, more easily than critics, could encourage first-time readers and rereaders alike to imagine (or reimagine) Austen's novels as more dramatic than comic. They could encourage readers to see her fiction as more intimate than social or as more whimsical than serious—as works of political commentary or as the furthest thing from it. Artists had the power to lead readers to anticipate that Austen's novels were stories centered on families and conflict, or horses and tea sets, or forested estates and the natural world. Whether in single images at the front of books or in copious illustrations throughout a novel, illustrators were there, at every step of the way, confronting a reader with ways to visually grasp the text. By comparison, those few pages of a critic's brief introduction to the novel could be quite easily skipped over.

Reasonable people may disagree over whether the situation I've just described is cause for celebration or worry, now or in the past. But from our vantage point, it's hard to know whether to cheer on Henry James or to boo him off the stage, especially when you realize how many illustrated Austen editions of the 1890s were marketed as young people's Christmas gifts. Should we really blame *those* artists for going in for the stereotypically unthreatening Aunt Jane approach? That kind of edition was never going to depict *Pride and Prejudice*'s Lydia Bennet eloping with Wickham or *Emma*'s Mr. Elton drunkenly proposing marriage in a carriage. Yet, believe it or not, Austen's earliest English illustrator did select some of her most sensational scenes of domestic terror for his Austen designs. Despite what some would have us conclude, there was no univocal, collusive "message" being promoted by nineteenth-century and early twentieth-century Austen illustrators. Each artist made his (and, in a very few cases, her) own imprint on the material, each with its own potential to shape readers' first impressions—and sometimes longer-lasting ones, too.

If you prefer your Austen-legacy stories to be neatly packaged accounts of inspirational development, or, à la Henry James, accounts of going to hell in a handbasket, then you'll be disappointed in the following chapters. The material I've uncovered and describe here doesn't provide us with a tidy tale about the making of Jane Austen through book illustration. It does move us, over the course of a century, from adult-themed serious gothic sensationalism, to a glut of charmingly humorous children's pabulum, and from there to books on (and of) the big screen. The history of Austen and book illustration is a challenge to pin down. There are surprising twists and turns, but there are also insipid repetitions and unaccountable anomalies. There are nearly forgotten representations and illustrators, as well as Austen artists whose images and reputations achieved enviable longevity. No responsible book chapter on Austen and illustration could carry forward through a single argumentative thread or set out to be encyclopedic without ignoring a great deal of visual evidence.[1]

There is at least one argumentative constant: the assumption that illustrations seen by Austen's first generations of readers shaped then-developing understandings of the author and her fiction. As a result, we should consider how—and speculate why—illustrators visualized (or visually interpreted) Austen's novels the ways they did. We don't know, and in many cases can't know, whether these illustrations had their genesis in assignments from publishers, in artists' perceptions of what to emphasize in Austen's fiction, in market-derived considerations and trends, or in artists' or publishers' own life experiences. The artists and publishers who made choices about what, where, and how much to depict in Austen may not have even read her novels! (In some cases, evidence would suggest they didn't or didn't very carefully.)

What we do know is that Austen-inspired book illustrations emerged at first in modest numbers. The early illustrations would have had an outsized impact, as they had little to no competition. As more illustrations followed, the size of their impact would presumably have been proportional to their sales and distribution. Then Austen images exploded in the midst of a larger craze for classic novel illustration in the 1890s.[2] This made any goal to make a visual impression more difficult to achieve for different reasons, as Austen images were so prevalent that illustrators began to compete with each other to gain oversaturated audiences and eyes. The following chapters describe some of Austen's momentous, trendsetting, and reputation–shifting images and their artists. I focus on those who were active prior to 1940, the moment that saw the emergence of her first film and television adaptations. It was then that screen images began visually to overwrite book illustrations, although the first Austen film drew directly on book illustration in its marketing. These images were anything but trivial in the process of building Jane Austen's place in culture and society.

The example of one early critic-fan illuminates how deeply such images could shape readers. Sheila Kaye-Smith acknowledges in *Talking of Jane Austen* (1943) that "for many years *Pride and Prejudice* was the only book of hers that I had seen."[3] Kaye-Smith uses the word "seen" and not "read" intentionally, she says, because she first took *Pride and Prejudice* off of the shelf, as a girl, to study its pictures (1). She continues, "I would turn the pages and look at the illustrations, which gave me a general impression of quaintness—a characteristic I still dislike but no longer expect to find in the pages of Jane Austen" (2). This idea of "quaintness," she admits, persisted "till after I should have known better," as Kaye-Smith describes going to a dance in a costume inspired by what was presumably an artist's rendering of Elizabeth Bennet (2). "Evidently," she concludes, "my mind still carried a simpering picture based on a merely ocular acquaintance with *Pride and Prejudice*," although she then owned and reread other editions of the novels beyond the illustrated one she'd studied as a girl (2). The quaint costume of an Austen illustrator stuck with Kaye-Smith more profoundly than Austen's own descriptions of the heroine.

Only a handful of such detailed accounts survive of the impact of Austen illustration on individual readers. But even without first-person testimony, we can and should speculate. Illustrations invited readers to envision or reenvision Austen's themes, words, and meanings. Studying the history of Austen and book illustration allows us to approach her words and others' images in tandem, to look at how each works with and comments on the other, especially as they're adjacent on the page.[4] In Austen's case, these adjacencies are far more fertile, substantial, and politically meaningful than we've given them credit for.

Just how many original illustrations have appeared in Austen's novels over the past two centuries? Prior to 1975, the number can be estimated at approximately fifteen hundred.[5] This rough count doesn't include images on book jackets and book covers or seek out Austen-inspired illustrations in works beyond the six novels. By way of comparison, Sir Walter Scott's *Waverley* novels had amassed fifteen hundred total illustrations by the end of the nineteenth century.[6] It's true that Scott published many, many more novels than Austen did—the Waverley novels series alone numbers twenty-six titles—and that he enjoyed immediate fame whereas she had late-dawning celebrity. But even after Austen's standing as a novelist outstripped his, she didn't catch up to Scott in number of illustrations. It's likely because classic book illustration was itself diminishing in importance with the onslaught of adaptations for TV, radio, and film.

The differences in illustrating Scott and Austen had their origins in the early nineteenth century. In the 1810s, Austen's novels were published unillustrated, something perfectly typical for the era's fiction. In that period, illustrations signaled a substantial financial investment. First, the publisher would pay an artist a modest amount for the designs, as they were called. Then, an engraver would receive a somewhat larger amount to transfer the artist's image to a plate, often on steel or wood. The choice to include an illustration in a novel could pay off in greater sales, making the title more desirable for purchase, but it could also cut into profits. Publishers weighed one risk against the other.

Adding to the risk was the fact that novels, especially those not written by a handful of then-celebrated authors, were considered ephemeral.[7] The genre's relatively lower status also played a role in its comparative lack of illustration. The works of Samuel Richardson, Henry Fielding, Ann Radcliffe, or Frances Burney are the ones a reader could expect to find published in new illustrated editions in Austen's day. But Burney's *Evelina* (1778) didn't receive a frontispiece until its fourth edition, and Radcliffe's *Mysteries of Udolpho* (1794) until its fifth.[8] Even Scott didn't see his first illustrated fiction title until 1819, five years after publication of bestselling *Waverley* (1814). Austen's fiction sold perfectly well but not stratospherically well. She could not have expected illustration.[9]

Copyright laws mattered, too. For *Sense and Sensibility, Pride and Prejudice,* and *Mansfield Park*, the copyright would have lasted twenty-eight years, according to an 1814 act. Those novels, published in 1811, 1813, and 1814, saw their copyright expire in 1839, 1841, and 1842. Her last three novels, *Emma* and *Northanger Abbey* and *Persuasion*, were published in 1815 and 1818, set to go out of copyright in 1843 and 1846.[10] But then this latter set of expirations was prevented by another act in 1842. That act extended the copyright of

Emma until 1857 and *Northanger Abbey* and *Persuasion* to 1860. Austen's nineteenth-century reputation was shaped by these acts and dates. As one perceptive critic in 1898 put it, in the mouth of a fictional interlocutor, "[Austen's] greatest vogue came when her copyright was expiring. Any publisher who likes can make money out of it."[11]

The moving target of copyright expiration had its greatest impact on Austen in limiting the potential for a collected edition. This curtailed the numbers of illustrations. Before 1833, no single British publisher had the right to make a complete set of Austen titles. After 1833 and until 1860, only one did. Mid-nineteenth-century editions of Austen's novels as single titles, however, turn out to have been far more common than we've previously realized, and some of them were illustrated.[12] Because the Austen copyright situation applied only in Great Britain, it was in new editions abroad that Austen's novels first began to be illustrated, four years after her death. Publishers who printed unauthorized editions abroad did exactly what they liked, allowing for several artists to create frontispieces for French and German editions.

The first illustration to an Austen novel was in a French translation of *Persuasion*, titled *La Famille Elliot* (1821), with its engraved frontispiece by Delvaux, after Charles-Abraham Chasselat (1782–1843), the historical painter and illustrator of Voltaire, Racine, and Molière. Chasselat would go on to create designs for several Austen novels.[13] His illustration of Marianne fainted away in the arms of Willoughby is strikingly similar to his depiction of Josephine's reaction after learning of her divorce from Napoleon, a visual convergence about which much more could be said. But of far greater importance to Austen's legacy were the circumstances that led to her first English illustrator, Ferdinand Pickering, described in the following chapter.

CHAPTER ONE

Austen's First English Illustrator

Ferdinand Pickering's
Victorian Sensationalism

Fifteen years after Jane Austen's death, in 1832, publisher Richard Bentley (1794–1871) purchased the copyrights to all six of her novels. Bentley's foresight changed the course of Austen history, as he secured a decades-long firm control on her print and visual legacy in Britain. He successfully negotiated with Austen's family executors—her siblings Henry and Cassandra—for every title except *Pride and Prejudice*, which he had to purchase from its copyright-holding first publisher, Thomas Egerton. Bentley paid the Austen family £210 and Edgerton's executors £40, an amount that at first might have seemed large for six outmoded novels that had never been runaway best sellers.[1] Bentley set about publishing each Austen title, one at a time, in his series called The Standard Novels. He also commissioned illustrations for all of them. These illustrations, too, changed Austen history, providing the first mass-produced visualizations of her novels. They would be encountered by decades of her readers in England and beyond.

It wasn't that Bentley thought about Austen's novels differently from other works of fiction. Every Standard Novel title was illustrated in precisely the same manner. Each featured a steel-engraved frontispiece and a title-page vignette, with captions using quotations from the novel to accompany their chosen scenes. The first Austen title to appear, in December 1832, was *Sense and Sensibility*. The other Austen novels came out in rapid succession in the months thereafter.[2] Then Bentley made an important decision. In October 1833, he reissued Austen's Standard Novels as a collected edition apart from the full range of Standard Novels—obviously envisioning a market for them. It was the first time her novels came out in a uniform edition from a single publishing house, making them attractive collectibles for those few who could afford them. The publication of Bentley's five Austen volumes

(*Northanger Abbey* and *Persuasion* shared one volume) meant that a total of ten illustrations were now in print, all of them produced by the same artist.

That artist and those illustrations had an oversized but little-described impact on Austen's growing reputation. As we'll see, they encouraged readers to imagine her fiction as Victorian. They promoted a sense that her novels were best understood as familial, female focused, and sensational. For decades, these illustrations would have served to steer readers away from the conclusion that Austen's fiction ought to be understood as social, comic, or didactic. Of course, we can't *prove* that the Bentley Austen illustrations alone set these outcomes. (It's difficult to know what that proof would even look like, a notorious problem in reception studies.) We can, however, surmise that a majority of readers would have approached these illustrations not as highly skeptical art critics but as avid consumers of text and image, prepared and hoping to be entertained. They would have turned to Bentley's illustrations in all of the Standard Novels as a kind of visual guide to reading, as an advertisement, preview, or a taste of the novel to come. Readers' sense of the novel would have been influenced by looking at an artist's designs. And in Austen's case, for decades of readers in Britain, there were pretty much just these ten images to go by.

These ten illustrations circulated widely. Bentley's custom was to print six thousand copies for a Standard Novels title. It ended up taking him about four years to deplete his Austen stock, making some critics wonder whether Bentley may initially have been disappointed in his investment.[3] However, Bentley couldn't possibly have felt anything like regret over the long term. Bentley's Austen titles were republished in 1836, 1837, 1841, 1846, 1847, 1848, 1851, and 1854. The collected edition was republished twice, in 1856 and 1866.[4] With Bentley's firm hold on Austen's copyright, with regular reprinting, and with her slow if steady growth in readership over the course of the nineteenth century, these illustrations enjoyed a virtual visual monopoly for nearly four decades, at a time when there was not yet a known portrait of Austen herself. These illustrations *were* Austen visualized.

We've long known that these illustrations were designed, as signed, by "Pickering" and engraved by "Greatbatch."[5] William Greatbatch (1802–72) was an active, respected engraver, doing frequent work for the keepsake book or gift book market, in annuals such as *The Cabinet* (1828) and *The Literary Souvenir* (1828). Although now largely forgotten, Greatbatch is referred to in a nineteenth-century source as "eminent."[6] One reviewer described Greatbatch's name alone as "sufficient guarantee for all that is perfect in that difficult style of art," engraving.[7] Greatbatch did a number of engraving commissions for Bentley, from portraits by Joshua Reynolds and George Romney to illustrations for the Bentley Walpole Correspondence; Greatbatch was even trusted with the engraving of Richard Bentley Sr.'s portrait. In choosing Greatbatch to engrave his Austen designs, Bentley was giving the task to a trusted craftsperson.

Pickering, the artist who created Bentley's Austen designs, has been the greater cypher of the two. He's previously been referenced either as an unknown Mr. Pickering or as "probably George Pickering ca. 1794–1857."[8] George Pickering is the only artist of the period with that surname who appears in the *Oxford Dictionary of National Biography*, which may be what led Austen scholar David Gilson to provide that provisional attribution. Gilson's tentativeness accords with the flimsy evidence. George Pickering was a landscape painter whose only other known frontispieces were for geographical works.[9] Unfortunately, Gilson's "probably" George Pickering has slid, in many scholarly sources—including his own bibliography's index, recent essays on Austen and illustration, and most library catalogue records—into a definitive attribution.[10] That attribution, however provisional, is in error.[11]

Little-known nineteenth-century biographical sources and other signed engravings indicate that the right Pickering—the one who served as the first English illustrator of Jane Austen—was Ferdinand Pickering (1810–89).[12] The attribution has been hiding in plain sight. He illustrated many other titles for Bentley's Standard Novels.[13] Sometimes identified on illustrations as "F. Pickering," he is listed simply as "Pickering" in the Standard Novels' Austen engravings. The images themselves indicate that the same hand is at work in both "Pickering" and "F. Pickering," collaborating frequently with Greatbatch as engraver.

The identification of Ferdinand Pickering as Austen's first illustrator rewrites her reception history in several important ways.[14] First, it allows us to move beyond speculation about and into concrete analysis of the artist responsible for images in an edition that was "frequently reprinted, in different binding styles and at various dates until 1869"; Bentley's Austen editions "led the field" for nearly as long as Victoria's reign.[15] It's crucial, therefore, that we get the Pickering attribution right, to properly study him and his body of work as each informs his Austen images. Second, the attribution allows us to see how the illustrations led to Austen's books being marketed and understood as early Victorian novels. Pickering's illustrations place Austen's novels among the more sensational, post-gothic, and fashionable fiction of the

1830s, not only in their costumes but in their intimate, female-focused, melo-dramatic situations. This mattered. It may even have slowed down the real-ization that Austen's novels were in any way different from (or better than) Victorian potboiler best sellers. After all, she was packaged and sold along-side some of them, and her illustrations certainly made her seem as if she were one of their kind.

It's unlikely that Ferdinand Pickering was given the Bentley commission as a result of any special insight into Austen. Bentley had hired Pickering as an unknown artist in his early twenties to complete a significant num-ber of illustrations for novels that have little in common thematically. The Standard Novels series began in 1831 and would eventually number 127 English, American, and Continental titles, published uniform and sold for six shillings.[16] Pickering was responsible for a large share of the series' illustrations, at least twenty-two volumes, or nearly a fifth of the titles pub-lished over the course of the 1830s. Bentley paid Pickering a modest amount for his artwork. The publishers' records indicate that the sum going to "de-sign" for each volume was usually five pounds, with thirty to forty pounds going toward steel engraving.[17]

Pickering provided images for Bentley editions of fiction by William Beck-ford, James Fenimore Cooper, and Jane Porter, as well as for bestseller *Paul Clifford* (1830), by Edward Bulwer-Lytton, famous for its first line, "It was a dark and stormy night." Pickering's images perfectly suited such an ethos; they depict not only storms but executioners, seafarers, and damsels in distress. His work lingers over classical folds in clothing and draperies, waves and clouds, tree branches and trunks, and he has a penchant for depicting human figures with gracefully pointed, delicate feet. The effect is theatrical, studied, and serious. Pickering's domestic scenes may recall Joseph Highmore's paintings for Samuel Richardson's *Pamela* from a century earlier. The outdoor adventure scenes, by contrast, suggest the influence of Napoleonic-era history painters, such as novelist Jane Porter's brother, Robert Ker Porter. Pickering was working in a variety of artistic and liter-ary registers in his many designs.

His Austen images have not been widely admired, called "artistically con-servative," "rather dark," and "unsuitably ponderous" (Carroll and Wiltshire 65). Critics remark on their "Gothic romantic gloom" and "wasp-waisted her-oines" (Cohn 219). It seems probable that Pickering's designs for Austen's fic-tion were heavily influenced by his other commissions from Bentley, for what were primarily melodramatic, historical, and adventure novels. It may further explain why Pickering's Austen images emphasize the novels' most sensational moments, considering the literary company they kept in the Standard Novels series. Nevertheless, previous critics seem to have missed the ways in which several of Pickering's images do attempt to visually capture Austen's dry humor, as we'll see shortly.

Pickering (or whoever chose the scenes that would be depicted) knew Austen's novels well enough to illustrate decisive dramatic moments. These scenes tend to be foreboding or foreshadowing ones, featured midway through the novels, most involving an inauspicious event or a looming crisis. Pickering's work for Bentley represents significant, climactic scenes, especially of shock and terror, either showing nature's sublimity (if outdoors) or moments when secrets are being revealed in private spaces, such as bedrooms. Moments of terror are depicted through his subjects' eyes, in a way that may today seem so broadly done as to be almost comic but which were unlikely to have been designed to provoke laughter then. Pickering's women have a delicate quality and remarkably even features. Most wear their hair up, dark curls framing their faces. All of his figures have exaggeratedly small and elegantly placed feet.

When studied together, the images indicate a preference for representing Austen's heroines with other women, rarely in direct contact with heroes, emphasizing moments of pain, illness, shame, or emotional distress. The *Sense and Sensibility* images, for example, focus entirely on female characters and their difficulties. First, the frontispiece represents the moment in which Lucy Steele reveals her hidden miniature portrait of Edward to Elinor, as the two women emerge from a path in the wood, with a large Georgian estate in the background. Lucy's words are highlighted in the captioned quotation, "Then taking a miniature from her pocket, she added, 'To prevent the possibility of a mistake, be so good as to look at this face.'" It is one of the novel's moments of greatest surprise and horror for Elinor. The quotation invites viewers into Elinor's position, listening to these words. So, too, does the image. The face that viewers look directly into is Lucy's calm, triumphant one.

Another moment of pain and terror is represented on the title-page vignette, which shows Marianne feverishly ill. She is in bed, bedclothes and cap draped as carefully as the curtains and counterpane, a visually controlled image for a scene that is otherwise so beyond control. The focal point is Marianne's raving, wide eyes, with her one hand wildly outstretched. Elinor is draped over her sister's shoulder, lovingly restraining her, with one hand

Figure 1.1. Frontispiece, Jane Austen's *Sense and Sensibility* (Bentley's Standard Novels, 1833), William Greatbatch, after Ferdinand Pickering. RB426640. The Huntington Library, San Marino, CA.

around her back and the other resting to the side of her sister's breast. Elinor's face is obscured and angled, drawing our eye to her cheek, her long neck, and her partially exposed back and shoulder. The caption is, "Marianne, suddenly awakened by some accidental noise in the house, started hastily up and with feverish wildness, cried out, 'Is mamma coming?'" It's an illustration

Marianne, suddenly awakened by some accidental noise in the house, started hastily up, and with feverish wildness, cried out "Is mamma coming?"

Figure 1.2. Title page vignette, Jane Austen's *Sense and Sensibility* (Bentley's Standard Novels, 1833), by William Greatbatch, after Ferdinand Pickering. RB426640. The Huntington Library, San Marino, CA.

that wouldn't be out of place in a gothic novel, in a scene in which a character had just seen a ghost.

The *Pride and Prejudice* frontispiece also features a familial scene: Elizabeth plaintively speaking to her father, Mr. Bennet. The caption reads, "She then told him what Mr. Darcy had voluntarily done for Lydia. He heard her with astonishment." Pickering doesn't show Mr. Bennet's astonishment through his eyes, in a departure from his other Austen images. His second *Pride and Prejudice* illustration, the title-page vignette, returns to his pattern in *Sense and Sensibility*. It depicts two women, Elizabeth Bennet and Lady

Catherine de Bourgh, emerging from a wood. Lady Catherine grabs one of Elizabeth's wrists and points a finger menacingly at her. Elizabeth holds a parasol, eyes wide. Both women are portrayed with a single artfully placed foot, daintily pointed toward the front of the frame. The captioned quotation reads, "This is not to be borne, Miss Bennet. I insist on being satisfied. Has he, has my nephew made you an offer of marriage?" As with the *Sense and Sensibility* frontispiece, this *Pride and Prejudice* vignette gives voice to the female villain.

Mansfield Park continues Pickering's selecting out of female-female interaction. Its frontispiece image shows Mary Crawford taking Fanny's hand, leading her toward a full-length mirror set in front of a window. The caption reads, "Miss Crawford smiled her approbation and hastened to complete her gift by putting the necklace round her and making her see how well it looked." The illustration emphasizes the moment of making Fanny see, although viewers aren't privy to her reflected image. There's no smile on Mary's face, as Fanny holds up the necklace, appearing to admire it—and herself—in a way that doesn't square with the original novel. Still, there's something ominous about the image, especially when viewed alongside the vignette for *Pride and Prejudice*. Mary's grabbing the heroine's hand looks a little like Lady Catherine's doing so to Elizabeth.

The *Mansfield Park* title-page vignette, in its use of male characters only, presents an anomaly in Pickering's work, although it showcases a characteristic scene of surprise and shock: the moment when Mr. Yates discovers Sir Thomas Bertram (or vice versa), as the patriarch returns home and disrupts the young people's ill-advised private theatricals. The caption reads, "The moment Yates perceived Sir Thomas he gave perhaps the very best start he had ever given during the whole course of his rehearsals." The line quoted is a funny one. The narrator comments on Yates's bad acting, in contrast to his believable and warranted display of everyday fright. Pickering's image communicates the humor of Austen's original, but it's possible to read the illustration without so much as a smirk if one has little familiarity with the original novel. (It's amusing, too, of course, because this is Sir Thomas's first meeting with his vacuous future son-in-law.)

There's some humor as well in Pickering's frontispiece to *Emma*, which shows Emma Woodhouse drawing Harriet Smith's portrait, while Mr. Elton looks on appreciatively. Emma is seated, pencil perched midair, studying Harriet from across the room. But the viewer's eye may be drawn first to Harriet, taking a Sarah Siddons–esque "Tragic Muse" pose, arm outstretched and mouth a little bit open. Mr. Elton hovers over Emma. The captioned quotation is, "There was no being displeased with such an encourager, for his admiration made him discern a likeness before it was possible." Emma studies Harriet, Mr. Elton leers at Emma, and Harriet looks either absent-mindedly out the window or surreptitiously over at Mr. Elton. For a reader familiar with this scene, Pickering's image presents a love triangle in which all the actors mistake the others' feelings and intentions—potentially a comic moment. But for a first-time reader on whom the humor of the image may be lost, the image shows a portrait painter and her subject watched by a curious man.

The title-page vignette of *Emma* is unusual in depicting hero and heroine together in a declaration of love. It's the only one of its kind among Pickering's Austen designs. This is the scene in which Mr. Knightley asks Emma, "Tell me! Then; have I no chance of succeeding." Emma stands to the side of Mr. Knightley, looking perhaps too demurely downward and away from him, given what we know of this scene. Mr. Knightley, carrying a riding crop, grasps her hand with his own and pleads. It could be a menacing image, like the others we've seen from Pickering that involve the grasping of hands. Informed readers would know otherwise, but uninformed readers might be left in suspense. Both lovers' feet are again arranged so neatly as to be something out of a dance, rather than an anxious, perambulatory proposal.

The Standard Novel's single-volume *Northanger Abbey* and *Persuasion* includes one scene from each novel, with the more melodramatic *Northanger Abbey* winning the larger frontispiece. It portrays the climactic scene in which Henry Tilney finds Catherine Morland on the Abbey's stairs, inspecting his late mother's off-limits chambers. The caption accompanying the image is from Henry's perspective, likening him to the villainous women quoted in the other Pickering images. It reads, " 'How came I up that staircase!' he replied, greatly surprised. 'Because it is the nearest way from the stable yard to my own chamber.' " Henry, one leg artfully draped over the top stair, points an accusatory finger at Catherine, looking her directly in the eye. He resembles Mr. Knightley down to his riding crop, but unsuspecting readers may mistakenly identify him as villain, not hero.

The title-page vignette from *Persuasion* shows the heroine again caught in an awkward moment that proves a turning point: Pickering's Anne Elliot, seated on a hill and against a rock, overhears Captain Wentworth and Louisa Musgrove talking about Anne's long-ago refusal of her brother Charles Musgrove's hand. The caption is the narrator's from Anne's perspective: "Her own emotions kept her fixed; she had much to recover from before she could move." Viewers look on Anne as her head rests on her elbow. Her eyes are closed cr cast down, much like Emma's were. Anne's feet are outspread in a manner suggesting fatigue or fainting. The image beautifully captures Anne's status as an outsider heroine for whom readers are meant to have sympathy.

Seen quantitatively, Pickering's Austen images focus overwhelmingly on female characters. His ten designs feature a total of twenty-three figures, fifteen of whom are women and eight of whom are men, making them 65 percent female. One, the vignette for *Mansfield Park*, features three men. There are more female villains or rivals depicted than male heroes, four compared to two or three. There are rarely more than two figures to an image. No group or social scenes are ever chosen. Later Bentley editions of Austen, those published after 1869, reproduced only Pickering's frontispieces, leaving out the vignettes. When the five frontispieces are studied together, the images are three-quarters female; only one of the five, *Northanger Abbey*'s, features a hero. Pickering's illustrations provided the basis for reengraved frontispieces in American editions, too, experiencing, in those derivative versions, a circulation abroad.[18] Over the course of the nineteenth century, thousands of new readers would have been invited to approach Austen's novels through Pickering's images, expecting a focus on put-upon young women, villainous-looking rivals, and sensationalized domestic conflict. It may well have led early audiences to downplay or misjudge the importance of humor, irony, sociality, or social criticism in her fiction.

Pickering's Austen illustrations are also noteworthy for employing then-contemporary hairstyles and costuming, rather than historically accurate Regency fashions. Pickering's women sport the large, flowing skirts, with puffed-sleeves and tight, neck-plunging bodices, gathered at the waists, of his era, rather than the empire-waisted and loose-flowing gowns of the earlier nineteenth century. The choice to put Austen's characters in the fashions of the 1830s was not peculiar to Pickering's Austen novels. He rendered almost all of his human figures in the Standard Novels illustrations in contemporary clothing, with exceptions being made for fiction set further back in the eighteenth-century past. Critics Carroll and Wiltshire note that this practice of putting Austen's characters in 1830s dress at first must have helped her novels seem more fresh and timely. Doing so avoided "casting [them] . . . as documentaries of past times or as distant museum pieces" (65). Pickering, in 1833, may even have intentionally set out to make Austen seem fresh and fashionable at the moment of Bentley's republication, whether that was his own idea or was done at Bentley's direction.

But, of course, the fashions of the 1830s were ephemeral, too. Pickering's designs, reissued as they were for some sixty years, set the stage for generations of readers to associate Austen's fiction with the 1830s. It's an interesting factor to consider when seeking to explain why, in the late nineteenth-century, Austen was so often grouped with the likes of Charlotte Brontë and George Eliot, all of them judged as Victorian novelists. Certainly, it had to do with these authors' common commercial and critical success and their common gender. But Pickering's widely circulating images, in effect freezing Austen's characters in the fashions of the 1830s, may also have added to the public's comfort in imagining her as a fellow (early) Victorian. Indeed, it is possible that Pickering's images had an even more enduring impact on the choice of Victorian costuming for Austen, carrying well over into the twentieth century, perhaps as far as the Victorian wardrobe choices for the 1940 film adaptation of *Pride and Prejudice*.[19]

We've amassed little evidence about how Pickering's images were judged by actual nineteenth-century viewers, but one prominent surviving account isn't favorable. Historian and critic Thomas Babington Macaulay (1800–59) reports in a private letter that he is reading from the Bentley edition of Austen in 1833, enjoying *Persuasion* ("charming") and *Northanger Abbey* ("a little less pure in manner than her later works"). We know that Macaulay thought highly of Austen; a decade later, he would make Janeite history by comparing her favorably with Shakespeare.[20] What Macaulay is most dismissive of are the Bentley edition's illustrations. He writes to his sister Hannah Macaulay (later Lady Trevelyan), "The publisher of the last volume of poor Miss Austin has succeeded in procuring two pictures decidedly worse than the worst that I ever saw before." It's hard to tell what images Macaulay is comparing Pickering's to—all novels? All Bentley illustrated novels? He couldn't have meant all Austen illustrations, as Pickering's were among the very few of the kind then available to see.

Macaulay especially skewers Pickering's melodramatic interpretations. He writes, "Get a sight of the Book next time you go to a circulating library at Liverpool; and tell me whether Henry Tilney be not the most offensive Varmint man that ever you saw. The artist must have read the book carelessly and must have confounded the adorable young parson with John Thorp. As to Miss Anne, sitting under a hedge, her appearance at once vindicates all

Captain Wentworth's doubts as to her identity with the pretty girl whom he had known, and renders the final triumph of his constancy so admirable as to be almost incredible."[21] Macaulay's response to Pickering's designs, whether typical or not, shows us the sort of challenges that early illustrators faced in trying to live up to readers' sense of their beloved characters' imagined looks and demeanors.

Pickering, as it turns out, faced many kinds of challenges. After the commission for Bentley, the artist led an eccentric and remarkable life. His Standard Novels designs would turn out to be his foremost artistic achievement, although records about his life and career are scant. Dictionaries of Victorian painting mention him briefly, noting that he flourished from 1831–82 as a "painter of genre and historical subjects," who exhibited at the Royal Academy, early on winning several silver medals. The titles of his exhibited works suggest that he specialized in painting women and scenes from the Far East or Middle East.[22] The rest of his artwork treated literary subjects, including Shakespeare, Molière, and Samuel Johnson, suggesting perhaps the force of habit, the recognition of a market niche, or the mark of an artist with a strong literary bent.

Pickering also tried his hand at portraiture. He was, according to Charles Dickens's letters, undertaking a portrait of that author, circa 1838–39, in a work either now lost or never completed. Pickering probably came into Dickens's orbit through Bentley, before Bentley and Dickens had their well-known falling out. Once, in a letter, Dickens mentions Pickering in the course of apologizing to a correspondent for the mean state of his own signature; he says it's the result of "writing under the soothing influence of Mr. Pickering, the author of that meek portrait still unfinished."[23] A year later, Dickens's assessment is far less sanguine. He refers to "Pickering the snobbish" and calls the portrait in progress "his practical joke against me."[24] With those anecdotes, we virtually exhaust the usual sources in which to research little-known nineteenth-century artists and illustrators.

Searching for Pickering in the *unusual* places, however, rewards the effort. An unnamed artist, writing a decade after Pickering's death, describes him as "a life student at the Royal Academy and artist of divers frontispieces and vignettes to some of the novels of half a century ago, who came from an old Yorkshire family." The "life student" part is worth unpacking first. We know that, at age twenty-nine in 1840, after his Bentley commissions came (for some reason) to an end, Pickering entered the Royal Academy Schools as a painter, and, it is said, never left them. He didn't have to. When he entered the academy, training there lasted for ten years, with no fees requested from the student. Only one's own artistic materials needed to be provided. But if you were awarded two medals, as Pickering was, then you won the right to a life studentship. Pickering was apparently one of the last—or at least one of the longest and most notorious—of a category thereafter abolished.

Further accolades didn't follow. As artistic success "eluded him," one critic speculates, "he . . . slowly sunk into a state of apathy and destitution." His becoming a permanent fixture as a life student at the Royal Academy Schools may well have been a matter of his having "nowhere else to go." It is reported that, "year after year, he pursued the same course, rubbing out whatever he had done at the end of each sitting because he only had one board."[25] Pickering became not only a legend but a target for tomfoolery. His fellow students are said often to have played cruel jokes on him. The Royal Academy Schools in the mid-nineteenth century offered a chaotic, even violent, learning environment. The students were "left entirely without control or supervision" and "quarrels, ending in stand-up fights would not infrequently take place" (Ormond 1349). Teachers were brought in to the school in a kind of revolving door, under the assumption that they would have "no time to get stale" and would provide "a variety of different ideas and techniques" (1348). This is the atmosphere in which Pickering spent a good portion of his adult life.

For a time he lived in an apartment in High Street, Camden Town, shared with his Spanish mother (which explains his unusual first name) and various siblings; he would end up living on the same street for more than fifty years.[26] Despite his not having made a great name for himself in the Victorian art world, we do have a sense of what Pickering himself looked like. His tenacious hold on his life studentship, not his own art, allowed his likeness to survive at the National Portrait Gallery. He became another artist's subject. Historical painter and academician Charles West Cope (1811–90) took a visiting duty in rotation at the Royal Academy Schools in the 1860s. During his rotation at the schools, Cope completed sketches of the students at work.

Several of Cope's images depict Ferdinand Pickering, an exceptionally eye-catching figure, almost exactly Cope's age. Pickering appears in Cope's drawings as an intense, disheveled person, near-sighted, hair wild. He seems tall, awkward, and uncertain how to manage his elbows and knees, which almost touch each other as he looks through his eyeglass onto his canvas. Another of Cope's drawings, labeled *Pickering; Painting School*, shows a somewhat more controlled man, although, again, with an eccentric, stiff stance and gangly limbs. It's interesting to speculate on whether Cope, who had himself been bullied as a boy, took a personal interest in Pickering during his rotation for sympathetic reasons.[27] Whatever led Cope to draw Pickering, it's a peculiar fact of history that we have a greater number of authenticated portraits of her long-forgotten first illustrator than we do of Jane Austen herself.

Ferdinand Pickering may have had many reasons for escaping his home life at the Royal Academy Schools and for not reaching what we'd call today his artistic potential. In October 1850, London newspapers covered a lurid story of a well-dressed thirty-six-year-old man, a linguist, accused of stabbing his mother in the neck and face, nearly killing her. The alleged assailant was Richard Pickering, son of Josephine Pickering. Offering evidence about the assault was a man named "Frederick" Pickering, of High Street, Camden Town, an artist, brother of the assailant. This was certainly Ferdinand. "Frederick" reports that one morning, after mother had called him down to breakfast in the home they all shared, he heard her screaming, "Murder." Mrs. Pickering had scolded Richard for his indolence. In response, he came

Figure 1.3. Ferdinand Pickering (1862), by Charles West Cope. ©National Portrait Gallery, London.

after her with a table knife. "Frederick" found his injured mother on the stairs. A doctor gave evidence to the court, testifying that her life was in danger. Richard was imprisoned. When his mother survived the injury and returned to court a week later, she indicated a hope that her son would not be hurt, despite wanting to protect herself from further violence.

Pickering's younger brother, Charles Louis, had his own troubles with the law. Early census data lists him, ten years younger than Ferdinand, in the same household, describing him as a tutor by profession. Later in life, he would call himself an artist and watercolorist. Newspaper accounts record that one Charles Louis Pickering, "a gentlemanly looking young man, an artist and author," pleaded guilty to bigamy and ended up doing six months' hard labor in 1867.[28] The newspaper also reported Charles Pickering's having previously been brought before the court for assaulting his (unlawful and bigamous) second wife.[29] With these details in mind, we might speculate that Ferdinand Pickering had biographical reasons for presenting fictional characters in scenes dark and stormy when he illustrated Austen's and others' fiction. The actual lives around him later seem to have been torrid.

Perhaps it is only fitting that Pickering himself, after his death, would become a character in a novel. Pre-Raphaelite artist William de Morgan (1839–1917) turned to fiction writing in his sixties, publishing several loosely autobiographical novels. One, *Alice-for-Short* (1907), features a character said to have been based on Ferdinand Pickering. The character, named J. W. Verrinder, is described as an "art-student of sixty-odd" "at the Royal Academy schools": "A strange connecting link with the past, a life-student of the schools, dating back almost if not quite to the days of Fuseli. His name occurs at the corner of copperplate illustrations of the days of our Grandmothers . . . By what slow decadence the unhappy artist had dwindled to his present position, Heaven only knew! But there he was, a perpetual life-student . . . [Who] had never completed a drawing or a study since the one that had won him his medal and gained him his position, early in the century."[30] The fictional Verrinder was said, at the end of each model's sitting, to use turpentine to wipe out his work on the only canvas he owned, in order to begin again with the next sitter. He's said to have worn always the same clothes and to have had an indifference to soap and water, leading to an unpleasant body odor. De Morgan writes, "An impudent youth once said to him, 'Why do you never wash yourself?' and he replied, 'Why should I?' and then added 'If you were me, *you* wouldn't.' " De Morgan's Verrinder never ate lunch and borrowed all of his paint tubes and brushes from others, retreating rapidly from his pictures as though to get an effect from afar, then accosting a nearby student for a squeeze of a particular color (119).

To what degree is Pickering's life reflected in the fictional character Verrinder? It's impossible to determine the boundaries. We may surmise that De Morgan and Pickering knew each other when the two men were together for some years at the Royal Academy Schools. But it's probable that de Morgan knew a great deal more about Pickering than that mere acquaintanceship would suggest, a supposition supported by two things. First, De Morgan's novel begins with a scene very much like that in which Pickering's mother was attacked. *Alice-for-Short* opens with a mother's being hit with a hammer on the head and neck, although, in the novel, it's by her husband, not her son. She screams, "Murder," and is assisted by the police and an artist-boarder who lives upstairs. Second, De Morgan was married to a famous Pre-Raphaelite painter, Evelyn de Morgan (1855–1919). Her maiden name was Pickering. Perhaps she was distantly related.

This much is certain: Ferdinand Pickering survived long enough to see his Austen images reprinted through many editions and iterations. They were his most famous, most viewed, and longest-lasting artistic contributions. When he died at age seventy-nine, a bachelor, his Austen images were still being widely reprinted. He himself was also still being referenced, by surname at least, in the advertisements for the Bentley Complete Austen. Their 1870 new edition was advertised as "illustrated by Pickering." But slowly, over the course of second half of the nineteenth century, posthumous Austen's first long-term, print-illustration partnership—Bentley, Pickering, and Greatbatch—began to lose its dominance. It gave way to competing editions and illustrators, as we'll see in the next chapter. Dozens of illustrator-publisher teams entered the field, ending Bentley's and Pickering's dominance. With it ended the dominance of the sensational, female-focused, intimate, and ominous illustrated Jane Austen. Yet some effects of Pickering's Austen images—especially his manufacturing of Austen's Victorian provenance—endured. The eccentric, slovenly, made-for-a-novel lifelong art student got neither credit nor blame.[31]

CHAPTER TWO

Visual Austen Experiments

From Lush Landscapes
to Bearded Heroes

A *Pride and Prejudice* book cover featuring a seated Lydia who flirts with three officers at once. A *Sense and Sensibility* frontispiece with a bearded Willoughby. Tiny human figures in lush landscapes drawn for an early *Mansfield Park* edition. In the mid- to late nineteenth century, Austen illustrations by artists other than Ferdinand Pickering began to emerge in print. They may now strike us as very peculiar. When Austen's novels were released, one by one, from copyright protection in Britain, new frontispieces and front-board illustrations with these idiosyncratic images appeared. They remain little known and rarely seen today, no doubt due to the paucity of surviving copies of these books.[1] After learning about these images, some readers may decide that their scarceness is all for the best. Some illustrations from this period were simply derivative. But others reveal curious innovations, depicting scenes and characters from Austen's novels in ways that shatter stereotypes and invite speculation.

The derivative illustrations are easier to explain. Victorian artists created designs for Austen's novels out of air that was, if not thin, certainly not oxygen rich. With few conventions in place, some artists just copied Pickering in substance and style. The old adage "If it ain't broke, don't fix it" may apply. But the raft of idiosyncratic illustrations presents a greater challenge to understand. One possibility is that Austen's reputation as a particular kind of novelist was debated, unstable, unknown, or malleable among artists, publishers, and reading audiences, creating much more of an "anything goes" historical moment. Some artists and publishers seemed almost to be casting about for new Austen representations that would strike a chord with audiences. They seem to have sought out images that would stick. As it turns out, very few did. This mid-nineteenth-century moment is sometimes called the "first golden age" of book illustration, but for Austen it was not.

The Austen illustrations that echoed Pickering prove his impact. American and British publishers from this period include illustrations in their single editions that are "reminiscent of those of the Bentley 'Standard Novels' issues of 1833, on which they may be based," as David Gilson puts it.[2] It's an assessment especially accurate for describing the images brought out by publisher George Routledge in its Railway Library series. These books themselves were imitative objects, designed for sale at bookstalls in train stations, copying the Parlour Library series.[3] Later editions in the Railway Library use wood-engraved illustrations on their front boards, in a style that came to be called "yellowback." These books seemed to do very well in the market, if only because they were cheap. Yellowbacks sold at a fraction of the price—one or two shillings—whereas Bentley's (formerly the "regulation cheap fiction") had gone for five or six.[4] Some yellowbacks also include interior illustrations.

One single title that deserves description in this context is Routledge's *Pride and Prejudice* (1851), with its frontispiece by Sir John Gilbert (1817–97). Gilbert would become a noted painter and engraver, creating a slew of designs—more than eight hundred—for a three-volume edition of Shakespeare.[5] Both prolific and successful, Gilbert may have known Pickering from their overlapping years at the Royal Academy Schools.[6] (Of course, nearly every nineteenth-century artist studying there would have overlapped some period of years with the perpetual student.) Gilbert was, in any case, at first following in Pickering's footsteps in illustrating Austen, before far outperforming him in a decades-long, successful career as an artist. Even with his large body of work, Gilbert brought to Austen and his other illustrations interpretations that weren't necessarily appreciated or enduring. Late nineteenth-century Austen critic Austin Dobson (1840–1921) would later make fun of Gilbert as old fashioned. Dobson has scorn for Gilbert's plain images, calling them ignorant of value, tone, and point of view.[7]

It's likely that George Routledge didn't fret overmuch about Gilbert's artistry. The publisher's approach to single Austen titles in the 1850s was hardly aiming for high quality or originality. Routledge advertised its own Standard Novels by echoing Bentley's earlier formula, touting that its (cheaper) titles featured an illustration by Gilbert. Gilbert's body of work is generally considered successful by today's critics, despite Dobson's snarkiness. One recent critic calls Gilbert an "illustrator of strength; especially in the area of historical

Figure 2.1. Frontispiece, Jane Austen's *Pride and Prejudice; and Sense and Sensibility. With an illustration by John Gilbert.* London: George Routledge & Co, 1851.

romance—an exciting, swashbuckling and often dramatic performer and one who, by sheer force of personality, can impress the reader with a thorough understanding of the literature." The critic continues, "Without a trace of facetiousness [Gilbert] may be seen as the Errol Flynn of mid-nineteenth-century literature."[8] It is amusing to imagine an artist in the mold of Errol Flynn, the early adventure film actor best known for his Robin Hood, illustrating Jane Austen.

The assessment may allow us to understand better why Gilbert's *Pride and Prejudice* frontispiece is so lifeless. Perhaps he didn't know what to do with a novel of manners. Gilbert's bonneted, flat-faced Elizabeth walks blankly through a wood, reading Darcy's letter. Wearing a neat Victorian dress, carrying a handkerchief, and wrapped in a shawl, she looks more like Little Red Riding Hood than a formidable heroine. Gilbert's illustration is a pale, emotionless half imitation of Pickering's image of Elizabeth in the woods. Pickering's design had featured her deep in conflict with Lady Catherine. Gilbert's Elizabeth, however, is tediously alone. She reveals little vivacity, resembling instead a forlorn damsel in distress. Elizabeth's lackluster depiction may even have arisen from Gilbert's chauvinism. As Thomas Wilcox puts it, "The chivalry [Gilbert] had glorified in fifty years of picture-making was based on the firm belief in the superiority of men over women."[9] Gilbert was not, from that vantage point, a very propitious choice for illustrating Elizabeth or Austen. He created a meek heroine who seems to be crying out for a swashbuckling rescuer. That visual version of her did not survive long in the Austen illustration corpus.

Gilbert's Austen image may now seem intriguingly boring, but others were just plain odd. Chapman and Hall's yellowback edition of *Pride and Prejudice* (1870) depicts a scene not even really in the novel. It's a cover illustration of Lydia Bennet at Brighton Camp, seated in front of the officers' tents.[10] In the novel itself, Lydia fantasizes that, once she gets to Brighton, she'll talk to six officers at once. The Chapman and Hall illustration (unsigned) shows her with a paltry three. One critic describes these yellowback-era cover illustrations as "surprisingly attention grabbing."[11] Another unusual (and also unsigned) image appears in Boston publisher Ticknor and Fields's dual edition of *Sense and Sensibility* and *Persuasion* (1863). It's a wood-engraved frontispiece, captioned "Willoughby's Farewell." The image represents a pretty, if generic, Marianne in Victorian dress with her hair gathered in a bun. She clasps the hand of a tall, dark, and perhaps handsome Willoughby. It is difficult to gauge his attractiveness, because he's presented from behind. His most noticeable feature is his beard. He may be the first bearded Willoughby—a depiction of that hero-turned-rake that did certainly not stick. Marianne shows no sign of spirit, fire, or romance, and Willoughby looks more like a clerk than a cad. This is one of those images of which we might skeptically wonder, "Did the artist really read the book?"

One landmark Austen edition from the period suggests greater artist involvement and direct engagement with the text: Alexander Francis Lydon (1836–1917) and his designs for Groombridge & Sons' *Mansfield Park* (1875). That edition has the claim to fame of being the first to go beyond a frontispiece and title-page vignette, something that took a full forty years after

WILLOUGHBY'S FAREWELL.   P. 270,

Figure 2.2. Frontispiece, Jane Austen's *Sense and Sensibility and Persuasion* (Boston: Ticknor and Fields, 1863), by unknown artist.

Pickering, and sixty years after first publication, to happen (Gilson, "Later Publishing" 135). Making the edition even more unusual is that it was a one-off volume; Groombridge & Sons brought out no other Austen novels. A publishing house that specialized in nonfiction titles, Groombridge made its name through lavishly illustrated editions of birds and fish, county seats, and ruined abbeys. The latter efforts were led by its star printer-engraver Benjamin Fawcett (1808–93). Fawcett's protégé was the younger Lydon, who went by the name Francis.[12]

How and why did Groombridge move from fish and fowl into the Austen market, and why was Lydon chosen to illustrate one of her novels? The publisher had dabbled in literary titles, including the Groombridge Classics series, "illustrated with vignette engravings," and its Miniature Classics, pitched to a growing student book market. Groombridge had also produced, with Fawcett and Lydon, a popular volume, *Gems from the Poets* (1860). Lydon had further literary experience, having done designs for single-volume works of Daniel Defoe, John Bunyan, Oliver Goldsmith, and James Fenimore Cooper. Knowing this, Groombridge's bringing out its *Mansfield Park*, with drawings by A. F. Lydon, looks a little less peculiar. The volume was marketed as an exemplar of artistic innovation. The publisher plugs its inclusion of "tint engravings in a new style." Gilson notes that the engravings were reproduced "apparently, lithographically, in tones of purplish grey" ("Later Illustrations" 135). The advertisement emphasized, "Be careful to order Groombridge's Edition, as it is the only one issued in this style." The book was presented as a cutting-edge artistic product, a collector's item.

Choosing *Mansfield Park* from among Austen's six novels might seem unusual for this purpose, because it's rarely her most acclaimed or beloved title today. But that novel ranked as her best for some nineteenth-century readers. We can see the appeal of *Mansfield Park* in an essay published in the *Atlantic Monthly* in 1863 and much reprinted thereafter. It describes an unattributed anecdote that "a party of distinguished literary men met at a country-seat." When "discussing the merits of various authors, it was proposed that each should write down the name of that work of fiction which had given him the greatest pleasure." On opening the slips of paper, "*seven* bore the name of 'Mansfield Park.'"[13] That this was an exercise in a country house may be the key detail. *Mansfield Park* might well occur to and appeal to men gathering in a provincial retreat. But it was also a male preference that would survive some years as a niche Janeite identity. Logan Pearsall Smith, for example, defined himself as a "Mansfield Parker" in 1936.[14] In 1875, though, a main point of interest for Groombridge may have been that *Mansfield Park* fit nicely alongside its geographical books.[15] The illustrations show that fictional place and the natural world were central to Lydon's vision of Austen.

Lydon brought his experience illustrating nature to *Mansfield Park*. The volume is in a gilt-edged, gift-book style, including a decorated title page and seven illustrated scenes. In three of these illustrations, the people are presented in miniature, dwarfed in relation to the English landscape. His illustrations include a total of six female and four male figures, most often either solo or in a courtship relation, but almost all overwhelmed in size by the natural world. It's a scale that may strike us today as an unusual choice for Austen. Why would novels now valued most for their characterizations include so many illustrations in which the characters are miniaturized against woods, estates, and distant church steeples? It's an emphasis that suggests an understanding of Austen that did not become mainstream—one that sees her tied to nature and geographical place, rather than to character and family conflict. It's almost an anti-Pickering Austen. Lydon's illustrations offer an artistic vision that helps us to reflect on what it would mean to have learned to read Austen's novels as fiction that emphasizes setting and landscape. It's clearly Lydon's dominant visual sense of her novel, and it ought to give us some pause.

Lydon's designs are detailed and striking. The scenes are labeled with page numbers that correspond to actions in the novel, which his illustration sets out to depict. A close examination of the frontispiece may stand in for the spirit of Lydon's entire body of design work on Austen. That image is captioned "p. 64," pointing reader-viewers to the scene in which Fanny Price, waiting for her turn to get her needed exercise on horseback, suspects that she's been forgotten by her cousin (and love interest) Edmund Bertram. Edmund has gone riding with his romantic interest Mary Crawford and has not returned on time with Fanny's promised horse. The novel's page 64 informs us that Fanny "could look down the park, and command a view of the Parsonage and all its desmenes, gently rising beyond the village road," and that what she sees before her is "a happy party." It's "Edmund and Miss Crawford both on horse-back, riding side by side, Dr. and Mrs. Grant, and Mr. Crawford, with two or three grooms, standing about and looking on."

In the novel, Fanny sees from a distance that Edmund takes hold of Mary's hand, prompting Fanny's speculation on others' motives and concern for her mare, in typically self-deprecating ways. It is a very detailed and psychologically complex scene that Fanny's perspective paints—both observing and imagining—as told through the narrator. Lydon captures this complexity but takes some liberties in placing Fanny in a remote wood, leaning against the trunk of an enormous tree, rather than in a location near the great house. The human figures she's observing, too, are so small that it seems impossible she'd be able to make out any of their gestures or actions. Yet Lydon gets at the grand anxiety of the scene, with Fanny positioned as a fragile outsider, looking on others' pleasure. Lydon's illustration accentuates the beauty and sublimity of both the natural and psychological landscapes. He gives us an illustration that makes clear how connected those landscapes are in the novel.

In a later, similar illustration, Lydon depicts Fanny seated on a bench, fatigued, at Sotherton, watching as Mary and Edmund go off to "determine the dimensions of the wood" without her. Lydon's illustration again mirrors the situation communicated in text, showing Fanny's dual status as both observer and observed. Two further Lydon illustrations cement the sense that his designs were crafted with an eye to the novel's confluences of physical and psychological landscapes. One shows the carriage that holds Edmund, Fanny, and Susan Price, as it returns to Mansfield Park. In the novel, Fanny invests the scenery (just as the viewer of the Lydon illustration might) with her multilayered emotional response. Lydon does include one landscape illustration from the perspective of a character other than Fanny: Henry Crawford's description to Edmund of his having happened upon Edmund's future clergyman's living and home at Thornton Lacey. In each case, Lydon emphasizes Austen's fiction as most important for its overdetermined natural and psychologized landscapes. The places mirror, or are invested with, the emotions of the characters.

Just three of Lydon's illustrations depart from this pattern of large landscapes and small figures, although they, too, juxtapose human and natural relationships. One is an outdoor scene, depicting Fanny and Edmund walking in the "shrubbery," here clearly transposed into a woods. Edmund guides Fanny on the path, trying to convince her to accept Henry Crawford's offer of marriage. Another illustration shows Henry with Fanny and Susan at the dockyards at Portsmouth, with Fanny again depicted as fatigued. Henry stands with his dog, looking on the two seated women, with wooden docks and ships' sails in the background. This may be Lydon's most striking image of human figures, not overwhelmed pictorially in the same way by the natural world. The people seem more central, with figures drawn in darker outline than the grayscale, wood-grained shipyard. Only one of Lydon's designs offers an interior—although it, too, might rightly be judged an interior landscape. It's the scene in which Fanny takes an inventory of all of the objects in her favorite room, the East room, her domestically isolated apartment.

Because he includes multiple illustrations, Lydon's plates, for the first time in the history of Jane Austen, offer reader-viewers the opportunity to read the pictures narratively, as a visual story within a story, separate from the

Figure 2.3. Frontispiece, Jane Austen's *Mansfield Park* (London: Groombridge & Sons, 1875), by A. F. Lydon.

text itself. Lydon's designs make up a kind of graphic novel, as we'd call it today, another first in the history of illustrated Austen. (Pickering's ten illustrations were separated, two by two, in different volumes, hardly making a "story," even if they reveal patterns of interpretation.) Lydon's designs, held within the pages of one book, provide an image story in sequence: A lone woman peers onto an estate and its inhabitants. She sits alone on a bench, while another couple has a tête-à-tête. A man hovers over the woman, inside the home. A man on horseback looks over another majestic landscape. A man and a woman on a wooded path are in deep conversation. At a shipyard, a man stands over a distressed-looking woman, whose hand is held by another female. A carriage approaches a great house. What appear to be—and are—landscape-driven images also, in this stand-alone reading, offer a story of a heroine's detachment, observation, engagement, conflict, suffering, and reintegration into the landscape, ending with her probable arrival at the great house. Lydon's images, too, interpret Austen's novel as a particular kind of fiction—a story of courtship that firmly puts the land back in landed gentry.

Lydon was both a talented artist and a model citizen. When he left the town of Driffield in 1883, its inhabitants gave him an award for his contributions there to its Mechanics Institute and Literary Association.[16] Lydon was also a poet, having published, as A.F.L., a book of verse about a butterfly's journey, titled *Fairy Mary's Dream* (1870). He illustrated the book, too, in exquisite color, with a peacock-feather motif title page. It includes an image of an estate that seems a precursor of his illustrations for *Mansfield Park*. *Fairy Mary's Dream* is described in one advertisement as a handsome gift book for a girl.[17] It was published, of course, by Groombridge. The verse tale is about a girl who dreams she is a butterfly, takes off on a fantasy flight away from home, and encounters dragonflies, spiders, a human boy, and other adversaries. At one point, as a butterfly, she vows to stay in a safe place, but vanity drives her forward on the journey. In the end, she decides it was all a dream. A "passing spirit" confirms this interpretation, encouraging the girl-butterfly to understand her dream teaches her

> that your state,
> Though humble, may be very great,
> And if you read the dream's intent,
> You'll cheerful strive and live content.[18]

This sentimental tale and its self-effacing moral lesson also make one wonder whether publishing *Mansfield Park* was a suggestion to Groombridge from Lydon himself. Fairy Mary has some of the same qualities as *Mansfield Park*'s Fanny Price.

Whatever led to *Mansfield Park*'s being its sole Austen title, Groombridge's not continuing with any further illustrated volumes of her work has raised questions for critics. Did the volume not sell? Did the publisher have second thoughts about Austen? A more likely explanation is that the publishing firm (run by a father and his sons) faced financial difficulties. The firm's setbacks included one son's death, a business reorganization, and, ultimately, a dissolution. Sometime in the late 1870s, Groombridge failed. One source reports that engraver-mentor Fawcett went into the engraving room and said to Lydon, in a quiet, restrained voice, "Groombridge have gone down, Francis."[19] The appearance of just one Groombridge/Lydon Austen may speak to the publisher's exigencies, the volume's profitability, or both. The choice of *Mansfield Park* as its single Austen title is intriguing, demonstrating, too, that *Pride and Prejudice* had not yet solidified with the reading public as a bookseller's best financial bet for an Austen one-off.

The fact that just one, and not all six, of Austen's novels was illustrated by Lydon in the 1870s ought also now to seem to us an opportunity missed. He could have packaged Austen in new ways and emphasized other aspects of her fiction. Lydon's vision of Austen's novel as a psychological character study communicated through landscape description seems distinctive for its time. Had Lydon's large-terrained, diminutively peopled illustrations of Austen become as dominant as Pickering's images, it may have advanced critical and popular perceptions of Austen in alternative directions. Lydon's illustrations of Austen's novels could have linked her fiction more solidly to rural topography, for instance, or to descriptions of the natural world. As it is, she's rarely *first* thought of in those terms now. Nudging forward such readings through Lydon's images could have made Austen seem far more like her renowned poet-contemporaries in the Romantic era, heightening the sense of her similar artistic sensibility for subsequent generations of readers. Instead, for years her fiction was classed by critics as an heir to the classically inspired Augustans of the eighteenth century, or she had her scenes depicted, as we've seen, as if Victorian. Ferdinand Pickering's wide-eyed, gothic illustrations prepared decades of readers to anticipate female-dominated, intimate, domestic scenes of anxious or terrible struggle in Austen. (As we saw, there was just a tinge of humor for those in the know.) Lydon's natural-psychological Austen landscapes were exercises in the sublimity of human relationships and geographical places. Despite their visual power, they seem not to have made much of an impression on readers, then or since, probably because of their modest circulation.

Books like Lydon's were collectors' items, gift books, and show pieces. They were out of reach of those of low or moderate income, as were most books. Austen had largely been left out of the serialization-illustration craze that brought the works of Dickens before so many readers, with a novel appearing in periodical-published parts at regular intervals. For Austen, more inexpensive editions (and newsprint serialization) began in the 1880s.[20] Austen's inclusion in the illustrated *Dick's English Library of Standard Works* was a momentous innovation. It is estimated that *Dick's* print run was twenty thousand copies an issue, and it was the first time, Annika Bautz argues, that owning Austen (and illustrated Austen) was within reach of the working classes (111). In terms of its circulation, the "sixpenny *Pride and Prejudice*" rivaled best-selling gift books of the 1890s, which were pitched to middle- and upper-class readers.[21]

Dick's English Library of Standard Works would include three of Austen's novels in its pages in the 1880s: *Pride and Prejudice* (1887), *Sense and Sensibility* (1886), and *Mansfield Park* (1884). *Mansfield Park* was first, suggesting again (along with Lydon's single volume) the primacy of that title for Victorian readers. *Dick's* reprinted well-known fiction in installments. For the *English Library of Standard Works*, weekly issues were sixteen pages long, with four total illustrations. Each issue included excerpts—in tiny-print triple columns—from multiple classic works. There was little rhyme or reason as to which texts were published in the same issue. Installments of *Mansfield Park*, for instance, sat alongside installments of Charles Lamb's *Tales from Shakespeare* and Harriet Beecher Stowe's *Uncle Tom's Cabin*, among others.

Comparing the *Mansfield Park* images in *Dick's* alongside those of Lydon is illuminating. Lydon, as we've seen, emphasized natural-psychological worlds, but *Dick's* illustrator centered entirely on heroine Fanny's moments of honorable humility and humiliation. Most of *Dick's* images of her, as the perfect Victorian woman in ornate surroundings, show her with her face and eyes cast down. One image has her observing Edmund Bertram and Mary Crawford from behind a tree. Another has her throwing her hands around her just-arrived brother's neck, looking up at him adoringly. But the rest are interior social scenes, with characters observing Fanny being humiliated or manipulated. You might caption half of them, "Fanny Price is modest." The traditional, modest, passive femininity on display is a visual pattern in the working-class Austen editions published at this time.

Owning Austen's fiction became tied up, during this period, not only with women's modesty illustrated for working-class women but with other kinds of consumer purchasing. The novels were marketed as giveaways by a soap company, as Janine Barchas has described.[22] Advertisements began to appear more prominently in and even on the covers of the novels. A Routledge edition of *Pride and Prejudice* (1883), as Deirdre Gilbert notes, "advertised patent medicines on its lower boards while its upper boards depicted the stomach-churning marriage proposal from Collins to Elizabeth—an unintended juxtaposition." Gilbert remarks on the humorous possibilities in reading these advertisers' wares along with the scenes featured. She describes this as a new era in which Austen was first advertised with "products independent of the novel" rather than with other books (para. 11). Austen's novels had become fictional products used to sell things other than books, a new moment in their commercial history.

Humor was not generally emphasized in these mass-market Austen illustrations pitched at middle- and working-class audiences from the 1880s. Instead, they featured more serious themes and imparted heavy-handed lessons, when they didn't include lurid teasers. As one critic puts it, these illustrations show "little sign of humour and instead impart strong moral messages about young ladies' conduct" (Bautz 123). Indeed, Austen's humor would not be given much visual expression at all, in novels pitched at readers of any income bracket, until the 1890s. Then, comic moments were centrally featured in editions sold to those with greater levels of disposable income, not to the working classes. Perhaps it's because such visual humor and whimsy would become the dominant mode that the Austen illustrators of the midcentury period now look so odd and out of place. This era and its artists produced illustrations that appear to us as either conservative moralizing throwbacks or puzzling eccentricities. Neither fits well with our present sense of Austen or with prevailing understandings of the spirit of her fiction, yet several generations of nineteenth-century readers may have felt perfectly at home imagining Austen otherwise. For a time, through her illustrations, Austen could easily have been conceived of as a novelist of the natural world, with markedly humble heroines and heroes who were facially hirsute.

CHAPTER THREE

A Golden Age for Illustrated Austen

From Peacocks to Photoplays

If you say "bird" and *"Pride and Prejudice,"* in a room full of Janeites, someone will surely exclaim, "Peacock!" You might think it's because pride is
associated with the peacock, but it's also because of one famously decorated
gilt-embossed book cover and title page. On it, the name of Austen's novel is
entwined with illustrated peacock feathers. We can thank Austen's highest-
profile celebrity illustrator, Hugh Thomson (1860–1920), for the enduring
association. Thomson's Austen illustrations from the 1890s are probably
among those you've seen most often and know best, whether you recognize
they're by him or not. For more than a century, Thomson's illustrations have
ended up on everything from Jane Austen House Museum postcards to
silver-plated Birmingham Mint reproductions (1976), to "tea towels, mugs,
cards, and other merchandise."[1] There's even a *Pride and Prejudice* Peacock
shower curtain. More than a century after the fact, Thomson still seems to
hold the record for the greatest number of published book illustrations depicting Austen's fiction.[2] His impact has been so great that it's difficult to
imagine anyone surpassing him, ever, despite the fact that his images attract
very little love from critics. Most seem to hold their noses as they describe his
achievement.

Thomson was in the right place at the right time. No period was more
vibrant and formative for illustrated Austen than the 1890s. In that decade,
sometimes called book illustration's second golden age, the vogue for the illustrated gift book grew; it lasted until the First World War.[3] Before 1892, the
largest number of Austen illustrations by any single known artist remained
Pickering's, at ten. By the end of the 1920s, four artists had published more
than one hundred Austen illustrations each over the course of their commissions and careers. One of the most significant things about this body of

illustrations, beyond its large quantity and wide circulation, is that it introduced new visual themes, including those iconic peacocks. More significant
still is the introduction of gentle humor and sociality. What may surprise is
that these artists also infused illustrated Austen with images of social criticism, overt physicality, war, and death. They pushed the envelope for what
it meant to visualize Austen and her fiction. But, for the first time, the illustration of her novels also moved toward a set of common tropes. Collectively,
these 1890s and 1900s images worked to shift the tone for characterizing
Austen's fiction from feminine moral seriousness and suspense-filled domestic sensationalism to mild comedy and genial satire.[4] That shift transformed, too, how Austen was conceived of as an author and, especially, how
she and her fictional characters were imagined as female role models. Of
course, it's difficult to determine whether illustrators were leading or following trends. In either case, they bolstered them.

High-income readers of this period were courted by publishers marketing "Christmas books." Their content, despite the name, was usually not
holiday related. These Christmas books were so called because publishers
timed their release to the end of the year, marketing them as the season's hot
gifts. By the 1890s, the illustrated book was a go-to present, a looked-for luxury item. As one critic puts it, "Many a Victorian aunt or godparent solved
their Christmas present problems with a pretty volume for 4s. 6d."[5] Such
books also began to be associated with particular publishers, signature artists, and classic novels. *Pride and Prejudice* was advertised as a Christmas
gift book title especially suitable for girls.[6] Libraries acquired the titles for
their collections. One finds many surviving copies with long inscriptions on
title pages and endpapers, indicating that so-and-so has won such-and-such
a school distinction or a prize and was given this gift of a book. That these
books were also kept over the years suggests they may have functioned
for their recipients as a kind of trophy, as material proof of an academic
accomplishment.

Four publishers brought out major new illustrated Austen editions in the
1890s, with varying levels of lavishness—London-based J. M. Dent, Macmillan, and George Allen, and the Boston-based Roberts Brothers. (The London
publishers usually marketed their editions simultaneously in New York as
well.) Macmillan's and George Allen's Austen titles were especially visually
transformative. These volumes not only had copious illustrations—sometimes
by the dozens and hundreds—but gilt edges and gilt-embossed covers. The
books themselves were works of art. A uniform set was a collectible. As

Dent put it in its advertisement, "A Set of a Standard Author" was "An Ideal Present." Wedding announcements of the era used to list the presents received by the bride and groom, and it was not uncommon to find a complete Austen edition given to the newlyweds. In addition to its Austen, Dent advertised sets for Brontë, Burney, Defoe, Dickens, Edgeworth, Fielding, Ferrier, Marryat, Peacock, Scott, and Sterne, among others.[7] Uniform novels had served as collectors' items long before this. Sir Walter Scott's titles were early examples. But, after the 1890s boom, Austen's novels stood unequivocally alongside them.

The outpouring of illustrated Austens during this period led to Henry James's 1905 grumbling about Austen's reputation being pushed over its natural high tide by "the stiff breeze of the commercial" and "the special bookselling spirit."[8] As we've seen, James's statement decrying Austen's early commercialization prominently imprecates her illustrators, painted with one brush as pandering opportunists. During this period, illustrations of Austen's fiction were widely described as spoiling readers' experiences. No doubt it was because, for the first time, there were so many of them to compare at once. Perhaps, too, it was because these images began to be describable as an illustrative type, something it was difficult to do during a period dominated by one illustrator (Pickering) or with the strange, disconnected Austen-inspired images that were prevalent before the 1890s. "Twaddle" is James's dismissive word for that new collection of images, but the word approving reviewers used most often was "charming."

To dismiss these illustrations with "twaddle" or "charming," however, is to ignore their significance and the landmark ways in which they shifted the tone for visualizing Austen and her fiction. One way the shift can be charted is by comparing J. M. Dent and Company's ten-volume edition of Austen's novels, edited by Reginald Brimley Johnson (1867–1932) and illustrated by William Cubitt Cooke (1866–1951), with those that came after it. The Dent Johnson/Cooke Austen edition was a milestone production in several ways. It also marked the endpoint of some previous trends. David Gilson identifies Dent's 1892 Austen edition as "the first, as far as I know, to have any editorial matter" and the first "to make any attempt at serious consideration of the text."[9] Claudia L. Johnson deems the effort "quasi-scholarly."[10] Illustrator Cooke's designs are described by Gilson as "sepia photogravure reproductions of almost monochrome grey-brown wash drawings" and "the first to attempt (however unsuccessfully) to represent characters in the dress and surroundings . . . of the dates of composition or first publication of each novel"

("Later Publishing" 138). Cooke's images move away from the flouncy Victorian dresses of Pickering and his imitators toward something resembling the empire-waisted simplicity of actual Regency fashion. Still, Cooke's images retain some hallmarks of 1890s fashionability, particularly in the characters' hairstyles.[11]

More remarkable is that the Dent Austen features thirty illustrations, the largest number produced by one artist to date. Cooke designed three plates per volume, with the four longer novels split into two volumes each. After Cooke, no single illustrator could count on his (and most were male) potential power to shape readers' experiences of reading Austen's fiction through his designs. The publication of more illustrations and the featuring of more illustrators meant that the competition for memorably depicting Austen's characters and scenes became fierce. Cooke didn't turn out to be a long-term winner in that contest. Dent's choice of Cooke for its Austen designs was not unlike Bentley's choice of Pickering to illustrate his 1833 Standard Novels. Both publishers plucked out an up-and-coming (and likely therefore cost-saving) rookie artist. Cooke's first published illustrations had appeared in 1892, the same year as his Austen edition. He worked in an artistic tradition that had proven a success with book buyers, in the mode of famed illustrators Randolph Caldecott and Kate Greenaway. Cooke's images are in that sense extraordinarily safe. They extend, rather than deviate from, previous trends in Austen illustration. Cooke's *Sense and Sensibility*, volume 2, presents precisely the same scene that Pickering chose, an illustration of Elinor at the bedside of a deathly ill Marianne. Its caption is, "A restless and feverish night."

Cooke's image is interesting to compare to Pickering's. Where Pickering incorporated a counterpane that overwhelmed the image with its undulant folds, the room that Cooke depicts is anchored instead by wall art. Pickering's frenzied fabrics gave way to Cooke's ordered rectangles. In Cooke's version, Elinor, not Marianne, is at the center of the frame. It is Elinor's eyes we can almost see, cast down, as she leans over in her chair, clearly wretched. Marianne lies in bed, only slightly visible beyond her bedcovers. Elinor stretches out her hand over her knee, but the two sisters don't touch. The illustration strips away both the Gothic suspense and the female intimacy notable in Pickering's version. Cooke emphasizes Elinor's solitary, contemplative fretting over her sister, not her sister's physical danger or their close relationship to each other. On the whole, Cooke, like Pickering before him, selects out small domestic scenes, primarily interiors—featuring just one male in six illustrations, one outdoor scene, and never more than two characters in

Figure 3.1. "A Restless and Feverish Night, Ch. 43," from
Jane Austen's *Sense and Sensibility*, vol. 2 (London: J. M.
Dent, 1892), 141, by William Cubitt Cooke.

the same image. He makes these the signature visual elements of the novel.
Cooke's edition now looks like a transitional moment in Austen illustration,
with one foot in the old and one in the new visual world. He was an inexpe-
rienced illustrator whose images fall within long-established patterns, but
they also appear in larger numbers than ever before in a new sort of edition.
Just two years later, another illustrator would change the tone and effectively
wipe from memory the work of Cooke and his predecessors.

That innovator is the aforementioned Hugh Thomson, who might be
called the Colin Firth of Austen-inspired book illustration. Once you've seen
publisher George Allen's *Pride and Prejudice* (1894), it's easy to come to the
conclusion that every other edition of the book must pale in comparison.

That book came to be known as Austen's "Peacock edition" because of its peacock-themed endpapers, title page, and gilt-embossed cover. It also features a total of 160 illustrations, counting headpieces, tailpieces, ornamental initials, and other decorations, including the drawn title page and dedication (Gilson, *Bibliography* 267). One reviewer describes the Peacock edition as "one of the richest, if not the very richest, reprints of the season in standard English fiction."[12] In the Austen canon, the Peacock edition remains among the most memorable and valuable of her illustrated titles. At this writing, well-preserved copies may fetch $500 or more.

Thomson's Austen edition is often called "Cranfordized," a term that deserves explanation. The word stems from Elizabeth Gaskell's novel *Cranford* (1851). But when we call a book Cranfordized, it has nothing to do with Gaskell's story. It refers to the commercially successful style in which Gaskell's novel was famously produced in 1891 by Macmillan, illustrated by Hugh Thomson. The series in which it was published featured books with "three edges gilt, bound in dark green cloth, front and spine heavily stamped in gold," illustrated by Macmillan's impressive stable of artists.[13] Macmillan's Cranford Series would come to include twenty-four titles, eleven of which were illustrated by Thomson. The series and style were so popular that they created "legitimate offshoots and numerous imitators."[14] Even Macmillan itself continued to cash in, with its New Cranford Series and Illustrated Standard Novels.[15] The latter is the series in which all of Jane Austen's generously illustrated works ultimately appear, most of them illustrated by Thomson. But the first and most famous Cranford-looking Austen edition was the Peacock edition. It was published not by Macmillan but by its competitor and imitator, George Allen. (We'll return to the story of Thomson's temporarily switching publishers shortly.)

What made Thomson's Austen Peacock edition so visually groundbreaking was its pioneering infusion of gentle humor. Austenian humor had been depicted prior to Thomson, as we saw in chapter 1 with Pickering's occasional sly designs. But light humor was not Pickering's dominant visual mode. Thomson's humorous style and tone brought the potential to change, and arguably greatly change, what readers came to expect from and believe about Austen and her novels. Of course, it's difficult to prove Thomson's or any illustrator's influence on actual reader-viewers. We are sometimes able to marshal anecdotal evidence, like that of Sheila Kaye-Smith, discussed in the introduction to part 2 of this book. Kaye-Smith admits that the *Pride and Prejudice* illustrations she pored over in her childhood—likely Thomson's—imprinted themselves on her psyche so that she unconsciously borrowed from them as an adult in making a "quaint" Austen-inspired costume. But, most often, when we consider an illustrator's influence on audiences, we're operating on the level of speculation and probable impact.

In Thomson's case, we also have the evidence of the edition's great commercial success, as well as its staying power. Its visual dominance—and its inspiration of so many copycat editions—suggests not just popularity but sway over readers' expectations. Thomson's illustrations would have encouraged viewers away from expecting to find female-focused moments of intimacy, conflict, or climax, as Pickering's had. Instead, Thomson repeatedly depicts groups of characters, four or five or more, arranging them in formal social situations (dances, musical performances, etc.), something previous artists rarely did but which many did after him, evidence of his impact. His Austen-inspired comic, social images may also have either paved the way or smoothed the waters for perceiving Austen's novels as more readily dramatized and cinematic.

Thomson's illustrations display a smirking sense of fun, appearing not to take themselves (or Austen?) nearly as seriously as his predecessors' had. There are many moments of levity, including multiple cupid figures placed throughout the text. Was Thomson serious with those, or were they tongue-in-cheek? It's indeterminate, which makes them fall somewhere between campy-amusing and condescendingly horrifying as Austenian commentary. Thomson clearly sets out to add whimsy, especially to his headpieces, which often consist of fantasy scenes not depicted in the novel itself. Characteristic of this visual pattern is the headpiece featuring the Bennets' status-conscious neighbor, Sir William Lucas, as he's being knighted. He is shown down on one knee before the king. The monarch's sword is raised over his bowed shoulders, reinforcing what the original text indicates about Sir William's obsequiousness. Another headpiece has two men holding and twirling a long laurel, as if it's a jump rope. At first glance, these images may seem juvenile ones better suited to children's books, but they speak to adults, too, with a knowing wink and a nod.

The most thought provoking and eye catching of these headpiece drawings precedes *Pride and Prejudice*'s chapter 15. In it, the five Bennet daughters are spaced evenly across the page. They sit in almost-unseen chairs, flanked on the left by their fussing mother. She arranges one daughter's hair, likely Lydia's. On the right is their more distant, bemused father. He stands, hand to chin, holding his hat and his walking stick. In the middle of the five sits the daughter who is presumably Elizabeth. Over her head is a small sign reading "NOT FOR SALE"[16] This image resembles Thomson's other quirky illustrations and may be compared with his fanciful headpieces. But it's unlike the others, too, in making overt Austen's social criticism, even suggesting an endorsement of it. Providing visualized, political readings of Austen's novels, or providing commentary on the economics of marriage, was exceedingly rare before Thomson. He was taking a visual risk by making it prominent, although it benefits from being placed among his other whimsical images. It may seem more lightheartedly clever than politically invested when it's set among the others he produced. On its own, it's jarring.

Still, it's difficult to tell Thomson's Bennet sisters apart as female products. In the "NOT FOR SALE" illustration, the women are virtually identical. Thomson was, at least, equal opportunity in this sense. His characters of both sexes are rather undistinctive, running one into the next, making it difficult to tell which one matches up to which of Austen's. A few do stand out visually, including his Mrs. Bennet, depicted as older, wizened, often hunched over. She's also presented as physically bold, inserting herself into every situation, arms and torso shown lurching forward. Yet there is a cold detachment in Thomson's illustration of most adults. He offers up images of children, carriages, and horses with greater care and warmth. It would seem he feels a greater affinity for them as an artist. He almost seems to have selected his

Figure 3.2. Headpiece from Jane Austen's *Pride and Prejudice* (George Allen, 1894), Hugh Thomson. University of Michigan Special Collections.

favorite objects, working to shoehorn them into the contents on quasi-suitable pages of the novel. As one recent critic puts it, Thomson set out in his art not to "give readers a parallel visual narrative" but rather to create "a series of vignettes which stimulate the readers' own imagination."[17] In this way, we might say that it's as if Thomson has written his own Austen novel in illustrations, using his own symbolic economy, rather than setting out to better discern Austen's. Their packaging, as Kathryn Sutherland argues, suggests that "these were [Thomson's] books, not Austen's."[18] That fact makes both his humor and politics more difficult to pin down, a feature that his illustrations hold in common with Austen's prose. It's a quality that may have led to the wide appeal of each at particular historical moments.

Knowing more about the man may also help us make better sense of the images. Thomson was an unlikely celebrity illustrator. Born in Ireland to a tea merchant and shopkeeper father, he was not formally educated as an artist, starting his working life as a clerk for linen manufacturers (Fitzpatrick and Shorley 14). He next did work for printers and publishers, including one of the first commercial Christmas card companies, from whom he learned the trade and the craft. At the suggestion of a mentor, he moved to London to pursue a career in illustration, married (and had one son), and worked for the newly formed *English Illustrated Magazine*, published by Macmillan. There he did nostalgic, sentimental line drawings of Covent Garden and Regency Bath. These images set the stage for his style for decades to come. He is said to have enjoyed researching Georgian costumes and settings at the nearby National Gallery and museums (17).

Thomson benefited from new technologies for artists and book production. He's been credited with designing "the first illustrations to be reproduced by photomechanical means in commercial periodical publications," on photoengraved blocks, eliminating the need for an engraver (Fitzpatrick and Shorley 7). Thomson cemented his fame with his illustrated Macmillan edition of the earlier-discussed *Cranford* (1891), finding a prominent place among a group of artists now referred to as the Wig and Powder school.[19] He worked hard as an artist; his only hobby was said to be golf (Fitzpatrick and Shorley 8). His biographers repeatedly refer to him as "modest."[20] A surviving photo of him from 1894 suggests self-assured, confident intensity, as he sits near a body of water, before his easel, legs spread apart and focused on his canvas.

He was not described by biographers as having much business savvy, despite declaring himself interested in "golden shekels," but he made at least

Photo: George Dallas, Garvagh, Co. Derry

Figure 3.3. "Hugh Thomson Sketching at Kilrea," 1894. Published in M. H. Spielmann and Walter Jerrold, *Hugh Thomson: His Art, His Letters, His Humour, and His Charm* (London: A. C. Black, 1931), 97. Arizona State University Libraries.

one shrewd decision (Spielmann and Jerrold 91). After having reportedly told his longtime employer Macmillan in the early 1890s that "he regarded Jane Austen's work as unsuitable material for illustration," he contracted with a rival publisher to illustrate just one Austen title. Thomson agreed to illustrate *Pride and Prejudice* for publisher George Allen. Macmillan was "understandably aggrieved" by this choice by its star illustrator, and Thomson was "predictably guilt-ridden" about his own defection (Fitzpatrick and Shorley 9). It was no doubt a change spurred on by financial considerations on the part of the illustrator.

Thomson's unpublished letters with Macmillan give us a sense of what he was previously paid for his work. At first, at Macmillan, Thomson's compensation wasn't that much more than Ferdinand Pickering's had been more than fifty years earlier—about five pounds per drawing. The difference is that Thomson was providing hundreds of them per book. For his edition of Oliver Goldsmith's *The Vicar of Wakefield*, for instance, Thomson contracted with Macmillan to provide drawings at the rate of £5 for a full page, £3 for a half page, and £2 for a tailpiece.[21] Sometimes the contract stipulated an amount for the edition as a whole, such as his agreement to be paid £400 for illustrating Mary Russell Mitford's *Our Village*.[22] That edition advertises itself as including one hundred illustrations, so Thomson would have been paid approximately £4 per drawing. He wasn't, however, getting a royalty from sales. Perhaps that became a sticking point for him.

The publisher Thomson fled to, George Allen, gave him more generous terms than Macmillan's by including a royalty percentage. Thomson was paid £500 for the *Pride and Prejudice* Peacock edition—on a par with Macmillan's previous lump payments—but he was also promised a royalty of seven pence on every copy sold after 10,000. One wonders whether George Allen anticipated how many copies would sell. In just one year, Thomson reached the threshold for receiving his royalties, with 11,605 copies sold, along with 3,500 sent to America. By 1907, a whopping 25,000 copies of the Peacock edition of *Pride and Prejudice* had been sold (Gilson, *Bibliography* 267). This was, as Kathryn Sutherland points out, more than the lifetime sales of all of Austen's books put together (*Jane Austen* 9).

But not long after his George Allen commission was completed, Thomson switched publishers again. According to his biographers, Thomson described himself as "compunctious" about having left Macmillan in the first place (Spielmann and Jerrold 86). He ended up returning to Macmillan to illustrate their editions of the remaining five Austen novels: *Emma* (1896), *Sense and Sensibility* (1896), *Mansfield Park* (1897), and *Northanger Abbey* and *Persuasion* (1897). Each Thomson Macmillan volume included a frontispiece and thirty-nine line drawings (almost all full page), for a total of 160 more Thomson-Austen illustrations produced. Macmillan had agreed to give Thomson a royalty percentage.[23] Surely this, along with his previous longstanding relationship with the firm, explains his return to Macmillan, although the slower pace of his completion of these illustrations has been chalked up to his "indifferent health" (Fitzpatrick and Shorley 9). It seems he had a severe case of influenza (Spielmann and Jerrold 85–86).

By all accounts, Thomson was ambitious and hardworking—a man with a sense of humor. But he was also continually dogged by money problems, even prior to the period of hardship most artists experienced during the war years. In 1912, he complains to his publisher that he's been working constantly, to the point of his drawings getting "stale," as he's not "been free from pencil and paper for a day, Sundays not excepted, for 2 years. Pathetic!

Almost Tragic!!"[24] Letters survive in which Thomson asks his publisher for advances, noting that his bank account balances have fallen very low.[25] Macmillan clearly felt concern for his financial plight, as it once sent him a "large sum of money" and later put in a "generous letter to the Prime Minister" to help him secure a Civil List pension of £75.[26] One surviving letter gives us some insight into an early financial blow in the year that Thomson temporarily switched publishers from Macmillan to Allen. That year he inherited from his recently deceased father a crushing £150 debt.[27] It may have motivated his switch.

Whatever Thomson's circumstances were, and from wherever they stemmed, his temporary defection from Macmillan put that publisher in a bind. Macmillan couldn't use Thomson's illustrations for its own edition of *Pride and Prejudice*, which it needed in order to have a complete Austen edition. So Macmillan commissioned one of Thomson's artist-competitors, Charles Brock, to undertake its illustrated *Pride and Prejudice*. It's why Thomson's and Brock's names both grace the Macmillan Austen edition's maroon covers. That does not explain, however, why Austen's own name (included on the spine) didn't make it to the front covers of Macmillan's editions of the novels at all. It's important to recognize that this was not a special dig at Austen. Macmillan regularly named the illustrator, rather than the author, below the work's title on its covers. Maria Edgeworth's *Castle Rackrent* and *The Absentee* (1895), for example, includes "Illustrated by Chris. Hammond," rather than Edgeworth's name. The illustrators' names being placed on the covers of these books—seemingly more prominent than the authors'—shows the artists' stature and marketability in this genre and era. Thomson was at the pinnacle of his profession, but his name on Austen's novels doesn't indicate in this instance his unique, personal power to overshadow her.

Thomson's commercial success, and critics' longtime disparagement of it, leads to the detail still most cited about him in Austen scholarship: that novelist E. M. Forster once dubbed him "the lamentable Hugh Thompson [*sic*]."[28] Forster, in the course of reviewing the landmark scholarly Austen edition edited by R. W. Chapman in 1923, expresses his gratitude for its period illustrations. Forster is grateful not only for their accuracy but hopes they will "purge his mind" of Thomson's illustrations, "which illustrate nothing" (Forster n.p.). Thomson was, for Forster and others, representative of all that had gone wrong with visualizing Austen by the 1920s. Illustrated Austens had come to be perceived as fetish objects, de-emphasizing historical authenticity and distracting from the author's own words. Chapman's edition, with its original period plates, was welcomed by Forster as a corrective. In Chapman, there wasn't a cupid or peacock to be found.

It is difficult to know just how widely held opinions like Forster's were. There is certainly a long history of intellectuals deriding popular things that sell well, especially when attached to material understood by some to be the rightful property of high-culture connoisseurs. For that reason, it's difficult to conclude that Forster's view was a majority one. Forster's "lamentable Thompson" insult had its greatest impact through its repetition in Austen reception histories, circulating after both the critic-novelist and the imprecated illustrator had died. The repetition has prevented our proper grasp of Thomson's mammoth contribution to the formation of Austen's twentieth-century image, putting us in Forster's shoes. Yet, depending on your vantage point, Thomson's illustrations may deserve some of the derision Forster doles out.

Most today describe Thomson's images as dainty, quaint, and sentimental, with the phrase "chocolate box" popping up frequently. Kathryn Sutherland puts it most succinctly: Thomson's Austen was "a whimsical, chocolate-box idyll, reflecting nostalgia for an idealized pre-industrial England just out of reach."[29] Claudia L. Johnson declares that Thomson's Peacock edition is "lavishly if inanely illustrated."[30] Claire Harman has disparaged him the most forcefully since Forster, accusing Thomson of "abducting *Pride and Prejudice* into the land of kitsch."[31] One sees in these assessments something that is both fair and unfair. It's fair in that Thomson's illustrations rarely prompt deep thinking or highlight interpretive complexity, qualities that many attribute to and value in Austen's fiction. But these dismissive assessments of his illustration are unfair in that, at the time, Thomson's Austen images were forward leaning in ways that have since become invisible to us. They propelled readers and future illustrators in new directions of emphasis, promoting an Austen more widely perceptible as fashionable rather than old fashioned, comic rather than serious, social rather than intimate, and gently satirical rather than gently sensational.

Thomson may have led the visual charge for updating Austen and expanding her popular base, but he had reinforcements. Other celebrity illustrators cobranding with Austen during this decade include the Brock brothers, Charles Edmund Brock (1870–1938) and Matthew Henry Brock (1875–1960). The number of Austen images the Brocks completed between them amounted to at least 212, in many formats and editions, over decades. Although it is not possible to do their work justice in a brief discussion, among their important "firsts" was colored plates for Austen. There had been previous color illustrations of her fiction used on front boards of yellowback editions but not multiple interior color plates. Mass-produced color illustration, reproduced by lithography, was a novelty in the 1890s. A new ten-volume Austen edition by J. M. Dent, illustrated in color by the Brocks, was published in 1898, immediately overshadowing Dent's previous Cooke-illustrated edition of 1892. Dent seems to have undertaken the new Brock-illustrated edition specifically to have a cutting-edge illustrated Austen edition on the market, rather than through any particular dissatisfaction with its 1892 edition. Whatever Dent's motivations, the Brock-illustrated Austen had the effect of eclipsing, if not extinguishing, Cooke's.

The Brock brothers evenly shared the Dent Austen assignment—five volumes each, six plates per volume, for a total of sixty plates. The edition proved a success and was republished several times. A decade later, from 1907 to 1909, the Dents produced yet another new Austen edition, and Charles E. Brock singly produced more illustrations. His commission for this project included 144 watercolors, which were also reprinted, in various iterations, for years thereafter.[32] In terms of design and subject, they were often in Thomson's artistic shadow. The Brocks' work has become known as derivative of, and less original than, his.[33] The Brock brothers followed Thomson's "attention to historical detail," although one critic describes their illustrations as "distinct," finding Thomson's more artificial and allegorical and the Brocks' more attentive to relationships and secondary characters.[34] This seems accurate, though the Brock illustrations are—regardless of which brother produced which—altogether visually busier than Thomson's.

Their busier look isn't just a result of the new coloration technique. Previous Austen illustrations invited the eye to focus on characters more than vistas or interiors. Even Lydon's from 1875, with his lush landscapes, produced images in which the eye was drawn to the human figure dwarfed by the sublime natural world. Brock-brother illustrations were, instead, what C. M. Kelly calls "over-decoration, that desire to fill all available space with patterns of some sort" (43). It's a bit like studying a very busy wallpaper. When viewing the Brocks' illustrations, it's a challenge for the eye to know where to look. In their efforts to achieve historical accuracy, the Brocks seem as interested in the settings as the characters. Their illustrations are a feast for the eyes but provide little visual content to chew on in interpreting the six novels. The number of umbrellas, parasols, and muffs the Brocks include borders on the absurd. They depict many of the same scenes that Pickering had, in a similar style to that of Thomson, but without sensationalism or smirking humor. Given the sheer number of images the Brocks created, however, there are exceptions to this general charge and even a few unexpected moments.

One startling image is C. E. Brock's version of Edward Ferrars and Elinor Dashwood's physical closeness in *Sense and Sensibility*. In a scene from late in the novel, the couple is shown next to each other on a love seat, knees touching. His arm is draped across her shoulder, with her hand reaching up to her own shoulder to touch his hand. Up to this point, Austen illustrations had not been nearly so bold in depicting physical intimacy or suggesting overt sexuality, even in the yellowback's Lydia-flirts-with-the-officers image discussed in chapter 2. In previous images rarely did opposite-sex characters touch each other beyond a hand on the arm. The captioned, quoted line, "The Enjoyment of Elinor's Company" prompts a less innocent interpretation of the original line, when paired with Brock's illustration. Brock's image makes us see the potential physicality of Edward Ferrars enjoying Elinor's company in this scene. Most of the Brocks' Austen images, however, are far less provocative.

The Brocks and Thomson had one more formidable 1890s Austen-illustration competitor: Chris. Hammond, born Christiana Mary Demain Hammond (1860–1900). One recent Austen reception study indexes her under "Hammond, Christopher," demonstrating how little known and how much in the shadow of Thomson and the Brocks she has become.[35] She was the first identifiably female illustrator of Jane Austen's novels, illustrating three Austen titles for two publishers.[36] Her first two were the heavily illustrated editions of *Emma* (1898) and *Sense and Sensibility* (1899) for George Allen, picking up where Thomson left off, after he reestablished his relationship with Macmillan. The last was a sparsely illustrated *Pride and Prejudice* for Gresham Publishing (1900), produced at the end of her life. An obituary of Hammond was accompanied by six of her Austen illustrations, showing how highly they were ranked among her artistic accomplishments.[37] The writer of the obituary, not wanting to label her art "woman's work," nevertheless celebrated its femininity, glamour, and sincerity. Of the three terms, "sincerity" seems most to apply to what she produced, especially in the images that deviated from Thomson and the Brocks.

Hammond's heavily illustrated editions emulate some aspects of her predecessors'. The hand-drawn title pages for both her *Emma* and *Sense and Sensibility* are near replicas of Thomson's Peacock edition. Of the three

Austen volumes she illustrated, Hammond's first, *Emma*, is the most derivative of Thomson, perhaps more by publisher George Allen's direction than
by her own inclination. Hammond's echoes of Thomson, when they occur,
seem far too ham-fisted to have been much more than an assignment. We
can see this as well in her two interior cupids. Hammond also makes liberal
use of parasols, horses, muffs, wall art, and people seated at desks. These elements seem directly Thomson-inspired, if not deliberately copied.

One illustration even seems a direct riff on Thomson's "NOT FOR SALE"
Elizabeth Bennet: Hammond's bride-price Emma and her inferior rivals
or knockoffs. Captioned "If Miss Woodhouse of Hartfield the heiress of
£30,000 were not quite so easily obtained . . . he would soon try for Miss
Somebody else with twenty or with ten."[38] The illustration shows Mr. Elton
looking over three prospective brides, sitting under signs 1, 2, and 3, holding
sacks of money labeled with their respective fortunes. The women are seated
on a stage, as if at a fair or auction. Mr. Elton holds up his hand and a marker,
ready to command one of them for his own, declaring her the "winner." Like
Thomson's "NOT FOR SALE" illustration, Hammond's image could be read as
broad-humored social criticism, lampooning the ways that marriage turns
women into chattel. It could be read as even darker still—as in comparison
to the sale of human flesh to which Jane Fairfax alluded in the novel. But it
might also be read less politically, as commentary on Mr. Elton's hubris and
greed, rather than as an indictment of marital economics or sexism. Perhaps the ambiguity was intentional.

Hammond's Austen illustrations are on the whole more serious, less
whimsical, and more visually surprising than Thomson's or the Brocks'.
She, too, emphasizes sexual desire and tension. Her illustrations for *Sense
and Sensibility* (1899) include a handful of quirky departures. One is her image of Willoughby cutting off a lock of Marianne's hair. It emphasizes the
intimacy of such an act, as he steps in close to touch her head from behind,
her clenched hand poised very near his groin.[39] In her *Emma*, Hammond
includes another scene that is shockingly serious and may also be seen as
political commentary, directly taking viewers from romance to realism—or
at least romanticized realism. Hammond illustrates the slain father of Jane
Fairfax, with the caption from the text, "The melancholy remembrance of
him dying in action abroad" (165). The deceased Lieutenant Fairfax, killed
when Jane was a girl, is depicted on the battlefield as a corpse.

Of course, there are deaths—and wartime deaths—in Austen's fiction. *Persuasion*'s unsympathetic mention of the late Dick Musgrove is unforgettable.[40]

If Miss Woodhouse of Hartfield the heiress
of £30,000, were not quite so easily obtained
. . . . he would soon try for Miss
Somebody else with twenty or with ten"

CHAPTER XVI

Figure 3.4. Headpiece from Jane Austen's *Emma*, ch. 16 (George Allen, 1898), 138, by Chris. Hammond.

But Hammond's illustration appears to be the first time that one of these scenes and characters is illustrated. Hammond's dead lieutenant is unsettling. It's indicative of her willing artistic foray into darker-toned, more weighty visual matters. Her corpse illustration may be in keeping with Pickering's gothic sensationalism, but it does more than shock. It foregrounds the tragedy that radically changed Jane Fairfax's economic circumstances and life prospects. Lieutenant Fairfax's corpse serves a function beyond shocking readers. It reminds them of the war dead who undergird Austen's story. This image may well even be Hammond's artistic response to the prominent critics then claiming that Austen's fiction was limited in its scope and

The melancholy remembrance of him dying in action abroad"

CHAPTER XX

Figure 3.5. Headpiece from Jane Austen's *Emma*, ch. 20 (George Allen, 1898), 165, by Chris. Hammond.

place. Her image gives the lie to the then dominant critical view that Austen's fiction was "small," that it contained "no event," and that it never touched on politics or the wider world. Hammond's illustration *shows* such blanket statements to be false.

Hammond had her own share of event and hardship. She died at age thirty-nine, a single woman, in the same year that her illustrated *Pride and Prejudice* (1900) appeared. Hammond's rise to artistic prominence would not have been predicted by her family of origin. She was born of a bank clerk father, himself the son of a surgeon. Christiana, the eldest child, was one of three artist siblings. An obituary of "Miss Chris Hammond," gives us a sense of her artistic education. Her mother having died when she was young, Hammon received her first art lessons from a governess. Success in later formal study at the Lambeth School of Art resulted in three years' free instruction at the Royal Academy Schools. Women had been able to enroll at the Royal

Academy Schools since the late 1860s, but Hammond (and her sister, who also attended) would still have been, to some degree, female trailblazers there. It's odd to think that Hammond, too, may have had at least a passing knowledge of life-student Ferdinand Pickering in his late years.

Hammond's time at the Royal Academy Schools was not without its challenges. Even after the abolishment of the life studentship, she would have had an opportunity to continue her studies there, free, for three further years, had she not become ineligible. She had performed well in her examinations, but she had poor attendance at the required lectures. It disqualified her from continuing. Although her absences were a result, it is said, of poor health and disability, these circumstances were not recognized as extenuating (Forman, "Chris" 347). Denied further training, she turned from oil painting to book illustration. She excelled at illustration and was in high demand for it. Like many other artists we've seen thus far, her Austen commissions would become her most lasting artistic contribution, as "Jane Austen's novels showed the gifted artist to the greatest advantage" (Forman, "The Late" 194).

Hammond's obituary includes many moving details, including this description of the exhaustion caused by pressing (and economically necessary) illustration commissions: "Few probably can realize to themselves how great a strain, mental as well as in some measure physical, must be undergone by an artist who undertakes to deliver within a given time a long series of illustrations for a novel. Miss Hammond sometimes felt this." The writer also includes this pathetic story: "It is a little sad now to think that, only a few weeks before her death, Miss Hammond had inherited a small sum of money which would have enabled her to devote more time to portrait-painting," an art form that she preferred and found less exhausting (Forman, "Chris" 349). Hammond was the pioneering illustrator who first depicted death and war in Austen, reminding viewer-readers that Austen's female characters, too, were shaped by grand political events and the world beyond Britain.

By the end of Hammond's career as an artist, it had begun to matter not only whether one read Austen but from which edition one read her. Consuming fiction in a cheap newspaper format, versus reading it in a luxury illustrated edition (and which one), could determine a reader's experience of Austen and shape others' sense of her or him as a reader. A few were in a position to compare and contrast the editions. One even constructed his own wish list of Austen illustrators that never were. In *Pages from a Private Diary* (1898), in an essay originally published anonymously in *Cornhill Magazine*, poet and deacon H. C. Beeching (1859–1919) assesses Austen's illustrators.

"Miss Austen," he concludes, "has suffered more than most authors at the hands of her illustrators." "How delightful," he continues, "it would have been if her novels had first appeared in *Cornhill* [*Magazine*] with [Frederick] Walker's or [John Everett] Millais's pictures!"[41]

This may at first seem Beeching's exercise in visual nostalgia. Placing Austen in the *Cornhill Magazine* in the 1860s would replicate the serialized, illustrated reading experiences of his childhood, of which he had fond memories. It wasn't necessarily more exciting to read in this way, he notes, but it would be a trip down memory lane. He continues, "For though it is undoubtedly a bore to read a novel for the first time in sections, nothing is pleasanter than to go back upon it in this way tasting it like old wine" (Beeching 110). For Beeching, illustrators and illustration are central parts of nostalgic rereading. He seems to invest more emotional energy in Austen's illustrations than in her words.

Without the benefit of childhood nostalgia to sugarcoat his illustrated reading (or rereading) experiences, Beeching declares himself disappointed with the Austen illustrators of the 1890s: "Mr. Cooke's persons are devoid of any character whatever, almost of expression; Mr. Brock's are not much better; and Mr. Thomson's, though they are more like real people, are not Miss Austen's people. Look at the conceited boy for instance who does duty for Darcy; Darcy was thirty" (110). These assessments are significant because they show us that Beeching was conversant in the most notable Austen illustrations of the 1890s. He knew them all. He had *studied* them. It was meaningful for an educated reader to have and publish opinions on the illustrations. It signals the arrival of a new moment in the history of Austen's legacy. To know and read (or reread) her was to know, view, and judge the work of her illustrators.

Jane Austen entered the twentieth century as a proven, illustrated literary commodity. The bulk of the illustrations that had emerged in the 1890s continued to circulate in reprinted or new editions in the early 1900s, but there were naturally more publishers who wanted to try their hand at becoming the next Austen-derived financial success, just as Henry James had feared. Individual illustrated Austen titles continued to reach print, too, but a new "complete" Austen edition was published in 1908 by Chatto & Windus, in its St. Martin's Illustrated Library of Standard Authors.[42] It set out to rival—and in some ways to copy—the 1907–9 Austen illustrated edition by J. M. Dent. That edition was Dent's third Austen edition in fifteen years, this time with extensive watercolors by Charles E. Brock. In response, Chatto

& Windus chose as its Austen artist the *Punch* and *Humourist* cartoonist A. (Arthur) Wallis Mills (1878–1940). The Chatto & Windus edition features its illustrator's name in gold on the cover, adding a miniature-sized women's portrait in color above it. This was marketed as a set for the fashionable set and not just for girls.

Several factors worked together to make Austen and her fiction a safe subject for satire, including images aimed at adult audiences. Thomson's illustrations certainly made this possible, with their winking tone, opening the door to see Austen as comic. Just as important was Austen's rebirth as a political figure and as a comic stage presence, as we'll see in later parts of this book. Social criticism in illustration had been nascent in the designs of Thomson and Hammond from the 1890s, but a dozen years later, Wallis Mills went beyond either one in his depictions. Politics, cartoons, and illustrated Austen became, in the early twentieth century, not just a conceivable but a desirable, marketable mix. His Austen edition would turn out to be one of Mills's few literary book illustration commissions. In his work on Austen, Wallis Mills wears his politics lightly, unlike in *Punch*, the satirical magazine. But publisher Chatto & Windus indicated it was capitalizing on the confluence of the two publications. In their Austen advertisements, Chatto & Windus touted Mills as the "well-known artist of London *Punch*."[43]

For each of the edition's ten Austen volumes, Mills provided a frontispiece and nine other plates, as well as his designed endpapers, making him the fourth artist to complete a set of Austen illustrations that reached into the triple digits. Mills's Austen illustrations show a caricaturist's sensibilities. He especially excelled at making Austen's ridiculous minor characters seem laughably awful, from Mr. Hurst's gluttony in *Pride and Prejudice* to Miss Bates's garrulousness in *Emma*. Wallis Mills included many images of men and boys engaging in senseless, and risible, violence. He depicted Austen's snooty women with particular energy and aplomb. Wallis's images are pronounced "rather insipid" by David Gilson, which seems off the mark ("Later Publishing" 148). Mills communicates the ridiculousness of Austen's most absurd characters, especially her most hateful, privileged characters, quite well. He is far more in his visual element when producing a send-up of *Mansfield Park*'s wealthy, daft suitor Mr. Rushworth than he is with a straight-up hero, such as *Pride and Prejudice*'s Mr. Darcy.[44] Mills is less successful in presenting gripping images of the characters and scenes most readers would approach with seriousness. He seems more adept at capturing Austen's buffoons of both sexes than her heroes or heroines.

These images wear their class-based and gendered politics lightly, too, but after seeing Wallis Mills's later suffrage cartoons, his depictions of Austen's characters should be revisited. His Austen edition completed, Mills drew further famed political cartoons for *Punch*. The best known of them may be "The Suffragette That Knew Jiu-Jitsu" (1910). It was an homage to the martial arts instructor who trained the female bodyguard unit at the Women's Social and Political Union, Edith Margaret Garrud (1871–1972). Mills depicts her in a fighting stance, before a small army of police officers, with the subtitle "The Arrest." But the image suggests that any arresting that is going on is Garrud's of the officers. She has arrested them by stopping them in their tracks, so they are unable to arrest her. She's already physically bested several of them, their bodies depicted tossed aside, in various states of vanquishment. Some half-hang over an iron fence, apparently tossed there by the suffragette. The police have lost their hats in the process. Others have landed on the other side of the fence, rubbing their heads from the fall. Tied to the fence is a placard reading, "Votes for Women." A frightened, out-of-shape officer is the largest character in the image, cowering at the front, with several smaller fellow officers crouched behind him.

Looking at the *Punch* jiu-jitsu image in comparison to Wallis Mills's Austen, there are moments of visual overlap. His jiu-jitsu suffragette resembles to some degree his Elizabeth Bennet, with her similarly styled dark hair, toned upper body, and determined-placid expression on her face. Like the jiu-jitsu suffragette, Elizabeth is frequently depicted in Mills's edition with well-defined arms in motion. She, too, locks eyes with her enemies across the room. She also clenches her fists. Wallis Mills's arresting/arrested police officer looks most like his Mr. Woodhouse from *Emma*, with arms raised in fright. Mills's suffrage cartoons are not merely propaganda images. They poke fun at the suffragettes, but they do so while consistently highlighting female wit and strength of body and mind. That similarity seems in keeping with emerging understandings of Austen and her fiction in this turn-of-the-century period. Mills may have been less commercially successful than Thomson as an artist, but he took Thomson's comic innovations for Austen and pushed them further, moving her from the realm of the whimsically humorous to the visual territory of the broadly humorous and satirical. Book illustration helped make the author a different Jane Austen, her fiction a different fiction.

What proved a visual turning point—gradually moving illustrated Austen from a popular product to a fine-art medium—was the emergence of Austen in film and television. The book and film industries began to work hand in hand to get Austen's name and image in front of new generations of readers and viewers, something that happened to many classic authors in this period, of course. In Austen's case, we might date the origins of this shift to 1931, when Grosset and Dunlap published its *Pride and Prejudice* edition, in a series called the Universal Library. That edition, like many books that would emerge over the decades to come, was otherwise unillustrated. It did feature a decorative book jacket cover meant to entice buyers, illustrated by the little-known Alfred Skrenda (1897–1978).[45] Today he might be most recognized for his cover illustration for Charlotte Brontë's *Jane Eyre*, still well enough regarded to have ended up on T-shirts and tote bags.

Skrenda's *Pride and Prejudice* book jacket cover illustration would not seem poised to have had much impact. It isn't visually unusual, with its glamorous, Art Deco–meets-Regency heroine and hero shown from the torso up. The hero dominates the frame, his aquiline nose and curved elbow arched toward the heroine and his hand resting on his just-visible knee. The lily-white heroine, reddish hair worn up, long neck prominent, seems not to notice the hero, as she gazes beyond him and the viewer. The couple's eyes do not meet, and their bodies apparently do not touch, yet their precisely matching

Figure 3.6. *Left*, book jacket cover, Jane Austen's *Pride and Prejudice* (Grosset and Dunlap, 1931), by Alfred Skrenda; *right*, official trailer still, *Pride and Prejudice*, 1940, Metro Goldwyn Mayer.

red lips seem on an inevitable crash course toward each other. Their lips are one of the few parts of Skrenda's image that are not encased in a dramatic black outline. The image doesn't break any illustration-history boundaries or explore new visual territory, for Austen or men and women. But it would end up being put before more eyes—gaining more "viewers"—than perhaps any book illustration before it. It was seen by millions when it was used in a film trailer, almost a decade after its first publication.

The Grosset and Dunlap edition was featured in the official trailer for Robert Z. Leonard's Metro Goldwyn Mayer film version of *Pride and Prejudice* (1940). The two-minute trailer's first image is of Skrenda's book cover, with its dashing man and movie-star beautiful woman. These characters even bear a coincidental passing resemblance to the film's actor-stars, Laurence Olivier and Greer Garson, down to their real-life hair color. After flashing on screen for a few moments, the book jacket image is covered over by a phrase: "One of the Most Famous Novels Ever Written!" Just how many people would have seen a film trailer at that time? One source estimates thirty-three million people in Britain were going to the movies on any given day in this period; in the United States, the estimate is that eighty to ninety million people went to the cinema each week in the 1930s and '40s.[46] That gives us a rough sense of how many millions would have seen this film trailer at their local cinema. The number jumps up further when we add the fact that MGM also used Skrenda's book jacket cover image in many of its print promotional materials for the film, posted in theaters and printed in newspapers.

Skrenda's *Pride and Prejudice* book jacket both died and was immortalized with its transition to film and film publicity. Grosset and Dunlap, the leading American publisher of film tie-in editions, was chosen as the imprint to publish the photoplay edition of *Pride and Prejudice* after the release of MGM's film. Photoplay editions were, as Deirdre Gilbert puts it, "advertised in the movie theaters during the film's run—right along with candy and gum."[47] After the film's release, Grosset and Dunlap almost immediately threw over Skrenda's image for a book jacket using a photo of the MGM film's stars, an oft-used formula at the time. At least ten photoplay editions were published for *Pride and Prejudice*, linking the movie and the book.[48] Most reproduced images from the film in their contents, although not necessarily on their book jackets. Two-dimensional Darcy was no longer represented only as drawn, engraved, or painted. He had also become a photograph.

One Grosset and Dunlap photoplay frontispiece is staged remarkably similarly to Skrenda's illustration, with Olivier's Darcy in almost precisely

Figure 3.7. Book jacket cover, Jane Austen's *Pride and Prejudice* (New York: Grosset and Dunlap, 1940?).

the same outfit, hairstyle, clothing, and position. Garson's Elizabeth differs from Skrenda's heroine in that she looks directly into Olivier's eyes, holding a fan up between them and preventing their bodies from touching. It allows her hands to rest inches away from his chest. The effect is a photographed human tableau that echoes, whether intentionally or not, Skrenda's *Pride and Prejudice* book jacket illustration from a decade earlier. It maintains the fiction (or fact?) that this is a novel that is both fresh and classic. The image puts its man and woman on an almost-level plane, as well as on track for coupledom. The big visual question seems to be whether their eyes and lips will meet.

Did Grosset and Dunlap, or MGM, set out to have the book that became a film, and the film trailer that featured a book cover, replicate that book cover seen on film as its photoplay? The dizzying visual traffic here, from print to book illustration to print ad to celluloid and back and forth, is remarkable, whether these echoed visual images were ever intentional. The Skrenda book cover and book trailer appearance marked the end of one era and the beginning of another for Austen and book design. Moving images meant that book illustration would never again be looked to as the medium that would showcase the author at her most fashionable and contemporary.

By the mid-twentieth century, illustrated Austen titles had traveled far from the objects they'd been at the time of Richard Bentley's Standard Novels in the 1830s, published for "a middle to upper-class audience," with their sensational, intimate, female-dominated images by Ferdinand Pickering.[49] A few editions of the mid-twentieth century followed in the tradition of the 1890s Cranfordization craze in their high quality and prodigious number of illustrations, such as the collectible illustrated Austens published by the Heritage Press (1940; illustrated by Helen Sewell), the Book Society (1944; illustrated by John Austen), or the Folio Society (1957; illustrated by Joan Hassall). But the Austen illustrated book changed perceptibly as her fiction traveled into new media. Media beyond the printed page increasingly became the Austenian point of reference, even for the print illustrated edition. As odd as it may seem now, there was a radio tie-in print edition. In 1951, Hodder and Stoughton published a "shortened version" of *Pride and Prejudice*, advertised on its book jacket cover (as well as in its introduction) as "prepared by H. Oldfield Box, whose radio adaptation of this famous novel enthralled millions of listeners."[50]

The copious photoplay editions—and the radio tie-in edition—demonstrate how Austen's movement into new media has long piggybacked onto old media. Charting such shifts in illustrated Austen ought to make it difficult for us to take seriously today's residual claims about Austen's being "ruined" by graphic novels or by massively multiplayer online role-playing games like *Ever, Jane*. Artists' images of Austen's fiction have served to shape each generation's sense of her material and thrust, her tone and politics. These images inevitably propelled weightier conversations about her fiction and its legacy to wider audiences. In renovating her and her fiction for emerging visual media, book illustrators of a century and more ago carried Austen's image forward by degrees, making the old fashioned into something newfangled. In each case, a few loudly expressed the worry that, in making the leap, Austen would be ruined. Thus far such skeptics have proved unlamentably wrong.

PART TWO

JANE AUSTEN, DRAMATIZED

I shall never again be able to read "Pride and Prejudice" with the old
pleasure. And all because of the mania for acting gridirons!
—A. B. (Arthur Bingham) Walkley (1901)

JANE AUSTEN TODAY ENJOYS far more viewers than readers. It seems not only
likely but probable that most now come by their first impressions of
her and her fiction via moving images. Yet few of us are aware that stage
adaptations once played a similarly foundational, reputation-altering role, a
century and more ago. By the early twentieth century, Austen on the stage
was a formidable presence, as well as a source of controversy. Dramatized
versions of her fiction—and of her—became trendy, caught up in the era's
"mania for acting gridirons," as A. B. Walkley puts it.[1] Thousands came to
know Austen not on the page, through text and illustration, but on the stage,
whether as audience members or as amateur actors themselves. Austen
on the stage has a vigorous, complicated, and storied history, going back
at least to the 1890s and lasting well into the film and television era.[2] That
history, too, transformed her into a different sort of author, especially for
those who first encountered her and her fiction in theatrical performances
of all kinds. Dramatizing Austen moved her and her fiction in even more
politically progressive directions than illustration had, emphasizing the
parts of her novels that celebrated women's independence, particularly
from the 1890s to the 1920s. By the 1930s, Austen on the stage also sexed
her up, in ways both predictable and surprising.

The influence of dramatized Austen is easiest to grasp at the moment of
its greatest popularity and commercial success: the mid-1930s. The stage was
so powerful a medium that the first Austen film adaptation even tried to
capitalize on its connection to the theater. This is evident in the film's casting.
Metro Goldwyn Mayer's *Pride and Prejudice* (1940) chose as its stars two

actors who were proven stage talents: resolute heartthrob Laurence Olivier (Fitzwilliam Darcy) and feisty sweetheart Greer Garson (Elizabeth Bennet). That was a common enough Hollywood move at the time, as the back and forth between stage and screen was frenetic. But promotional materials for the *Pride and Prejudice* film took the stage-movie connection even further. In one set of ads, two authorizing images hover over the fictional couple's heads. The first image is a book jacket cover, discussed in chapter 3. The other is a theater marquee. An early version of MGM's publicity poster reads, "One of the most famous novels . . . One of the most famous plays . . . And now, it will be one of the most famous pictures ever filmed!" The three-minute trailer for the film tweaked it a little: "One of the most famous novels . . . One of the most famous plays ever produced . . . Now, one of the screen's happiest events!"[3]

MGM's self-fulfilling prophecy about its film's road to greatness bore fruit. For the film's 1962 rerelease, its slogan was made into a fait accompli. As a reprise of the publicity poster puts it, this was "one of the most famous novels . . . One of the most famous plays . . . One of the most famous pictures ever filmed!!!" The Austen legacy mapped out in these marketing materials is perfectly clear: first book, then stage, and now film. It's clever Hollywood advertising ("You enjoyed X and Y, so now enjoy Z!"), but it's also a fascinating claim. *Pride and Prejudice* could once have been understood not just as a famous book or as a landmark film but as *one of the most famous plays.* Who among us today imagines *Pride and Prejudice* as having been a famous play? Yet, after 1935, it was.

This matters for many reasons, some of which lead us directly to Colin Firth's Mr. Darcy in the landmark BBC TV series *Pride and Prejudice* (1995). Firth has indicated that, when considering whether to accept the role of Mr. Darcy, he was at first intimidated at the prospect of trying to supplant Laurence Olivier's portrayal of the character.[4] Olivier was one of the great actors of his day—or any day—and he influenced all of the film and TV Darcys who came after him. Firth's Darcy shows evidence of a debt to Olivier in dress, demeanor, and expression. But we rarely recognize that Olivier's portrayal of Darcy wasn't invented out of Austen's original novel alone. It also emerged from previous stage portrayals. Olivier, the film's screenwriters, the producer, and the director would have had stage-actor predecessors in mind as they put Mr. Darcy in scripts and on film. Olivier's performance owes its screen success not only to his striking looks and matchless acting but to the versions of the character as he was played in Helen Jerome's

Broadway and West End hit, *Pride and Prejudice* (1935–36). Jerome's play, officially credited as the film's progenitor, was that most famous of plays referred to on the publicity poster. Jerome's *Pride and Prejudice* laid the groundwork for the infamous wet-white-shirt Firth-Darcy sixty years on. It's not farfetched to suggest that it all started on the stage.[5]

Austen's novels came to the stage much later than those of her most successful contemporaries and rivals, authors such as Sir Walter Scott, Charles Dickens, George Eliot, and Charlotte Brontë. Dramatic adaptations of Scott's Waverley novels, nearly everything by Dickens, and Brontë's *Jane Eyre* (1847) were mounted on professional stages almost immediately after their first publications. Scott expressed no interest in dramatizing his own work, but others knew an opportunity when they saw one. Dramatists attempted stage adaptations of Scott's fiction with lightning speed. Thomas Dibdin is said to have completed his dramatization of Scott's *Kenilworth* (1821) in just two days, yet another stage version was mounted before his.[6] More than 20 dramatizations of Scott's *Ivanhoe* (1820) were published in the nineteenth century.[7] At least 40 versions of Brontë's *Jane Eyre* were staged in the 1880s.[8] Provisional counts of the average annual dramatic productions of nineteenth-century novels make one thing clear: Scott dominated the scene. *Rob Roy* averaged 12.2 per year, making it "the most frequently dramatized novel of all time" (Bolton xx). *Guy Mannering* was just behind it with 10.8. Dickens was staged half as often. *Oliver Twist* averaged 4.3 per year, and *Nicholas Nickelby* 3.4. The rate for *Jane Eyre* was 1.5, with Mary Shelley's *Frankenstein* close behind it, at 1.4 productions averaged per year (xviii).[9] Jane Austen's fiction was absent. In the nineteenth-century fiction-to-stage boom, her novels appear to have been entirely passed over until 1895. That may seem to coincide with her fiction's slow growth to acclaim, but something more was going on, too.

We know this because many famous women authors, like Austen, experienced a dramatic emergence or resurgence in the early twentieth century. Previously collected provisional data from the book *Women Writers Dramatized* offers a snapshot of how Austen's dramatic legacy compared with fellow female novelists. Both Elizabeth Gaskell's *Cranford* (1851–53) and Emily Brontë's *Wuthering Heights* (1847) joined *Pride and Prejudice* in getting a slow start, with "virtually no nineteenth-century dramatizations" (Bolton 95). It wasn't until after *Wuthering Heights* appeared on film in 1939 that it experienced its first stage transformation. *Cranford*, however, followed the same path to the stage as *Pride and*

Prejudice, with dramatizations emerging at the turn of the century (206). No doubt the skyrocketing popularity of both titles in the 1890s book illustration craze spurred on new stage versions. Unlike Austen, however, Gaskell earlier enjoyed novel-to-stage success with her *Mary Barton* (1848), dramatized on the heels of its first publication. Even George Eliot, who objected to stage adaptation of her work in general, saw her novels translated to the theater, with *Adam Bede* (1859) appearing in 1862 and 1884 and *Silas Marner* (1863) in 1871, 1876, and 1881 (200–11). Then Eliot's fiction, like Austen's, experienced a dramatic resurgence in the first decade of the twentieth century.

Staging Austen wasn't just an idea long overlooked. Some believed her fiction not only shouldn't but couldn't be put on the stage. It's evident in the remarks of Catherine J. Hamilton (b. 1841), who discusses the subject in print in 1892—just three years before the first dramatization of Austen was published. Hamilton writes, unequivocally and erroneously, "Not one of [Austen's] novels could possibly be dramatised."[10] Two years later, George Saintsbury—in his preface to the Hugh Thomson–illustrated Peacock edition of *Pride and Prejudice* (1894)—echoes the sentiment in part: "I do not know whether the all-grasping hand of the playwright has ever been laid upon *Pride and Prejudice*; and I dare say that, if it were, the situations would prove not startling or garish enough for the footlights, the character-scheme too subtle and delicate for pit and gallery."[11] Still, Saintsbury doesn't deny the *possibility* of Austen's fiction on the stage or doom any attempt to total failure. "If the attempt were made," he writes, "it would certainly not be hampered by any of that looseness of construction, which, sometimes disguised by the conveniences of which the novelist can avail himself, appear at once on the stage" (xii).

Attempts were made. Dramatic adaptations of Austen began to appear in modest numbers in the 1890s and early 1900s, in both Great Britain and the United States. By 1975, there were at least fifty published plays based on Austen's fiction.[12] The first were designed for the amateur actor and became fashionable, long before they experienced professional stage acclaim. It's an order of dramatic appearance that is highly significant. One scholar dismisses these early Austen plays as "trifling attempts . . . apparently intended only for the schoolroom" (Gilson, *Bibliography* 405).[13] But whether considered trifling as works of art or not, these plays were significant because of where and by whom they were performed. Early Austen plays (often short scenes, rather than full-length adaptations) served as tools of education, especially for young women. These schoolroom and amateur plays were bellwethers of Austen's growing cultural consequence, of how the old was being made new. They set the stage, as it were, for the full-length plays that appeared afterward. Whether designed for amateur or professional performance, these plays created new understandings of Austen and her texts that resonate to this day.

It's especially odd that scholars have disregarded Austen dramatizations, because most now believe that she herself adapted a novel for the stage: a version of Samuel Richardson's *The History of Sir Charles Grandison* (1753–54). That text, *Jane Austen's Sir Charles Grandison* (1980), was first edited by Austen critic B. C. Southam, who argues, contra family legend, that the play is by Austen herself, not by her niece Anna Austen Lefroy. Everyone agrees that the play is in Jane Austen's handwriting. The question is whether the composition is her own. The five-act play does not resemble the short dramatic burlesques of Austen's juvenilia. It is "over fifty pages long" (albeit on small paper) and "bears the stamp of an adult mind," rather than a child's, which is what Anna Austen would have been at the time of her supposed authorship.[14] There are other reasons to suppose the play Jane Austen's. The Austens had "a long tradition of family theatricals," including putting on Richard Brinsley Sheridan's *The Rivals* (1775) when Jane was nine and "a number of later productions" (Southam, introduction 13). Knowing this, we might see portions of her fiction as incorporating the conventions of stage direction, as Joseph Roach has argued.[15] But there is no evidence that she dramatized her own works of fiction.

That sort of effort would begin nearly a century later. The most significant dramatic innovator of Austen, Rosina Filippi (1866–1930), is the subject of chapter 4. Filippi was a pioneering actor, director, writer, and teacher who repurposed Austen for the stage for "every cultivated amateur," through seven short scenes in dialogue—what she called "duologues."[16] Duologue was a fashionable term that had been around since the 1860s, although it seems to have experienced renewed vogue in the 1890s. Filippi's contributions to the genre, published in 1895, were meant to be staged simply and without scenery—no stage, proscenium, footlights, or curtain. A spare approach meant that almost anywhere could be turned into an Austen performance space. Filippi argued that her scenes were complete in themselves, but they were also excerpts that served to amplify selected characters and moments of the plot. These short plays presented Austen as the author of material that emphasized—and celebrated—female domestic protest. Filippi, and those who came after her, shaped the ways in which Austen's fiction was learned by young people, and young women especially, for decades. Untold thousands of students and young women would have voiced, or heard voiced, three-dimensional Elizabeth Bennets recast on stage as agreeable, quasi-feminist role models.

As Austen adaptations arrived in the professional theater, new patterns of representation and meaning arrived, too. In chapter 5, I follow one iconic character as he appeared on stage: *Pride and Prejudice*'s Mr. Darcy. Several decades of the dramatization of Austen's most famous hero provide a window onto how stage adaptations changed the extent and kind of emphasis on Darcy versus Elizabeth over time. I focus on the actor-Darcys of the 1890s to the 1930s, including one who approached him as a Dickens hero, another who took the stage at a surprisingly advanced age, and the little-known amateur female Darcys. Decades of playwrights, directors, and actor-Darcys paved the way for Laurence Olivier's star turn for MGM's film.

Austen's legacy in the theater wasn't all about Elizabeth and Darcy, as I show in chapter 6. Another important milestone in the history of staging Austen is the first full-length biographical play based on her life, which opened at New York's famed Civic Repertory Theater in 1932. With fewer than a dozen performances, the play wasn't a success in theatrical terms, but it fascinates in every other way. Written by Eleanor Holmes Hinkley, first cousin of modernist poet T. S. Eliot, the play *Dear Jane* (1919) has never been published and is rarely given more than a mention in Austen studies. Copies of it survive, however, inviting an extended analysis. *Dear Jane* depicts its subject as both a dedicated writer and an unrepentant flirt. Austen was dramatized as a flapper, a figure night-and-day different from the Christian spinster and old-maiden aunt put forward by early biographies. Hinkley's Jane entertains a series of suitors, before choosing to throw them all over to commit to a life of writing with her sister.

The play itself is interesting, but its little-known performance history is stunning. The first known actors to play Cassandra and Jane Austen in *Dear Jane* in 1932 were themselves an off-stage romantic couple. Cassandra was played by acclaimed director and actor Eva Le Gallienne. Leading lady Josephine Hutchinson, recently divorced from her first husband, played Jane Austen. Le Gallienne and Hutchinson's romantic relationship adds a crucial chapter to the history of Austen and queer studies. Examining *Dear Jane*'s unpublished script in conversation with its history of performance changes how we understand the female-intimacy and marriage-rejecting elements of Hinkley's play. That the first two women known to portray Jane and Cassandra on stage were publicly outed as lovers contributed to critics' mixed response to *Dear Jane*. It also paved the way for Helen Jerome's hyperheterosexualized stage version of *Pride and Prejudice* (1935).

After MGM optioned Jerome's play for film, it needed to come up with its Hollywood screenplay. MGM turned from one screenwriter to another, producing one rejected script after another. These unrealized 1930s scripts are the subject of chapter 7, offering us a wider window onto how Austen was being reimagined as a potentially hot Hollywood property. Each screenwriter or set of writers tried to update Austen's plot and characters, to broaden their appeal to moviegoing audiences. Whether proposing the use of Western-movie style scenes with guns and dogs, or suggesting broad comedy with Elizabeth falling into a mud puddle, or adding smallpox, masquerade balls, and dog-monkey fights, screenwriters grasped at straws. They tried to make Austen's original story more humorous, thrilling, and contemporary. Their ideas never saw the light of day. But their failed efforts reveal where Austen was then envisioned by pop-culture makers as falling dramatically short.

MGM's film was not the end of Jerome's dramatization of Austen on the professional stage. Two decades after it was translated to the screen, Jerome's play inspired a Broadway musical flop, *First Impressions* (1959), by Abe Burrows of *Guys and Dolls* fame. Jerome's play and the MGM screenplay also inspired a never-made Universal television film project in 1974. Each playscript had its innovations and its own visions and versions of Austen, but both were also derivative of dramatizations. We've so overvalued telling the history of Austen adaptation on screen that we've missed the signal ways in which professional and amateur stages paved the way for them. As Austen on stage once again proliferates in the early twenty-first century, we ought to recognize that it's a dramatic resurgence, not an emergence.

CHAPTER FOUR

Austen's First Dramatist

Rosina Filippi's *Duologues* for Every
Cultivated Amateur

Mr. Collins: Your wit and vivacity, I think, must be acceptable to [Lady
Catherine de Bourgh], especially when tempered with the silence and
respect which her rank will inevitably excite.

Elizabeth (*aside*): How am I to stop the man?
—Rosina Filippi, *Duologues and Scenes from the Novels of Jane Austen:
Arranged and Adapted for Drawing-Room Performance* (1895)

If you've read *Mansfield Park* (1814), then you'll find humor in knowing that
the history of performing Jane Austen's fiction begins with private theatricals. It didn't happen in the toniest theaters. Austen's characters and stories
first came to be performed for live audiences on makeshift stages in people's
homes, in community groups, and in schools, especially in the growing
number of girls' schools. In some ways, it's an amusing, real-life echo of the
performance planned at Mansfield Park. A signal difference is that the responsible elders involved in these first 1890s Austen-inspired amateur plays
weren't there to crack down on dramatic impropriety. Instead, the older
generation served as directors, teachers, and impresarios—benign versions
of Austen's officious, unfair Mrs. Norris.

Nor were the fin-de-siècle amateur actors using their thespian turns as
excuses to flirt with each other. Few of these early Austen dramatizations involved acting out romance. They more often staged failed proposals, like
Mr. Collins's to Elizabeth Bennet. Most involved short dramatic or comic
scenes, especially featuring Austen's heroines (and Austen herself) at their
most forthright and bold. In drawing-room performances, before friends and
family, amateur Austen actors denied not only heinous suitors but defied traditional gender roles and the old-fashioned powers that be who would
enforce them. In short, these actors were not channeling *Mansfield Park*'s
righteously timid heroine Fanny Price.

What they were channeling, through selected and adapted portions
of Austen's dialogue, was the era's New Woman movement. It called for

greater personal freedom, more economic independence, and expanded public opportunities for women. Once you notice the pattern, it becomes surprising that so few have realized it before. These amateur dramatizations at first sliced and diced Austen's novels into select chunks of dialogue, with small scenes featuring mostly female actors, performed in female-focused spaces. In the late nineteenth and early twentieth centuries, many people, especially young women, would have first "read" Jane Austen aloud, in excerpts, as amateur actors or in elocution courses.[1] Many more would have heard these scenes read aloud as audience members or classmates. It's not an exaggeration to say that early stage adaptations of Austen's fiction determined how massive numbers of young people first came to know the author and her writings in this period. It profoundly shifted Austen's reputation, making her, despite being "old fashioned," seem a natural ally for the New Woman. No longer an author of politeness, repose, and quietude, the early dramatized Aunt Jane was loud, clear, and funny. For those acting on amateur stages, it was not their mothers' Jane Austen.

Pride and Prejudice's heroine Elizabeth Bennet became a performance staple of amateur theatricals, especially in the scenes in which she proudly—and without being punished for it—chose to say, "No!" We have not previously processed what this meant: young English-speaking women of the early twentieth century were literally ventriloquizing the carefully selected and dramatized words of an Austen heroine who charmingly but firmly spoke her mind, stood her ground, and would not acquiesce to the expectations of those around her. Amateur actors and audiences in the United States, United Kingdom, and beyond were introduced by the uncountable thousands to *Pride and Prejudice* as a tale of admirable female domestic protest. Then, as now, such first encounters would have had a profound effect on how audiences came to understand the themes of the novel, teaching them how to value (or devalue) its author. Yet we've almost entirely written this phenomenon out of our records, probably because drawing-room amateur theatricals went out of style by the mid-twentieth century. We might also blame the fact that later critics would carry the day, with their exaggerated complaints that these dramatizations deserve the historical dustbin as mangled, garbage versions of Austen. It's a story that deserves to be told without the usual condescension.

Thousands may have contributed to the surge in Austen's dramatic popularity, but exceptional individuals led the charge. Pioneering visionary Rosina Filippi (1866–1930) first dramatized Austen for print and adapted it for the stage.² A successful actress who also ran an acting school and taught elocution, Filippi published *Duologues and Scenes from the Novels of Jane Austen: Arranged and Adapted for Drawing-Room Performance* (1895), after having directed many of her own adapted comic scenes, probably with an amateur acting group in Oxford. Oxford was at this time a "hive of amateur dramatic activity," and Filippi was directing at least one group, the Christmas Dramatic Wanderers. There was genius among them. One of her actors, "Dolly," became the famed Dorothea Baird (1875–1923).³ Filippi herself was already a proven stage talent. In 1895, Baird and Filippi appeared together in the London Haymarket Theatre production of *Trilby*, with Baird in the lead role.

Just one year before Filippi's *Duologues* saw print, and during the period in which they were likely being performed by her troupe in Oxford, an American critic was opining that Jane Austen should be drama-proof. The critic exclaims in 1894, "Miss Jane Austen seems to say *Noli me tangere* to biographers, critics, illustrators and literary or artistic embroiderers of every sort. Most of all does she cry hands off to the intending dramatist."⁴ But "hands off" did not hold, on either side of the Atlantic. The critic suggests that there may have been an American rival or forerunner to Filippi: "A well-known man of letters told me the other day, that some intemperate girl had sent him a stage version of 'Emma'! Even the newest woman could not make such an experiment a success" (737). The names of this critic, as well as the well-known man of letters and upstart "girl" dramatist of *Emma* he references, seem to be lost to history. But mere months later, Filippi did exactly what raised hackles. She became the new woman who made the experiment of dramatizing Austen a success.

Some since have called Filippi's book lightweight, but, in its repurposed scenes and illustrations for actors and directors, it was brilliantly conceived and executed. Reviews and wide circulation suggest, too, that its impact was great, regardless of how any reader then or now might assess its literary or dramatic quality. Filippi developed a passion for Jane Austen, and she envisioned dramatizing the author's fiction as filling a cultural need and creating a marketable opportunity. Dickens had long been incredibly popular in dramatic dialogues for private theatricals.⁵ Why not Austen? Filippi brought together her knowledge of Austen and her expertise in stagecraft, expressing confidence in her product. In her introduction to the *Duologues*, Filippi declares, "I am convinced that Jane Austen *as a play-wright* will fascinate her audiences as much as she has her readers *as a novelist*."⁶ The London

Times's reviewer agrees, declaring "We share Miss Filippi's conviction."[7] To some today, this may sound like an absurd fantasy, but Filippi's prediction came true and held true. It did so well into the twentieth century.

Filippi brought to the project her skills as a storyteller and as an artful narrator of her own past. She claimed Italian and French descent, having been born in Venice, the daughter of the Italian music critic Filippo Filippi (1830–87). Rosina's father was best known as the man who gave Puccini his first positive review, and he was an ardent supporter of Verdi and Wagner.[8] Her mother, Paolina Vaneri, was a renowned singer, said to be French by birth, who married Filippi in 1868 and became the first woman professor (of singing) at the Royal Conservatory in Milan in 1878.[9] Vaneri's mother—Rosina's grandmother—was the writer Madame (Georgina) Colmache (c. 1811–1904), described as "a connecting link with the times of the first Napoleon" because she was the widow of the private secretary of Prince Talleyrand.[10] This all sounds very cosmopolitan and high culture—aristocrats, Italian opera stars, professors, French diplomats, and the like. For an aspiring stage actress in London like Rosina Filippi, that sort of European cachet and those cultural connections would have been of no small value.

She was not initially forthcoming—at least not publicly—about the fact that she was also of British descent and grew up in England. Filippi was raised for some years by her grandmother, the aforementioned Madame Colmache, rather than by her French singing professor mother or her Italian music critic father, both of whom seem to have lived in Italy. But Madame Colmache was English, not French, by birth, having been born in London as Georgina Alicia Lee. A mother of four, said to have been widowed in France, Colmache returned to Britain, supporting herself as a writer and journalist. She contributed a weekly column for forty years to the *Birmingham Daily Post*. Madame Colmache's obituary describes her as a friend to George Sand, Gioachino Rossini, Charles Dickens, Agnes Strickland, Lady Rosina Lytton, and Frédéric Chopin, with William Thackeray particularly mentioned as a "personal friend."[11] In published accounts, presumably created with her cooperation, Filippi rarely mentions her British ancestry or anything with a whiff of the *Birmingham Daily Post*. The glamour quotient of these parts of her pedigree were lacking.

To be fair, Filippi's mysteriousness about her English heritage seems tied to a lack of clarity about how and where she was raised. Some accounts mention a Paris education, but Grandmother Colmache seems to have been the one more closely involved in rearing the Filippi daughters. Filippi's obituary reports that she and her grandmother escaped from France together at the outbreak of the Paris Commune in 1871, when the girl would have been in her fifth year. Rosina Filippi was said to have first set out to be an opera singer like her mother, having afterward turning to acting.[12] Census records show that, as a teenager, Filippi was living in England in a household with her grandmother, her unmarried uncle Morris (or Maurice) Colmache, the manager of a telegraph company, and her unmarried aunt Laura (or Laure).[13]

In published features about Filippi's life as an actor, she liked to emphasize her foreign roots and was often described in the press as olive-skinned, as if to concretize that heritage. In 1898, when proposing the creation of a drama school, she touted her dual French and English training.[14] Filippi was cast in outsized minor comic roles, not as a leading lady. Surviving photographs suggest a charismatic woman in the mold of the jocular Mrs. Jennings from *Sense and Sensibility*—a peculiar combination of iconoclastic and maternal. Her son-in-law's sister, famous actor Dame Sybil Thorndike, candidly describes Filippi as having "*such* a temper, a terrible temper," but the surviving stories suggest someone driven more by a benevolent artistic-educational vision than an oversized actor ego.[15] A fellow actor, E. Harcourt Williams, says Filippi was "a woman who put up with no nonsense" and "a forthright character tempered with great humour" and a "rich chuckle."[16]

Filippi became beloved by many greats of her generation. George Bernard Shaw was a fan. His letter to her of June 21, 1905, trying to persuade Filippi to accept the role of Cleopatra's nurse in his play *Caesar and Cleopatra*, flatters her enormously. Shaw writes, "Do try to get free. There is nobody like you. All I want is the best of everything; and you are not only the best, but something more—something different in kind & quality."[17] A letter from Filippi to Shaw shows that she was a free-spirited woman who presents herself as flighty and unreliable, though not entirely unwilling to please. She responds to Shaw, "I am never quite sure of what I *say*—I speak at random—I *mean* what I say when I *say* it, but as I never remember *what* I say I also can't remember what I *meant* when I said it," but she concludes, "when you want me I shall be proud to play for you."[18] It's hard not to read each of them as playing calculated, self-serving parts in this exchange, but the details may be telling. Filippi understood the extent to which correspondence, self-fashioning, and career management might be handled in the manner of an early nineteenth-century country dance.

That is one reason we might not be surprised at her attraction to Jane Austen's life and writings. Filippi lived a kind of public-private double life.

In the public eye as an actress on the London stage, she also took pains to create a more conventional private life as a wife and mother in Oxford. The other name she used was Mrs. H. M. Dowson. On the title page to the *Duologues*, she uses both names: "By Rosina Filippi (Mrs. Dowson)." Four years earlier, in 1891 (after having been on the stage for nearly a decade, much of that with famed actor-manager F. R. Benson's Shakespearean company), Filippi had married Henry Martin Dowson. He's been described as a man who "lived in Iffley, a village outside of Oxford, played the viola, and was a brewer"—a Nonconformist—who just happened to be married to "one of the best-known stage actresses of the time."[19] It's not clear how the two met, but outward signs suggest a successful marriage, raising four children. Filippi led a full life. When she is discussed by recent scholars, it's usually for (unsuccessfully) trying to establish a people's theater in London, to bring Shakespeare to the masses at low cost.[20] Few realize how interesting a woman Austen's first dramatist was.

Reviewers praise Filippi's *Duologues* for how little they tinkered with Austen's prose. In her preface to the *Duologues and Scenes*, Filippi describes herself as an arranger of the material, but she obviously takes license with the seven scenes she adapts from four Austen novels: two from *Pride and Prejudice*, three from *Emma*, and one each from *Sense and Sensibility* and *Northanger Abbey*. (*Mansfield Park* and *Persuasion*—arguably Austen's least comic novels—are the ones that Filippi passes over.) Filippi retitles each scene with a capsule phrase describing its theme and characters, such as "Literary Tastes: Duologue between Catherine Morland and Isabella Thorpe" (1) or "Lady Catherine's Visit: Duologue between Lady Catherine and Elizabeth Bennet" (123).

Filippi's *Duologues* are a pleasurable read. One can easily imagine the scenes enjoyed by audiences, as well as by fledgling actors. In giving asides to Austen's characters (often while they're alone on stage), Filippi makes them more broadly comic than they are in the novels. This may not be to everyone's liking, but she renders them and their thoughts refreshingly directly. It's hard not to take pleasure in Elizabeth, listening to Mr. Collins's proposal, vocalizing asides such as "I may as well get it over as soon and as quietly as possible" (109) and, dripping with sarcasm, "The idea of this man being run away with his feelings" (110). Along with these amusing exaggerations, there are false notes, such as when Filippi has her Mrs. Elton, in an aside, declare her own husband "foolish" (62). (Then again, perhaps Filippi has a valuable insight. We don't get much information from the original novel's narration as to what Mrs. Elton really thinks of her much-vaunted Mr. E.)

Filippi's compact, octavo book, at 140 pages, provides a smattering of Austen, not a deep reading experience. It's in keeping with her reasons for the project: "The idea of compiling this small book arose from the dearth of good duologues and one-act plays suitable for amateur performance" (Filippi vii). The *Duologues* present an Austen cleverly packaged for the everyday reader, not for the well-trained aficionado and critic. Filippi's focus is on Austen's humor and on the villainous characters' delectable awfulness. This approach played well to Filippi's own talents as an actor, but it also catered to a range of contemporary theatrical tastes. The *Duologues* repurpose Austen for, as Filippi puts it, "every cultivated amateur" (viii).

To the publisher of the *Duologues*, Filippi's book was also Austen repurposed for new readers and collectors, designed to sell. J. M. Dent made a crucial marketing decision when it brought out her *Duologues*. Three years earlier, in 1892, as we saw in the previous section, Dent published its ten-volume edition of Austen's novels, edited by R. Brimley Johnson and illustrated by William C. Cooke. When Dent published Filippi's *Duologues*, it designed the book to match its earlier edition. The *Duologues* were widely advertised as "uniform" with the Dent Austen, meaning that one could neatly line up one's Austen books on a shelf, as nearly identical. In effect, Filippi's *Duologues* was marketed as an eleventh volume of Austen's fiction. It was made to seem as if, in buying Filippi's book, you were completing your Austen set. In this way, Dent could appeal to those already loyal to Austen. But Filippi's book was pitched to the novice, too. Reviewers understood well that the book would be used, as one put it, by the "uninitiate in Miss Austen."[21] The *Duologues* served as both an extension of Austen's own writings and as an introduction to them. They appear to have been designed, by author and publisher, in the hope of capturing established and new audiences.

The historical moment at which the *Duologues* appeared was also of consequence. As mentioned earlier, Filippi's dramatized Austen was born on the heels of what came to be called the New Woman movement, a time when many, particularly well-heeled, well-educated women in Great Britain and North America, were roused to advocate for and seek what they believed would be more meaningful lives for females, including employment or activity outside of the home, political representation, and greater personal freedoms. Young women of privilege—and their teachers—were hungry for dramatic texts that developed speaking skills and gave expression to the idea that females are strong, capable, and intelligent. Finding a woman writer whose words, characters, and stories could advance these projects served the New Woman's political ends. Austen's fiction also had the advantage of having been pre-endorsed as great by great men, including Walter Scott, Thomas Babington Macaulay, and Alfred, Lord Tennyson. Austen could at once be packaged as old and new, old guard and New Woman. Filippi's book pulled it off.

Early dramatized Austen was often by, about, and for women. Filippi's Austen duologues are, like Ferdinand Pickering's early Austen illustrations, noticeably and profoundly female focused, with a dearth of successful suitor-heroes. In all, Filippi's Austen duologues and scenes contain sixteen character parts—twelve female and four male. Those four male parts are Mr. Collins, Mr. John Dashwood, Mr. Knightley (talking to Mrs. Elton), and a second Mr. Knightley (talking to Emma, after Emma speaks to Harriet). Seven scenes, then, include just one set of lovers, and that set for just half of a scene. Romance is not at all the point of these dramatic texts. Women's self-confident voices, in the face of domestic and familial conflict, are.

One reviewer, acknowledging that the volumes would "assuredly be welcome and popular," nevertheless believes they could not be successful with well-known amateur theater groups in Cambridge, "for the obvious reason," the reviewer writes, "that the women characters are all-important."[22] That reviewer does, however, make a joke that Austen's descendant, Richard Arthur Austen-Leigh (1872–1961), might make it work.[23] President of the Amateur Dramatic Club at Cambridge, Austen-Leigh was well known for taking female dramatic roles, with his Mrs. Malaprop being especially well received.[24] The reviewer declares (surely cheekily) that Austen-Leigh would make "an excellent Lady Catherine."[25]

The *Duologues* also guided its amateur directors and producers, not just its actors. It features eight illustrations, ostensibly so that actors will not make the mistake, as Filippi puts it in her preface, of choosing inappropriate, anachronistic costumes. (Shades of Pickering's illustrations may be perceived here.) But the *Duologues* offer images that go far beyond guidance on dress. They indicate potential cues for blocking—positions of bodies, physical interpretations of scenes, and other entertaining flourishes. Some illustrations are also broadly comic, rather than strictly functional, such as that of Emma on her knees, execution style, being shot through the chest by Cupid's arrow (Filippi 100). This image surely derives from the fashionable cupids in

Thomson's Peacock edition, published the previous year, rather than as a guide to actors or directors.

Considering the *Duologues'* illustrations in comparison with William Cooke's allows us to see how they move beyond the functional and into the interpretive and political. Cooke's illustration, from his 1892 Dent *Pride and Prejudice*, is captioned, "Lady Catherine beaten." It shows Lady Catherine in a dominant physical position, lording over Elizabeth. Elizabeth Bennet is "beating" her by sitting calmly and coolly on a bench, as Lady Catherine points a finger and foments. If this is victory, it's an intellectual one. It is otherwise quite physically passive for the heroine. Comparing Cooke's illustration to the one that Margaret Fletcher produced for Filippi's *Duologues*, we see the potential for an alternate interpretation of the scene. Fletcher's version depicts a very different physical arrangement from Cooke's. Fletcher's Elizabeth stands as her Lady Catherine sits, almost hunched over. Elizabeth's position could be read as deference, but it also puts her in a position of physical dominance on the stage. Fletcher's Elizabeth stands back, bemused,

Figure 4.1. Left, "Lady Catherine Beaten," Jane Austen's *Pride and Prejudice*, vol. 2 (London: J. M. Dent, 1892), frontispiece, by William Cubitt Cooke; *right*, "Lady Catherine and Elizabeth Bennet," Rosina Filippi's *Duologues and Scenes from the Novels of Jane Austen Arranged and Adapted for Drawing-Room Performance* (London: J. M. Dent, 1895), 125, by Margaret Fletcher.

hands perched on the sofa. Her stance suggests her ownership of the object, the room, and the situation.

Cooke's and Fletcher's illustrations offer us almost opposing Elizabeths. The only clues Austen's novel itself gives as to the placement of the characters' bodies do not exactly accord with either illustration. Lady Catherine commands Elizabeth to sit, but it's not said whether she does so. The narrator also indicates that at one point during this scene both women are sitting down, but when Elizabeth rises, Lady Catherine immediately rises also. It's hard to imagine either illustration as attempting fidelity to Austen's prose, given these details. Cooke's and Fletcher's images both must be understood as loose, albeit telling, visual interpretations of the text. Published within three years of each other, these illustrations represent the dueling ways in which images of Austen were circulating. Crucially, only one, Fletcher's, was designed with intention of being physically reenacted.

That Fletcher would put her Elizabeth Bennet in a more active, forceful position accords with the life and politics of the illustrator. Margaret Fletcher (1862–1943) was a social critic who pushed the envelope for what was then allowed for women. She and Filippi must have known each other in Oxford, where Fletcher was raised as an Anglican clergyman's daughter. She later become an art teacher, gaining at the same time a name as a talented amateur actor. It's tempting to imagine Filippi and Fletcher collaborating not only on the printed *Duologues* but on their earlier staged test runs.[26] There is evidence that the scenes were being performed by Filippi "and her friends" as the "Jane Austen Comedies" in Oxford; the amateur stage seems a likely place for the author-artist collaboration to have had its genesis.[27] A decade after the *Duologues* were published, Fletcher would convert to Catholicism. She went on to found the Catholic Women's League and wrote several works advocating for the enlargement of women's roles in the church. One of them was *Christian Feminism: A Charter of Rights and Duties* (1915).[28]

Like Fletcher's illustrations, Filippi's *Duologues* stress Austen's female protagonists as assertive women. Filippi repeatedly chooses to emphasize the moments in which Austen's female characters are most direct and rebellious. Her short scenes may ostensibly teach students about elocution, history, or literature, but they were also teaching comportment and behavior. Filippi adds emotional descriptions in parentheses for the characters to play that make evident their self-confidence. Filippi's Elizabeth is given many asides with the audience that highlight her knowing rebellion. When told that she must stay in the drawing room to hear Mr. Collins's addresses, she replies, "I am going away by myself." When commanded by her mother to stay, she says in an aside, "Well, if it has to be—I may as well get it over as soon as possible" (109). After Mr. Collins makes his declaration, Elizabeth says, in another aside, "How am I to stop the man?" (111). Elizabeth's strength and humor are accentuated—we might say modernized—as they are communicated and embodied beyond Austen's original prose.

In her conversation with Lady Catherine de Bourgh (misspelled as De Burgh in Filippi's text), Elizabeth is assigned emotional responses to assist actors that also reshape scenes into moments of calculated rebellion. When Lady Catherine asks Elizabeth whether she's engaged to Mr. Darcy, Filippi's Elizabeth responds with emotions not clearly specified in the original text:

> ELIZABETH (*surprised and angry*): If you believed it impossible to be true, I
>   wonder you took the trouble of coming so far. What could your ladyship
>   propose by it?
> LADY C: At once to insist upon having such a report universally contradicted.
> ELIZABETH (*coolly*). Your coming to Longbourn to see me will be rather a
>   confirmation of it, if, indeed, such a report is in existence. (Filippi 130)

In addition to adding cues for Elizabeth such as "*quietly,*" "*surprised,*" and "*rising angrily,*" Filippi gives the heroine several asides to deliver in this scene, too. About Lady Catherine, Filippi's Elizabeth says, "Heaven! how could I think her like her nephew" (129), where the original has the more emotionally equivocal, "How could I ever think her like her nephew?"[29] When Lady Catherine takes her leave of Elizabeth without sending regards to her mother, the heroine is given a cheeky reply in closing: "Good-day to you, Lady Catherine." In the original novel, Elizabeth makes no answer. Filippi goes further, providing Elizabeth with the last line of the scene. In an aside about her eagerness for Darcy to arrive the next day, Filippi's Elizabeth declares, "Perhaps I, too, may learn to think the Bennet family lucky in spite of Lady Catherine de Burgh" (139). Elizabeth's sassy self-determination comes through even more clearly in Filippi's version, despite its using, in the bulk of the scene, Austen's original dialogue.

It's impossible to chart how many actors and audiences became familiar with Austen through Filippi's *Duologues*, but the number seems potentially, even astoundingly, large. The book went into a second edition in 1904. Two duologues were anthologized, by permission, in *The Reciter's Treasury of Prose and Drama* (1904).[30] A third edition was published in 1907. Then a new edition appeared in 1929, reedited and introduced. This time, it was presented as a textbook, with a series of study questions as its appendix. This is an interesting evolution of the text, although it's clear Filippi brought a teacher's sensibilities to the project from the first.[31] There is also evidence of 1920s radio versions of the *Duologues*, suggesting an even wider impact, for both Filippi and Austen.[32] The *Duologues*, from their original publication to their last edition thirty-five years on, functioned as more than a dramatization of Austen. They served as a powerful teaching tool for those seeking to impart, or to gain, an education in literature, history, acting, public speaking, and female self-assertion.

One source from the period gives us a glimpse into how Filippi's text and others like it may have been used. Former high school headmistress Fanny Johnson published her essay "School Plays" in 1909, describing herself as one of the "increasing number" of people who "believe in the drama as an instrument of education." She notes "the superiority both in quantity and quality of the plays provided for the use of girls," recognizing that "even plays specially adapted for boys . . . have for the most part been written by women."[33] Johnson also mentions Filippi's Austen *Duologues*, calling it "well known" and "chiefly suitable for small classes in girls' boarding schools" (101). School plays, then—not just Austen adaptations—were perceived as written by, and geared toward, girls and women, particularly privileged ones.

This is demonstrably the case in Austen dramatic adaptations. Of the fifty texts of this type that Gilson catalogues, published between 1895 and 1975, 62 percent were written by women, 30 percent by men, and 4 percent by collaborator couples. (A further 4 percent have not yet been sex-identified.)[34] As Gilson acknowledges, however, he kept track of printed adaptations only, not known performances in which a script—which may or may not survive— was registered. The Lord Chamberlain's Plays Correspondence file at the British Library shows an additional seven dramatic versions of *Pride and Prejudice* alone, at least four of them authored by women, in this period.[35] Other versions can be inferred, such as *Pride and Prejudice* script authored by "Miss Booth" that actor Sybil Thorndike describes in an unpublished 1933 letter as "well done." Thorndike nevertheless turns down the opportunity to be a part of it, because, as she tells the author, "I already have another 'Pride and Prejudice' play which I have promised to use if I ever want to do such a one."[36]

As these examples show, many began to join Filippi in the Austen dramatization effort, the aforementioned Fanny Johnson herself becoming one of the number.[37] These writers may have been acting on what one reviewer called "a feeling of good-natured envy" of Filippi's "excellent" and "simple" idea, one that "might so easily have occurred to them."[38] There were further stage versions of Austen almost immediately on both sides of the Atlantic, with most of them written by amateur playwrights. A few were full-length plays, such as *Pride and Prejudice by Jane Austen Arranged in Dramatic Form*, registered with the Copyright Office in November 1901, by Ohio librarian Hortense Fogelsong (d. 1915).[39] It was performed by a group of women teachers in Dayton, Ohio, who called themselves the Helen Hunt Club. They were devoted to dramatizing literature.[40] The play does not seem to have been published. The most successful full-length American version of Austen was by Mary Keith Medbery MacKaye (1845–1924). She wrote and published *Pride and Prejudice: A Play, Founded on Jane Austen's Novel* (1906) in four acts, which was frequently staged in American schools.[41] (Its actor-Darcys will be discussed in chapter 5.) Far more common were single scenes or miniature plays based on Austen's novels.

There were soon dozens of these Austen scenes and plays for amateur actors, published both as stand-alone texts and in collections of texts drawn from "classic authors." As we saw earlier, Austen was by no means alone in being used this way, as other novelists' work was similarly transformed. The fiction of Dickens and Scott proved enormously popular for selected scene dramatization in this period, as did that of Eliot and Gaskell.[42] These stand-alone scenes for the amateur stage were often made available simultaneously through agents in the United Kingdom, the United States, and beyond, suggesting a global market. Even the *Duologues* began to include an inserted slip prior to the title page that read, "Permission to perform these duologues in Great Britain, whether singly or otherwise, must be obtained from the publisher."[43] There was a growing, and probably lucrative, Austen amateur drama licensing market.

By far the most popular Austen text staged by the amateur or student actor during the early twentieth century was *Pride and Prejudice*. Particularly prevalent were the novel's scenes featuring Elizabeth's sizzling dialogue, including her conversations with Mr. Collins, Mr. Darcy, and Lady Catherine de Bourgh. These are among the most famous sections of the novel, presenting readers with evidence of the heroine's strength, intelligence, and right to self-determination in courtship. These adaptations presented dialogue-rich sections as *stand-alone scenes*. Typical among them is Sophie Trasel and Elizabeth Williams's "Mr. Collins in Search of a Wife: Being Scenes from Jane Austen's Novel 'Pride and Prejudice'" (1903), which describes its focus through its title. Registered for US copyright, the script survives, although its performance history is murky.[44] Other examples of the type were published by lawyer, writer, and critic Phosphor Mallam. His two short dramatic pamphlets, *Mr. Collins Proposes* and *Lady Catherine Is Annoyed with Elizabeth Bennet* (1912), also use their titles to reveal their dramatic thrust.[45] In each case, the scenes echo Filippi's choice of female-focused, power-struggle-centered Austen content.

Nowhere is the early emphasis on Elizabeth Bennet's staged defiance made clearer than in the title of the play *Elizabeth Refuses* (1926), adapted by feminist-socialist-pacifist playwright Margaret Macnamara (1874–1950).[46] Her play features five actors and is described as "shaped to play in Five-and-twenty minutes, on a stage lacking front curtain and scenery." Its innovation is to have Elizabeth refuse Mr. Collins and Lady Catherine in the same scene. To Mr. Collins, Elizabeth says, "I know I should make you miserable" (14). Macnamara's play also demonstrates the extent to which such early dramatic works were designed to be performed to small audiences, catering to girls and women. The text of *Elizabeth Refuses* gives directions for how to pay royalties for amateur use but also indicates that "special facilities are given for public performances by Girls' Clubs and Women's Institutions" (1). Macnamara would later publish another Austen dramatization, *I Have Five Daughters: A Morning Room Comedy in Three Acts Made from Jane Austen's novel "Pride and Prejudice"* (1936). As in her earlier effort, Macnamara's dialogue works to make Elizabeth even more "pert" and "saucy," as the character calls herself. Rewritten scenes emphasize Elizabeth's courage, outspokenness, lack of sentimentalism, and wit—hallmarks of the New Woman and the first wave of feminism, leading up to the widespread passage of women's suffrage. Macnamara's plays are later examples of this kind, but they're representative of many ongoing trends in dramatizing Austen, in showcasing Elizabeth at her most defiant and independent.

Readers at this time who came to Austen's novel *after* having seen or acted in these short plays would have gone into the original text anticipating a story about a heroine who exerts her own strong will, proudly saying no. In the novel, of course, Elizabeth also apologizes, accepts, and expresses gratitude. But what many in this generation of readers would have had imprinted on them, through performing or watching amateur drama, is the image of a witty Elizabeth thwarting the wishes and imperatives of the traditional and the powerful, in favor of her own desires and will. In these scenes, Darcy seems almost beside the point, a fortunate afterthought, a just dessert for Elizabeth's cleverness, self-assertion, and confidence. These dramatic scenes and plays were written by a far more politicized set of progressive (and largely female) authors than we ever suspected. They compel us to expand, if not overturn, our sense that Austen's early celebrity depended on establishment conservative male literati. The Austen dramatists' reach was arguably larger, in the short if not in the long term. While the literati were arguing over whether Austen and her novels ought to be appreciated or depreciated as politically limited or narrow in scope (as we will see in chapter 8), dramatists were tweaking her characters and plots to more directly empower girls and young women. Although we've been slow to realize it, it was the opposite of trifling, lightweight work.

CHAPTER FIVE

Playing Mr. Darcy before
Laurence Olivier

Cross Dressing, Consuming Passion,
and Cracking the Whip

From 1940 to 1995, the screen actor who *was* Darcy was Sir Laurence Olivier (1907–89). Viewers of a certain age might remember and appreciate David Rintoul's Darcy (1980), but Olivier's position was secure before the arrival of Colin Firth in the BBC *Pride and Prejudice* mini-series (1995). Olivier, a star for whom words like "incomparable" seem inadequate, attracted the greatest critical acclaim for his Shakespearean stage roles. His best-known film roles include turns as Heathcliff in William Wyler's *Wuthering Heights* (1939) and as the brooding widower in Alfred Hitchcock's gothic thriller *Rebecca* (1940), with its *Jane Eyre*–esque plot. For many years, Olivier was the filmgoer's favorite broody, mysterious, tall-dark-and-handsome hero. Among Janeites, Olivier's Darcy may stand out as his most memorable role, despite the film's being largely derided today, except for his performance.

Even Colin Firth was at first intimidated by Olivier. Firth said that, once he learned from his brother that Darcy was "supposed to be sexy" and re-searched the role, he started to think, "Oh, God, Olivier was so fantastic and no one else could ever play the part."[1] Olivier famously hated the role of Darcy and the resulting film, but, like Firth after him, he couldn't escape his star turn as Austen's hero. In a book of autobiographical reminiscences written in his late seventies, Olivier wrote, "I'm still signing autographs over Darcy's large left lapel." Olivier modestly attributes that fact to MGM's sumptuous costumes, rather than to his own powers of attraction; he certainly didn't think the quality of the film accounted for it. He thought the film missed "the best points in the book."[2]

The dominance of Firth and Olivier in the pantheon makes it easy to for-get that there were many three-dimensional Darcys prior to Olivier.[3] Most of those living, breathing Darcys played the character in front of live audi-

ences, on the stage. We saw in chapter 4 how the amateur theater had a previously unrecognized impact on Austen's legacy, particularly in amplifying
the themes of women's independence and in celebrating admirable domestic
protest. Dramatic versions of Elizabeth Bennet were reshaped by stand-alone
scenes and amateur theatricals presented in the wake of increased educational
opportunities for women, the New Woman, and the women's suffrage movement. But as Austen's novel came to the professional stage, her hero, too, took
new shape. Over the course of the first half of the twentieth century, stage
adaptations of *Pride and Prejudice* shifted the focus of the reader-viewer
away from envisioning the plot as centered on the admirable rebellion and
growth of a witty, saucy heroine. Instead, these adaptations moved toward
a focus on audience members' witnessing the heroine's gradual realization
of what they'd seen all along: a sexy, misunderstood hero.

We often hear claims today about the groundbreaking nature of Colin
Firth's sexualized portrayal of Darcy. Screenwriter Andrew Davies is credited with creating the first version of the character that presented him as
perceptibly in touch with his manly desires.[4] Davies imagines himself as
being able to "help" Austen with audiences by "writing such a pro-Darcy
adaptation . . . If they saw him suffering or just doing something very physical, the audience would treat him more like a real person, and not just have
Elizabeth's view."[5] But the history of stage Darcys shows that Austen's dramatic adapters were running with this idea long before Davies. Darcys on
the professional stage date back to 1901, although at first in what Davies
might call anti-Darcy adaptations. They were Darcys who spent much of
the play acting in ways that reinforced Elizabeth's most uncharitable views
of the character. In this chapter, we'll examine stage Darcys as they moved
from pompous stiffs who turn out to be marriageable in end-of-play big reveals, to becoming lusting hotties roiling with passion throughout the action.
These later Darcys were meant to be irresistible to everyone except Elizabeth, until she finally gives herself over to him, too.

In the early years of Austen on the stage, Darcy seems to have been a difficult stage part, both as the character was written by playwrights and as
he was interpreted by individual actors. The first three-dimensional, professional actor Darcy was conceived for the stage by Rosina Filippi, the
same innovator who published the first Austen adaptations for dramatic
amateurs. Filippi wrote *The Bennets* (1901), staged as a special matinee at the
Royal Court Theatre on March 1, 1901. She gave it the subtitle *A Play without a
Plot*. The script doesn't appear to have survived, but both subtitle and published

reviews suggest it was not a stand-alone retelling of Austen's novel. It appears to have consisted of connected scenes that relied on an audience's familiarity with the novel. One reviewer dubs it "a play with a plot indifferently handled," although he credits the work with being "the most interesting" of the week's new shows in its novelty. He also concludes that the play was at least as "cheerful a meeting with old friends as is afforded by many inappropriate book illustrations," showing the extent to which the three media—novel, illustration, and play—were then seen as in conversation.[6]

The surviving program and reviews indicate that Filippi doubled as the cast's comic Mrs. Bennet. The play's codirectors, E. Harcourt Williams (1880–1957) and Winifred Mayo (née Winifred Monck-Mason; 1870–1967), doubled as its Darcy and Elizabeth. That the first professional *Pride and Prejudice* on stage was codirected by the actors who played Elizabeth and Darcy itself seems like a fairy-tale piece of literary and theater history.[7] That the play was written by the woman who played its Mrs. Bennet seems almost the stuff of fiction. (We've already heard about Filippi in chapter 4.) Her partners in the first professional stage Austen were just as intriguing. Mayo would later become a leader in the women's suffrage movement and take the stage *as* Jane Austen, as we'll see in chapter 9. Harcourt Williams, too, would later direct suffrage plays.[8] But much of the rest of the cast was drawn from the troupe with which Filippi had had a long association: F. R. Benson's company of Shakespearean players, now understood as a training ground for many of the era's most accomplished actors.

The Bennets' Darcy—the first professional stage Darcy—was often cast as a Romeo or an Othello. Harcourt Williams was one of the players "borrowed," as the program puts it, from Benson's troupe. His turn as Darcy was early on in his career, when he was an emerging talent in his early twenties. He eventually achieved renown as a character actor and London theater director. We can gather only a little about the sort of Darcy the play offered audiences, primarily from reviews. One reviewer describes *The Bennets'* Darcy as "becomingly superior," suggesting that he was not played as entirely unlikeable to the audience, even when Elizabeth dislikes him.[9] A later critic would dub Williams "one of the ideal younger heroes of the romantic drama."[10] Another describes him as "refreshingly youthful," with "grace and a pleasing personality."[11]

Not everyone embraced his Darcy, beloved actor though he may have been. Drama critic A. B. Walkley reports being extremely disappointed. He suggests that dramatizing Austen is a "ghastly crime," writing, "My own

Figure 5.1. Collage of Austen Actors, *clockwise from top left:* Rosina Filippi, undated photograph; E. Harcourt Williams, undated postcard; Winifred Mayo, undated postcard (permission of Aurora Metro Press); Ben Webster, undated postcard.

private pleasure in the book is marred by associations with the real and contemporary. I have, like all readers, my own ideas of Darcy and Elizabeth; I have lived with them for years, and return to them year by year. Henceforth I shall always be bothered by recollections of Mr. So-and-So at the Court Theatre, representing Mr. Darcy as if he were Mr. Martin Harvey."[12] Another reviewer, too, thought Williams's Darcy "curiously alike in voice and manner" to Martin-Harvey, finding the performance "to the end" "rather incomprehensible."[13]

The likening of Harcourt Williams's Darcy to the style of a fellow actor is worth untangling. The man who became Sir John Martin-Harvey (1863–1944) was best known for starring as Sydney Carton in an 1899 adaptation of Charles Dickens's *A Tale of Two Cities*. Martin-Harvey's climb to the guillotine was said to have made women in the theater audience openly weep. He specialized in "costumed romance and melodrama," which hints at the kind of mannered, larger-than-life, pathetic Darcy that Harcourt Williams may have brought to the part.[14] Apparently, however, Williams could not pull off Martin-Harvey's version of winningly, tear-inducingly somber. One review judged that Williams's Darcy lacked dignity.[15]

It's impossible to know what precise embellishments Filippi brought to Darcy in her script, so we shouldn't blame only Williams's acting for any perceived deficiencies. Other actors came in for greater praise in the reviews. Filippi herself is much admired, as vivacious and delightful. The actor who played Mr. Collins, Lyall Swete (1865–1930), is lauded for his comic relief, and the *Saturday Review* focuses its review of the play around him.[16] Mayo was not so universally approved. The *Times* reviewer complains that her Elizabeth Bennet is too pert and petulant.[17] The *Athenaeum* declares her "not quite an ideal Elizabeth" but "destitute neither of humour nor charm." It finds the play as a whole "open . . . to the charge of amateurishness" but still "an agreeable and moderately refreshing entertainment" (443). With these mixed reviews, it's no surprise that this is the play's only known performance.

Perhaps because of its lackluster showing, Filippi's professionally staged Austen adaptation did not immediately spawn massive numbers of imitators, as had her amateur dramatizations. Over the course of the next two decades after 1901, only a trickle of professional-actor Darcys followed Harcourt Williams to the stage. But there were *amateur* actors playing Darcy, a few of whom may be identified from surviving records. At an elite American women's institution, Wellesley College, a student and alumni production of *Pride and Prejudice* was mounted in 1899. The corporate authorship of the play by the women of the Zeta Alpha Society, a literary society at Wellesley, seems implied. Theirs was a five-act version, in which Darcy was performed by alumna Miss Willis, class of '96. Her performance is described as having been "especially artistic and finished" in a difficult role.[18] A photo survives of the cast, although it's not clear which of the two crossed-dressed swains is Willis's Darcy.[19] It's possible that the first—certainly one of the first—identifiable amateur-actor Darcys was a woman.

Figure 5.2. Photograph, "A Scene from Pride and Prejudice as Dramatized and Performed at Wellesley," in "Drama at the Women's Colleges," *Puritan* 8, no. 2 (May 1900): 155. Courtesy of University of Michigan Libraries.

We have no clear sense of what kind of Darcy the women of Zeta Alpha Society decided to put on their stage. Several years later, Mary Keith Medbery (Mrs. Steele) MacKaye published a four-act play, *Pride and Prejudice* (1906). It became the first full-length version of the novel to reach print, providing us with a text to study the ways that Austen's hero was likely staged. (Filippi's *Duologues* did not include a Darcy.) MacKaye knew the theater and theatrical life. Her husband, Steele MacKaye, was a famed playwright and theatrical inventor, the man who patented the folding theater chair.[20] The MacKaye men are well-known figures in Shakespearean theater history; the MacKaye women deserve to be better known, especially among those who care about Jane Austen.[21] Despite the fact that MacKaye's Darcy gets first billing in her list of characters, her "Fitzgerald Darcy," as he is renamed, is not a major presence in the script. He bursts out from time to time in speeches featuring exclamation points.[22] As one reviewer put it, MacKaye's Elizabeth is the play's "bewitching" character, both "a stimulating yet mollifying cohesive force."[23] Perhaps that's because MacKaye's Darcy demanded mollifying.

MacKaye's Darcy is most unusual in his second proposal scene, for which he arrives to the Bennet home with a whip in his hand. He carries it with him in his conversation with Elizabeth, occasionally banging it against his knees in anger. He cracks the whip when Elizabeth tells him that it was his aunt, Lady Catherine, who revealed that Darcy helped Lydia secure a marriage to Wickham. (This is obviously an important deviation from the original novel, in which it is Lydia who inadvertently lets that fact slip.) After he cracks his whip, Darcy utters a "Damn!" (MacKaye 164) and exclaims furiously to Elizabeth that he will "settle matters" with Lady Catherine and that "*she* shall be set right, I assure you" (166). This scene shows, among other things, that the Heathcliffing and Brontëization of Austen is not a recent invention.[24] But MacKaye's Darcy is only briefly explosive, as mysteriously violent behavior doesn't dominate his character in the play.

Instead, MacKaye offers audiences a profoundly Elizabeth-centric version of the story. The following dialogue makes clear who holds the power:

DARCY: I really am not the pretentious prig I must have seemed to you. I wish you could forgive my abominable pride.

ELIZABETH (*Looking at him with a half smile*): I will, on one condition.

DARCY: Name it.

ELIZABETH: That you forget my unwarrantable prejudice.

DARCY: Oh, Miss Bennet! (*He goes impetuously forward—then restraining himself, smiles and looks down on her.*) I really think, after all, I shall have to be grateful to my aunt. She has done us an enormous service.

ELIZABETH (*Smiling still more*): Well, Lady Catherine loves to be useful! (167)

MacKaye's Elizabeth has all of the play's best lines. The action may end with Darcy holding Elizabeth in his arms, but he's the one who careens emotionally between "faltering" and "furious," until she in the end changes her mind about him, as does the audience, through her eyes (166).

MacKaye's play became immensely popular. One 1916 catalogue describes MacKaye's play as "widely used by colleges and schools," primarily in the United States.[25] Performances are difficult to trace, but records survive of some notable features, including, again, some all-female casts. The script calls for ten women and ten men, but there are records of twenty-woman productions. A copy of MacKaye's *Pride and Prejudice* in my own collection of Austeniana pencils into the margins identifiably female names next to the male parts on its list of characters. In 1907, Mr. Darcy was played by a University of Michigan senior named Lulu Liesemer.[26] The Lulu Liesemer Darcys— these hundreds of actor-Darcys, female and male—may now be untraceable, but they, too, played a signal part in establishing Austen's legacy and popular reception. First, they ensured Austen's continued relevance and cultural reach fully as much as—and perhaps more than—the dramatically skeptical Austen-loving literati. Second, these actors gave audiences performances that offered more than a comic crash-course to marriage. All-female casts may have made it possible to put the story on stage as a vehicle for exploring relationships of all kinds. That casting made for a dramatic story about power, control, and self-determination, taking *Pride and Prejudice* beyond the interpretive confines of heteronormative romance.

The next full-length *Pride and Prejudice* dramatization recorded in Gilson's *Bibliography of Jane Austen* is a Marathi-language text published in India in 1913. Gilson describes *Vichar-vilasit*, by Gopal Chiminaji Bhate, as an Austen dramatization. That text is presently untraceable, but its title is similar to one given to a Marathi *Hamlet* translation.[27] A previously unrecorded *Pride and Prejudice*–based text was published in Marathi in that year. It is not, however, a dramatization: Kṛshṇājī Keśava Gokhale's *Ājapāsūna Pannāsa Varshānnī Āṅgla Kādambarīkartrī "Jena Ôṣṭina" Yāñcyā "Prāiḍa êṇḍa Prejuḍisa" Yā Kādambarīcē Rūpāntara* (1913). Gokhale was a Kokanasth Brahmin who, after his education, took service in Jath State, became a judge, and ultimately served as the divan (or dewan) of Jath.[28] His title roughly translates to *Fifty Years from Today: A Conversion of "Pride and Prejudice," by English Novelist Jane Austen.* His text does away with the character of Kitty Bennet and renames Lydia as Sundari. His preface describes a hope that Austen's scenario will apply to Indian society fifty years in the future.[29] Gokhale's conversion or adaptation of Austen would no doubt be interesting to study in conversation with Gurinder Chadha's Bollywood-style film of a century later, *Bride and Prejudice* (2004).

There was a professional stage lull for new Austen dramatizations after Harcourt Williams in Filippi's *The Bennets* (1901). The next recorded professional-actor Darcy, twenty years on, was the highest-profile performance yet. He took the stage before Her Majesty the Queen. This *Pride and Prejudice* dramatization, too, had a connection to women's education and progressive women. It was staged as a benefit for the Bedford College for Women in London, with one matinee performance at the Palace Theatre on March 24, 1922. The performance drew a very large audience, including

Bedford's patron, Queen Mary, consort to King George V. The play was coauthored by husband and wife Eileen and J. C. Squire. Eileen Squire (1884–1970) was a writer who had published novels under her maiden name, Eileen Harriet Anstruther. Poet and editor J. C. Squire (1884–1958) may be best known for his one-liner, "I am not so think as you drunk I am."[30] The Squires' play, as it was first performed, featured among its cast the seventy-five-year-old actor-luminary Ellen Terry (1847–1928). This was one of her last roles. The play was produced by Terry's daughter, Edith Craig (1869–1947). (More discussion of Terry, Craig, and their significant involvement in staging Jane Austen is found in chapter 9 of this book.)

The Squires' *Pride and Prejudice* was not published until 1929, seven years after its production.[31] From that print edition, we learn more about the Squires' Darcy. He appears to have been almost a comic character, the butt of Elizabeth's jokes, given stage directions that involve standing silently and looking around the stage through his eyeglass (Squire and Squire 20), delivering his lines *"solemnly"* (22), *"gravely"* (37), and *"firmly"* (58), as well as *"smiling superciliously"* (23), and *"smiling at last"* (38). He must have been broadly drawn and noticeably stiff, because at one point, behind his back, Elizabeth is given directions to imitate him walking (31). When, during his second proposal, the Squires' Darcy is directed to kiss Elizabeth's hand and then to embrace her, sitting down next to her and putting an arm around her, he concludes by saying *"softly,"* "My dearest and loveliest Elizabeth" (114). Elizabeth is characterized by wit and energy, as Darcy changes from a haughty stiff to a conquered stiff. The Squires' version also lumps all three suitors together in the end, having them deliver the play's penultimate line in unison, addressing themselves to Mr. Bennet with a robotic, "Oh, thank'ye, sir" (120). Elizabeth not only gets all of the play's best lines but most of its vigorous physical movements.

The Squires' Darcy proves a milestone in another way. In the 1922 performance, he was played by famed actor Ben Webster (1864–1947), who was then fifty-seven years old. Webster was an unusually aged Darcy by our standards. So, too, was his Elizabeth Bennet, played by Mary Jerrold (1877–1955), who was a surprising forty-four years old. Webster's real-life wife, Dame May Whitty (1865–1948), was cast as the play's Mrs. Bennet.[32] A Darcy and a Mrs. Bennet married to each other offstage is definitely something new in the history of Austen. (It makes offscreen couple Elinor [Emma Thompson] and Willoughby [Greg Wise] from Ang Lee's *Sense and Sensibility* [1995] seem practically ho-hum.) The play's positive reviews, which name Filippi as a precursor to the Squires, don't mention the actors' ages. It would seem that their ages didn't bother anyone: the Squires' version of the hero, at any age—with his ogling eyeglass and stiff walk—could not have been staged with the primary intention of making audience members drool over him.

For some few years longer, minimizing Darcy's role and appeal onstage continued, even as dramatic treatments of the novel became more frequent. Anne Johnson-Jones's *Pride and Prejudice* (1930), for example, is very buttoned down. Recycling much of its dialogue from Austen's original, Johnson-Jones also strings it together in an exceptionally clipped, cool way. The character of Lady Catherine de Bourgh is entirely dispensed with, and Elizabeth is given the play's last word, as Darcy takes her hand. Critic Andrew Wright notes of this version, "It is regrettable that in the play as a whole there is very little Darcy."[33] But the phenomenon was by then a common dramatic approach. Perhaps playwrights imagined that by making him, or the Elizabeth-Darcy romance, more central, they would move too much of the story away from the guiding perspective of Elizabeth. The intention of these early playwrights seems to have been to put the audience in the same emotional boat as Elizabeth. The play would communicate her skewed view of the hero and then overturn it at play's end. In these plays, the heroine and the audience simultaneously realize that they've been mistaken in Darcy, recognizing that he is both lovable and marriageable. Elizabeth was presented as the most valuable part of the story on the stage.

That changed in 1935, when *Pride and Prejudice* came to Broadway. Helen Jerome's play became a New York hit, running for 219 performances.[34] The following year, it traveled to London's West End, where it enjoyed 317 more.[35] It toured thereafter. Jerome's play had come close to being staged earlier in the 1930s. It was first optioned by a producer who hoped to use it as a stage vehicle for Katharine Hepburn. When Hepburn proved unavailable, Jerome's play was picked up by another producer, the legendary Max Gordon. It was said that Gordon had "the backing of certain motion picture interests, which served reasonably to strengthen his normally gambling instincts."[36] Hollywood was then on the lookout for literary classics and stage hits to take to the screen. The success of Jerome's *Pride and Prejudice* was at least in part a case of right author, right novel, right play, right time. When seen in those terms, the play may appear to be an almost accidental success. But its popularity—and the enduring cultural presence of some changes Jerome made to the original—proves that she pushed just the right buttons, too. Her sexy Mr. Darcy reshapes audiences' sense of the character's proper role in dramatic versions of the story, moving him into new territory. (Jerome's innovation of a weepy Elizabeth was less successful and had little staying power.)

Helen Jerome (1883–1966), like Rosina Filippi before her, may seem an unlikely pioneer of dramatized Austen. Unlike Filippi, Jerome doesn't seem to have had much theater experience. Her previously published writings had attracted little notice, yet somehow she put her finger on the pulse of the cosmopolitan theatergoing public, becoming "the unexpected playwright success of the year."[37] Jerome reinvented Austen's story to appeal to contemporary tastes and, especially, desires. Reinvention was part of her own life experience. Raised in a large Irish Catholic family living in Australia, the former Nellie Bruton married young. Her husband, Armand Jerome, appears to have been in the mold of a Wickham. One account from the 1890s refers to his "bursting upon Sydney like a brilliant meteor."[38] He became a publisher, threw lavish suppers and picnics, and claimed to be a relative of English writer Jerome K. Jerome.[39] Whatever his ancestry, Armand Jerome turned out to be a con artist and a convicted forger. He married Nellie Bruton not long after having been released from prison.[40] It seems they first met when he served as poetry editor to young Helen (then still Nellie) when she was in her early teens. They had one daughter.[41] Armand Jerome became a music promoter and faced a bankruptcy.

Later in her life, Helen Jerome was described as "demurely wise, distractingly petite" although, when angry, someone who "towers like a monolith."[42] In the 1920s, her con-artist husband dead, Jerome published a treatise on sex questions, a novel, and more verse.[43] She immigrated to the United States. Then her *Pride and Prejudice* debuted. By 1936, she had a new identity. *Vogue* described her as "white-haired, English born, and married to George Ali."[44] After her *Pride and Prejudice*, she would go on to write a dramatization of *Jane Eyre* (1937), subtitled *A Drama of Passion in Three Acts*.[45] That play was no hit, but staging classic literature with contemporary passion became Jerome's most successful venture. Her Austen play was subtitled *A Sentimental Comedy in Three Acts*, with "sentimental" being an adjective more appropriate to Jerome's Elizabeth than to her steamy Darcy.[46]

Thanks to producer Gordon and his Hollywood interests, Jerome's play was mounted on a scale unlike any previous Austen production. It was the first *Pride and Prejudice* to use serious set designs, props and costumes. It also featured more amusing dialogue for all of its characters than had pre-vious plays. Even Jane, Charlotte, and Darcy are each given their own zing-ers. (The play does away with Kitty and Mary.) Jerome's biting, memorable line, cattily delivered by Lady Lucas to Mrs. Bennet, that some men prefer women to have character over looks, made it into the 1940 Metro Goldwyn Mayer film. Jerome liberally used nonverbal embellishments, too. Her Darcy and Elizabeth do a great deal of eyebrow raising to communicate mutual disdain (18–19).

Reading Jerome's play alongside the Austen dramatizations that came before it, rather than against the original novel, better reveals its nov-elty.[47] There are a few holdover elements from Old Stage Darcy in Jerome's play. For instance, Jerome's Darcy is frequently directed to act bored. When Darcy declares Elizabeth tolerable, the directions say he is to do so indiffer-ently, while examining his fingernails (Jerome 49). When Miss Bingley de-clares Elizabeth to be ill bred, Darcy again examines his fingernails (59). The overly jocular Colonel Fitzwilliam, in defending Darcy to Elizabeth, dubs him "old sobersides" and the "old solemn owl" (127). These lines were designed for laughs, but there is seriousness, too, as the Colonel excuses Darcy's snobbery and faults as arising from his nursemaids, governesses, and impossible mother (128, 129). So far, so similar to many earlier staged versions of Darcy.

The changes are most evident in Darcy's approach to Elizabeth. When Jerome's Darcy comes for Elizabeth in his first proposal, he comes on strong and physically. He approaches her and stands close; he holds out his hands. He paces. He delivers his lines *"slowly and passionately."* He refers to "this love for you that consumes me." He declares, *"white with emotion,"* "Eliza-beth, I love you" (Jerome 132). But then we're told, after she objects to his manner of proposing, he speaks to her *"as one would tell a child [about] some-thing astonishing"* (133), a response that more than excuses her rebuff. Stage directions describe him as being filled with *"hidden yearning,"* *"hurt for the first time in his life"* (135). When he leaves the stage, Elizabeth sheds tears (138), something she does in Jerome's version with cloying frequency.

In the second proposal scene, Elizabeth is directed twice to tremble, and Darcy twice to deliver lines humbly, as well as *"passionately"* (Jerome 190). Elizabeth declares to him, with a bowed head, "I am abased" (192). As they come closer and closer to each other physically, Elizabeth again cries. Darcy delivers the last lines of the play:

DARCY: Dare I ask you . . . again?

ELIZABETH (*Smiles up at him through her tears*): My father says you are
the sort of gentleman whom one would not dare refuse anything he
condescended to ask.

DARCY (*Moved to his depths. Takes her in his arms*): My cruel . . . my kind . . .
oh, my lovely Elizabeth! (*Folds her close, his lips on hers*)

CURTAIN (193)[48]

The play was by no means ahead of its time in terms of its gender politics, as
Filippi's *Duologues* had been. Jerome's play reinforced traditional gender
roles, doing more to shame the heroine and put her in her place than Austen's original did. (Can you imagine Austen's having her Elizabeth bow her
head and declare herself abased, not to mention all of that crying?)

Staged *Pride and Prejudice* had long been recycling the same dramatic patterns. Most plays featured rebellious Elizabeths, cardboard Darcys, and lifeless interactions between them. Jerome transformed all of these, the latter
two with success. Augmenting parts of the original text where desires might
be located between the lines, and keeping parts of Austen's story intact, Jerome changed the potential for immediate sympathy with hero *and* heroine.
Audiences did not spend several hours imagining a powerful man as a distant
enemy only to decide they were wrong. Instead, they were encouraged
to empathize with Darcy's thwarted desires and to enjoy watching them be
fulfilled, as he slowly conquered Elizabeth's high standards with his worthy,
palpable passion. But witnessing his desires and struggle to control his now-
readable, laudable attraction also had the effect of making Elizabeth's rejection
of him seem less sensible. Jerome had crafted a story about Elizabeth's awak-
ening to her own desires, propelled forward by Darcy's long-perceivable feelings for her. Perhaps this shift is what led Jerome to make her witty Elizabeth
noticeably weakened and weepy. Elizabeth's abasing herself before Darcy
makes more sense when she is as emotionally volatile as he is.

Jerome's Darcy, then, required an actor who could carry the production,
not tread around the stage as a caricature of tall, dark, and distant. The directors cast several men who tried to carry the piece, some apparently more
successfully than others. When Jerome's play began to tour in the late 1930s,
it would end up featuring many different actors playing Darcy. But the first
one, in New York, was Colin Keith-Johnston (1896–1980), an Englishman of
nearly forty. Keith-Johnston was best known for his Shakespearean characters, especially his avant-garde modern-dress Hamlet, played as rebellious,

snarling, cigarette smoking, and violent. Photographs of Keith-Johnston as Darcy suggest an actor sensual and dashing—absolutely Olivier's equal in projecting sex appeal. When he leans in to Elizabeth (Adrianne Allen [1907–93]), he strikes a pose that shows he finds her far more than "tolerable." In one promotional still, Keith-Johnston's Darcy seems to be sniffing Allen's Elizabeth. Reviewers understood the change. As one put it, "Both the play and the performance are said to scotch the old libel that Elizabeth was strong in her resentment of Mr. Darcy's arrogance until she saw the splendours of Pemberley."[49] Playwright Jerome must have shared the critical view that Austen's Elizabeth would have taken Darcy "as willingly without Pemberley as with it."[50]

Keith-Johnston traveled the United States with the touring production for a time, which means he did not serve as the West End Darcy. When

Figure 5.3. Photograph, Colin Keith-Johnston and Adrianne Allen. Publicity still from *Pride and Prejudice* (New York, 1935).

Jerome's *Pride and Prejudice* opened in London, it was with Hugh Williams (1904–69) as Darcy and Celia Johnson (1908–82) as Elizabeth. Williams was significantly younger than Keith Johnston, not quite thirty, but he was already an international stage and screen star. Despite the play's longer run in London than in New York, British reviewers were on the whole less glowing about Williams's Darcy and about the play. This is perhaps because London's theater critics expressed greater attachment to the fidelity model of adaptation or because they were more conversant with the original novel. Either way, they were not as pleased with Jerome's deviations from the original as were American critics. The *Observer*'s reviewer declares the play "potted Austen." The review acknowledges that Williams as Darcy "triumphantly holds our interest," yet saves its greater praise for Johnson's Elizabeth.[51] In general, British critics seemed to want to hold on longer than American ones to the centrality of Elizabeth in *Pride and Prejudice* stage adaptations. (A. A. Milne's ill-timed play, completed just as Jerome's appeared, shows this with its very title, *Miss Elizabeth Bennet* [1936]. His play's focus remains squarely on the heroine.) But audiences internationally would soon come around to a *Pride and Prejudice* driven by Darcy's desires.

Did Laurence Olivier crib some of his Darcy from Colin Keith-Johnston or Hugh Williams, from Jerome's steamy stage Darcy, whether consciously or not? It's hard to imagine otherwise. Reviewers who liked Jerome's play—and most found things to like—express surprise at its being so like "a comedy of to-day," calling it "a play that pranks deliciously," "beguiling," and a "love-duel."[52] After Jerome's Keith-Johnston, the character of Darcy would emerge as the visual and emotional center of most *Pride and Prejudice* adaptations. His portrayal drove the play away from the blueprint of stand-alone, refusing Elizabeths prevalent in the earlier twentieth century. The new Darcy made the story so unmistakably about heterosexuality that female Darcys would become straight-out unthinkable. Thanks to Jerome's Darcy and those who played him, the hero of *Pride and Prejudice* became irresistible eye-candy for female audiences. It's a position the character holds on stage and screen to this day. Olivier might be credited with many things—and so might screenwriter Andrew Davies and Colin Firth—but inventing sexy Darcy is not one of them. For that, we must turn to the history of Austen on the stage, especially to the literary woman who seems to have lived her own life more in the mold of a Lydia than an Elizabeth Bennet: playwright Helen Jerome.

CHAPTER SIX

Dear Jane

Christian Spinster, Feminist Flirt, and Shadow Actress

In her Broadway hit *Pride and Prejudice* (1935), Helen Jerome dramatized Darcy to emphasize heterosexual desires roiling beneath the surface of the hero. Jerome's characterization provided one way to answer nagging questions about Jane Austen herself. It came at a time when readers and critics were confused about how to make sense of an author who had been presented to the public by critics as a sheltered Christian spinster but whose fiction vividly depicted romantic love. Some suspected that the author of *Pride and Prejudice* must have been Elizabeth-like—that she'd had a real-life, Darcy-like lost love, an experience on which she drew in writing her fiction. Others wondered what Austen could have known of desire, never having married. Examining what made Austen tick as a woman became a matter of robust speculation. Was she, as D. H. Lawrence would have us believe, a "thoroughly unpleasant" "old maid"?[1] Were the passions "perfectly unknown" to her, as Charlotte Brontë charged?[2] It was a literary historical detective story to investigate, with Austen's letters and her fiction used as clues. For many, it remains an intriguing mystery, whether unsolved or unsolvable.

Jane Austen's sexuality had become subject to debate among critics by the mid-twentieth century. "Because Austen's heterosexuality was not guaranteed by marriage," as Claudia L. Johnson argues, "doubts about her sexuality have been played out in different historical moments as asexuality, as frigidity, and as lesbianism." Johnson calls this ambiguity "queerness," noting that it "has been used to account for her fiction since the get-go."[3] Austen's indeterminate sexuality or queerness gained wide public notice in 1995 when the *London Review of Books* advertised a review with the headline "Was Jane Austen Gay?" Terry Castle's review (also titled "Sister, Sister") suggests that the novelist's close relationship with her only sister, Cassandra, had an "unconscious homoerotic dimension."[4] The *London Review of Books*' sensational headline and Castle's review kicked up a lot of dust, not to mention a fair amount of conservative Janeite ire.

Newspapers and television stations worldwide picked up the story. Castle explained to audiences the difference between "homoerotic" and "homosexual," as well the fact that editors, not authors, write headlines. She describes the response to her piece as "incredibly homophobic," which seems, with the hindsight of two decades, entirely right. "People have reacted as though I'd desecrated the temple or something," Castle writes. "Many people still consider it a terrible slur if you suggest that a person like Jane Austen might have had homosexual feelings."[5] One would hope that we're in a different place today with such suggestions, even if we find ourselves no closer to answers about Austen's sexual desires or practices—or lack of them. What we do know now that we didn't know twenty years ago is that the first two women to play Jane and Cassandra Austen on the professional stage in the 1930s were lovers.

In November 1932, famed theater director and actor Eva Le Gallienne (1899–1991) mounted a now little-known play, *Dear Jane*, a fictional stage treatment of the life of Jane Austen. *Dear Jane* featured the stage's earliest actor speaking as Jane Austen and was the author's first biographical dramatization.[6] Performed in 1922 in Boston with an unknown cast, *Dear Jane* made its New York debut a decade later at the innovative Civic Repertory Theatre. The Civic Rep was a theater designed to bring classics to the masses, known for its low-priced seats and high-quality performances. The theater's visionary founder and director, English-born Le Gallienne, was considered such a national treasure that her face had appeared on the cover of *Time* magazine in 1929.[7] As director of *Dear Jane*, Le Gallienne cast as her Jane Austen the beautiful actress Josephine Hutchinson (c. 1898–1998). Le G (as she was called) cast herself in the role of Cassandra Austen.[8] Audiences at the time would have understood this as a highly interesting set of stage sisters. Le Gallienne and Hutchinson had already been publicly outed as a lesbian couple.

The relationship of the two actors was made into titillating newspaper fodder in the coverage of Hutchinson's divorce in 1930. Her estranged husband was Robert Bell, the theater-obsessed nephew of inventor Alexander Graham Bell.[9] Robert Bell, the first of Hutchinson's three husbands, alleged her extreme cruelty in his petition, something most biographers agree was a "necessary fiction concocted to gain the divorce" from his wife (Sheehy 198).

The newspapers had a field day. The *New York Daily News*, scandalmonger-
ing, ran the headline "Bell Divorces Actress, Eva Le Gallienne's Shadow."[10]
"Shadow" was then a code word for lesbian, originating from the controversial play *The Captive* (1926). In the coverage of Hutchinson's divorce proceedings, Le Gallienne is said to have spent time with Hutchinson "morning,
noon, and night," ruining the marriage to Bell. Worldly readers of the time
would have understood precisely what was being implied.

Le Gallienne and Hutchinson were a couple for five years, acting and living together.[11] Friends worried that, in the wake of Hutchinson's divorce,
negative publicity about the two women's intimacy would end both their
working and personal associations. As one source later put it, "I remember
how stunned everyone was in the 1920s when Le Gallienne's affair with
Josephine Hutchinson hit the headlines. People thought it was simply fright-
ful and I wondered how they would have the courage to go on with their
careers or simply to go on. But they did."[12] Hutchinson herself later declared
their years as a couple "good and normal and healthy," noting, "There was
never any shame connected with our relationship" (Sheehy 167). *Dear Jane*
would turn out to be an important moment for them as a couple. Playing the
Austen sisters offered a first chance to act out private devotion to each other
as adult characters on the public stage.

It was also an important moment in the history of Jane Austen's legacy.
Dear Jane puts forward a portrait of the author that veers sharply away
from the stereotype of the perfectly pious Christian spinster. The play offers audiences the novelist as feminist flirt, testing and throwing over her
male suitors. She actively chooses a writing life at the side of her beloved
sister. The play carried further potential meanings for Civic Rep audiences,
if they knew the putative sisters were also an offstage couple. The production
opened on November 14, 1932, and ran for just eleven performances. Theatri-
cally, it was deemed a failure.[13] Since then, it has been almost entirely forgotten. *Dear Jane* "often appears as a bibliographic entry in books and papers
about adaptations of Austen," as recent critics Russell Clark and Williams
Phillips note, "yet no one seems to have read or seen it, or to be familiar
with its contents."[14] The previously unpublished play survives in typescript,
allowing us to examine its themes and effects.[15]

Dear Jane was written by Eleanor Holmes Hinkley (1891–1971), a playwright based in Cambridge, Massachusetts, who was the beloved first cousin
of poet T. S. Eliot. Hinkley attended Radcliffe College and eventually joined
Professor George Baker's famous 47 Workshop of playwrights. By then

she'd gained a reputation for hosting energetic private theatricals. For Hinkley, Jane Austen was both a literary and a dramatic interest. On February 17, 1913, in one of her theatrical salons, Hinkley staged her stand-alone *Emma* scene, "An Afternoon with Mr. Woodhouse." T. S. Eliot himself is said to have played the valetudinarian Mr. Woodhouse—a literary historical fact better known in Eliot than in Austen studies. Adding to the significance of that day is that the amateur actor who played Mrs. Elton was Hinkley's talented classmate, Emily Hale. Eliot was already falling in love with her.[16] It's hard to say which of these details is most arresting: T. S. Eliot as a Mr. Woodhouse, or a Mr. Woodhouse of any kind falling in love with a Mrs. Elton.[17] Hinkley's *Emma* scene was apparently never published. But for Hinkley, it would be the character of Austen herself, rather than those in her novels, that would prove the more enduring dramatic interest. It was also Hinkley's greatest stage success. *Dear Jane* was the one piece of writing mentioned in her brief obituary.[18]

Hinkley's *Dear Jane* was registered for copyright in 1919.[19] A notice of its first performance dates to 1922. The *Cambridge Tribune* trumpets the headline, "LOCAL PLAYWRIGHT LAUNCHES SUCCESS: Eleanor Holmes Hinkley's Romantic Comedy, 'Dear Jane,' Given Twice." The newspaper declares that the play was performed at Boston's National Theatre (a 3,500-seat venue), where it was "unanimously voted a delightful success by all who had the pleasure of witnessing it." *Dear Jane*, it was said, "was built up from an idealization of Jane Austen's early life, and the famous authoress was depicted in a series of youthful adventures and love affairs, calling out a range of acting talent, scenic setting and costuming, constituting, with the text, a very fine entertainment. The comedy . . . might almost be one of Jane Austen's own novels boiled down to fit the stage."[20] Further details of the performances are difficult to trace.

When Le Gallienne bought the rights to produce *Dear Jane* early in 1932, she was under the mistaken impression that Hinkley's was a "new" play. Le G wrote excitedly to her mother to report that she'd acquired it: "I have bought a new play—a charming comedy written by an American woman called Miss Hinkley—about Jane Austen. The play is called 'Dear Jane'—a good title I think, and is quite *delightful*—gay & amusing & of course a period full of character—1798. Jo [Josephine Hutchinson] is to play 'Jane Austen' a part ideal for her, she is very pleased about it. I am to play her elder sister 'Cassandra' an important and difficult part."[21] Le G was said to have chosen the play "mainly because the role of Jane Austen provided a good vehicle for Josephine Hutchinson."[22] Hutchinson was just as excited at the prospect, because the part of Jane Austen would be among her first playing an adult role; she'd previously been cast most often as a young girl. Her notable roles at the Civic Rep were Wendy in *Peter Pan* (with Le G playing Peter Pan) and Alice in *Alice in Wonderland* (with Le G as the White Queen). Playing Jane Austen as a woman in her twenties excited Hutchinson as a new professional challenge. Hutchinson expressed this in her own letter to Le G's mother:

> Eva told you, of course, about "Dear Jane." I am really excited and pleased about it as I haven't been for years. I will be able to open in a grown-up part! I don't think I have ever discussed my work with you at any length, but one of the things that has been worrying me is that a whole side of me has never been exercised ... I may be rotten in it, but it won't be because I haven't tried. I had never read Austen and if for nothing else I am grateful for being introduced to her. I have finished "Sense and Sensibility" and am almost finished with "Pride and Prejudice." All the way through I have seen Eva as "Elizabeth." If it were ever dramatized it would be a lovely part for her.[23]

Although both Hutchinson and Le G were drawn to Austen, neither seems to have been aware of the dynamic amateur history of dramatizing her works in homes and schools, in the earlier suffrage movement, or on the professional stage in England.

Le Gallienne was well versed in—and well known for staging work by—dramatists such as Ibsen, Shakespeare, and Chekhov. That Le G chose to stage *Dear Jane*, a "new" original play by an American woman, may seem a curious choice, but Le Gallienne had previously given living playwrights the opportunity to showcase work before her large audiences. Most significant among them was Susan Glaspell, whose play *Alison's House* (1930) debuted at the Civic Rep. Inspired by the life and work of Emily Dickinson, *Alison's House* would go on to win the Pulitzer Prize. Perhaps Le G saw in *Dear Jane* a chance to repeat that formula. It was not to be. Of the thirty-four plays Le Gallienne staged at the Civic Rep between 1926 and 1932, *Dear Jane* had the second-lowest number of performances (Cooper 305–06). Despite its "stylishness" and Hutchinson's "winsome gaiety," the play proved neither a critical nor a popular success (21).

The play opens with an intriguing scene, in a pub on December 16, 1775, Jane Austen's birthdate. Gathered there are four of the eighteenth century's most famed intellectual, artistic, and theatrical men—Dr. Samuel Johnson, James Boswell, Sir Joshua Reynolds, and David Garrick. They sit at a table at the Cheshire Cheese, gossiping and arguing about women's talents. Johnson beats the table with his coffee spoon, absentmindedly and impatiently. The men describe their opinions of the actor Sarah Siddons, the novelist Frances Burney, and even Johnson's late wife. It leads them to the collective conclusion that "there breathes no female alive who is, or ever shall be capable of true creation."[24] This proclamation sets up the story that follows: a female genius was born in Britain at the precise moment these male luminaries declared it impossible.

Next *Dear Jane* fast-forwards to 1798, introducing the now-adult Jane Austen as an unapologetic feminist flirt. She's declared an embarrassment by her imperious, moralizing, and sexist brother James, who wants to rein her in and marry her off. Three suitors present themselves in succession: charismatic rake Tom Lefroy, stolid childhood friend James Digweed, and handsome baronet Sir John Evelyn. (Evelyn was the only one of the three men not closely connected to the Austens in life.) Over the course of the play, Cassandra tries to help Jane judge each of the suitors, to decide which one among them to marry. Along the way, the Austens are visited by educational philosopher and author Richard Lovell Edgeworth (father of famed novelist Maria Edgeworth), as well as the mother of novelist Mary Russell Mitford. Both offer further commentary on marriage. Edgeworth comically suggests that perhaps he ought to marry Jane Austen himself, despite then being married to his fourth wife.

First, Jane considers and rejects Lefroy. She discovers him cavorting with a shopgirl and declares to Cassandra that although Tom is a dear, delicious man, he is fickle as the wind. Jane next rejects Digweed. He proposes, but she decides that he's inviting her to slavery and calling it romance. In confidence to Cassandra, Jane compares Digweed's treatment of her to her fictional character Mr. Collins's of Elizabeth Bennet. The last and most promising of Jane's suitors, Sir John Evelyn, seems her best match, intelligent, handsome, and passionate, not to mention rich and titled. But he, too, is rejected by Jane. She discovers that he's not really listening when she describes the plot of her novel *First Impressions*. (Jane tells him that it's Cassandra who wants her to rename it *Pride and Prejudice*.) Jane admits, "Sir John, I write," to which he replies that he loves her and not her novel (6-12). Sir John kisses her ardently, but he brushes aside the part of her she most values. After the kiss, Jane looks into his eyes "and saw he did not know me" (6-18). She tells Cassandra that she could not marry and be a stranger to her husband (6-20).

By the end of the play, Jane has rejected three eligible men—one like Wickham, one like Collins, and one a defective Darcy—in order to go on to write her genius fiction and prove the opening scene's famous pub conversationalists wrong. But another thematic thread runs throughout the play: Cassandra and Jane's close relationship. The two are almost always on the stage together. When Digweed comes to propose to Jane, he mistakenly believes her to be alone. Realizing Cassandra is there in the room, he tells the sisters that he thinks of the two of them as one. There are other moments, too, telegraphing their future together. When Cassandra declares she's leaving, Jane says to her, "You go, my better half?" (2-19). Digweed may imagine Jane and Cassandra as interchangeable women, but Jane's joking words imply that the sisters already see themselves as like a married couple. Hutchinson's Jane referring on stage, in character, to Le Gallienne's Cassandra, her real-life lover, as her "better half" cannot have been lost on the most knowing viewers or on the actors themselves for its momentousness.

The character of Cassandra, too, is shown as Jane's stalwart partner, asking Jane to investigate her views toward matrimony. Cassandra nudges Jane to examine her feelings for her suitors, to determine whether she is in love. At one point, Cassandra asks Jane whether she is fickle. Jane says, "I always love you Cassy, do I not?" (2-18). Cassandra, "embracing her tenderly," cries, "Dear Jane!" echoing both surviving real-life letters and the play's title. The two women hold each other on stage, in character, as Jane and Cassandra. As their onstage banter continues, Cassandra asks Jane whether she means to marry sometime, to which Jane replies, "Do I look like a spinster?" (2-24). There's no moment in the play that better highlights Hinkley's subtle work to reimagine marriage and to recast prevailing notions of single women. It's an even more fascinating line when understood as delivered by a recent divorcée to her female lover.

The success of that line on the stage depended on Hutchinson's not "looking like" the negative stereotype of a spinster. She was a stunning young woman, described as "slim and long-legged, five feet five inches tall, with amber eyes in a heart-shaped face and a cloud of reddish-gold hair" (Sheehy 155). Her character didn't resemble a stereotypical spinster. But what was the difference in "looks" and demeanor between a spinster and a stereotypical lesbian, in Austen's day or in the then-present? Both actor and character in *Dear Jane* would seem to be working to undo prejudices. Adding to the multilayered reading possible here is the fact that Hutchinson's personality offstage was said to be very like Jane Austen's, "as defined by Eleanor Hinkley," with the part's "swiftly changing humors" giving Hutchinson the "chance to demonstrate the suppleness and finish she had acquired" as an actor (Cooper 119–20). Audiences, however, did not seem to connect readily. A Civic Rep stage manager thought that *Dear Jane* failed not because of the actors' talents or suitability for the roles but because the script "read much better than it played" (151). Perhaps audiences also had a hard time making sense of how to judge a flirtatious, intentionally single Jane Austen, not to mention one played by a winsome actor.

Figure 6.1. Josephine Hutchinson, publicity still from *Dear Jane* (New York, 1932).

It's even possible that Hutchinson and Le Gallienne meant for audiences to envision their relationship on the stage through *Dear Jane*'s sisters. The play ends with Jane declaring, "Cassy, we must leave tonight!" They run away together from Sir John Evelyn's Pemberley-like home, where both are staying as his guests. Jane breaks down and drops to her knees beside Cassy, crying, declaring that she cannot marry without love. Cassy emphatically responds, "No!" Then the two sisters, after having trouble opening a massive bolted door, bust it open and bust out together. Jane declares her "old quill pen" to be her destiny, and the audience sees, as a last tableau, the couple creeping past a window—shadows of themselves. They head off, as anyone who knew Austen's life story would have known, to an unmarried future together. The play's final scene, as it's described, also mirrors a marriage proposal. It produces a no rather than a yes, yet it's also a love scene. It involves a declaration to a loved one (about not being in love elsewhere) and a dropping down on one's knees. It provides a twist on the couple riding off into the sunset happily ever after, substituting a running off into the darkness. In this play, Hutchinson and Le Gallienne played a same-sex couple mock-eloping before an audience, in the guise of Jane and Cassandra Austen.

The play's theme, its "celebration of female creativity and independence," would have "appealed to Le Gallienne," according to biographer Helen Sheehy, but at the time "it was not a popular view." This is a play better suited to a less anxious and more open time than Depression-era America, as "independent women threatened male status and power." Sheehy makes another claim that's important to understanding the shift from Le Gallienne's and Hinkley's Jane in 1919, 1922, or 1932 to Helen Jerome's and Keith-Johnston's Darcy in 1935. One critic in the *New York Telegram* in 1932 complains that the era's "playwrights . . . are giving all the character and strength to the women's roles and transforming the men's roles into pallid shadows." It's an interesting twist on the word "shadow," as Sheehy remarks (219). *Dear Jane,* play and production, was everything that this reactionary critic fears. It was a female-run, female-dominated, female-independence-promoting, disposing-with-men sort of a play. That was true from the play's direction and opening scene on down.[25]

Other reviewers suggest discomfort with the gender-bending nature of *Dear Jane.* In one review, Hutchinson's Jane is preferred to Le Gallienne's Cassandra. The *Brooklyn Daily Eagle* concludes that Hutchinson was "so delightful a picture that you can't very well forget her" but that "almost constantly beside her in a fairly colorless subdued role, is Eva Le Gallienne as her devoted sister and adviser."²⁶ The most remarkable review, however, directly hints at the Le Gallienne–Hutchinson scandal. The last line of the play, as quoted above, has Jane embracing her quill pen as her destiny. But the *New York Herald Tribune*'s reviewer claims he heard a different word at play's end. He writes, " 'To freedom!' as the enfranchised Jane cried as the final curtain was just about to fall, and if I understood Miss Josephine Hutchinson aright, 'And my queer own pen!' Well, it made a pleasant evening for all that."²⁷ The word "queer" was no accidental mishearing. This is smirking, homophobic in-speak, buried in a theater review. When the same reviewer later refers to Le Gallienne's Cassandra as a "watchdog elder sister," there's absolutely no mistake. Some theatergoers saw a queer Austen in 1932. With the Civic Rep's seating capacity of 1,100 and its eleven performances, it was an Austen viewed by a significant number of playgoers.

The history of *Dear Jane* might end there. But in an interesting coda, further romance and failed romance emerged from the play's cast. Hutchinson, in her third and final marriage in 1972, wed former Civic Rep and *Dear Jane* actor Staats Cotsworth (1908–79). A man some years Hutchinson's junior, Cotsworth is listed in the program for *Dear Jane* as one of the cast's dancers. He'd then moved on from the Civic Rep to make a name for himself in radio. After Cotsworth's death, Le Gallienne wanted to reunite with Hutchinson, whom she thought of as the love of her life. Le G hoped they would live out their days together, much like Jane and Cassandra had. She approached Hutchinson with an offer, but Hutchinson declined (Schanke 266). When Le G passed away, she left her wealth to many people and organizations, but to Hutchinson she left a sapphire ring (Sheehy 461). In an imaginative frame of mind, we might see it as the missing prop from *Dear Jane*'s backward proposal scene.

Hinkley's *Dear Jane* offers a vision of the woman writer, of the creative life, and of sisterly love that is iconoclastic, performed by two female actors who were in love. The play shows that, for a time, Austen's life and writings inspired and showcased romance between women, outside of the confines of traditional marriage, onstage and off. This ought to give pause to those who would scorn Austen, in her own right and in her legacy, as an author of reactionary "chick lit." It's also a wake-up call to those quick to dismiss her and her fiction as hopelessly heteronormative. Yet Hinkley's *Dear Jane* did not prove enduring as a play.

Hinkley seems to have been interested in continuing to work with Le G. An unpublished letter survives from Hinkley to Le Gallienne. There Hinkley writes that she regrets not connecting in person on her recent trip to New York. Next they do get together, Hinkley promises not to bother Le G with Charlotte, Aphra, or "any other dead lady."[28] Perhaps Hinkley had pitched plays on Charlotte Brontë and Aphra Behn to Le G. But the collaboration of the playwright and director would not continue. It's difficult to determine what long-term effect, if any, *Dear Jane* had on Austen's reputation or on future adaptations in any medium. Playwright Helen Jerome, who was living at the time in the New York area, may have known of *Dear Jane* before writing her hit play, *Pride and Prejudice* (1935). Whether she knew it or not, Jerome managed what Hinkley couldn't or wouldn't—a play centering on the desires of the mesmerizing hero. Jerome did not test, as *Dear Jane* did, the public's readiness for a sex-role-bending, free-thinking heroine or author. Jerome's lust-filled, passionate-kiss ending stands in sharp contrast to Hinkley's runaway sisters. *Dear Jane* dropped off of the Austen-legacy charts, while Jerome's sexy Darcy endured. Quill pens conquered queer pens.

CHAPTER SEVEN

Stage to Screen *Pride and Prejudice*

Hollywood's Austen and Its
Unrealized Screenplays

Helen Jerome's Broadway hit dramatization of *Pride and Prejudice* (1935) was optioned for film for a staggering $50,000.[1] Over the next several years, Metro Goldwyn Meyer worked to create its own Hollywood version of Austen via Jerome. The film that emerged would bear only a passing resemblance to either. Still, the film advertised itself as "based on Helen Jerome's dramatization of the Jane Austen novel. Screen play by Aldous Huxley and Jane Murfin." It proclaimed that it would "be one of the most famous pictures ever filmed!" as we saw earlier. At Radio City Music Hall in New York City in August 1940, crowds lined up around the block to see *Pride and Prejudice* (1940), giving the film its greatest weekly attendance numbers that month.[2] The program featured the grand organ, the symphony orchestra, a Technicolor Walt Disney cartoon, and a musical stage revue with dancers, a life-sized automobile, and a towering lighthouse, followed by the screening of the film.[3] If Jerome's Broadway play left any lingering doubts about Austen's marketability, *Pride and Prejudice* at Radio City Music Hall chased them away. Jane Austen had experienced another encore as a hot property in a new medium.

Once again, the leap came after a lull. Austen's fiction was a late arrival to radio and film adaptation, just as it had been to book illustration and dramatization. Despite their popularity in print, Austen's novels were overlooked by filmmakers during the silent movie era, perhaps because her stories were "too static in terms of location, too reliant on conversations and lacking in grand narratives, like those of Shakespeare and Dickens," as one recent critic puts it.[4] Shakespeare's work was adapted in a feature-length talkie as early as 1929 (*Taming of the Shrew*, dir. Sam Taylor) and in a brief early film advertising a theatrical production of *King John* (1899).[5] The fiction of

Figure 7.1. *Pride and Prejudice*, publicity poster, Metro Goldwyn Mayer, 1940, loose clipping.

Dickens was, for a time, everywhere on film, silent and then talkie. Brontë's *Jane Eyre* was adapted for silent film in 1913, 1915, and 1921, with its first sound version in 1934.[6] Jane Austen's fiction moved from big-time stage to big-time film property in just a handful of remarkable, transformational years.

Even that road was not smooth. MGM's *Pride and Prejudice* went through a considerable number of versions and would-be screenwriters before being green-lighted for production. These draft scripts and their proposed changes to Austen's original (and Jerome's play) offer us a chance to look not just at failures or false starts—although there were certainly those—but to investigate how leading screenwriters thought an Austen-inspired dramatic success ought to be rewritten to appeal to film audiences. These once-imagined but never-made film versions demonstrate the dangers of our arguing that Austen was being repurposed for some kind of Hollywood-initiated ideological plot.[7] For instance, recent critics have suggested the film was intended as loosely veiled war propaganda, setting out to make Britain appealing to an America hesitant to join forces with it against Germany. Surviving scripts show no such consistent political effort. Other critics describe *Pride and Prejudice* (1940) as an Austenization of Margaret Mitchell's *Gone with the Wind* (1936) and the 1939 film based on the novel. A few even mistakenly suggest that *Pride and Prejudice* recycled *Gone with the Wind*'s Southern belle costumes to be economical.[8] Such arguments aren't supported by the surviving scripts either. (*Little Women*, as we'll see, is *Pride and Prejudice*'s more likely film progenitor.)

What a close examination of surviving drafts of the script shows is that there was never one Austen-inspired "message" being packaged by a Hollywood cabal of political conspirers, commercial opportunists, or hired hands. If one of these groups must be identified as the most influential among them, it would seem to be the commercial interests. Hollywood producers, as Harriet Margolis puts it, "think less in terms of ideology and aesthetics than of financial success," as much as those things can be separated.[9] But Hollywood also wanted to push its family friendliness, as well as its profits, in the wake of criticisms that its products appealed too often to the baser human instincts. Examining the dizzying number of MGM-commissioned scripts for *Pride and Prejudice* suggests that producers may have been guiding writers to "freshen up" Austen, to make the novel and Jerome's script more appealing to viewers of all tastes and ages—and both genders. Hollywood's top screenwriters continued to experiment with the path that Jerome had started audiences down: expanding the role and screen centrality of Mr. Darcy.

Many writers tried to infuse elements into their scripts to make Austen's story speak to present cinematic trends. Unfortunately, they often displayed little knowledge of history in the process. Turning to film genres and conventions of their own day, they incorporated stereotypes they thought audiences held about the nineteenth-century past (Bonnets! Horses! Sheep!). They mixed in elements of screwball comedies and Hollywood Westerns. They masculinized plot points to appeal more directly to boys and men. Most re-

tained Jerome's new visual and dramatic emphasis on the handsome, brooding Darcy, instead of presenting the story from the perspective of Elizabeth.
They invented entirely new scenes to showcase his flawed but redeemable
manliness. Some still flirted with the baser instincts. Yet who or what was
responsible for the attempt to bring *Pride and Prejudice* to the screen remains
subject to debate.

One improbable version of the story says that it was Harpo Marx. It's a
stage-to-film fairy tale that's been repeated far and wide in recent Austen
film criticism.[10] The story originated with film critic Kenneth Turan, who
first wrote about it in 1989. Harpo Marx saw Helen Jerome's play in previews
in Philadelphia in October 1935, Turan reports. Marx thought that Norma
Shearer, the actress-wife of MGM cofounder and producer Irving Thalberg,
would make a great Elizabeth Bennet. Marx reportedly sent the following
telegram to Thalberg: "Just saw Pride and Prejudice. Stop. Swell show. Stop.
Would be wonderful for Norma. Stop" (Turan 140). The interpretive leap
made next is that, thanks to Marx's telegram suggestion, Thalberg had a
lightbulb go on. It led him to snap up the play for Hollywood and for his wife.
(Thalberg would, in fact, become the first Hollywood producer associated
with the *Pride and Prejudice* film and Shearer the first actor entertained for
the role of Elizabeth.) In a recent e-mail communication, Turan writes that
he believes he never saw the telegram in question but rather saw it mentioned in another archival source, which remains presently unidentified.[11]
But even if this telegram—or the source that quotes it—surfaces in the future,
we should question the interpretive leap.

Jerome's *Pride and Prejudice* seems to have been headed to the stage for
at least a year prior to its Broadway debut in 1935—a year prior to Harpo's telegram. The play was first optioned by producer Arthur Hopkins, who wanted
Katharine Hepburn for his Elizabeth Bennet.[12] When Hopkins failed to lure
Hepburn to Austen or back to the stage, Hopkins dropped the play. It was then
picked up by producer Max Gordon, with "the backing of certain motion
picture interests, which served reasonably to strengthen his normally gambling instincts," as we've seen.[13] It was Gordon who is said to have sent to
England for his stage stars, Colin Keith-Johnston and Adrianne Allen. This
much was reported at the time in reliable yearbooks of drama, as well as in the
Washington Post.[14] Producer Gordon's stage efforts were supported by motion
picture interests from the first, long before Marx's telegram in October 1935.
Why, then, would Marx contact a Hollywood producer to whom he'd been
under contract when the *Pride and Prejudice* play was in previews?

Perhaps it's because Marx, a close friend of Broadway producer Gordon, already knew of Hollywood's plans for *Pride and Prejudice*'s play-to-film transition. If so, then Marx may have simply been ratifying previously discussed casting ideas. (Thalberg and Marx were tight; Thalberg had just produced the Marx brothers' nationwide hit, *A Night at the Opera* [1935].) Or if Thalberg wasn't already on board with producing the *Pride and Prejudice* film, or was wavering about it as an MGM project, then perhaps Marx was working a stage-to-film angle on Max Gordon's behalf, to lock in producer Thalberg's involvement. Taken together, these connections make it highly unlikely that the first film version of Austen's *Pride and Prejudice* originated with a suggestion in Harpo Marx's telegram. It's too bad, because it makes for a spectacular origin story.

A less fabulous version would begin by noting that MGM's interest in *Pride and Prejudice* dates back to 1933. MGM's files show that it had been trolling Austen for material for a couple of years before Jerome's play appeared. (Jerome herself is not mentioned in those first memos.) Initially, there was skepticism about an Austen film. As MGM's Edward Hogan wrote in his synopsis report early in 1933, "Since when have novels and comedies of manners been screen stuff? There has been talk, with some reason but to no purpose, of WHUTHERING [*sic*] HEIGHTS and JANE EYRE, roughly in this same period; they are dramatic and PRIDE AND PREJUDICE isn't."[15] "Roughly," indeed. Helen Jerome's play also obviously proved Hogan wrong. But several factors suggest that Hollywood had expressed some interest in *Pride and Prejudice* even before Jerome's play had proved a hit. Hopkins, who we saw above was the play's first would-be producer, had a track record of flipping scripts from stage to screen. His involvement itself might be said to signal the belief that a film would emerge from the play. In discussing Hopkins's role in another stage-to-screen deal, one scholar concludes, "A lot of flop plays were purchased by the movies and fell into the plus column when MGM purchased the rights."[16] Hopkins understood and capitalized on stage-screen commerce.

There are further details that add credibility to the idea that Jerome's *Pride and Prejudice* was intended all along to move from stage to film. In March 1934—a year and a half before the play debuted and before Harpo Marx's alleged telegram—the president of the Motion Picture Producers and Distributors of America announced publicly that *Pride and Prejudice* would be an upcoming cinematic release. The Austen title was listed in a spate of literary classics said to be in the process of adaptation to film that would be suitable for children and would be "pictures of the better kind."[17] The intention was to "raise standards of the industry," in the face of criticism of its immorality. The article doesn't name which studio was involved in moving forward with *Pride and Prejudice*, but MGM, of course, seems a likelihood. The motion picture industry was eager to publicize the release of more culturally weighty and family-oriented fare to shore up its credibility with critics. That Hollywood chose Jerome's version of *Pride and Prejudice* as its putative Austen text is amusing, because family friendliness is hardly the steamy play's calling card. But Hollywood's push to present screen offerings suitable for the young does explain a great deal about what would (and would not) happen to Jerome's play and Austen's novel during its dizzying five-year journey to the screen.

Some of the most skilled screenwriters in Hollywood took a stab at *Pride and Prejudice*. Today's critics find many things to deride in the 1940 film.[18] It is no longer a favorite with most Janeites, whether because of its erroneous Victorian costumes, its flibbertigibbet Elizabeth, or its making of Lady Catherine de Bourgh into a fairy godmother who's only out to test Elizabeth's love for Darcy. To comply with the Motion Picture Production Code, MGM also changed Mr. Collins from a clergyman to a librarian, so that there would be no whiff of criticism of men of the cloth.[19] But once you learn about the versions of the film that *weren't* made, the fact that the final cut of *Pride and Prejudice* hews as close to Austen's original as it does may seem a minor miracle.

From the outset, MGM's focus was on the would-be scripts and the would-be stars. Many possible actors were considered for *Pride and Prejudice*'s leads, and many scriptwriters were cycled in and out of the project. That was business as usual for this period. It was common Hollywood practice to assign a script to a number of different writers in succession, "in hopes each would improve and refine the earlier work."[20] Screenplays were regularly passed from one set of hands to the next until something stuck, just as possible stars came and went from a project, based on the studio's needs, desires, and whims.

A great number of stars were considered for Darcy and Elizabeth. The earliest MGM plan was to use as its Darcy a pre–*Gone with the Wind* (1939) Clark Gable, then in his midthirties. He was to star opposite Norma Shearer as Elizabeth, with her husband Thalberg producing. But when Thalberg tragically died of pneumonia in 1936, at only thirty-seven years old, the widowed Shearer's involvement in the film ended, too. The project stalled. Rumors of many possible new leads and directors followed, with an especially impressive list of possible Darcys, including American actor Melvyn Douglas (who was, like Gable, in his late thirties), Robert Donat (a British actor in his early thirties, who would become an Oscar winner in *Goodbye Mr. Chips* [1939]), and American actor Robert Taylor, then in his late twenties. MGM ended up casting Taylor in its film *Waterloo Bridge* (1940) instead of *Pride and Prejudice*. All of these possible Darcys were swoon-worthy and box-office preapproved.

MGM wound up going with yet another actor who fit that bill: Englishman Laurence Olivier, then in his early thirties. He was pulled into the project on the heels of starring in MGM's *Wuthering Heights* (1939) and *Rebecca* (1940). Olivier hoped he was going to star in *Pride and Prejudice* opposite his then-lover, Vivien Leigh, and that they would be directed by George Cukor, who'd had success with *Little Women*. Instead, worries swirled about Olivier and Leigh's extramarital affair. The studio was apparently concerned that if audiences had knowledge of the stars' offscreen liaison, it would lead to the rejection of the film. So Olivier found himself starring opposite Greer Garson, then thirty-five. The new producer on the film was MGM's powerful, handsomely paid, proven Academy Award–winner Hunt Stromberg. Reliable MGM director Robert Z. "Pop" Leonard was brought in to see the film to the finish line.

While all of this jockeying and negotiating was going on over actors and directors, at least eight writers were paraded in and out of the film. The screenplay went through a staggering number of versions that, for a time, seemed to get successively more absurd with each new set of hands. "Everything about the making of *Pride and Prejudice*" meant "mounting a spectacle," as one critic argues.[21] The problem is that it took MGM quite a while to agree on what the spectacle should be. The earliest screenwriters involved were husband-wife team Sarah Mason (1896–1980) and Victor Heerman (1893–1977), who had a few years earlier won the Academy Award for their adaptation of Louisa May Alcott's novel *Little Women* (1933). MGM's notes on Jerome's play show that this was exactly how Hollywood was thinking about using Austen. It imagined a *Pride and Prejudice* film as "a sort of 'Little Women' of early nineteenth century English middle-class life."[22] Mason, who had been involved in the film industry's transition from silent film to talkies, had been its first "continuity girl," or script supervisor. Heerman had experience in comedy, having directed the Marx Brothers' *Animal Crackers* (1930). (Those Jane Austen connections to the Marx Brothers do keep popping up!)

The Mason-Heerman script offered several innovations. One was an early scene in which Elizabeth and Jane meet the newly arrived Bingley and Darcy in the Bennets' stables. There, the four have a rousing conversation about dogs, especially Elizabeth's favorite dog, Kate. Darcy obnoxiously opines on Kate's inferior breeding, which he says means that her puppies will never amount to much. This is an idea from which Elizabeth naturally recoils, saying that her beloved dog's finer qualities are her work in the field, disposition, intelligence, and affection. "That may be so," says Darcy, "but I prefer a superior strain."[23] Despite the popularity of 1930s screen dogs, that inelegant bit did not make it to the screen. Perhaps it asked viewers to imagine Elizabeth as breeding material a bit too directly, making Darcy a bit too distasteful. Another Mason-Heerman version has Lizzy singing "Oh Dear, What Can the Matter Be" to Darcy, followed by the two of them singing it together, as if the film were veering toward a musical.[24] Finally, there is direct evidence that Mason and Heerman drew script ideas from Hugh Thomson's Austen illustrations, notably Bingley's chaise.[25] The film's title sequence shows that Thomson's influence endured from the play's stage designs to the final Hollywood screen cut. (One recent critic has compared the MGM *Pride and Prejudice* to Thomson's illustrations; it's a connection we can now identify as intentional.[26])

Hollywood wanted more hands on the *Pride and Prejudice* deck. In 1936, Tess Slesinger (1905–45) was briefly involved in revising Mason and Heerman's screenplay. Slesinger, known for publishing groundbreaking semi-autobiographical fiction about the experience of having an abortion, would also be involved in cowriting the screenplay of Pearl S. Buck's novel *The Good Earth* (1937). (That film was produced by Irving Thalberg, recipient of Harpo Marx's telegram.) Slesinger's innovation on *Pride and Prejudice* was to create a scene in which Elizabeth and Darcy first met in the "Misses Anderson's Book Shoppe," with its maxim posted on the wall: "Silence is golden."[27] Darcy and Elizabeth are shown standing back to back, browsing the shelves, as the female proprietors bring out their wares to each customer. Darcy asks for Macaulay's *Essays* (1843) and is brought instead essays by Charles Lamb and Thomas De Quincey. He is informed by the first Miss Anderson that these books are almost the same thing. Darcy expresses his surprise that the Misses Anderson do not keep the very latest books in their store, although today we might express our own surprise that the screenwriter doesn't know the difference among works of the 1810s, the 1820s, and the 1840s.

This sort of historical sloppiness, or perhaps ignorance, was a problem that MGM would continue to have in its *Pride and Prejudice* scripts and production department. It turns out star Greer Garson herself complained about it on set. She once gently let the set decorator know that he'd made a historical error. He explained to her that for the set's bookshop illustrations, he'd chosen images by George Cruikshank, the illustrator of Dickens. She asked him, "Don't you think [Thomas] Rowlandson would be better for the period?"[28] In Slesinger's historically fast-and-loose script, when Elizabeth tries to guide Darcy to find his desired book in the Misses Anderson's Book Shoppe, he expresses surprise at her knowledge of literature. Young ladies, he arrogantly quips, generally prefer bonnets to books. The conceit of a bookshop made it to the final version of the film, but the action would ultimately revolve around Mary Bennet, not Darcy.

Although it is unclear why—perhaps it's related to Thalberg's death—Mason and Heerman ultimately exited the project. Playwright Zoe Akins was the next writer on board, starting in 1937. She'd recently adapted Edith Wharton's *The Old Maid* (1935) for the stage, winning the Pulitzer Prize. Akins was also fresh from having cowritten the screenplay adaptation of Alexandre Dumas's *Camille*, directed by Cukor and produced by Thalberg. This would seem a promising talent and a good MGM fit. But Akins's changes to *Pride and Prejudice* are among the most bizarre of the lot. One Akins version opens with an unidentified girl arriving to a dissolute tavern. There she finds a drunken Wickham, and she begs him to make good on his promise to marry her, lest her brother kill him in a duel.[29] When she gives him a gift of a lock of her hair, Wickham callously blows on his hand to scatter it. Beginning the story by immediately revealing its villain was a new tack, never before seen in Jane Austen adaptation. One imagines that the cast-off mistress was also not what Hollywood had in mind in cleaning up its act for children and the classics.

One version of Akins's draft screenplay ends with a mirror image of the Wickham tavern scene. Where the first scene was male centered and dissolute, the final scene is virginal and female centered. Both scenes are set at night, but the last features two women in bed together, talking about the men they love. In it, Jane and Elizabeth contemplate their respective future happiness in upcoming marriages to Bingley and Darcy. The final image, in contrast to Wickham's hurtfully blowing away a lock of his mistress's hair, is of the two women blowing out their candles and laughing. This proposed ending is the version most in keeping with the spirit of Hinkley's *Dear Jane* (1919; 1932). Perhaps unsurprisingly, it was soon scrapped. Two women in bed together may have sent the wrong kind of moral message, historically accurate as it was and as innocent as it may have been meant to seem. In another version of the script, Akins depicts the two Bennet sisters sitting together alone on a hill, with Elizabeth reciting "Rule, Britannia" and Jane inexplicably sketching "the Castle of Edinbourgh [*sic*]."[30] It's hard to know what is more preposterous here—the caricatured exhibition of patriotism or the apparent ignorance of British geography.

Akins also toyed with adding elements of the melodrama and the Western. Another version of her script includes a scene in which the newly arrived Bingley orders a group of gypsies at Netherfield to get off of his land. The gypsies, however, are good guys, unbeknownst to Bingley. The head gypsy, Tony, pleads with his friend Elizabeth Bennet to provide a character reference for him. Elizabeth then pleads with Bingley, pressing him to let the gypsies stay. But the snobbish Darcy insists that Bingley must evict these beloved neighborhood gypsies. In another plot twist, Akins's Jane Bennet turns out not to have caught cold but to have come down with smallpox. It leads to the delicious line, delivered by Miss Bingley to Elizabeth, "Do you not realize this disease destroys the beauty of the complexion if one is so unfortunate as to live at all?"[31] Adding to the movie's Western flavor, Wickham teaches Lydia how to shoot a gun, a scene that is laughable but which may have been the genesis of the final film's famous Darcy-Elizabeth archery scene. In other innovations, Kitty and Lydia sing a dirty ditty at the pianoforte, and Mr. Collins proposes to Elizabeth while they are on horseback. Akins was, by the end of her many drafts, seemingly throwing things at the proverbial wall to see what might stick.

Akins also wrote a draft trying to make the film more directly appealing to men. She invented a series of scenes in which Darcy and Colonel Fitzwilliam transport the depressed and lovesick Bingley away from Jane and Netherfield to London for some male-bonding time. The three lads would experience together a male fantasy night of worldly adventures. First, they go to a masquerade ball, where they dress up as cavaliers of Charles II. There, Bingley flirts with a pearl-wearing sultana temptress. Then the men head to a cock fight to watch the wagering crowds. At the cock pit, they discover they're in for a real treat. There will be a fight featuring the celebrity monkey, Jacko Macacco, who takes on the best dogs in England. This leads Colonel Fitzwilliam to deliver such zingers as, "Wait and see. I bet on Jacko!" The colonel bets ten pounds on the monkey, but Darcy bets twenty on the dogs.[32] Perhaps meant to shore up the male characters' manliness, the scenes also give the heroes space to exhibit their good looks and attractiveness to women.

After Akins exited the project, there was a period of stasis, until screenwriter Elaine Ryan provided an outline of action in 1939. (She was involved in screenplay projects that featured Judy Garland and, later, Fred Astaire.) Ryan keeps much more strictly to the original novel, despite including a prodigious number of exclamation points. Finally, in summer 1939, screenwriter Jane Murfin was brought on board. Murfin was both a proven playwright and a proven screenwriter. She'd once been nominated for an Academy Award, but the film project she had just been involved in cowriting, George Cukor's *The Women* (1939), is likely what led MGM to tap her for the Austen adaptation. *The Women*, adapted from the Clare Boothe Luce play, is a female-centered film. There are no men in it, although the women talk about men. It might seem that, fresh from this screenwriting experience, Murfin would have tried to bring Elizabeth Bennet back to prominence in the Austen film. For some reason, Murfin did not work the material in that direction. She did, however, work to give Elizabeth and Darcy more dramatic episodes together.

Murfin had a number of inauspicious beginnings with her script, too, including a pathetic scene with Mr. Bennet on horseback feeding gruel to sheep, making him out to be a poor farmer. Another unforgettable version of Murfin's script has Elizabeth dressed up in a milkmaid's costume. She sits outdoors with her friend, the Scotch shepherd, old Jamie, feeding baby lambs and quoting Robert Burns. They are startled when the hunt rides past them.[33] It turns out to be Darcy and Bingley on horseback. The scene would seem to presage the one that opens the 1995 BBC *Pride and Prejudice*, with Elizabeth watching Darcy and Bingley riding from afar. But Murfin dialed it up by having Elizabeth actually encounter the two men on horseback. In one Murfin version, the encounter with Elizabeth throws Darcy off of his horse, and he must crawl out of a mud hole. In another version, it's Darcy's horse that splashes Elizabeth with mud. Because she's dressed up as a milkmaid, he treats her roughly and as a servant, tossing a shilling at her before he rides off.[34] If this was supposed to be comedy, it was an unpromising scenario. We seem to be back in Zoe Akins's Austen-Western territory.

By mid-1939, however, scenes begin emerge in the drafts that would make it to the final film. In October, Aldous Huxley was brought in to work with Murfin on the dialogue, at the rate of $1,500 a week.[35] That handsome sum is the equivalent about $25,000 in today's dollars. It was the satirical novelist's first foray into Hollywood. He was irreverent about the remunerative work in his private letters, telling his brother Julian that "Jane Austen's masterpiece" was referred to by MGM as "Pee and Pee." Some may be surprised that Huxley, author of the futuristic, dystopian *Brave New World* (1932), would take on a Hollywood Austen, but there was a Janeite in his family. Huxley's father wrote an introductory essay to a book on Austen, in which he suggests that males who don't understand the power of her fiction have not yet matured as men.[36] Even so, Huxley's reluctance to take on the Austen film job is well documented. He changed his mind about joining the "lunatic industry" in part to use the money he would be paid to help those suffering in war-torn Europe.[37] His involvement improved the script, making the dialogue far more crisp. It also appears to have brought parts of the screenplay closer to the novel than either the previous screenwriters or, in some cases, playwright Jerome had done. For example, the character of Elizabeth returns to some semblance of her original reasonableness—hard to imagine given the flighty character that emerges in the film. Most of Jerome's weeping Elizabeth is removed. Working together, Murfin and Huxley returned many of the novel's original scenes to the script. Huxley and Murfin crafted some new material at this time, too, including the famous archery scene, in which the surprisingly skilled Elizabeth and her would-be teacher Darcy point, shoot, and converse, cheek to cheek.

The final film, like the earlier Jerome play, made Darcy-ogling a recreational activity for both Elizabeth and the audience from the very first. The film opens with Mrs. Bennet, Elizabeth, Jane, Aunt Phillips, and the Lucases gossiping in a dress shop. The most important shopping they do is out of the window, as they gaze on Darcy and Bingley's carriages in the street. They are, as Deborah Cartmell notes, set up as "consumers," first of clothes and then of men (*Adaptations*, 50). In a close-up from the vantage point of the women looking out the shop window, Darcy wordlessly rises in the carriage, walking stick in his hand, ostentatiously tipping his hat at Mr. and Miss Bingley. Then Darcy alone is seen making a graceful step out of the carriage. The camera cuts away to the ogling women. All thought of purchasing dresses is pushed aside in consideration of the novelty of the fashionable male commodities. Elizabeth's presence in this Darcy-gawking scene, and her expressed interest in learning more about the extent of his wealth, shifts the terms on which sparks first fly between them. Elizabeth may make leveling comments about class in the film, but she's repeatedly shown as a full and curious participant in scenes that involve sizing up Mr. Darcy's assets.

The Murfin-Huxley script did make Elizabeth less sentimental and perfectly clever. There are several scenes in which Elizabeth and Darcy quote Byron together. Darcy himself plays a Byronic hero. One scene direction indicates that "Darcy is the center of all feminine attention."[38] The archery scene indicates that the actor playing Darcy should turn toward Elizabeth with a "surprisingly charming, almost boyish smile" (62). We can see most clearly what Murfin and Huxley were trying to get at with his character in a scene that was deleted from the final film. One script version reveals that Darcy was originally to have had a *second* archery scene that was either never shot or didn't make the cut. Part of that scene shows Darcy alone, at night, reliving his afternoon archery "lesson" with Elizabeth. He repeats their dialogue as a soliloquy, pining for her as he moves his lips. He then recites Byron's "She walks in beauty, like the night," in the dark. At the same time, he ineffectually shoots arrows, including one directly up into the night sky (79–80). If it had been included, this scene would have given Olivier even more space to demonstrate, alone with his audience, the depth of his passion for Elizabeth. The shades of Shakespeare here must certainly be intentional. The fact that Darcy, and not Elizabeth, gets a stand-alone scene to reminisce speaks volumes about how *Pride and Prejudice* was being more deeply reimagined in the 1930s as a story centered on Austen's hero, not her heroine.

The deleted scene would also have taken audiences even further inside Darcy's head and in a far darker direction. The plan was to make him turn Brontë-brutal. After his soliloquy, he was to bump into Miss Bingley on his night walk, still holding an arrow in his hand. The two of them were to have had a conversation, conspiring about how to break up Jane and Bingley, for Bingley's own good. This scene would have made directly visible one of Darcy's ugliest acts, described secondhand in the original novel. Darcy's nefarious plotting against his friend's happiness would have been made not only disturbingly visible but directly violent. Darcy was to have said to Caroline Bingley, "We're like a pair of conspirators, plotting a murder—the murder of a man's feelings. Well, seeing it has to be done, let's do it quickly." Then Darcy was to have raised the pointed half of the arrow in his hand and "driven it savagely into the bark on the tree under which they have been sitting, as though he were stabbing a man." He was then to have turned without a word and walked off (Murfin and Huxley 82). This episode is a darkly sexualized one, echoing a figurative rape as much as it does a figurative murder.

This scene's being omitted must have been equal parts disappointment and relief to Olivier. It echoes both Romeo and Heathcliff, at which he excelled as an actor, but it's decidedly un-Austen-like and makes Darcy even less admirable a figure. The scene was likely cut from the film for budgetary reasons, not because anyone had second thoughts about adding Shakespearean tragedy and Brontëan shock to Austen's iconic hero. As the script indicates, "NOTE: do not schedule the above scene and do not include it in the budget. We will wait until the picture is finished to determine whether or not the scene is needed" (Murfin and Huxley 82). There's no evidence the scene was ever shot. But this new knowledge of the full script makes evident the kind of sexy, brooding, boiling-just-below-the-surface Darcy that Huxley and Murfin were going for, as they built up those few retained aspects from Jerome's play. The film was scripted as Darcy's, not Elizabeth's, *Pride and Prejudice.*

Despite the film's moderate success, Olivier later disparaged it. He said, "I was very unhappy with the picture. It was difficult to make Darcy into anything more than an unattractive-looking prig, and darling Greer seemed all wrong as Elizabeth. To me, Jane Austen had made Elizabeth different from her affected, idiotic sisters; she was the only down-to-earth one. But Greer played her as the most affected and silly of the lot."[39] He's not wrong about Garson's Elizabeth, but he is wrong about his Darcy. The play's groundwork for an expressive, passionate Darcy, which Olivier echoed and amplified in the film, has been recycled in almost every script and acting performance after it. Garson's affected, silly Elizabeth has not.[40]

Jerome's play would prove even more lasting. A later stage version used her script as a springboard but did not prove a success: *First Impressions: A Musical Comedy* (1959). It was described as "adapted by Abe Burrows, from Helen Jerome's dramatization of Jane Austen's novel." Burrows (1910–85), who made his mark with *Guys and Dolls* (1950), claims critics panned his Austen-admiring, satirical stage musical because they thought, "Why would a guy who writes the hilarious stuff Burrows writes take on this tired costume drama?"[41] Some of Burrows's Austen is certainly hilarious, but his script takes odd turns.

The script reveals Burrows's Elizabeth (Polly Bergen) to be far more spirited and rebellious than Jerome's was, with lines such as, "Well, I don't like to do the things that are the things to do."[42] But Burrows's Darcy (Farley Granger) isn't written as Jerome-level passionate. He communicates his longing for Elizabeth primarily through lyrics and dance. His song "A Gentleman Never Falls Wildly in Love" is a horror. Mr. Collins has a brilliantly funny song, "Fragrant Flower," but it wilts under Elizabeth's repetitive chorus of "Nos."

One doesn't have to listen too far beyond Mrs. Bennet's whiny, half-spoken-word "Five Daughters," about her unsuccessfully having prayed to give birth to sons, to see why the musical wasn't a smash hit. In the end, Elizabeth too easily capitulates to the "things that are the things to do," as Mrs. Bennet joins forces with her daughter to scheme and snag Darcy as a husband. The musical even gives Mrs. Bennet its last spoken line (Burrows, *First Impressions* 90). Mrs. Bennet (played by Hermione Gingold) wasn't destined to become the precursor female version of Tevye from *Fiddler on the Roof* (1964).

Despite the failure of *First Impressions*, Jerome's famous play was still having an indirect impact as late as forty years after it first opened on Broadway. In 1974, Universal TV went some distance toward a remake of the 1940 film, just a dozen years after MGM's widely publicized 1962 rerelease. (That rerelease is further discussed in chapter 11.) Although the 1974 version of *Pride and Prejudice* was never made, its strange screenplay/teleplay survives in the Academy of Motion Picture Arts and Science's Margaret Herrick Library's unrealized scripts collection. It was cowritten by Jerome Lawrence (1915–2004) and Robert Edwin Lee (1918–94), and the project's producer was to have been Hunt Stromberg Jr. Stromberg was primarily a TV series guy, having worked on popular shows such as *The Beverly Hillbillies*, *Hogan's Heroes*, and *Gilligan's Island*. He is best known for having discovered Vampira and for producing the cult classic TV film *Frankenstein: The True Story* (1973). His follow-up to that movie was slated to include one Dickens and one Austen adaptation. The Austen project was on his plate for very specific reasons. It was clearly a son's nostalgia trip. Hunt Stromberg Jr.'s namesake father, Hunt Stromberg, had been the famed producer of the MGM *Pride and Prejudice* (1940).

Lawrence and Lee weren't the first screenwriters associated with Stromberg Jr.'s project. It was to have been written by novelist Christopher Isherwood (1904–86). Stromberg Jr.'s *Frankenstein: The True Story*'s teleplay had been cowritten by Isherwood and his partner Don Bachardy (1934–). That show was broadcast in two 90-minute episodes. Stromberg Jr. wanted to move forward with his Dickens and his Austen adaptations on the same model. He approached Isherwood about writing the script for *Pride and Prejudice*, Isherwood's diaries reveal, as early as November 1971.[43] But the experience on *Frankenstein* had so soured Isherwood on Stromberg Jr. that he refused. Isherwood writes, "Hunt Stromberg called from Texas, wanting us to do another script for him: *A Tale of Two Cities*. It is really unthinkable that we could work with him again. We can't trust him" (439).

Stromberg went with another pair of writers, Lawrence and Lee. They were highly experienced and poised for screen success. The two men would write thirty-nine plays together, the most famous being *Inherit the Wind* and *Auntie Mame*, the latter brought to film as *Mame*. Their *Pride and Prejudice* screenplay gives us a sense of what a popular Austen film adaptation of the 1970s—had one been made—might have looked like. The Lawrence and Lee *Pride and Prejudice* kept some elements and changed others from the MGM 1940 film. It calls its Elizabeth Bennet "Liz" through much of the script. It retains the carriage race between the Lucas and the Bennet women, but it moves it to the opening scene. Liz holds the reins of the horse, as her mother goads her to drive the carriage faster and faster. Then we learn that she's racing against Charlotte Lucas in the next carriage. The two women compete to see who can reach home first to send their fathers to meet the new eligible-bachelor neighbor, Mr. Bingley.[44] Liz and Charlotte's racing the family carriages was the film's attempt at a feminist back-formation, but it was used in a scene with equally sexist elements. The carriages next crash into each other. When no one is discovered hurt, the farce continues. Now carriage-less, the two mothers engage in a footrace across the fields, jumping stiles, to their homes and husbands.[45]

Far more ought to be said about this script, which involves a red-hot, love-hate Elizabeth and Darcy. In one scene, Darcy forces himself into Elizabeth's carriage. In another, he broodingly skips rocks in a stream. The film was to have featured a masquerade ball. Its Lady Catherine de Bourgh was to travel everywhere in a sedan chair. In the concluding scene, Lady Catherine was to dance with Sir William Lucas in what's described in the script as an eighteenth-century precursor to the twist. The two- to three-hour TV film was to have ended with Mr. and Mrs. Bennet happily dancing together, very much in love. Mr. Bennet gets the last word, declaring his garrulous wife's unusual silence on the dance floor to be "heaven."

A surviving casting memo makes clear the collective vision for the movie. Lawrence and Lee wrote to Stromberg with their ideas as to who would play what role. They wanted Peter Sellers as Mr. Collins and John Gielgud as Sir William Lucas. They hoped for Margaret Leighton as Lady Catherine de Bourgh. Their ideal Darcy was Peter O'Toole. For Elizabeth Bennet, the screenwriters had no one in particular in mind, which is itself telling. They inserted a question mark for her. Their suggested alternatives for the above actors, if these first choices were not available, included James Mason for

Mr. Bennet, Ralph Richardson or Michael Redgrave as Sir William Lucas, and Peter Cook as Rev. Collins. What is most remarkable however, are the actors they sought for their Mr. and Mrs. Bennet: Laurence Olivier and Greer Garson.[46]

To imagine Darcy and Elizabeth transformed into Mr. and Mrs. Bennet might seem anathema to some. But for those generations who had grown up seeing Austen on stage and screen—who might remember these plays and films from their youth—what could be better than a movie that ended with an aging Mrs. Bennet, played by a one-time Elizabeth Bennet, giddily dancing with her once-Darcy-husband? The Bennets' marriage never looked better. It was turned into the story's most enduring happy ending. This unrealized 1974 *Pride and Prejudice* would have been a movie pitched to the conservative middle-aged nostalgic, at a time of cultural revolution, hence its few requisite nods to the contemporary women's movement.

From the time of its origin at the end of the nineteenth century, *Pride and Prejudice* on stage had gone from being a text that revolved around a strong heroine's admirable rebellion, to one in which she steps aside to let the hero exhibit his smoldering passion, to a story about her devolving into a Mrs. Bennet herself, as either she or her once-hot (still hot?) husband gets the last word. (It involved laughs at her expense in either case.) By 1974, Elizabeth Bennet could even become a witty question mark, an everywoman "Liz." Thanks to Helen Jerome's hit Broadway play, and MGM's enduring film, *Pride and Prejudice* would become less and less a story centered on the self-actualization of a "not for sale" heroine, gradually falling in love with her intellectual equal. Instead, Jerome's innovations accelerated opportunities to identify with, or just gaze longingly at, Austen's once less-conspicuous hero. In that sense, Jerome's *Pride and Prejudice* is still with us, serving to suppress other possibilities for reimagining Austen's multilayered masterpiece of a novel.

PART THREE

JANE AUSTEN, POLITICIZED

ON MAY 1, 1872, the House of Commons was debating an oddly named and controversial piece of legislation: the Women's Disabilities Removal Bill. It would seem a difficult thing for a politician to come out against, the removing of women's disabilities. Who could be for keeping disabilities in place? The bill had been cleverly named. It proposed to expand the franchise, giving women property owners (e.g., the unmarried and widowed) the right to vote.[1] With a petition in favor of the bill having reached almost a quarter of a million signatures, wide public support was claimed. The proposed legislation had supporters in both houses, among both Tories and Liberals, but it also had strong opponents in each. On that day in May, members of Parliament engaged in heated debate, touching on such questions as whether women were more illogical—or had better control of their passions, or greater sobriety—than men. In making their arguments for and against the Women's Disabilities Removal Bill, the politicians also repeatedly name-checked Jane Austen.

Austen's name was first mentioned on that day in 1872 by Conservative MP John Henry Scourfield (1808–76), of Pembrokeshire, Wales. A published account gives us a sense of what he had to say. He believes "the incomparable Jane Austen" would have been staunchly against the bill and against women voting at all, just as he believes the majority of British women then were.[2] Scourfield uses a quotation from one of Austen's novels to support his claim: "Goldsmith tells us when lovely woman stoops to folly, she has nothing to do but to die; and when she stoops to be disagreeable, death is equally to be recommended as a clearer of ill-fame" (38). Scourfield doesn't say where this line appears in Austen, but it's from *Emma*. It's used by the narrator to describe Highbury's response to the death of the much-maligned

Mrs. Churchill, the wealthy, controlling aunt and guardian of Frank
Churchill. The quotation continues, "Mrs. Churchill, after being disliked at
least twenty-five years, was now spoken of with compassionate allowances."
This seems a satire on the population of Highbury, not a seriously
communicated universal truth. As a result, it's hard to recognize in this line
what Scourfield wants it to mean—that Austen was skeptical of women's
wisdom. It's even more difficult to imagine it as suggesting that women's
disagreeableness or ill-fame ought to disqualify the entire sex from voting.
Yet that's precisely how Scourfield would have us interpret it, and he
expected to carry the day.

Once Jane Austen's would-be opposition to the Women's Disabilities
Removal Bill had been alleged, another MP set out to claim, on the contrary,
that Austen would have been a solid supporter of the bill. Those trying to
defeat it said that it was only women who were "failures in life," those
who were not wives, who sought the franchise. In response, John Francis
Maguire, Liberal MP for Cork, takes issue with the idea that "Miss Austen
was opposed to the idea of such a concession," that "failures in life"
shouldn't get the vote. Maguire points out that the alleged female "failures" have "awfully increased of late, for they may be reckoned by tens of
thousands." Moreover, he argues, "Among those failures who are bent on
obtaining this right for their sex are many of our deepest thinkers and our
most brilliant writers." It leads him to refer to Jane Austen once again: "As
to Miss Austen, she wrote good works some half-century since; but if that
lady were now alive, would she not be found with the women of this day
who are her equals, if not her superiors, in intellect and in cultivation?"
(*Hansard* 45).

Could this be the earliest argument over Jane Austen in a legislative
body?

There's one more wrinkle worth mentioning. Referring to Austen in
parliamentary debate was no innocent act on that day. Just after Maguire
spoke, claiming that Austen would have been in favor of so-called failed
women getting the vote, the MP for Sandwich was roused to respond.
Edward Hugessen (E. H.) Knatchbull-Hugessen makes it clear that *he* is
voting against the bill. He argues at length against Maguire and the bill,
concluding, "I am against 'woman's rights' because I wish to retain women's
privileges" (*Hansard* 54). Knatchbull-Hugessen doesn't refer to Jane Austen
directly in his remarks, but perhaps it's because he doesn't need to. Many
would have known that Knatchbull-Hugessen was there speaking *as an*

Austen. He was the author's great-nephew, the man who would later become Edward, Lord Brabourne, first editor of Austen's *Letters* (1884).

Parliamentary debates using Austen were the most prominent places to demonstrate her growing political legacy. Between the 1870s and the 1920s, there was such frequent mention of Austen in political argument and public speech that one critic expressed his exasperation with it. As G. K. Chesterton puts it in his 1929 essay, "There was a remark about Jane Austen in connexion with the General Election. We have most of us seen a good many remarks about Jane Austen in connexion with the Flapper or the New Woman or the Modern View of Marriage, or some of those funny things. And those happy few of us who happen to have read Jane Austen have generally come to the conclusion that those who refer to her have not read her."[3] Chesterton's essay takes issue with the journalist who'd used *Pride and Prejudice*'s charismatic villain, George Wickham, to make a political point. The journalist is said to have claimed that women who were part of the "Flapper vote" would have been able to see through a charlatan like Wickham in five minutes. Chesterton disagrees. He argues that Wickham is exactly the kind of man who might "make a success of political elections" in their own day, who was "made for Parliamentary life." Chesterton concludes, "So vividly do I see Mr. Wickham as a politician that I feel inclined to rewrite the whole of *Pride and Prejudice* to suit the politics of today."

Making his own capsule political novel out of Austen's characters, Chesterton would send Elizabeth and Jane Bennet out to canvass. Elizabeth would go "with amusement" and Jane "with dignified reluctance." For Lydia Bennet, Chesterton expresses the highest of hopes: "She would be a great success in modern politics," he declares (200). But it's Wickham's triumph over Darcy that brings Chesterton the most amusement in crafting his cynical work of speculative fiction. Chesterton, a conservative, shows utter disdain for the politicians of his own day, while reinforcing Austen's importance to contemporary understandings of them. George Wickham, Chesterton argues, "would be the greatest success of all" as a politician: "He might become a Cabinet Minister while poor Darcy was sulking in the provinces, a decent, truthful, honourable Diehard, cursing the taxes and swearing the country was going to the dogs—and especially to the puppies" (200). In Chesterton's worldview, Austen's *Pride and Prejudice* serves as the foundational text among a Conservative's tragic political fables.

Austen's legacy in politics—on podiums, signage, and soapboxes—has a far deeper and richer history than most of us realize. We can't say that

Austen came late to being referenced in political speech. It's not because it's untrue but rather because there's little basis for judgment. One might assume that, because she was so often said to be an apolitical novelist, she was also slower to be brought into political conversations. In fact, the opposite argument holds up to scrutiny. Austen was labeled apolitical in highly politicized ways. Her fiction was quoted by politicians and political activists, becoming a touchstone in institutions of the modern state. And for more than a century and a half, those who became invested in a political Austen (whether they called her that or not) have clashed.

Among the late nineteenth- and early twentieth-century elite male literati, many of whom were socially if not politically conservative, Austen tended to represent a lost golden age for courtship and marriage.[4] She was envisioned as a cultural emissary from once-smooth domestic waters, to which some hoped society might yet return. For feminist activists and suffragists of the time, however, Austen was a foremother—a foregrandmother—whose very existence and achievements proved the rightness of their cause for expanding women's rights and opportunities. In chapter 8, I turn to one of their more prominent clashes. In 1902–3, a private men's club speech about Austen spilled over from a jovial dinner onto the public page. The men's club author pitched his remarks to others of his group and kind. The most prominent public response, however, came from a feminist woman, starting a print controversy. In chapter 9, I look at the direct ways that the women's suffrage movement used Austen's name and image in propaganda plays, street activism, and costume parties. Dressing up *as* Jane Austen for women's rights turns out to be one of the earliest forms of Janeite cosplay. I look at how establishment figures, peaceful activists, and radical protesters brought Austen into their lives and writings. They used her to wildly different ends—all claiming her allegiance to their causes—to ratify their most deeply held political passions. At signal moments of political debate in the past, especially debates over gender roles, it sometimes seems as if everyone wanted to claim Austen for his or her side.

Now we've again become used to talking about Jane Austen and politics in the same breath. Twitter death threats over Jane Austen's being put on the ten-pound note are merely the most sensational of such conversations. Hollywood stars now claim Austen for feminism. Scholars and students regularly engage in readings of her fiction using political theories, whether Marxist, feminist, queer, or postcolonial.[5] We've even become more accustomed to the idea that Austen was taken up by politicians and for political purposes in the past. Rudyard Kipling's short story "The Janeites" (1924) has enjoyed renewed popularity.[6] It considers the officers, soldiers, and nurses of World War I as devotees of Austen, exploring how they used her fictional characters to make sense of human follies and tragedies in the trenches. The fact that Winston Churchill read Austen as an escape from worry and illness during World War II is now frequently cited.[7] It turns out that Jane Austen—an author for so long described as having nothing to do with war and politics—definitely got around in wartime, as many now realize. But she was debated and got around politically beyond those signal moments, too.

That's why it's so surprising that, by the time of the bicentenary of Austen's birth in 1975, there was scant cultural memory of her onetime centrality to heated polemical or meaningful political thought, war related or not. Once again, if Austen were imagined as having a politics at all, she was believed to be conservative, due to her fiction's seeming endorsement of traditional marriage. It took years to change those widely held conceptions, too. It's one reason why understanding Austen's repoliticization in our own time as the doyenne of girl-power feminism requires our resituating her among more distant debates. To tell the story of Jane Austen in politics means providing a history of the intense conflicts over her, in clubs of all kinds, and in activism and political protest, as well as in establishment print commentary, oral speech, and political cartoons. Whatever party Austen may or may not have affiliated with during life, her legacy puts her all over the political map. If history is any guide, your sense of whether that would have pleased her or left her nonplussed may hew more closely to your own political beliefs than to anything we can prove about hers.

CHAPTER EIGHT

The Night of the Divine Jane

Men's Club Clashes and Politics
in the Periodical Press

High-profile Victorian and turn-of-the-century men were deeply commit-ted to securing Austen's reputation. That made her, for a time, the darling of discerning male literati—at least according to the literati themselves.[1] We can see its effects in microcosm in an anecdote of 1920s expatriate Paris. The Canadian novelist John Glassco writes about having been an uninvited guest at a party hosted by American author Gertrude Stein. It was quite a party to crash. Dada artist Man Ray was there, at one point holding forth about his enthusiastic discovery of Jane Austen's novels. He was thinking about doing an imaginary portrait of her, he told fellow party guests. In his image of her, she'd be wearing a long white dress, looking at a mushroom, and, he said, "the focus of the whole thing will be the mushroom . . . It represents the almost overnight flowering of her genius—also its circumscribed quality, its sug-gestion of being both sheltered *and* a shelter."[2]

Glassco listened attentively to Ray's odd description of how he'd depict Jane Austen, in a portrait that would feature mannish trees, simmering sexuality, and possibly some elves and witches. Not everyone listening was amused, however. A tweedy Englishman opined, "You are talking of Jane Aus-ten and sex, gentlemen? That dried-up lady snob lived behind lace curtains all her life . . . Isn't that so, Gertrude?" (Glassco 81). Then Stein approached the group.

She asked Glassco, "Do I know you? . . . No, I suppose you are just one of those silly young men who admire Jane Austen."

Glassco replied, "Yes, I am . . . And I suppose you are just one of those silly old women who don't."

Stein turned on her heels and walked away. The tweedy man threw Glassco out (81).

Did young men admire Jane Austen more than old women did in the 1920s? If it were true—something that's not at all clear—pigeonholing her devotees based on sex is a phenomenon that had begun many years earlier. They were first stereotyped as male. In 1870, the same year that J. E. Austen-Leigh's *Memoir* of his aunt was published, reviewer H. Lawrenny suggests that men who loved Jane Austen were an already-formed subgroup. Lawrenny writes, "Miss Austen has always been *par excellence* the favorite author of literary men. The peculiar merits of her style are recognized by all, but, with the general mass of readers, they have never secured what can fairly be called popularity."[3] The "general mass of readers" would seem, in this formulation, to include all women and nonliterary men. Amusingly, this reviewer was a woman. Lawrenny was an early pseudonym of Edith Simcox (1844–1901), the prolific essayist and early feminist.[4] Apparently, for a time, even an educated woman could see educated men as Austen's most enthusiastic reader class.

Lawrenny isn't alone in this opinion. Scots literary critic Andrew Lang voices a similar view a decade on. In his imaginary letter to Austen in *Letters to Dead Authors* (1886), he tells her, "You are not a very popular author: your volumes are not found in gaudy covers on every bookstall; or, if found, are not perused with avidity by the Emmas and Catherines of our generation" (76). For Lang and others, knowing and loving Austen marked a reader as a member of an exclusive male enclave. Austen was happily inaccessible to the less-discerning, naïve female readers, a group he seems to imply wouldn't properly appreciate her anyway. There are definitely age- and class-based inflections at work in all of this stereotyping as well. But in the midst of Austen's apotheosis among the (young? middle-aged?) male establishment, her name, image, writings, and characters began to attract young female readers, too—Lang's dreaded Emmas and Catherines. These two groups, well-heeled men and upstart women of a wider range of class backgrounds, both read and loved Austen. But they didn't always see eye to eye, and factions sparred. Today it might all seem very Darcy and Elizabeth. In this case, however, the pride and prejudice involved was not inclined toward an enlightened meeting of the minds. It was more like a war of ideas. At issue was not just to whom Austen belonged but whose view of her life and her fiction's political meanings would prove more persuasive and lasting.

In this chapter, I refer to "men's club Janeites" as a shorthand for the attitudes expressed by the likes of Andrew Lang. A number of the period's culture-making men saw themselves as the keepers of Jane Austen's eternal flame. They express no small amount of anxiety that others not like them will discover or claim her, as well as a fear that others like them won't. The anxiety was actually well-founded on both counts. Like Lang, some of the literati imagined the Emmas and Catherines as rare reader-enemies. By 1900, rarity could no longer be alleged. Girls and women had discovered Austen en masse, especially, as we've seen, on the stage and in the Christmas book market. But whether these readers deserved to be imagined as enemies or friends by those who imagined Austen as their longtime property was another matter. Not all elite literati in the Anglosphere belonged to men's clubs, not all men's clubs were politically homogenous, and not all elite literati were men. As for the Emmas and Catherines—as their Austenian fictional names seem to imply—they certainly came from varying economic circumstances. Could they properly appreciate her? A professed love of Austen had become deeply political.

The longstanding caricature of Jane Austen as an apolitical writer was based in *something*, some set of widely held beliefs about her and her writings. In trying to make sense of it, we might start first with the question of how one defines "politics." If we define it narrowly, in an understanding that the *Oxford English Dictionary* labels as "the science or study of government and the state," then Austen's surviving writings can hardly be said to engage contemporary politics frequently, directly, or intentionally.[5] She might mention a county magistrate (*Emma*'s Mr. Knightley), joke about adding a chapter on Napoleon to *Pride and Prejudice* (truly a lost opportunity for hilarity!), or wryly describe a member of Parliament in her letters, but her fiction is not heavily invested in statecraft. Yet if one means by politics "actions concerned with the acquisition or exercise of power, status, or authority" (following a secondary definition in the *OED*), then Austen may appear one of our *most* political novelists. The *OED* tells us that both definitions of politics were current in Austen's era and thereafter.

Today's understandings of Austen as a political author follow the second definition. It has become common to regard her fiction as commenting on the exercise of power, status, and authority, particularly in regard to families, economics, and gender roles. We sometimes mistakenly believe that our generation deserves credit for first recognizing the Political Austen. We view the present or the recent past as responsible for it, spurred on by late twentieth-century feminist literary criticism, by Marxism and cultural studies, or by postcolonial criticism in the wake of Edward Said's *Culture and Imperialism* (1993). Imagining these origins for Austen's political reputation, however, could not be more wrong. Once again, there is a longer and largely untold history of making Jane Austen mean something more (or something else) in the service of one's preferred dogma.

During the period 1870–1940, as B. C. Southam rightly concludes, "Austen was enrolled in many causes and seen in conflicting roles—sometimes as heroine of the feminists, sometimes as a champion of domestic values."[6] We ought to describe this "enrolling" for what it was—the profound politicization of her life and writings. For conservatives, men and women alike, Austen supported the notion that seeking any kind of cultural and political change in gender roles was wrongheaded. Austen stood as a beacon of past political sanity, contrasted to present political lunacy, especially where women, men, and relationships were concerned. She harkened back to what was imagined as a less complicated and more right-thinking time for courtship and marriage, when women belonged in the home and men in the wider world. She was particularly embraced by the most highly placed of those men in the wider world. Austen was, for a time, an incredibly popular figure in London's ubiquitous private men's clubs, where men of privilege ate, drank, sang, recited, argued and generally escaped from their domestic or professional lives.

Southam's *Critical Heritage* volumes catch some of the flavor. In the early twentieth century, men who criticized Austen were engaging in a dangerous activity, or so novelist Arnold Bennett (1867–1931) claims. In 1927, Bennett wrote in his column in the conservative London newspaper the *Evening Standard*, "The reputation of Jane Austen is surrounded by cohorts of defenders who are ready to do murder for their sacred cause. They are nearly all fanatics." He continued, "They will not listen. If anybody 'went for' Jane, anything might happen to him. He would assuredly be called on to resign from his clubs. I do not want to resign from my clubs. I would sooner perjure myself."[7] Not willing to label Austen "great," Bennett saw her instead as a "great little novelist," admitting that he usually prevaricates in conversation with his highly placed male club friends, feigning a reverence for her, rather than speak the unpopular truth of his actual views. He suggests that his private men's clubs are filled with members who think "Jane Austen was the only estimable author who ever lived."[8] Southam includes Bennett's piece in *The Critical Heritage*, under the heading "a great little novelist" (2:viii).

Bennett's dismissive description of Austen and of the knight-errant, Austen-loving male reader were caricatures, but he was responding to what had been described as a long tradition of Austen-loving men and to highly placed male champions of Austen. Among these champions we ought to count George Saintsbury (1845–1933), the Edinburgh professor said to have coined the term "Janeite."[9] He also names Austen the "mother of the nineteenth century novel."[10] William Dean Howells, dubbed Austen's "foremost American champion," calls her "the divine Jane."[11] Oxford professor A. C. Bradley has been called (exaggeratedly) "the starting point for the serious academic approach to Jane Austen."[12] These and other Austen standard-bearers made revering Austen de rigueur among the male cultural elite. Apparently they also made club life rather uncomfortable for men like Bennett, who did not share their zeal.

Any list of the era's most zealous men's club Janeites must also rank G. K. (Gilbert Keith) Chesterton (1874–1936) very highly.[13] In his essay "On Jane Austen in the General Election" (1929), Chesterton explains away progressive and feminist understandings of Austen with the imputation that anyone who holds them either has not read her or has not read her well.[14] Chesterton sets himself up as the right (political) reader of her novels and her characters. Chesterton, a public figure who delivered speeches on contemporary issues, had long made Jane Austen one of his favorite touchstones, using her to communicate his dim view of expanding women's education and rights. It's an odd thing to happen to a nineteenth-century author who was then believed by many (Chesterton included) as entirely uninvested in politics.

When Chesterton toured the United States in 1930, one newspaper ran a headline "Chesterton Thinks Women Will Tire of New Freedom," with the subtitle, "Place Is in the Home."[15] For Chesterton, Austen's fiction was on the front lines of this battle. For him, it advocated against any kind of social change, particularly for women. We see this in his essay "The Evolution of Emma," where he offers up heroine Emma Woodhouse as Austen's cautionary tale against both strong women and political movements that seek freedoms for those who are allegedly unready for them, such as working-class women.[16] In Chesterton's reading, Emma learns that the social order belongs just as it was, because those who go mucking about with it only harm those they would help. Chesterton's Austen shows readers how to stay in their (class-based, gendered) places. His Emma teaches us to resist social change. There are, of course, other ways to understand the positions that Emma comes around to by the novel's end. In any case, Chesterton was a controversial figure. Some years earlier, the periodical *Current Opinion* expressed itself unsympathetic to Chesterton's "medieval" and "gloriously fantastic" conservative views on women; it ran an illustration of him in its June 1913 issue with the caption, "He Idolizes Jane Austen."[17] For a set of powerful

HE IDOLIZES JANE AUSTEN

The author of "Emma" could "keep her head," writes Mr. Chesterton, "while all the after women went about looking for their brains."

Figure 8.1. G. K. Chesterton, "He Idolizes Jane Austen," in *Current Opinion* 54, no. 6 (June 1913): 495, by Alfred Priest.

male readers of the time, the two opinions were very much related: to idolize Austen and to hold conservative views on women's rights and roles went hand in hand. There was nowhere better for such men to express and argue over these views than in tony private men's clubs.

Several factors came together to make Austen popular in "Very Important Men's Clubs."[18] One was the fashionability of recognizing her fictional powers, proving one's aesthetic good judgement. Another was that Austen and her heroine-creations were widely seen as romantically (if not sexually) attractive to men. Saintsbury believed that there were a handful of female protagonists with whom it might be a pleasure to fall in love, but none rose above Elizabeth Bennet "to live with and to marry."[19] As a reviewer points out, Saintsbury "waxes almost erotic."[20] The shared private judgments meant that public pronouncements—establishment critics publishing in establishment periodicals—often read like clubby, knowing in-speak. Disagreements about her politics were there, but they were expressed in a shockingly small range, from "she had none" to "she was conservative." Some, like liberal politician and essayist Goldwin Smith (1823–1910), saw Austen's fiction as having "not the slightest tinge of politics," her "general tendencies" "evidently conservative," although with "a flash of something like Radical sympathy with the oppressed governess."[21] R. Brimley Johnson (1867–1932) thought Austen represented "unaggressive conventionalism and conservatism."[22] With few exceptions, the way these club men loved Austen mirrored the ways they approved of women's roles in their own time. For those traditionalist men who appreciated her, Austen and her fiction were to be celebrated not only in spite of her being limited but *because she upheld limits*.

Men's expressing a common love of Austen could be an act not only demonstrating their collective opposite-sex attraction to her or their mutually held views of her fiction's achievement as it mirrored proper sex roles, but also an act of homosocial bonding. As Claudia L. Johnson rightly puts it, "Austen's novels appear often to have facilitated rather than dampened conversation between men."[23] Johnson's work troubles over an emerging undercurrent of these conversations that serves to contextualize a minority of male Austen-haters. She examines how anti-Janeite men, like Mark Twain, imply that a man who enjoyed Austen was engaging in an unmanly activity, marking any devotee of hers as a "pansy."[24] Some anti-Janeites would have had it that a shared male love of Austen stemmed from men's wish to romance *each other*. Johnson's exploration of the queerness of Austen's legacy is a groundbreaking one. It does, however, leave further areas for investigation. Another way to get at the complicated status of Austen among elite men during this period is to study the conversations, images, and arguments about her that arose in the context of an actual turn-of-the-century men's club.

On May 27, 1902, an evening dinner and lecture were organized by a prominent private men's club, the Sette of Odd Volumes, for its forty-two members and their male guests. The Sette was a social and dining club for enthusiasts of the "writing, illustrating, and publishing of books."[25] Since its establishment in 1878, the Sette had dined together once a month, although arguing, drinking, singing, and other antics seem to have been as important as the food and sharing of ideas. The Sette's famous members included Sir Edward Sullivan (of Book of Kells fame), the publisher John Lane, and

Vyvyan Holland, son of Oscar Wilde.[26] Prominent guests in 1902 included Bram Stoker, various knights, and a viscount.[27] The dinner on May 27, 1902, became known in the club's privately printed records as the Night of the Divine Jane. But the Sette's Night of Divine Jane was not an homage. It was, as we'll see, designed as a Janeite takedown.

The Sette's evenings included collectible menus.[28] "The Divine Jane: Domine" features an illustration of Jane Austen in ruins.[29] It is an illustration drawn by Sette member John Hassall (1868–1948). He's been called the "epitome of the good all round English clubman," a hail-fellow-well-met heavy drinker, who later became known as the "Poster King" (Cuppleditch, *London* 78, 81–82). Recently widowed and spending his evenings in all-male company, Hassall was a commercial artist of great industry, who regularly designed menus, invitations, and logos for a number of his clubs (72–73). He had a fun-loving or eccentric side and enjoyed dressing up, whether as a police officer, a Turkish refugee, or as St. George, in a costume made out of old biscuit tins (70, 78). He was also very industrious. Hassall produced during this period some six to seven hundred commercial posters and eight hundred book covers, as well as two hundred book illustration commissions (75, 79). His Jane Austen menu illustration for the Sette—previously unnoticed by scholars, perhaps because it was privately printed—makes clear how fraught a subject Austen's political reputation had become in turn-of-the-century men's clubs.

Hassall chose to create for this menu a busted bust of Austen.[30] In Hassall's illustration, a disheveled, large-eared, and comic-looking maid looks askance at a broken Austen bust, fallen from a book title–filled plinth. Hassall was known for his sense of humor, so whatever else this image is, it was certainly an irreverent Austen send-up. The maid, as she stands in front of the Club's signature "O V" symbol, looks squarely at the place where Austen's head had been. The first bits of "broken Jane" have been swept up, but other pieces lie scattered on the floor. The image is ambiguous. It may suggest the maid is responsible for the mess. If so, then Austen is being ruined for the (male) elite by the (female) working classes. But if the maid is cleaning up someone else's mess, then Austen's head has been smashed by some other force. It's unsettling that the maid's head is just to the right of where Austen's would be if it were still attached at the shoulders. The visual play encourages us to imagine the maid's head atop the plinth, and her cap even resembles the one from Austen's imaginary portrait. The maid carries in her pocket a menu, positioned as a parallel to the names of Austen's six novels, mentioned opposite. If Hassall's image is any kind of homage to a "Divine" Jane, it's an odd one, in that it depicts her destruction, whether by the maid (or the working classes) or by the privileged men whose maids clean up their messes.

Hassall's other artwork doesn't give us much guidance on how to read this image. The image most associated with him is his "jolly fisherman" for *Skegness Is So Bracing* (1908), an influential design purchased by the Great Northern Railway.[31] The poster was commissioned to attract tourists to travel by train to a struggling seaside resort, in an echo of Jane Austen's

Figure 8.2. "The Divine Jane: Domine," *The 236th Meeting of the Sette of Odd Volumes: 27 May 1902* (London: Sette of Odd Volumes, 1902), menu by John Hassall.

unfinished seaside novel *Sanditon* that can only make us smirk. Hassall specialized in humorous designs and "wasn't concerned with politics," according to his biographer (Cuppleditch, *John* 93). But that doesn't mean that the Austen menu is devoid of political import. The more we learn about the evening for which Hassall designed the menu, the more Hassall's ruined Austen seems highly politicized.

A further and crucial piece of evidence is the fact that lectures were always featured at the Sette's dinners. Hassall's busted Jane was created in conjunction with that evening's scheduled talk, delivered by fellow Sette member Walter Frewen Lord (1861–1927).[32] The night was described as "The Divine Jane: Domine" because the word "domine" (meaning lord and master) was also Lord's club nickname. Lord was a literature and law man (Inner Temple), having been invalided out of the Civil Service in India. He would eventually leave London to become a history professor at the Durham College of Science at Newcastle-upon-Tyne.[33] It was with a historian's sensibility, and as a privileged, well-traveled man, that Lord approaches the subject of Austen's fiction. He found much to criticize in it in his lecture. For Lord, William Thackeray was the greatest novelist, the one most deserving of comparison to Shakespeare.[34] Austen, Lord thought, was overrated among his brethren. Lord would later publish an essay taking down the Austen-lovers Thomas Babington Macaulay and W. D. Howells. We get a sense of Lord's disdain for their praise when he asks, "But really? Shakespearean? Divine? Are there any two qualities more entirely lacking to Miss Austen?" (*Mirror* 79). It seems likely that on that night in 1902, Hassall knew that Lord's lecture was going to knock Austen's head off. Hassall created an image meant to accompany a rousing verbal depreciation.

The Sette of Odd Volumes, in addition to its privately printed menus, also privately published an annual *Year-Boke*. It is from that volume that an account of Lord's Austen lecture may be found. It reports that Lord spoke on "the merits and defects of 'The Divine Jane.'" He took the floor "with a narrow table in front of him, on which were displayed a set, uniformly bound, of the works of Jane Austen, with carefully arranged and disposed book-marks in each" (*Year-Boke* 16). Lord read aloud "illustrative extracts." He poked fun at Hassall's drawing, which he described as "representing an imaginary night of the *Dominie* [Lord] with a most Undivine Jane." Lord sarcastically declared himself "much offended" with the image, taking his revenge by reading what he himself called "a Paper of vast length and appalling dulness"

(17). He predicted his own poor performance as a lecturer. He reports that he prosed on "until his voice was drowned in universal execration" (18).

Lord did precisely what Arnold Bennett would later say he feared to do. He went into his men's club and prodded his Janeite friends with the sharp stick of an anti-Janeite lecture. He dared to criticize Jane Austen in front of his club men. After he spoke, there was a discussion. Records tell us that two guests declared against Lord's arguments, in "untimely [*sic*]" and "unreformed" condemnation (*Year-Boke* 19). They reputedly pronounced Lord "Advocatus Diaboli"—devil's advocate—and wanted to retitle his paper "The Diabolic Dominie and the Divine Jane" (19). Not all in attendance were enraged, however. According to club records, one member mistakenly thought Lord must have been joking. Another confused Charlotte Brontë for Jane Austen. Yet another gave "a carefully prepared impromptu musical rendering of the spirit of Jane Austen's work" (20). The men argued. They laughed. No doubt some drank heavily. The night of the Divine Jane came to an end.

Lord's Austen-hating argument, however, lived on. What started as a confrontational lecture among forty men who met for a monthly dinner in a hotel ended up seeing print. A version of it was published in the periodical the *Nineteenth-Century and After*. In his published essay, Lord describes in specific terms his political motivations for writing. Lord was crafting an anti–women's fiction, anti–women's rights, and simply antiwoman argument, ostensibly in response to what he saw as wrongheaded in his brethren's Janeite assessments. In the print version, Lord imagines both his audience and Austen's enthusiasts in masculine terms. He complains that Austen's "devotees, more numerous with every year that passes by, stand round with drawn swords and compel our homage."[35] These devotees appear to Lord as multiplying Don Quixotes, protecting their beloved Jane Austen.

No matter how much Lord seeks to distance himself from the Austen-quixotic, his opinions have some *political* commonalities with these sword-drawn worshippers. Most, like him, imagine Austen as a "lady" who "wrote like a lady," finding her "ignorant . . . of what was really going on around her." Like them, Lord believed that Austen either ignored or was ignorant of war and that she deserves to be understood as small, limited, and apolitical. Where Lord differs from Janeites is that he does not conclude these things and then nevertheless argue *for* her greatness. To him, such "ignorance" precludes greatness. Lord describes Austen's ignorance in geography, naming places she never traveled to or mentioned: Japan, China, the South Seas.

He lists the world events of her day that form no part of her stories ("Jane" 666). For Lord, Austen's "smallness" is not a sign of miniature perfection or of artistry. He sees Austen's downsized fiction as a feminine limitation.

Lord makes his own politics clear. He continues, "All honour to her for not writing about what she did not understand," such as "an imaginary mutiny at sea" or an "imaginary conspiracy of the colored folk" (Lord, "Jane" 670). His male-centered conservativism and class- and race-based privilege and bigotry lead to his greatest problem with Austen's (female-authored) fiction. He opines that "each of her stories is exactly like the last, and that much of her narrative is hopelessly uninteresting" (669). Although he believes that she is as admirably conservative as he is, Lord finds her subject matter boring. In fact, he thinks her writings are boring *of necessity*. Femininity is boring and apolitical. Masculinity is exciting, global, and political. As a result, only masculine fiction writing could effectively grapple with weighty subject matter like mutinies of working-class sailors and conspiracies of the racially marginalized—and, presumably, express relief about how they are put down in the end or nod at a warning about exactly what disasters might befall if they aren't.

Lord considers himself an "iconoclast" where Austen is concerned: "I should not be surprised to find myself acclaimed as the Devil's Advocate," he concludes. Of course, we now know that he was declared precisely that at the Sette's Night of the Divine Jane. Rhetorically, Lord still seems to imagine himself in the periodical essay as speaking to the same audience he addressed at the Sette of Odd Volumes. It does make one wonder just how many Austen essays published in leading periodicals had their origins in private men's clubs. (If this were a common practice, it might explain in part why so much conversation on Austen in this period appears to us to be written in a man-to-man, urbane, and knowing argot.) Lord ends his 1902 depreciation with the ratifying point, as he characterizes it, that Austen herself described her work as "small" in her private correspondence. He must be on the mark about her shortcomings if the author agrees with him, he suggests. Lord discerns no humor or irony in any of Austen's correspondence with Royal Librarian James Stanier Clarke, instead seeing her as freely admitting her "essentially feminine" smallness, to which Lord is only too happy to accede ("Jane" 674).

If we read Lord's published essay alongside Hassall's image on the 1902 dinner menu, the Sette of Odd Volumes night looks quite different. The talk sought to crush—and the menu illustration to accompany and make fun of those who would crush—men's club Janeites. Lord envisions himself as performing a political public service, a needed literary execution. Illustrator Hassall set out to poke fun at Lord and Janeites all at once. His image was created as a private in-joke among club men, viewed by very few eyes in the years since its publication. Lord's essay, however, ended up, five months later, in the hands of tens of thousands, in a leading periodical.[36]

The *Nineteenth Century and After* was a nonsectarian, high-circulation, and well-regarded monthly, featuring work by leading writers and intellectuals. At its helm was noted editor-publisher and architect Sir James Knowles, who also just happened to be Walter Frewen Lord's father-in-law.[37] Yet even that cozy connection did not prevent Lord from coming under subsequent attack in the periodical's pages. Instead of inflaming the ire of the men's club literati, as Lord anticipated, his essay called out a far different opponent: a feminist Janeite. The writer who responded most directly to Lord's Austen essay signed herself, "Miss Annie Gladstone." Her response appeared in the *Nineteenth Century and After* several months after his, titled, "Another View of Jane Austen's Novels."[38] It was widely reprinted in periodicals in the United States and United Kingdom, attracting still further commentary.

Why editor Knowles would have chosen to publish a cutting rejoinder to his son-in-law's Austen essay may seem puzzling. It may simply have been a choice made to sell more copies of the magazine. It may also have been because the journal's reputation for nonpartisanship would be upheld by publishing a riposte to a controversial piece by the editor's son-in-law. Perhaps it was even a result of Knowles and his son-in-law Lord not getting on very well (Metcalf 343). Whatever the reason, the dueling essays provide us with a rare moment in which the men's club and first-wave feminist Janeites exchanged direct fire over how to classify the political meanings of Austen's image and fiction at a crucial time in the reformation of her political legacy.

Annie Gladstone rails against those who would use "feminine" as an insult. She weighs in on the Janeite and anti-Janeite wars: Austen "has been placed by the enthusiastic votaries on the very pinnacle of literary achievement; she has been accused by equally fervent detractors of being commonplace, monotonous, and, worst of all, feminine!" It's the last insult—feminine—that leads Gladstone to take Lord apart with force. She turns his argument on its head: "To say that Miss Austen's work is feminine is indeed its highest praise." She suggests that expecting Austen to write in a manly way is to seek inauthenticity. Gladstone criticizes Lord for suggesting "a woman should . . . avoid being feminine . . . [that] her work is only valuable as it apes the characteristics of a man's mind" (113). Genius may be masculine or feminine.

A later review of Lord's 1906 book laid this bare as a distinctly political problem: "Mr. Frewen Lord appears to have waded through a vast quantity of novels seeking not literary merit but the political or moral lesson they conveyed."[39] It's amusing, because this is exactly the sort of criticism later made of feminist literary critics of the late twentieth century. Lord himself makes clear his own views on the early twentieth-century's women's movement: "Forty years of the Women's Movement—which was to do so much for us—has wrought little but mischief" (*Mirror* xiv). Gladstone, in her trailblazing 1903 response on Austen, focuses on Lord's faulty, gendered litmus test for testing Austen's artistic merit. He misjudges her achievement by measuring her fiction for a demonstrated interest in (masculine) government or statecraft, for worldliness and cosmopolitanism.

Gladstone takes Lord to task for finding Austen's fictional world small and for criticizing her lack of travel. Wordsworth and Shakespeare wrote of children and women, she points out. Shakespeare wrote a whole play about "the doings of a girl of fourteen who had probably never been out of her native Verona." "Why, pray," Gladstone asks, "is a girl of seventeen who has never been outside her own village less interesting than any other theme?" The problem, she argues, is in the beholder's eye: "We must not forget that when the subject is not interesting to us we are really expressing not the defect of that subject, but our own limitations. We mean that we have little knowledge of it and less sympathy" (Gladstone 115). Gladstone maintains that Lord is the one hampered with limitations, not Jane Austen.[40]

It's a decisive intervention in a conversation that usually excluded feminists, yet Austen critics have had trouble identifying her. Southam refers to her as "a Miss Gladstone" (2:73), indicating his uncertainty.[41] She was, in fact, Annie Martha (Gladstone) Wilton (1857–1932), a passionate educator of girls. She may have had reason to conceive of Austen as a precursor or a role model. At the time she published her Austen essay, Gladstone was a single woman, a teacher, and a pseudonymous writer in her early forties. The daughter of a bank clerk, Gladstone still lived with her parents and several talented siblings, all of whom had benefited from the systemic educational changes of their lifetimes. Gladstone ran a small secondary day school for girls in a London suburb.[42]

Her Austen essay appears to be the first she published using her own name as a byline, departing from her previous practice, an interesting choice for an essay defending an author who, a century before, did not use hers.[43] In later years, Gladstone would break away even further from Austen's example. Her young first cousin, the gifted mathematician John Raymond Wilton, came to England from his native Australia. Together, Gladstone and Wilton would read aloud, with literature providing them an "ever-developing intimate bond."[44] When Wilton proposed to Gladstone on her birthday in 1908, it is said that she was surprised by it. Gladstone was fifty; Wilton was twenty-four (Stevenson 83). She told him to wait two years to see whether he felt the same. The two would marry in 1910 and move to Australia, where she published editorials under her married name.[45] I provide these details here not only because they are interesting but because it helps us to rethink our stereotypes of middle-aged spinster writers. Gladstone-Wilton doesn't seem to have published further work on Austen, but she deserves a more prominent place in our histories of Austen's reception for the one essay alone.

Gladstone's rejoinder anticipates not only the suffrage movement's later claiming of Austen for their cause (as we'll see in chapter 9) but the decades-later, far better-known, and oft-cited arguments on Austen by 1920s and 1930s feminist critics Virginia Woolf and Rebecca West.[46] History (and literary history) would prove to be more solidly on Gladstone's side than on Lord's where Austen and politics were concerned. At the time, however, opinion was far more divided. One source deemed Lord's essay a "clever analysis," another a "clever criticism."[47] But those who commented at greatest length supported Gladstone. Lord's "depreciating," "patronizing articles," while not seen as "really severe or ill-natured" were nevertheless neither "very valuable or very true," according to one periodical reviewer.[48] Another critic called Gladstone's essay "the most interesting article" of the volume and notes that it is "an answer to the impertinences—to use the word in its correct sense—of the [man] who . . . wrote flippantly against Austen."[49]

Gladstone's Austen essay may have taken some of its inspiration from W. D. Howells's discussion of Austen in *Heroines of Fiction* (1901), as Southam has charged (2:73). But it's certainly not the case, as Southam further suggests, that Gladstone had nothing new to say about Austen. Gladstone's defense of Austen against political attacks goes far beyond anything Howells published. She employed more rhetorically pointed, indignant language, in an essay that was a direct shot at Lord, who was himself admittedly responding to some extent to Howells. Gladstone broke the chain of men's-club-responding-to-men's-club Janeites in a high-profile periodical. Whether it worked or not, she forced the conversation out of its single-sex rhetorical confines.

There's at least one way, however, in which Howells went further than Gladstone in his discussion of Austen's politics. Howells directly identified Austen's fiction as liberal or progressive, although labeling her *unconsciously* political. Of *Pride and Prejudice*'s Elizabeth Bennet and her interactions with Lady Catherine de Bourgh, Howells writes that Elizabeth's "triumph is something more than personal: it is a protest, it is an insurrection, though probably the discreet, the amiable author would have been the last to recognize or acknowledge the fact."[50] Howells as much as calls Elizabeth (and, by extension, Austen) a feminist revolutionary, "whether she knew it or not," because she "was in her way asserting the Rights of Man as unmistakably as the French revolutionists whose volcanic activity was of about the same compass of time as her literary industry" (49). It is hard to know whether Annie Gladstone would have agreed with this assessment of a progressive political Austen. (Austen's first dramatic adapters certainly seemed to.) Gladstone lived her life in sympathy with those who saw the potential for triumph in protest and insurrection among the less privileged, rather than, like Lord, seeing it as a form of wrongheaded revolt (mutiny, conspiracy) that great political literature ought to serve to put down.

We might say that W. D. Howells served as an ideological bridge between the men's club Janeites, many of whom saw Austen as safely apolitical, and feminists, who were unabashed about using Austen in support of progressive causes. The origins of these divergent opinions date back even further, as we saw in the introduction to this section, in the discussion of Austen in the House of Commons. There were also differences of political opinion about Austen among literary women. In her work on Victorian women's periodicals and Austen from the 1870s to the 1890s, Marina Cano-López notes that "Austen emerges as one of the fields where battles over female identity—liberal and conservative, professional and domestic—were fought."[51] As Victorian women's periodicals, and women themselves, debated women's proper rights and roles, Austen's fiction became a political field to mine, as well as a political minefield. Twenty years and more later, in the early 1900s, these conflicts had not been resolved. Sixty and more years later, by the 1940s, rousing debates over Austen's politics had faded from historical memory, along with the amateur dramatization craze and the memory of most of Austen's illustrations, save Thomson's and the Brocks'.

In the early 1900s, however, Howells and Gladstone were advocating for Austen against the dominant political positions of conservative elite clubmen. These men—speaking with the authority of their positions, and often speaking among themselves—were working to paint Austen into a very cramped literary corner. They were putting her on a pedestal, or, we might say, on a plinth. The likes of Walter Frewen Lord and G. K. Chesterton shaped the conversation about Austen as harmless and apolitical from their own powerful perches, inviting readers to weigh in on how to value Austen's conservatism, rather than asking whether she was conservative. They set the terms of the debate in the day's most respected cultural venues, but they could not dominate it. Their attempts to limit its terms prompted others to seek to widen them.

Today, when we repeat the early arguments about Austen made by conservative men, positioning the likes of West and Woolf as precocious feminist outsiders, we're misrepresenting the past. We're missing opportunities to record a wider range of statements. We're also missing the chance to understand how Austen became a political touchstone in an era of thundering debate, especially on gender politics. Those debates swirled vigorously around Austen, who, although long dead, was certainly a party to them. Her novel *Northanger Abbey* records a humorous conversation in which it's called an easy step from politics to silence.[52] But in the first century of Austen's afterlife, the easy step was more often from her supposedly apolitical novels to loud political debate.

CHAPTER NINE

Stone-Throwing Jane Austen

Suffragist Street Activism, Grand
Pageants, and Costume Parties

On June 13, 1908, suffragists took Jane Austen to the streets of London. The National Union of Women's Suffrage Societies (NUWSS) held its Great Procession, a demonstration march and rally, in what would become known as a "new style."[1] It was ordered, majestic, and artistic. An estimated ten thousand women representing forty-two organizations participated, marching across London for an hour and a half to Royal Albert Hall, where speeches were given by the movement's high-profile leaders. The visual centerpiece of the march was "a thousand beautiful banners and bannerettes, each different, each wrought in gorgeous color and in rich material."[2] Most of the banners used in the march advertised place names, as thousands of women had arrived in special trains from Liverpool, Manchester, Sheffield, Leeds, Hull, Birmingham, and Bristol, with representatives from America, France, Hungary, South Africa, India, and many other countries taking part as well. A significant albeit smaller number of the banners depicted "famous woman leaders and pioneers" (9). It's on one of these banners that Jane Austen's name was blazoned.[3]

Austen's name and image were used prominently in the street activism, political stage, and issue-oriented fundraisers of the women's movement's first wave, yet you'd never know it from our histories of her legacy. Histories of Jane Austen's critical legacy describe feminists of the 1970s and afterward with great care, but the political uses of Austen by suffragists have been almost entirely neglected in our Austen reception studies. A Virginia Woolf here, a Rebecca West there. There's little sense given in our literary histories of Austen's place among hundreds and thousands of Victorian and early twentieth-century feminists—among an entire political movement across several continents.[4] Putting Austen's suffragist champions back into the conversation about her legacy is not only right and just; it also reorients our sense of how Austen has been used for political purposes. We can't possibly understand political struggles over Austen in our own day without grasping just how long—and how loudly—debates over her and the political meanings of her writings have ranged.

Dating from the mid-nineteenth century to the moment when women's suffrage was achieved in many industrialized countries by the end of the 1920s, first-wave feminist activists sought female role models in history. Austen was, for those purposes, a perfect fit. Where the men's club Janeites saw in Austen a safe, admirably domestic figure whose life and writings were often seen as without political intention, the suffragists' Austen was almost always cast as a rebel. The more accurate phrase for the way many suffragists imagined and used her, as we'll see, may be "demure rebel." We saw in chapter 4 how amateur dramatizations of Austen drew on the tropes and ideas of the New Woman movement. Many of these dramatists were or would become suffragists. It's no surprise that they'd bring a strong, independent-woman-loving version of Jane Austen with them, from the amateur theatricals to the streets of London.

On that day in 1908, the marchers, nine out of ten of whom were female, represented "every class in society, from the highest (not Royal) to factory workers and working women of all grades, including domestic servants" (Fawcett, "Woman" 9). Among the professional women's groups represented was the Women Writers' Suffrage League (WWSL). This "very merry lot" wore signature red badges crossed with quills.[5] Its impressive banner was designed by artist and member of the Artists' Suffrage League, Mary Lowndes (1856–1929). The WWSL's large banner was carried by at least three women: actress and playwright Cicely Hamilton (1872–1952), novelist and New Woman essayist Sarah Grand (1854–1943), and American actress and playwright Elizabeth Robins (1862–1952). The WWSL's smaller bannerettes featured names from literary history, such as Maria Edgeworth, Fanny (Frances) Burney, and Mary Wollstonecraft. The stunning beige and reddish-brown banner commemorating Jane Austen featured a quill design, echoing the quills on the large banner and badges of the WWSL.

The banners used in the march were reportedly an awesome sight, creating a memorable event for participants and onlookers alike. "The striking sights of women's suffrage activism, their spectacular actions, banners and symbols," as a recent critic has put it, "made an immediate impression on public consciousness."[6] A witness reports that the crowd was "ready to scoff

Figure 9.1. Jane Austen Suffrage Banner, 1908, by
Mary Lowndes. Courtesy of the Women's Library at
the London School of Economics.

and jeer" but that "the flaming beauty of the procession smote them into a
reverent silence."[7] Lowndes had designed the banners to do just that. As she
wrote, poetically, "A banner is not a literary affair . . . A banner is a thing to
float in the wind, to flicker in the breeze, to flirt its colours for your pleasure,
to half show and half conceal a device you long to unravel."[8] The banners of
famous women were designed to be a moving spectacle. By all accounts,
they were.

The very act of carrying them was also a spectacle. It apparently involved
a significant feat of strength. Holding the banners for any distance walking,
particularly in the strong wind said to be blowing that day, was challenging
work. "The Men's League for Women's Suffrage," leader Millicent Fawcett
reports, "have volunteered help in the carrying of the banners," but the
plans called for "the young stalwarts among the women" to "bear their own

burdens" ("Woman" 9). Novelist May Sinclair (1863–1946) is said to have "seriously hurt herself by carrying a heavy banner for many miles in a Suffragist procession," perhaps on this very day.[9] The stakes of letting the banners drop were high. One newspaper account makes this clear: "At one point the guiding cords of a banner broke away," and "seeing the distress of the [female] bearer," a spectator called out, "You want a man's help." The woman carrying the banner is said to have replied, "No, I don't," as she successfully "wrestled with the intractable folds of the flapping silk" and, as the reporter puts it, "shows that she did not speak in vain" (qtd. in Tickner 293). Not everyone was impressed with such feats of female strength. As another periodical writer argues, "A woman who will walk five miles on a hot day and wave a banner all the time may be plucky, but the admirers of such pluck are not exactly deep thinkers, being, in short, persons whose intellects are of a mediocre caliber."[10] Not only exhibiting but just admiring female strength, for this writer, is a sign of intellectual weakness.

At the end of the march, the banners were placed carefully in Royal Albert Hall "in terraced ranks of raw and flaming color." As reporter James Douglas put it in the *Morning Leader*, "The names wrought upon the delicate silk were the names of women whose power was the power of the intellect and whose strength was the strength of the soul" (qtd. in Tickner 86, 89).[11] The official program doesn't reprint all of the names that were represented on banners, but it highlights several. After the banners of Vashti (called the first suffragist) and the "Three Great Queens" (Boadicea, Elizabeth, and Victoria), the next group advertised was the "Women Writers," with Elizabeth Barrett Browning, Jane Austen, George Eliot, and the Brontës chosen as representative.[12] Austen was prominently listed on the banners and program.

Including Austen's name among the Great Procession's banner honorees had everything to do with what scholars have called "an acute awareness during the period of the weight of literary history and precedent against which they were struggling . . . Significant literary and historical figures were identified and appropriated in this revisionist phase."[13] Austen, despite having only recently achieved the designation of "significant" to literary history and women's history, had quickly become one of the most frequently and prominently used "great women," chosen to serve as an "effective role model" to the women's suffrage movement.[14] No doubt this is because of her wide appeal, across political lines and among both men and women.

Public complaints arose about the propriety of featuring some of the women's names on the banners. The complaints centered on speculations about what was (or would have been) their positions on women's suffrage. For instance, a relative of Caroline Herschel (1750–1848) wrote a letter to the *Times* to complain that Herschel did not believe in women's suffrage or would not have supported it then. The relative suggests this was also the case with Mary Somerville (1780–1872). That relative, a grandniece, objects to Herschel's and Somerville's names being included on banners.[15] Another letter writer makes much the same argument for Mary Kingsley (1862–1900).[16] Fawcett, as NUWSS president, replies, explaining that the intention of naming them on banners had been to make a wider point: "Suffragists believe that the names of 'distinguished women who did noble work in their sphere' are in themselves an argument against relegating a whole sex to a lower political status than felons and idiots."[17] Further, "This is quite independent of whether the particular distinguished women named on the banners were suffragists or not. The names of Joan of Arc and Queen Elizabeth are found on the banners. The inference is surely clear" (Fawcett, "To the Editor," 9). Fawcett also rebuts Lady Gordon by outlining what she sees as Somerville's direct involvement in women's rights causes.

Such complaints were further addressed by the suffragists in their printed materials. In its *Programme of Banners*, the NUWSS explains, "This was regarded as an occasion for women to honor women. The banners are commemorative, and involve no assertion that the women whose names are inscribed upon them advocated the enfranchisement of their sex, though there are many such among them." The writer states, "It is said that Queen Victoria and Mary Kingsley were opposed to the franchise movement and that Caroline Herschel would certainly have been so. None the less do their sisters honour them for the good work they did." Jane Austen should be honored, the pamphlet suggests, whether her relatives endorse it or not.[18] It does not appear that collateral descendants made public comment on the 1908 banner with her name.

Perhaps the lack of public comment was a result of the Austen family descendants themselves being divided on the question of suffrage. In 1889, a Miss Austen-Leigh (otherwise unidentified) was a signatory to approve the extension of the parliamentary franchise to women.[19] The surname is unusual enough that it seems probable she was a collateral descendant. That there was a descendant active at this time who was prominently *anti*suffrage is, however, a certainty. Mrs. Florence Emma Austen-Leigh (1857–1926) was the president of the Cambridge Women's Branch for Opposing Woman Suffrage in the 1910s.[20] She was the widow of the late provost of King's

College, Cambridge, Augustus Austen-Leigh (1840–1905), great-nephew of Jane Austen, descended through her nephew James Edward Austen-Leigh, the *Memoir* author. But Florence Austen-Leigh herself was the daughter of George Benjamin Austen Lefroy, so she, too, was a descendant of the Austens, through Jane Austen's niece Anna Lefroy. (The Cambridge Austen-Leighs were first cousins, once removed.)

Florence Austen-Leigh worked against women's suffrage before the war, but, once World War I started, she spoke out more extensively, arguing that war was a reason for all other political work to cease. In 1917, she wrote to the *Times* that "a great war is not a time when so controversial a matter [as women's suffrage] can be properly discussed."[21] She did not invoke Jane Austen's name, but for many she would not have had to. She was well known in Cambridge as the widowed, Austen-descended "Provostess."[22] She also served nationally as an antisuffrage leader, having been one of a delegation of anti-suffragists to the prime minister in 1910, along with novelist Mrs. Humphry Ward, Mrs. Arnold Toynbee (widow of the economic historian), literary historian Sir Alfred Lyall, and a number of other activists.[23] Austen-Leigh would appear to have been there, with that group, in her guise as a literary descendant of Jane Austen, as well as a leader in her own right.

Early feminists didn't seek approval for their use of dead women writers' names and images. Not long after the 1908 procession, the suffrage banners went on tour across the country.[24] Soon after that, many of the prominent marchers took their idea of exhibiting famous women in support of women's rights from the streets and the lecture hall onto the stage. Just a year later, an actor first took the role of Jane Austen, portraying her on the stage in a new suffrage play. Cecily Hamilton's *A Pageant of Great Women* (1909) would become one of the most prominent and popular of its kind, an indoor political extravaganza. The brisk thirty-minute production debuted on November 10, 1909, at the Scala Theatre in London. It was said by the *Times* to have drawn a "large audience" "in enthusiastic sympathy with the movement," although two trade theatrical newspapers attacked it as propaganda.[25]

A Pageant became fashionable with suffrage groups, nationally and internationally. Organizations "up and down the country" asked for the chance to stage it (Whitelaw 89). Edith Craig would travel to these locations with her small number of principal actors and the needed wardrobe, serving as the play's producer. Most of the large cast was drawn from local women. One source suggests *A Pageant* was produced more than a hundred times in England between 1906 and 1914.[26] Presenting audiences with a vivid spectacle, the idea was to offer a celebratory piece that would "cast the largest number of actresses possible," to raise funds for the cause and rouse audiences to action (Gandolfi 54). Hamilton's play (said to have been coauthored with producer Craig) originated from a suffrage cartoon and featured three leads: Woman, Justice, and Prejudice.[27]

It had a good versus evil plot, with the allegorical Woman pleading her case before the female figure of Justice, while battling her male nemesis, Prejudice. These three characters speak most of the play's lines. Prejudice is "the sole male in a cast of forty seven," and the rest of the cast consists of "a display of exceptional women through history."[28] *A Pageant of Great Women* begins with Woman accusing Prejudice of trying to squelch her spark and glow of intellect with jeers and laughter: "Oh, think you well / What you have done to make it hard for her / To dream, to write, to paint, to build, to learn," celebrating those women who nevertheless "fought their way to achievement and fame!" (Hamilton 25–27). The play makes the figure of Jane Austen prominent among those exceptional historical women who fought.

In the original production, the role of Jane Austen, like almost all of the pageant's great women, was a nonspeaking part. The only one with lines of her own was famous actress Ellen Terry, the mother of the play's director, Edith Craig. (Craig and Terry had later experience with staging Austen, in the 1922 Squires' play *Pride and Prejudice*, discussed in chapter 5.) It's unclear whether it was Craig or Hamilton who chose to write the character of Jane Austen into *A Pageant*, but it seems likeliest that it was Craig. Craig's associations with Austen on the stage often involved her mother but turned out to be lifelong as well. Craig's last production, staged in July 1946, was a pageant based on classics of literature, beginning with Julius Caesar and ending with a garden party for Jane Austen.[29] Austen's inclusion in *A Pageant* was surely a calculated, deliberate literary and political choice.

The original cast list of Hamilton's *Pageant* reads like a who's who of the suffrage movement. The roles these activists played in public also seem either directly or dimly to echo the historical women they played on stage. The extensive cast list gives us a hint of what must have been its spectacular visual effect. Beyond the three leads, the remaining cast members are divided into six categories: "Learned Women," "Artists," "Saintly Women," "Heroic Women," "Rulers," and "Warriors," representing many centuries and countries. Austen is placed among "The Learned Women," and she's the only British woman writer among the forty-four. She is just one of four literary figures, alongside Madame de Staël, George Sand, and Madeleine de Scudéry.

The character of Woman announces that it was a female hand who had penned the first novel (de Scudéry) and that "English Jane Austen and George Sand of France" were her disciples. This role positions Austen as the most important Englishwoman in a feminist history of the novel. At the end of the *Pageant*, after being faced with all of these famous, accomplished women, Prejudice goes silent and "slinks away" (Hamilton 43).

This international impulse of the play illustrates the extent to which the suffrage movement was forging global connections and communities. Publicizing the countries that had earliest passed some form of women's suffrage, such as New Zealand, Australia, and Finland, put pressure on other nations to do the same. (Britain would allow some women the vote in 1918, followed by universal women's suffrage in 1928. In the United States, women's suffrage was achieved in 1920.) It was in this global framework that Jane Austen served as the exemplar of Englishwomen's literary and intellectual accomplishments. It's likely that these suffragists singled out Austen and her novels for feminist recognition in *A Pageant* because they "were popular and pleased the majority," as one critic puts it, in a more contemporary context.[30] We could rail at this as a dilution of feminism or of Austen. We could see it as pandering to the masses in the name of progress or as misrepresenting Austen in the name of politics. Perhaps it makes best sense to recognize it, however, as a canny understanding of how to use a liberal though not radical author to widen the audience for a progressive political cause. In any case, Austen was made to stand in for Britain in *A Pageant* because of her wide appeal. She had already developed name recognition that was attracting a following beyond its borders.

A Pageant of Women became not just a national but an international performance phenomenon. Nationally, as we've seen, it traveled across Britain and was staged in regional theaters. It was "one of the most successful and widely performed" suffrage plays, according to Katharine Cockin, serving to educate "its audiences about role models."[31] Cockin has documented at least fifteen different locations in which the play was performed between 1909 and 1912. She also describes a failed attempt to stage the play in translation in Hungary (Cockin, introduction x; "Cicely"). There may have been an Irish production, and, as late as the mid-1920s, requests to stage the play were still being made to its playwright (Cockin, introduction x). Five suffragist actresses played Austen across England in 1909–10, the best known of whom was Edith How Martyn, the woman who tried to make a speech in the House of Commons in 1906, one of the first militant acts of suffragist protest (Cockin, "Cicely" 539). A 1911 performance of *A Pageant* was mounted at the Women's Reform Club in Johannesburg, South Africa.[32] Americans, too, staged versions of *A Pageant* in May 1913, including one at the New National Theater in Washington, DC, derivative of Hamilton's play and retitled *Woman*. Its Jane Austen was played by Mrs. Alexander Jenkins.[33] Jane Austen had become, in the 1910s, a transnational figure used in support of women's suffrage. To call her the darling of the male literati of the period may be accurate from one vantage point, but to leave it at that tells a partial story.

A Pageant was performed in venues large and small, designed for ultimate adaptability, without scenery. It guaranteed large audiences, many of whom would come to see the local suffrage activists who made up the majority of its cast. As Roberta Gandolfi has put it, "Imagine all the friends and relatives of more than sixty women" amateur actresses (58). Producer Craig was very clear about the reasons that plays like *A Pageant* were mounted: "The plays have done such a lot for Suffrage. They get hold of nice, frivolous people who would die sooner than go in cold blood to meetings. But they watch the plays, and get interested, and then we can rope them in for meetings" (qtd. in Gandolfi 55). Another source suggests this may be overstated and that "audiences were mostly enthusiastic suffragettes."[34] In either case, nowhere is the use of history, culture, and performance—and the use of Jane Austen as part of it—to sell feminist politics to conventional middlebrow audiences put more condescendingly or clearly. *A Pageant* gained a name for "converting unbelievers" (Gandolfi 55). Jane Austen's presence in the play tells us not only about her prominence among lauded historical women and in a history of women writers but also about her perceived potential for political repurposing and impact. Significant numbers of actresses impersonated her, as untold thousands saw Learned Woman Jane Austen in a powerful feminist stage tableau. Meanwhile, some establishment men went on obliviously writing their essays in establishment periodicals about Austen's small fiction and safe domesticity.

The first actor to play Jane Austen on stage in *A Pageant* was Winifred Mayo (Winifred Monck-Mason; 1869–1967). Mayo had served as the codirector of the first professional stage version of *Pride and Prejudice*, Rosina Filippi's *The Bennets* (1901), as we saw in chapter 5. Mayo not only directed but played the heroine Elizabeth Bennet as "pert and petulant."[35] Born in India, Mayo was the daughter of a flautist and opera producer. Her father was a man who serially gained and lost fortunes, also known for his contributions to the history of ballooning.[36] In the end, he left his widow and daughters with some financial means. Winifred Mayo used them to become an actor, a prominent women's suffrage leader, and one of the founders of the Actresses' Franchise League. She gave elocution lessons to suffragists to improve their public speaking.[37] Her obituary describes further ways in which her stage background allowed her to assist the cause: "A little known aspect of the [Actress's Franchise] league's work was the skilled advice on make up and dressing up," the obituary writer reports, "which enabled many women 'on the run' from police to successfully disguise themselves and elude recapture."[38]

Mayo also became active in the Women's Social and Political Union, the militant wing of the suffrage movement. A friend of leader Emmeline Pankhurst, Mayo engaged in demonstrations that landed her three times in prison.[39] The year before the *Pageant* and her taking the stage as Jane Austen, Mayo published a moving autobiographical essay, "Prison Experiences of a Suffragette" (1908).[40] In late life, Mayo discussed these activist experiences with the BBC, describing her participation in the stone-throwing campaigns in November 1911. On a foggy night, a group of activists decided "it would be a good thing to wake up the Club Men."[41] They set out to break windows at London's tony men's clubs. Mayo chose a large, glass-paned door, not knowing which club lay behind it, took a stone out of her pocket, and hurled it. "To my great joy and satisfaction, it broke the window," she later reported. She did not run, as the point was to get caught and imprisoned. The club's porter ran out and seized her, asking what she was doing. She explained her political purpose.

She was asked, "Why the Guards? They don't know nothing about woman's suffrage?"

Mayo responded, "Well, that's exactly my point. Now they will!"

When a policeman finally arrived on the scene, he reportedly said to Mayo, "Did you do that?"

She answered, "Yes," as she tells the interviewer.

"What did you do it with?" the policeman asked.

"I did it with stones."

"Have you got any more stones?" he asked.

"Yes," she replies, in a matter-of-fact tone (BBC).

Then, with the police officer holding one of her arms, she reports that she took a stone out of her pocket and broke yet another window. As a result, she was imprisoned for a fortnight. Mayo notes with glee that some young guardsmen afterward attended a suffrage meeting. An obituary writer describes her as "Dainty and dignified, with a clear, carrying voice."[42] Mayo's activities, and their attachment to Jane Austen as a figure, show us that Austen was enthusiastically embraced by both the militant and the nonviolent wings of the women's suffrage movement.

The Great Procession of 1908 and *A Pageant* may turn out be Austen's highest-profile public political appearances of the day, but she played a role in several related minor women's suffrage events as well. One was an evening fundraiser—a dinner in London. Winifred Mayo attended it, too. It was billed as a "Costume Dinner of Suffragists." This time, Mayo dressed up as Charlotte Brontë. The June 1914 dinner at the Hotel Cecil is described in the newspaper, *Votes for Women*, as a Pageant of Famous Men and Women, arranged by *Pageant* director, Edith Craig. It was sponsored by both the Actresses' Franchise League and the Women Writers' Suffrage League, designed to attract an audience of the suffrage-supporting public. We might call it an alternative society event put on to further the suffragists' cause. Newspaper coverage billed it as an evening's spectacle featuring "rebels of all the ages impersonated by rebels of to-day."[43]

That night, novelist May Sinclair—the one who had been injured once carrying a banner in a suffrage march—came dressed as "a very demure Jane Austen."[44] Sinclair seems a more likely impersonator of Austen than does Mayo. Reviewers were then comparing Sinclair's writings to Austen's, one wondering "if in future years the quiet little English woman may not be recognized as a new Jane Austen."[45] The adjective "quiet," as dismissive as it seems, was also a word that suited Sinclair's self-concept. Her biographer calls her an "unlikely suffragist," due to her reluctance "to appear in public or to draw attention to herself."[46] The costume party in which she dressed as Austen would seem to be something of a departure from her preferred habits, but it was also an understanding of Austen's politics that was then taking hold among suffragists. Austen's status as a demure rebel might sound oxymoronic, but she was increasingly understood as a genteel, widely palatable, literary exemplar promoting social change for women.

This idea of Austen as a behind-the-scenes suffragist (nevertheless one who was squarely on the public stage, as in *A Pageant*) was a change of focus from earlier representations. From the 1890s to the 1910s, descriptions of Austen in progressive political rhetoric gradually shifted from imagining her as a pert, petulant, pioneering comic satirist, like her Elizabeth Bennet, to a quiet, demure, suffrage-friendly, but not suffrage-active, social critic. This shift is very much on view in Bertha Brewster's centenary-celebrating essay "The Feminism of Jane Austen" (1917), published in the suffrage newspaper *Votes for Women*. It sets out to establish the level and kind of the author's contributions to the cause.[47] Brewster—a militant, hunger-striking suffragist who was subjected to forced feedings in prison—is today best known for her 1913 letter in the *Daily Telegraph*:

> Sir, Everyone seems to agree upon the necessity of putting a stop to Suffragist outrages; but no one seems certain how to do so. There are two, and only two, ways in which this can be done. Both will be effectual.
>
> 1. Kill every woman in the United Kingdom.
> 2. Give women the vote.
>
> Yours truly, Bertha Brewster.[48]

Brewster was no stranger to political humor and satire in print. She also engaged in public speaking of a sort. It was then a common suffrage tactic for women to seek means to interrupt men's political speech. Brewster and another suffragist once hid in the rafters of the House of Commons to interrupt Chancellor of the Exchequer Lloyd George's speech. One of them shouted down from the rafters a criticism of the chamber's being unrepresentative where women were concerned. In the ensuing uproar, George addressed the men present. He dismissed the protest with, "I see some rats have got in; let them squeal, it does not matter."[49] Brewster, as "rat," was arrested and jailed.

This provides us with further context for understanding Brewster's remarks on Austen. In her essay, Brewster revisits old debates, such as its being "usual to speak of [Austen's] writing as feminine." Her commentary is reminiscent of Gladstone's rebuttal to Lord in 1903, which we saw in chapter 8. Brewster argues, "We frankly confess we do not know what exactly is meant by the term in her case." Austen's writing, according to Brewster, shows "strength and decision" and "robust common sense." Brewster, too, is engaged in rewriting the term "feminine" where Austen is concerned. Yet Brewster casts Austen as an independent thinker, rather than an activist: "We may admit her independence of thought: we cannot imagine her capable of equal independence of action" or "claim her as a fellow-suffragist." Brewster concludes, "We cannot picture Miss Austen addressing, far less interrupting, a public meeting; indeed, we fear she might consider it an unpardonable breech of decorum. But we can very well imagine her making fun of [Conservative MP] Mr. Arnold Ward's speeches" ("Feminism" 282). (Arnold Ward himself was the son of the famous antisuffragist novelist, Mary Augusta [a.k.a.

Mrs. Humphry] Ward [1851–1920], part of the antisuffrage delegation that included Florence Austen-Leigh, as we saw earlier.) Austen is assessed and lauded by Brewster. The author is cast as a demure suffrage satirist, an appreciative observer. To Brewster, Austen powerfully uses humorous words in print, rather than public oratory, to effect political change.

Whether this characterization is accurate to the "real" Austen may not matter in this circumstance; the women's movement in this period set out to use Austen to attract supporters to the cause, just as the men's club Janeites used her for their political purposes. The early feminist version of Austen was differently empowering and inspiring. She gave cautious or introverted women the option of being demure feminist rebels—Jane Austen suffragists. If unwilling to serve as public orators, they could still snicker at the lack of common sense in speeches by Conservative MPs. In the first decades of the twentieth century, Austen served as an exceptionally useful rallying point for progressive women's causes. Later and better-remembered feminist literary critics, such as Woolf and West, inherited the feminist Austen that Mayo, Hamilton, Brewster, and others had created, shaped, and sustained, yet in subsequent years the forerunners lost the credit for their labor and innovation in building Austen's legacy, neglected even in second-wave feminist literary histories of the 1980s and afterward.

The conversation shifted in wartime. The repeated criticisms leveled at feminists that wars ought to halt any other political activity but war had an effect. The repetition of views like Chesterton's about Austen's conservatism and views like Winston Churchill's on Austen's value for escapist pleasure had a lasting impact. The going out of fashion of the Austen-inspired amateur dramatizations, with their independent-spirited domestic protester heroines, likely played a role, too. Austen's increasing commodification and memorialization in ways aligning her with commercialism, luxury, and tourism served to help readers forget her earlier political legacy. We can see this in an Author Series set of role-playing bridge tally cards from Charles S. Clark Company in New York in 1924. It features Austen's name above an image of a book-cradling, hair-in-curling-papers bookworm flapper, reading in bed. Inside the tally card, the player is instructed, "You are Jane Austen" and told to find and partner with John Ruskin. We can see it in 1935, when London tobacco manufacturer Carreras Limited's Celebrities of British History series put out a fifty-card set that included Jane Austen.[50] In 1957, Benson and Hedges used Jane Austen's name to link expensive elegance, romance, and cigarettes, using a misquoted line from *Pride and Prejudice*.[51] By the early years of second-wave feminism of the 1960s and 1970s, Austen's former importance to suffragists had become virtually unknown.

For a time in the late twentieth century, Austen served less as a poster child than as a problem child for feminism. When Lawrence Mazzeno describes feminist critics as having had "a love-hate relationship with Austen," he's summing up late twentieth-century, second-wave feminist debates over Austen, marriage, and class, not the largely approving attitudes toward Austen of the women's movement in the early 1900s (107). It's easy to see why the second wave became impatient with Austen. Her fiction seemed to reinforce traditional marriage, to advocate for the heteronormative. All of those happy-endings marriages! Austen's novels didn't appear to have enough righteous feminist anger at systemic and everyday sexism to suit the prevailing political mood.

Only in the late 1970s would late eighteenth-century feminist influences on Austen start once again to become readable, palatable, and repeatable. An essay linking Austen and Wollstonecraft, by Lloyd Brown, had appeared in 1973–74.[52] But it was after Sandra Gilbert and Susan Gubar's feminist revision of literary history in *Madwoman in the Attic* (1979), Margaret Kirkham's *Jane Austen, Feminism, and Fiction* (1983), and Mary Poovey's *The Proper Lady and the Woman Writer* (1984) that the notion of a feminist Austen returned to literary criticism with vigor.[53] Unfortunately, few seem to have recognized that Austen had enjoyed a long popular feminist history. Second-wave feminist work on Austen and its greater circulation and acceptance among all literary critics did lead to her being widely used once again in public rallying cries for progressive and feminist causes. We might say that it culminated in Austen's face being chosen for the British ten-pound note, an act that famously prompted antifeminist, Austen-related death threats on Twitter in 2013.[54] We could see these events as bizarre oddities. But they are not isolated events in a political history of Austen. Waving banners, righteous pageants, political cosplay, and rats in the parliamentary rafters stand demurely behind today's feminist Austens. They need no longer stand silently.

PART FOUR

JANE AUSTEN, SCHOOLED

ONE LOOSE-LEAF PHOTOGRAVURE IMAGE was chosen to represent Jane Austen to curious readers in the June 1915 issue of the educational periodical, the *Mentor*. It was Hugh Thomson's illustration "Mr Darcy and Sir William Lucas" from *Pride and Prejudice*. This must have been a deliberate selection. The *Mentor* liked to feature author portraits, too. It used a small reproduction of what then passed for Austen's face in the pages of the journal itself. But when it came to choosing the suitable-for-framing, large-format image to represent Austen in the *Mentor*'s pages, Thomson's illustration won out over the imaginary portrait. That choice communicates a few things. First, it speaks to how thoroughly Hugh Thomson had come to stand in for Austenian authenticity, twenty years after his Austen-inspired illustrations were first published.[1] But the framable image also suggests the kinds of themes and ideals that the *Mentor* set out to promote to its reader-learners. Thomson's Austen image is of a social scene. It depicts six people, highlighting two men. One looks like a toady and the other a snob. The question is, what lesson was this image supposed to be teaching?

Thomson's Sir William bends forward, his hands clasped together in an obsequious pose. Next to him stands Mr. Darcy, one foot artfully set out before the other. The hero scrutinizes Sir William with an upturned chin, through an artfully held monocle. There is something both funny and sinister about the illustration. It may have been a difficult scene for a reader new to Austen to interpret. The full-page explanatory text on the reverse side of the illustration wrongly describes the picture as "a graceful social scene," which doesn't exactly inspire confidence in the caption writer. In fact, Thomson's illustration depicts one of the novel's *least* graceful moments, when Sir William Lucas awkwardly attempts to flatter Darcy and Elizabeth

Bennet into dancing together. The *Mentor*'s choice of image is a meaning-ful visual alternative in an era that was also promoting Austen and Eliza-beth Bennet as feminist role models. We might even see it as a response to that phenomenon, especially since this reproduction was designed not only for framing and appreciating as a work of art but was being sold as a teach-ing tool. Teaching Jane Austen in 1915, the *Mentor*'s illustrated plate seems to suggest, means emphasizing social graces and examining how men support, flank, and enable women in social situations. Its emphasis differs from what readers, viewers, and audiences were getting in other repackag-ings of Austen in the era's dramatic adaptations and some political speech.

The *Mentor*, with a circulation of more than fifty thousand, was an early twentieth-century magazine of the New York–based Mentor Association. The magazine and the association used as its slogans "Learn One Thing Every Day" and "Make the Spare Moment Count."[2] Touting its benefits and its smorgasbord curriculum to reading groups, the *Mentor* claims to be "instructive" for "those who want to gain knowledge by an easy and agreeable method." Each issue, a dozen or so pages long, had its own theme, ranging from Napoleon, to sporting vacations, to angels in art. The *Mentor* also features loose printed plates with each issue, and British authors had a fair amount of play in the contents. Shakespeare and Dickens were each subjects of an early issue. Although Jane Austen did not get her own issue—nor did any one woman—the first June 1915 number was devoted to famous women writers of England. Austen is presented as the most important member of that celebrated group.[3] Edgeworth is described as being before her, showing that Austen wasn't the first, but Eliot, Brontë, Gaskell, Barrett Browning, and Ingelow take a back seat to her in the *Mentor*'s account of prominence and famousness, as well as in chronology.

The *Mentor*'s Department of Literature Austen expert—the one who wrote its contents for the issue—was Hamilton Wright Mabie (1846–1916). Mabie was a prolific critic, editor, and magazine writer, then at the end of his career. In his essay, he rehashes old saws that were becoming standard fare about Austen in reference works, textbooks, and schools—her country village upbringing, her producing timeless fiction, her modest two inches of ivory statement, Scott's big bow-wow strain response to her, and so on.[4] Mabie presents Austen to reader-students as talented, narrow, quiet, and humble. He makes a few downright errors, but he also takes great pains to sell Austen without reservation to those unfamiliar with her.[5] He emphasizes her quality and her popularity. Mabie's Austen is a novelist of "intrinsic interest," read by "a host of people" (3).

The *Mentor* describes Austen on the back page of the loose-leaf Thomson image (in text that may or may not have been authored by Mabie) as "charming and lovable," "shy and often very grave," despite having seen "a great deal of society," in what seems a mishmash of then-circulating stereotypes—the delightful Aunt Jane mixed with the pious old maid.[6] When mentioning her never having married, the *Mentor* makes sure to indicate that she had options. Her life's "one romantic story of a love who died is veiled in mystery," as it cryptically notes. In the last paragraph, the *Mentor* paraphrases the *Encyclopedia Britannica* (unattributed) on the subject of why readers should tackle Austen: "It was not until quite recent times that to read [Jane Austen] became a necessity of culture. But she is now firmly established as an English classic." Seven great men who admired Austen are listed—Coleridge, Tennyson, Macaulay, Scott, Sydney Smith, Disraeli, and Archbishop Whately—to reach the oft-repeated conclusion that "she was always admired by the best intellects" and that "Disraeli read 'Pride and Prejudice' seventeen times" (n.p.).

The history of Jane Austen in schools—even of Jane Austen in encyclopedias, as we see here—is rife with the endorsements of Great Men. It would seem that to know *who* loved Austen was to know *how* to love her. Jane Austen became a "necessity of culture" not only on her own merits but because Macaulay believed her to be a rival to Shakespeare or because Scott was envious of her talents. Austen was taught to schoolchildren as a great author whose greatness was time tested because Great Figures said she was great. It wasn't as if such statements were absent from other kinds of printed materials about Austen. These endorsements appeared in many other venues. What's unusual is how central and how oft-repeated they were in educational materials about Austen. The Great Men endorsing the Great Austen had become a common schoolbook (and reference book) refrain. That, too, shaped her image profoundly.

Not everyone was happy about Austen's fiction being turned into schoolroom fodder. As one writer put it in 1917, Austen's "most delightful book [*Pride and Prejudice*] has been most unsuitably made into a schoolbook in the twentieth century."[7] Yet, in fact, Austen's novels had been made into school texts well before they were made into scholarly ones. As we'll see in chapter 11, Austen's novels appear on recommended reading lists for schools as early as 1838. The reason she became the subject of the first "dissertation," as we'll see in chapter 10, is because a Harvard professor was teaching Austen's writings to his male students in the 1880s. Austen arguably came more forcefully into classrooms and curricula of many kinds before she became an object of extended literary scrutiny and historical study. Even that milestone moment in the history of Austen's scholarly profile, the publication of what would become the standard edition of Austen's novels, edited by R. W. Chapman in 1923, might be said to have grown out of the schoolroom phenomenon.[8]

To some degree, however, making sense of Austen's position in English-language schools provides us with a chicken and egg question. What came first, we might ask, the growth in popularity of Jane Austen or the growth of English literature instruction in schools of all kinds? Austen's rise to celebrity coincided with great changes in the position of literary texts at all levels of the curriculum. She and her works benefited from the humanities becoming less focused on classical texts and more anchored in English literature over the course of the nineteenth century. The appeal of Austen's fiction as a subject for children also happened in sync with profound changes in educational institutions, particularly the rise of women's education in the second half of the nineteenth century. Some sought greater opportunities for female learning in formal settings, while others wanted to stop it in its tracks. As arguments over "the woman question" took new turns, women writers' stature in schools took on new importance and visibility. Austen's somewhat mysterious and malleable life story, and the wide appeal of her writings, put her in the right place at the right time for both escalating fame and wider school exposure.

We can't claim that Austen came early or late to the classroom in comparison with her literary peers. Because there was no standard practice for the formal teaching of novels in her lifetime, all novelists of the early nineteenth century in effect "came late" to textbooks and schoolrooms. Novels were long considered low trash or light entertainment, not educational tools, meaning that fiction of the Romantic period emerged in educational settings decades after its first publication, introduced as de facto passé. We'll see in chapter 11 how Austen fared when literary instruction expanded to include novels and when educational opportunities expanded for girls and women. By the early twentieth century, Austen was being put before tens of thousands of young people, many of them at ages that mirrored those of her heroes and heroines—in their teens. She was imagined as both a good literary and moral influence on the young. Few suggested that her fiction was interested in youthful rebellion or social change. In textbooks, her humor was lightened. Her satire was downplayed. It was a thrust that led to Thomson's images of Austen being perfectly suited to the period's educational texts.

The story of Austen's reputation as it was established, grew, and was debated in schools, universities, and author societies cannot be described in a straightforward line or an overarching sound bite. Once the question was no longer *whether* to teach Jane Austen in schools, it became *how*—in excerpts, abridgments, whole works, or, later, adaptations. Most authors of extended-length works faced similar questions, as educators tried to figure out how much and what literature to assign to their students. *Why* Austen should be read was similarly debated. Should the focus should be on understanding her in her own time or on translating her to the present? Should she be taught for manners, morals, or patriotic feeling?

In the early years of her fame, Jane Austen was presented at her most moralizing, straitlaced, and serious in literary instruction in schools. Textbooks and essays designed for teachers described Austen as the kind of woman that a student should want to become. Rarely presenting her as a demure rebel, they peddled Austen's characters as models of polite elegance. They suggested that reading and appreciating her fiction was a sign of taste and accomplishment. Many textbooks show an investment in advancing ideas of her literary quality, proper morality, and cultural safety. It was an approach that would last. For a few pioneering educators of the mid-twentieth century, even Austen's works adapted to film were perceived as a cultural good for instructing the young. In the following two chapters, we'll see the trailblazing individuals who had an impact, and specific trends that made a difference, in the history of Jane Austen education.

CHAPTER TEN

The First Jane Austen Dissertation

George Pellew and the Human Telephone

"Jane Austen Studies." David Lodge made fun of it in his academic novel, *Changing Places: A Tale of Two Campuses* (1975). The novel's blowhard protagonist, Professor Morris Zapp, concocts a plan to write commentaries on Austen's novels from every conceivable angle. Not "to enhance others' enjoyment and understanding of Jane Austen," he thinks to himself, but to "put a definitive stop to the production of any further garbage on the subject."[1] Zapp's plan for literary criticism is the project of a killjoy, one of Casaubon-esque *Key-to-All-Mythologies* proportions. It's hilariously wrongheaded, something Lodge's novel relishes sending up. Zapp seeks to quash Jane Austen studies, to serve as its terminus ad quem.

It's difficult now to imagine Jane Austen studies in its infancy, when the territory was a young scholar's for the taking. That's precisely the situation in which William Henry George Pellew (1859–92) found himself as a student at Harvard in the 1880s. There, George Pellew (as he was called) wrote himself into the history books of Jane Austen studies, earning a generous footnote. He is credited with having written the very first Jane Austen dissertation, a claim to the honor that's been oft repeated and that has gone long uncontested. The claim itself is worth our investigating further, and Pellew deserves greater mention in Jane Austen studies. But it's not only because what he did is important to the world of ideas. He also deserves to be a protagonist in an Austen-inspired campus novel.

Pellew's contribution to Austen scholarship was a very short book titled *Jane Austen's Novels* (1883).[2] It deserves the label pioneering. There seem to have been only two book-length studies devoted specifically to Austen prior to his, Austen-Leigh's *Memoir* (which went through several editions) and prolific novelist Sarah Tytler's (Henrietta Keddie) *Jane Austen and Her*

Works (1880), a book geared toward young readers. Pellew's book was early enough to be notable, both at the time and in retrospect. Today's Austen reception histories mention Pellew in passing. They often immediately go on to quote from a private letter to Pellew from novelist Henry James (1843–1916). James writes to thank Pellew for the present of his "thin red book" on Austen, half-praising it as "an attempt in scientific criticism of the delightful Jane." James admits he opened the younger man's book with trepidation: "When I read the first page or two I trembled lest you should overdo the science," but he happily declares he had nothing to fear.[3] For James, Pellew was "if anything, too mild" in his criticisms of Austen.

Jane Austen's Novels and the exchange of letters it prompted was a seminal moment for the author's entrée into higher education, yet few have looked more deeply into its circumstances. That deserves remedying, as the story of the first Austen dissertation might be said to resemble *Pride and Prejudice and Zombies* more than it does literary criticism. We think of dissertations and of Austen in schools as staid, even stolid, affairs. Yet the world of academia and the world of popular culture for Jane Austen were sometimes not so far very apart in the late nineteenth century. At least that is what the story of Pellew and Austen suggests. There was a time when Austen's name flitted between town and gown in ways that show we've drawn too hard a line in our histories between the two arenas, particularly prior to the 1920s. Pellew would go on to be famous in ways that are stunningly peculiar, drawing Austen's legacy into the paranormal. If you choose to believe the least skeptical of these sources, then the man who wrote the first Jane Austen dissertation came back from the dead. Frequently.[4]

Before getting to those mystical details, the staid literary criticism part deserves its exposition. As a Harvard undergraduate, Pellew had taken a course, English Literature in the Eighteenth Century, with a man who would become his mentor and friend, Thomas Sergeant Perry (1845–1928). Perry was a "cosmopolitan Back-Bay Brahmin," the great-grandson of Benjamin Franklin, who delivered lectures that must have been the catalyst for Pellew's Austen work.[5] The warm dedication to Perry at the beginning of Pellew's Austen book suggests it (*Novels* 3). His well-informed, highly allusive fifty-page study of her novels reads her alongside authors ranging from Richardson, Walpole, Radcliffe, and Lewis, to Fielding, Smollett, Burney, and Edgeworth. Pellew shows impressive familiarity with the novels, verse, and nonfiction to which Austen was responding, making extensive comparisons of her, too, with Eliot and Brontë, usually to Austen's detriment. In ranking the three women in this way, Pellew was by no means going against the grain. Eliot and Brontë were seen by most literary experts as Austen's superior in the 1880s. Yet Pellew was doing new things, too, as we saw Henry James note in his calling the book an attempt at scientific criticism of the delightful Jane.

Pellew certainly had his opinions about Austen and about her literary achievement. He gives us a window into his literary values when he remarks on how *Persuasion* is "to my taste, the most mellow and charming of all the novels." He criticizes *Pride and Prejudice* as containing "unsympathetic wit" but finds in *Persuasion* "for the first time in Miss Austen, an element of pathos" (*Novels* 33). He also takes up the commonplace belief that Austen's novels are without a politics, arguing that they aren't fully developed as art as a result. He sees her characters (especially the females) as limited (40). But what redeems that shortcoming is Austen's ability to describe "accurately what she saw" (47). He expresses disappointment that her fiction cannot "extort tears or compel admiration," but he concedes that "her novels give a real though unexciting pleasure" (50). (Here he echoes Charlotte Brontë's negative assessment of Austen as without passion, fast becoming a refrain in criticism of the day, but he gives it a more positive spin.[6])

Pellew's careful close readings of Austen's novels in his published work nevertheless suggest that he finds her brand of "real," "unexciting pleasure" to be highly compelling. He sympathetically links a sense of Austen's technical discussion of method with domestic confinement, as one of the few critics to study his book puts it.[7] He opines that her circumscribed life must have been tedious and commonplace. But he doesn't see that as preventing literary achievement. In her fiction, Pellew argues, "she anticipated the scientific precision that the spirit of the age is now demanding in literature and art" (*Novels* 49). She admirably avoids artifice. At a time when elite men—especially those in Pellew's circle of male champions—seemed either firmly pro or con Austen, Pellew's criticism sets out to be more measured. He seeks to do in literary criticism what he argues Austen did in her fictional method—to describe accurately and scientifically.

In life, Pellew was almost a male Emma Woodhouse. He was the definition of well born. His upper-crust father, Henry Edward Pellew, was born in England. His mother, Eliza Jay, was a Founding Father–descended American. Toward the end of his life, George Pellew's father became Viscount Exmouth. His mother—granddaughter of John Jay, first chief justice of the United States—didn't live to see it. She died in 1869, when George was just a boy. Widower Henry Pellew later married his late wife Eliza's sister,

Augusta, a union that was then illegal in England.[8] The Pellews' forbidden marriage prompted their immigration to the United States, where Henry became involved in charitable projects serving former slaves and families in poverty. Eliza's two young sons were enrolled in St. Paul's School in New Hampshire. George eventually matriculated to Harvard, taking an AB in 1880 and earning a law degree in 1883. By all accounts, he was a remarkable student, graduating first in the class of '80, writing the class ode, and distinguishing himself in classics and English.[9] His classmate Theodore Roosevelt is said to have found Pellew "*very* nice" (qtd. in Kenny 115).

Pellew's Austen book was completed when he was at Harvard's law school, ultimately winning the Bowdoin Dissertation Prize. A few subsequent Austen critics have largely misunderstood the term "dissertation," seeing Pellew's work as the culminating project for a doctoral degree in English literature. It wasn't. "Dissertation" refers here to a long essay. The Bowdoin Prizes, "some of Harvard's oldest and most prestigious student awards," were established in 1810, given to the likes of Ralph Waldo Emerson, Henry Adams, Arthur Schlesinger Jr., and John Updike.[10] Yet Pellew's being awarded such a prize for a study of a British woman novelist—even if it was not the first English literature PhD awarded on Austen—is unquestionably significant. It was momentous in that it proved she had entered academia as an object worthy of extended study.[11] On the basis of his award-winning Austen essay, Pellew was awarded an MA.[12]

Pellew's mentor in this work was its dedicatee, the aforementioned Professor Perry, lifelong friend of Henry James. This connection explains how an unknown Harvard law student's thin red Austen book could prompt a response from a famous novelist.[13] Perry opened many other doors for Pellew, beyond what was customary for student and teacher. Perry refers to Pellew in print as "my friend."[14] Perry had been on annual appointments at Harvard, but he was dismissed after 1881, despite his own protestations, along with those of public figures and students, with whom he was popular.[15] Shortly after Perry was dismissed from Harvard, he went into a deep depression. At that time, Pellew became a boarder in Perry's Boston home, living with his wife and their two young daughters (Kenny 116).

Mrs. Perry's name would become the most enduring among them as the noted American Impressionist painter, Lilla Cabot Perry (1848–1933). The years in which Pellew lived in the Perrys' home were difficult ones for both husband and wife. Thomas, scrambling for money, wrote for periodicals and taught courses at Radcliffe, and Lilla had two miscarriages. She spent a great deal of time lying down.[16] Eventually, Thomas's father died, leaving him a sub-stantial inheritance, making frequent trips abroad possible for the family (Haralson and Johnson 429). Pellew seems to have become like family to the Perrys. One gossipy source claims the younger man kept a photograph of Lilla in his pocket and that she and Pellew were in love, a suspect conclusion reached through a reading of their cryptic, amorous poetry.[17] Pellew ultimately left the Perry household and the practice of law, but he stuck with his poetry.

Pellew was a poet of "contemplated emotion," a man angelically singular; at least that is the estimate of Pellew's friend and mentor, William Dean Howells (1837–1920) (introduction viii). Howells, the "Dean of American Letters," is a man who features prominently in studies of Austen's legacy, because he seems, throughout his life, to be everywhere Austen's legacy is. Howells, James, and Perry were all close friends, further explaining how up-and-comer Pellew entered Howells's circle. In a private letter to James in 1886, Howells mentions that Pellew has "come back to town, & I find him very interesting. He's a very able fellow, and distinctly a literary promise."[18] Howells took a special interest in Pellew, twenty years his junior; they had in common an enthusiasm for Austen. Howells would later spearhead the American arm of the Austen centenary memorial campaign for a plaque in Chawton, England, unveiled in 1917. George Pellew, however, wouldn't live to see it. He died in 1892, at age thirty-two. By then he'd published several books, but he never quite found his niche or his fame.

It is Howells, again, who gives us the most sustained account of Pellew's stellar qualities and his fall from social grace. Pellew had become a source of negative gossip, perhaps for indulging in drink. In a private letter from 1888, Howells writes so colorfully of Pellew that it's worth quoting at length:

> I've known Pellew for three years, and I've never met him in the state in
> which too many others seem to have met him. He was in and out of my house
> familiarly, and was the delight of us all, for from youngest to oldest, we felt his
> rare quality and admirable ability and learning, which were almost without alloy
> of egotism. He has had a hard time since he left college, and discouragement has
> been, I'm sure, a large element in any temptation to which he has yielded ...
> [A]t times he has been quite shabby—slovenly he would be in purple: he would get
> a leg in one sleeve and an arm in another, and rest in absent-minded content.
> He often came with a single overshoe: I dare say his stockings were heedlessly
> put on. But he was always full of high discourse, to which one could not listen
> without profound respect for his extraordinary mind.[19]

Pellew would live just four more years, with Howells remaining steadfastly his supporter, in life and in death.

Conflicting accounts of Pellew's last hours have prompted questions. Some sources have him being thrown from a horse.[20] One account has him "falling into a construction site on the way home from a dinner party" (Kenny 114). News reports said Pellew struck his head and was killed by a concussion, after an inflammation of the eyes made him partially blind. This account adds that his watch and other valuables were found with him, with "no marks of violence," to rule out foul play.[21] Yet another account suggests Pellew was found dead outside of a gambling establishment, possibly with his head bashed in and neck broken. These details were then left out of a falsified coroner's report (Munves 148). Whatever its circumstances, Pellew's death was sudden and newsworthy. He was a young man of promise unfulfilled, who might one day have become a viscount and a literary lion. His death inspired not only printed obituaries but moving posthumous tributes.

The most enthusiastic encomium was from Howells. He extolls Pellew as the popular ideal of the literary man. To Howells, Pellew was friendly, unpretentious, and "just as one imagines De Quincey, Lamb, or Hunt must have been," often failing at the "practical and the commercial" side of life (introduction v). This tribute was eventually published as an introduction to Pellew's posthumous book of poetry. There Howells mentions Pellew's Austen essay, which he identifies as winning the Bowdoin prize and taking "one of the first steps in the direction of the new criticism—the criticism which studies, classifies, and registers." Just six years after its publication, with Pellew now dead, *Jane Austen's Novels* was being primed to take an honored place in a growing literary critical movement. According to Howells, Pellew's second book, *In Castle and Cabin; or, Talks in Ireland in 1887* (1888), was completed as "faithfully, directly, and impartially as he had studied the novels of Jane Austen" (vii).

What Howells neglects to mention—and certainly it was intentional—is Pellew's impassioned political writing. In private, in the 1888 letter quoted above, Howells praises Pellew's "masterly" woman suffrage pamphlet. Howells admits to his correspondent, "I must hereafter count myself a believer in the reason as well as the right of women's voting, and I must own that [Pellew] has persuaded me."[22] Pellew's *Woman and the Commonwealth; or, A Question of Expediency* (1888) is a remarkable book in support of women's right to vote. In his treatise, Pellew makes direct reference to Austen: "For one individual, or for any number of individuals, to assign arbitrary, definite limits to the activity of another or of others, is an act of bigotry and injustice obviously indefensible on scientific principles. The so-called 'proper sphere' of women has, moreover, been perpetually changing. In the time of Jane Austen it was thought improper for women to write novels, twenty years ago it was thought improper for women to study medicine and anatomy, and even to-day there are many people who think it improper for women to lecture" (25–26). Each generation must overcome its prejudices, Pellew suggests; his embrace of Austen resonates with his antisexism. Pellew had served as secretary of the New York Woman Suffrage Party; he had corresponded with women's rights activist Lucy Stone (1818–93) and had addressed a Boston suffrage meeting.[23] He was ahead of his time in the "science" of Austen criticism, and he was precocious in linking Austen's name to women's suffrage in the 1880s.

Yet Howells's hagiographic essay steers away from discussing his friend's politics and lauds his rather regular poems. What comes through in Howells's essay is a portrait of the lovable, inquisitive man who wrote the verse. Howells claims children loved Pellew and that he captivated all in his orbit (introduction vii–viii). In the end, Howells can't imagine Pellew dead, fancying him somewhere "disputing with kindred minds, and making the celestial echoes answer the glad laugh with which he either won or lost a point" (xi). Howells, who also enjoyed imagining Austen as an immortal, had no way of knowing how prescient he would be with this posthumous vision of his young friend Pellew.[24] Pellew's early death and hidden-in-plain-sight feminism are not the only things he had in common with Austen. His afterlife, like hers, also took an unanticipated turn toward unlikely celebrity.

Pellew had other interesting friends, including the parapsychologist Dr. Richard Hodgson (1855–1905). Hodgson was a Cambridge-educated Australian bachelor who'd joined the English Society for Psychical Research, or SPR. He left England for America, sent by the SPR to serve as the secretary to its Boston branch (Kenny 113). Hodgson was a man of animal spirits, laughter, repartee, and gesticulation, with a decided love for poetry, which no doubt drew him to Pellew and vice versa.[25] The two men were said to have argued frequently over whether spirits might survive bodily death. Hodgson believed it conceivable, if not probable, but Pellew was skeptical. In what may have been either an ongoing joke or a dead serious matter between the two, Pellew promised Hodgson that if he died first, he'd try to return to offer evidence of the afterlife (Kenny 119).

According to some sources, Pellew did just that. Weeks after his sudden death, Pellew began to communicate with Hodgson beyond the grave.

(This tidbit has gone unnoticed in Austen studies, but it has long been known among parapsychologists, suggesting the two groups don't communicate often enough.) Pellew's beyond-the-grave communication came through "the most famous, most trustworthy, direct-voice medium who ever lived," Leonora Piper (1859–1950), known as the "human telephone to the spirit world."[26] Pellew's spirit was said to inhabit Mrs. Piper's body, using her hand to write down his words, in what was called "automatic writing." For years, Piper channeled Pellew's spirit through pen and paper. In the 1890s, the author of the first Jane Austen thesis became the era's most prominent visitor from the great beyond.

Piper—described as a "housewife" who never finished high school, a married mother of two—was paid for her services. In the early years, she earned a dollar, and in later years as much as twenty dollars per sitting (Gardner 215). In the "automatic writing" phase of her mediumship, she was a high-ranking member not just of a movement but of an industry. Just four years after the fad of automatic writing took off, it is estimated that there were two thousand automatic writing mediums in the United States alone (McCabe 137). The number of noted intellectuals who came to test Mrs. Piper's powers, to witness her at work, may now seem astonishing to us. Piper spent time in private rooms, putting on displays of her supernatural powers, particularly for members of the intellectual class who were investigating spiritualism. Piper came to prominence through the notice of William James, brother of novelist Henry. William James, the well-known Harvard psychologist, was a founder of the American Society for Psychical Research. James's association with Piper may have made her famous, but in Richard Hodgson she would find her most fervent believer.

Hodgson is said to have visited Piper three times a week to communicate with the dead, assiduously transcribing the details of each visit.[27] He had detectives follow her and her husband, to determine whether they were secretly researching the lives of their clients.[28] Early on in her mediumship, spirits had appeared to Piper while she was in a trance, and "controls," as they were called, took over her speech. One control was a Native American maiden who went by the name "Chlorine" (Kenny 113). Piper was especially susceptible to controls who had been famous, such as Martin Luther, George Washington, Abraham Lincoln, Johann Sebastian Bach, and Sarah Siddons (Gardner 217; Kenny 113). She also channeled writers such as Henry Wadsworth Longfellow, Sir Walter Scott (who talked about the sun and planets), and George Eliot, whose spirit reported that she'd seen Adam Bede.[29]

Figure 10.1. Above, "Mrs. Piper a Human Telephone to the Spirit World," *New York Herald,* 18 June 1899, sixth section, 1; *right,* George Pellew, *Cosmopolitan* 13, no. 5 (September 1892): 527.

Pellew's spirit was one of the first controls to communicate with Piper through automatic writing and one of the first identifiable as a once-living, nonfamous person. Recently deceased, he was a "clear and lucid" visitor from the dead.[30] Parapsychology, like literary criticism, was then enamored of appearing scientific. Most of the spirits who visited Piper are recorded in the parapsychological literature with pseudonyms or initials, to protect their identities. George Pellew was given both: the pseudonym George Pelham, and the initials G.P.[31] G.P. was said to recognize with accuracy whether a visitor was someone he'd known in life. Thirty friends visited and were correctly recognized by his spirit, among a hundred decoys.[32] Hodgson was convinced that his friend G.P. had returned from beyond the grave. Some believed that Piper was merely telepathic, reading her visitors' minds. She herself even offered this as a possible explanation of her powers. Others were entirely skeptical of all of it.

Some of Pellew's Harvard professors were skeptics, but others were apparently believers. A number of them came to visit Mrs. Piper to see whether their former student was indeed making contact from beyond the grave. Both Perrys—Pellew's Austen professor and his poet-artist wife—joined an early sitting with Mrs. Piper. They were said to have been "intrigued," and they ultimately invited the medium into their own home. The Perrys devised authenticity tests that Piper seemed to pass, suggesting it was Pellew who was speaking through her pen (Kenny 120). The Perrys would end up having fourteen recorded sittings with Mrs. Piper in their home, in order to talk to Pellew. These were events that one SPR writer claims had a "lasting influence" on the Perrys' lives (Munves 146). Given the frequency described, this certainly seems plausible.

One of Pellew's Harvard professors, in a session with Piper, brought up the subject of Jane Austen. Skeptical Harvard art professor Charles Eliot Norton (1827–1908) asked G.P. to name the subject of his prize-winning essay. But G.P. "did not give the name of Jane Austen," instead offering that of John Jay, the subject of another book Pellew had written, about one of his maternal ancestors (Hodgson 525). But when Norton noticed the mistake and mentioned Jane Austen to G.P., that hint took hold. From that point on, Jane Austen herself began to appear in G.P.'s spirit writing. Hodgson reports that several times thereafter, at the end of a sitting, "when the writing became particularly dreamy, the name of Professor Norton appeared in connection with that of Jane Austen" (333).[33] University professors in the 1890s were arguing over whether a medium's written references to Jane Austen were proof of their former student's spirit visits.

Other Austen critics came to test Piper. Most entertaining to imagine among them was Andrew Lang (1844–1912), who had himself written a book called *Letters to Dead Authors* (1886). That book included among its contents a fictional letter written to the spirit of Jane Austen. Lang, too, visited Mrs. Piper to test G.P.'s genuineness. He came away concluding that Pellew had *not* returned from the dead, believing Mrs. Piper deluded but honest, illustrative of "savage phenomena" and a "secondary personality."[34] Pellew's spirit was said to visit the living through Piper's writing for many years. But eventually he began to dash in and out of her communications, as if he had "passed on" a second time (W. James 38). Where Pellew left off, other dead stepped in. Just eight days after a robust Hodgson died suddenly while playing handball at a boat club in 1905, Piper began channeling Hodgson's spirit, too (15).

Records of Hodgson's afterlife as recorded through Piper come down to us from the alternately skeptical and credulous accounts of Henry James's brother William James, who painstakingly collated sixty-nine sittings with the spirit of "R.H." One of the subjects R.H. communicated about was "dear old G. Pelham [Pellew], who did so much for me—more than all the rest put together" (W. James 9). Hodgson's spirit explained why G.P. had disappeared from Piper's cast of trance characters: he'd risen to the seventh sphere, or what we would call heaven (Robbins 94). Later readers came to know about G.P. and Mrs. Piper from Sir Arthur Conan Doyle's *History of Spiritualism* (1926). In fact, Doyle would credit Hodgson's "George Pelham" séance records with being the first phenomena that made his "mind receptive and sympathetic" to spiritualism.[35] Piper, who retired on a modest trust fund from the SPR, was never charged with committing a fraud, quite a rarity in her line of work.

It's an odd fact of literary history that the first published full-length study of Austen that came out of a school setting and her first young student-scholar led to the author making an appearance in paranormal history. In recent years, scholars have written eloquently about Jane Austen's being imagined as a ghost and what that might mean to her celebrity and legacy.[36] But we tend to forget how tightly the scholarly and the pop-culture paranormal, like the scholarly and popular-education Austen, were once intertwined. George Pellew's bizarre afterlife brings Jane Austen's legacy not only into the history of education but into the history of spiritualism. When we talk metaphorically about being haunted by Austen—when we imagine her speaking beyond the grave or ask, "What Would Jane Do?"—we might keep in mind that there was a time in the 1890s when professors set out to test whether their star student had returned to mention Jane Austen from beyond the grave, through another woman's pen. As skeptic Andrew Lang himself notes in 1909, Mrs. Piper's automatic writing was "more amusing than most novels."[37]

CHAPTER ELEVEN

Textbook Austens

From McGuffey's Readers
to *National Lampoon*

CliffsNotes, SparkNotes, and Googling for knowledge shortcuts, rather than reading the textbook, may seem a sadly modern student practice—"sadly," at least, to teachers. It's true that some aspects of it form a *modern* practice. In other ways, however, these sources sound new notes in a very old key. The late nineteenth century had its own pamphlets and books designed to help students take and pass that era's interminable tests. Because exams might determine a young person's future, the stakes were high. One way we can tell that Jane Austen had arrived in late nineteenth-century school curricula is that she began to be featured in study guides for the resourceful Victorian cribber.

H. A. (Austin) Dobson's *The Civil Service Handbook of English Literature* (1874), describes itself in its very subtitle as "for the use of candidates for examinations, public schools, and students generally." Dobson acknowledges that most of his information is recycled from previous sources and that several competing titles have appeared in the previous three years. His contents are limited to a discussion of principal English authors, the leading characteristics of their productions, and the prominent events of their lives. In his introduction, he articulates what he and his readers already knew: these books were necessary because students' "time and opportunities were restricted."[1] Dobson was offering them time-saving and expanded opportunities, giving them material to answer successfully the questions that would be posed. In his half page devoted to "Miss Austen," Dobson describes her as a "quiet and placid clergyman's daughter," using the funny line that her "life of retirement" was only once broken by four years of "mild dissipation" in Bath. Dobson uses G. H. Lewes's words of praise of Austen, along with Sir Walter Scott's, to buttress her inclusion among the major greats, but he also names her as a novelist (or, once, a "lady novelist") whose works "have not even yet been surpassed" "on her own ground" (184).

Little commentary exists on Austen's place in nineteenth-century English curricula and textbooks. Dobson's *Civil Service Handbook of English Literature* is unusual in that it's mentioned briefly by Austen critic B. C. Southam. He notes that Dobson's textbook was many times reprinted and that its account of Austen as "the quiet and placid clergyman's daughter" would have been seen by "students by the ten-thousand," which "must have assisted in the transmission of this touching fantasy."[2] We might add something else, too, after letting that idea and that enormous number sink in. Late nineteenth-century students by the tens of thousands would also have seen the assessment that Austen had "not even yet been surpassed." Making these conclusions all the more powerful is the fact that textbook authors frequently echoed the work of their predecessors. In a "new" college textbook published more than fifty years later in 1925, Benjamin Brawley recycles every one of Dobson's key words in his own Jane Austen entry.[3]

The few lines on Austen that made it into the early textbooks were immensely important. What details would be emphasized? How would tens of thousands be led to think about, to label, Austen's fiction? Descriptions like "quiet and placid" were, for a time, fighting words. "Not even yet been surpassed" was a judgment of greatness and achievement but also an indictment of the present age for fiction. What would the textbooks tell students about how to understand Austen's scale, scope, and place in the (small and/ or large? literary and/or political?) world? Whether writ large or small, Austen's position in these textbooks communicated things—often conflicting things—about literary value, educational aspirations, or sex and society. The word and phrase "novelist" versus "lady novelist" mattered and still does.

We've overestimated the extent to which Austen's established critics served to create her legacy in schools and elsewhere. Critics mattered. But the textbook authors, the teachers using the materials, and the students reading them were imprinting their own versions of Austen, too. This chapter looks at the history of using Jane Austen's writings in textbooks and schools, an arena in which she has tended to be presented at her most conservative, although we haven't previously set out to document much of it. (The story of Austen *adaptations* in education is far more complicated, given the school dramatizations described in chapter 4 and the work with Austen and film described at the end of this chapter.) As a closer examination of Austen in English curricula and textbooks of the late nineteenth century and after shows, they often shared rhetorical features with the men's club Janeite set. Teaching materials depreciated Austen's small life and her fiction's limited scope, while touting her artistry and citing her most visible Great Male fans. School editions had a profound impact on the emergence of scholarly ones. Once we uncover this, we can see some of what the drama-in-education boosters and the suffragists were up against. That stage and street activist work was antithetical to the safe, small Austen who was most often presented in nineteenth- and twentieth-century literature textbooks.

The "lessons" taught by late nineteenth- and early twentieth-century print excerpts and abridgments of Austen's writings tended to reinforce existing social structures, especially in terms of class, culture, and "taste." They made those choices rather than highlighting her satire, hints toward social change, or examination of gender roles in courtship or marriage. When questions of social power were taken up in these teaching materials, it was most often to suggest that Austen's work reinforced individual self-determination and warned against vulgarity or greed. Of course, this was a view that could be embraced by progressive reformers, as well as conservative traditionalists. Inculcating "taste" in the working classes through literary reading could be advanced as a mechanism for social change. But few of the textbooks describe their educational aims quite that directly. What they are more easily read for is their omissions. Because the early teaching of English literature also stressed elocution, Austen's humor was occasionally featured, but it was usually her gentle humor (as with Thomson's illustrations), rather than her most satirical or biting humor. *Emma* proved a far more popular text to excerpt in early textbooks, with early abridgments favoring *Pride and Prejudice* above all others.

It remains challenging to trace the teaching of Austen over time.[4] In part, it's because the materials to do so fly further under the radar than is the norm. Many illustrated editions of Austen's novels have become collectible objects, but early teaching editions of her novels (usually unillustrated) tend to be among the least prized or consulted. We could, however, learn a great deal about the teaching of Austen in a historical frame by studying the library holdings, gift and school inscriptions, and marginalia located in these teaching editions, whether for Austen or other authors, were we able to compile it. It's clear, as we saw in the discussion on illustration, that Austen's novels were often used as prizes for school competitions. Many classroom copies also include students' penciled endpaper notes, often trying to keep the names of characters straight or taking notes on themes. Few have attempted to collect this sort of information from extant individual copies of Austen's novels, although the Reading Experience Database and Book Traces crowd-sourced web projects would be models for doing so and could allow further patterns of classroom use to be identified.[5]

Despite an incredibly rich (and impossibly large and diffuse) amount of data, we know comparatively little about Austen's entrance into schools and colleges.[6] That's true whether we're talking about studies of recommended curricula, institutional practices, pioneering pedagogues, or teaching texts. Various kinds of documentary and anecdotal evidence survive, including the school affiliations of many early editors of Austen teaching editions, who presumably sometimes also taught Austen themselves. At the least, we know their editions were implicitly or explicitly recommending that *others* do so. What we can establish with certainty is that there was talk of including Jane Austen's books in a system of mass public instruction far earlier than most of us would assume. As early as 1838, an American author turned educational philosopher, Enoch Cobb Wines (1806–79), was recommending Austen's books—in a long list of others—as appropriate reading in a course of "popular education." There may turn out to be others before him, but he seems a remarkably early voice advocating for student reading of Austen's fiction, as teachers began to incorporate instruction in literature in English.

Records survive to help us understand what Enoch Wines valued in Austen. Wines, a Congregationalist, aimed at inculcating morality, good citizenship, and religious belief in the young. He saw education as a social good for its potential to lessen criminality, and he would later become involved in penal reform.[7] In his published writings on education, Wines proposed new standards for everything from teacher salaries to the architecture of school rooms. In his appendix of literary reading suggestions, he lists four novels by Jane Austen (twice misspelled as Jane Austin) among the two hundred works of fiction he counsels teachers to teach and students to read. (*Emma* and *Sense and Sensibility* don't make the list.)[8] We don't know how often Wines's reading suggestions were adopted, but his list offers evidence of an earlier start to *recommending* Austen to teachers and pupils than we might expect to find, given her relatively more modest popularity and name recognition from the 1830s to the 1860s.

It's recently become clear that we've overstated the extent to which the years prior to the publication of the first Austen memoir in 1870 were a "dark ages" for Austen's readership. So it shouldn't come as a surprise that, even in the mid-nineteenth century, there were those who imagined a future in which

Austen's novels would be used to educate. In his *Novels and Novelists from Elizabeth to Victoria* (1858), John Cordy Jeaffreson (1831–1901), the novelist, *Athenaeum* journalist, and manuscript scholar, describes how a student (especially a male one) might learn from Austen's work. Jeaffreson begins by noting that Austen's novels are "now but little read, and even when read gain few sincere admirers, notwithstanding that it is now the fashion indiscriminately to praise them."[9] It's hard to know how to parse that series of contradictions. But his own praise, apparently, is sincere and informed. It's certainly prognosticating. Austen's novels, he declares, "are however amongst the best specimens of one department of the fictitious art in literature, and will, we doubt not, be much studied five hundred years hence." Educating studious readers is not only something that Austen's novels will do in the future, according to Jeaffreson. They also have what he sees as an educational function in the present. He suggests that men can learn how to manipulate women by reading Austen, because she reveals what women desire in the "manly character." By learning from Austen, Jeaffreson concludes, "we are instructed how to flatter, feign, and win" women (2:84). Whether he's serious or joking almost doesn't matter. He's certainly teaching Austen against what would become the moralizing grain.

More serious Austen-inclusive educational materials emerged as well. Her fiction began to feature especially in literary encyclopedias or manuals, once a dominant format in English instruction. An account of the ways in which Austen appears in survey manuals from 1896 to 1915, a moment when Austen had already gained a place in emerging literary studies, may be found in the work of Lawrence Mazzeno.[10] Her place in them was advocated for by association, as we've seen previously. She was great because she was appreciated by other greats. The names that came up most often were Scott's and Macaulay's. (Scott was mentioned for his positive review of *Emma* in 1816, as well as for his laudatory comments in his posthumously published life writing. Macaulay was referenced for comparing Austen to Shakespeare in 1843.) Baptist minister and educator Joseph Angus's *Handbook of English Literature* (1865) includes Austen in its section on middle-class life. Her importance in this class of novels, too, was based on those who approved of her: "Scott and Whately and Macaulay agree in giving her the highest praise."[11]

Despite early suggestions from Wines and Angus, and Jeaffreson's claims for the value of Austen's novels as educational (however perverse), there was a slower path to wider acceptance for Austen in schools. Indeed, it would prove slow for all of English literature and for novels in particular. It was the case for novels by women most especially. The rise to prominence of Austen's fiction in formal school settings resulted from her novels being caught up in larger educational shifts. The novel and Austen both became part of the emerging category of classroom-appropriate English literature, at almost precisely the same moment that opportunities in the education of girls of many backgrounds began to expand.

The reputation of Austen's novels was enhanced by changes in education. The publication of Austen-Leigh's memoir in 1870 "coincided with the passing in the same year by the British Parliament of the Education Act," as William Baker has noted. As he writes, "This made mandatory the statewide foundation of elementary schools, insisted on universal literacy and the use of literary teaching as a national heritage, and the fostering of the awareness of national pride. A consequence was the opening of a wider reading public for Jane Austen."[12] Others have noticed similar changes. In a fine chapter titled "The Stigma of Popularity," H. J. Jackson notes that "successive Elementary Education Acts between 1870 and 1893 ensured universal education for children in Britain; the act of 1880 made schooling compulsory to the age of twelve . . . Austen's [novels] were judged suitable for children, and editors, abridgers and publishers were quick to capitalize on the new market."[13]

Questions arose about how teachers ought to teach Austen—how she would be positioned in literary history and in lectures, as well as how learning about her would be assessed. Essays for teachers were published in educational periodicals for just such a purpose. "A Novel Course for Teachers: Jane Austen" appeared in the Atlanta-based *Southern Educational Journal* in 1898. The piece, signed E.S.H., is made up of talking points for teachers to use in their classrooms. E.S.H. is concerned about the extent to which Austen is becoming almost *too* popular, musing, "What does this mean—that we are beginning to have a Jane Austen cult? How the idea would have amused the innocent subject of it all!"[14] The London-based *Journal on Education* published a 1902 essay with a similar end in view—to inform teachers so that they might lecture on Austen in class. The authors, M. and C. Lee, are critical of Austen's less firmly didactic approach and note her lesser popularity with young readers.[15] In 1897, writer-professor Arlo Bates (1850–1918) argues that Jane Austen is among the dozen novelists "which it is taken for granted that every person of education has read." A male reader without such experience, Bates concludes, "will find it difficult to hold the respect of cultivated men."[16]

But Austen was then gaining in popularity with younger readers of both sexes from a wider range of class backgrounds—at least if the growing number of school editions and abridgments of her novels are a reliable indication. The Christmas gift book phenomenon, described in part 1, also played a role in the circulation of Austen's fiction among the young. The first single Austen volume specifically prepared and packaged for school use appears to have been edited by an American, Josephine Woodbury Heermans (later Greenwood) (1859–1928). Heermans's edition of *Pride and Prejudice*, published in the Macmillan Pocket Classics series in 1908, sold enormously well over the years.[17] It identifies itself as edited for use in elementary and secondary schools, and Heermans's preface suggests she was a careful, knowledgeable scholar. She refers to the three editions of *Pride and Prejudice* published during Austen's lifetime, indicating that her own edition draws on the 1817 text. (This fact alone pokes holes in the assertion that famed Austen editor R. W. Chapman was the first to pay a scholar's meticulous attention to Austen and textual editing.) Heermans shows enough familiarity with the primary Austen materials, and care for the correctness of her text, that she mentions quotations from Austen's letters and describes misprints made in the early editions.

Heermans's introduction, too, is accomplished. She gathers brief quotes about Austen's positive reception ("appreciations") (xx). She provides a list of bibliographical and critical references and suggestions for study (xxi). Her edition includes copious annotations, adding up to serious textual treatment. Why has this edition not been given its due as a precursor to the 1923 Standard Edition of Austen edited by R. W. Chapman? One wonders whether the fact that one edition was published by an Oxford man and the other by a Missouri female schoolteacher may have something to do with it. That said, not everything in Heermans's edition was pitched to please scholars more than students. Heermans's suggestions for study are hardly weighty, offering insight into the ways in which Austenian knowledge was assessed in the early twentieth century.

In the Heermans edition, reading the novel allows for the mastery of literary terms and techniques through close reading analysis. The study questions ask, for instance, "How many chapters comprise the 'beginning' of *Pride and Prejudice*?" They direct students to "analyze the plot into single actions." They ask for a reader to "give instances of balanced sentences" and query, "What is the artistic value of the last chapter?" (Heermans xxvi). Yet Heermans's endnotes are learned and helpful, including explanations of card games, like vingt-et-un, or modes of transportation, such as a hack chaise. Sometimes the notes also include difficult interpretive questions, prompting students to have opinions, such as the note for "happiness in marriage" being a matter of chance. It asks students, "What is your opinion of Charlotte's argument?" concluding that "Charlotte's own future is interesting in light of the opinion expressed in this chapter" (327). Heermans chooses judiciously what deserves further explanation and provides students with sound information.

Heermans was herself a beneficiary of increasing nineteenth-century opportunities for women's education. She held a master's degree from Columbia University and served for many years as the principal of the Whittier School in Kansas City. The Austen edition was not her first book, as she had published *Stories from the Hebrew* (1903). A Christian Scientist, Heermans's approach to literature was highly spiritual.[18] She saw it as the fifth window onto the soul, concluding that a "graded system of education without literature is as the body without spirit" (Heermans 207). Her reputation in educational circles was high, with one positive review of the Austen edition claiming, "She is one of the best teachers of elementary grades in the country and a skilful [*sic*] author."[19] Heermans was a teacher of teachers, as well as of students, and she was said to have "shown that pupils need not wait until they are in high school to learn something of books and authors" or to learn "the good from the bad in literature."[20]

Some of the concerns in early Austen education discussions were practical. Educators approached Austen wondering how much reading their pupils could reasonably be assigned and at what grade level her fiction would be best introduced. Excerpts were pitched as a good compromise between solely descriptive manuals and lengthy complete works. Excerpts had benefits because they could get the author's own words into the hands of readers, rather than only summaries and assessments of them. Few educators saw excerpts as anything other than a concession, although plenty of booksellers and editors saw it as an opportunity. Everyone was looking for the sweet spot between too little exposure to an author's work and too overwhelming a reading assignment for students.

We can see this in *The Austen-Gaskell Book: Scenes from the Works of Jane Austen and Mrs. Gaskell* (1926). Designed for "older children," the book provides almost one hundred pages of excerpts from three Austen novels: *Pride and Prejudice*, *Northanger Abbey*, and *Mansfield Park*, along with its portion of Gaskell and illustrations for the fiction of throughout.[21] (It makes sense that the novel with the older heroine, *Persuasion*, and the heroine it was difficult to love, *Emma*, would be excluded, but the absence of *Sense and*

Sensibility must have been about perception of role-model suitability for the young.) The book's editor, the teacher and children's book author J. (Joseph) Compton (1891–1960), explains what's behind his method by acknowledging the obvious "objections to the books of snippets" and the drawbacks of abridged and simplified editions of entire novels (v–vi). Longer, connected extracts, he suggests, are the right solution. They alone are suitable for teaching eleven- through fifteen-year-olds the difference between good and bad literature and likely "to lead children to wish to read the complete work" (v, vii).

Laying the groundwork for a lifetime of reading and rereading was Compton's goal, telling the young that Austen and Gaskell "will be your friends for life if you will have them for your friends" (xiv). His was not the first volume of representative Austen extracts from multiple novels designed for initiates to Austen's fiction, but the *Austen-Gaskell Book* was more clearly geared to younger readers than previous editions had been. Lady Margaret Sackville's *Jane Austen* (1912), "a series of extracts from the six novels," had been pitched to those readers not previously exposed to Austen but aimed at, as the series ad put it, the "general reader and the busy man," suggesting an intended adult audience.[22] *English Prose, Chosen and Arranged by W[illiam] Peacock* (1921) also published eleven Austen extracts from four of her novels in its volume 3, with the project's selections "intended for readers of all classes and of all ages," for general readers, students, young and old.[23]

Excerpts were used not just for silent reading but also for elocution lessons. As Donald E. Stahl describes it, in late nineteenth-century English courses, "instruction most often consisted of studying a textbook composed of many short selections which were read aloud."[24] This practice is, in fact, what led to their nickname as "readers." By some estimates, readers sold from the mid-nineteenth to the mid-twentieth century into the millions of copies in the United States, putting them on a par with sales of the Bible. In Great Britain, the "most successful popularization of English literature for the mass market ever embarked upon" was Cassell's Library of English Literature (1875).[25] It eventually reached five illustrated volumes, under the editorship of Henry Morley (1822–94), professor of English literature at University College, London.

Morley, an apothecary and a journalist, was a supporter of child labor laws and women's higher education. "It is as a populariser of literature that he did his countrymen the highest service," concludes the *Dictionary of*

National Biography.[26] Morley included a selection from Jane Austen in Cassell's Library of English Literature as early as 1876, in his volume covering longer works in verse and prose. He included "a passage or two from her novel of Emma," as the best way to illustrate Austen's "manner," introducing it with, "The central thought of Jane Austen's 'Emma' is that each of us has his own life to live; we cannot make ourselves dictators of the lives of others." For Morley, the message of *Emma* appears to have been "leave well enough alone." Morley describes the entirety of the plot in a long paragraph and includes three passages: the "poor Miss Taylor" section, the introduction of Harriet Smith, and Mr. Knightley's conversation about Emma with Mrs. Weston. *Emma* is dispensed with in just a few hundred words.[27]

For a time, excerpts in prose readers seemed to have focused particularly on *Emma*. The best selling of the American readers were McGuffey's Readers, so named after William Holmes McGuffey (1800–73). McGuffey's Readers began as tools for elementary schools. When the series branched into high school instruction, Austen came to be featured. The excerpt in *McGuffey's High School Reader* (1889), in its Eclectic Educational Series, was also from *Emma*, a five-page selection in which Mrs. Elton and Emma have their long conversation about married women and music, at the end of which Emma declares Mrs. Elton insufferable.[28] *McGuffey's* titles it "A Parvenu English Woman," describing it as "an excellent picture of the presumption a certain class of people make on short acquaintance" (135).

The scenes selected from Austen's writings for dramatization were more likely to emphasize women's independence, but the *McGuffey's* scene from *Emma* emphasizes admirable class discrimination and stratification. *McGuffey's* recommends the value of staying in one's place or, if one gains wealth, of not acting the vulgar parvenu. The thousands of American high school readers who came to this scene without having read Austen's *Emma* would not come armed with the knowledge that Emma Woodhouse's snobbery is chastised later in the novel. The student is asked to identify with Emma's discrimination, learning how to be "classy," rather than learning how not to be class-presumptuous. The impact of McGuffey's in America cannot be overestimated. It's believed that 120 million copies of his readers sold between 1836 and 1920, reaching readers of all classes and regions.[29] Some of those millions were spoon-fed an Austen who endorses the existing social order.

This was a common enough textbook move, although the scenes varied and sometimes overlapped with those selected for dramatization. Where they differentiated themselves was in their prefatory matter. Editor George Saintsbury also turned to *Emma* for his selection in his *Specimens of English Prose Style from Malory to Macaulay* (1886), another early textbook. In what he describes as "The Strawberry Party," Mr. Knightley's tamps down the presumptuous suggestions of Mrs. Elton in that famous scene. Saintsbury's introduction to the excerpt describes those he sees as Austen's right readers. Her style, he says, is "not striking to the vulgar."[30] The same sentiment is touted in the prominent and commercially successful *English Prose Selections* (1893–96), edited by Sir Henry Craik (1846–1927). Craik declares Austen to be appreciated by those who "have acquired something of literary judgement," not the "average reader of fiction," enjoining students to approach her with patience.[31] Craik includes two Mr. Collins scenes from *Pride and Prejudice*, *Emma* on the Coles' party, and the defense of novels from *Northanger Abbey*. Craik addresses not the cultivated amateur but the cultivated.

In Britain, Craik's volumes were among the most powerful of their kind. As one recent critic puts it, "It was merely the admired top of an enormous iceberg whose foundations rested in the literary extracts of the elementary school readers which sold in the millions."[32] Craik's introduction declares that Austen holds "the most secure place in our roll of female novelists," a statement that, in the 1890s, might have seemed wishful thinking but that, by the 1910s, would have encountered few skeptics (54). Craik was a Scot, educational reformer, and politician, as well as a literary man who served as a Conservative member of Parliament for the universities of Glasgow and Aberdeen. His six-volume set became a standard. By the first decade of the twentieth century, there had been a flood of beauties, specimens, and extracts from nineteenth-century prose, many designed for use in schools. Austen was made a standard selection.

Despite the ubiquity of readers as English textbooks (and despite Austen's own criticisms of what Leah Price calls the "pedagogical anthology" in books like *Elegant Extracts*), there was a movement against excerpts and abridgments promoting the value of whole works.[33] A middle ground between the two was the abridged novel, which began to gain steam. Between 1890 and 1970, more than a dozen abridgments of *Pride and Prejudice* alone were published.[34] The most notorious among them are those that remove Austen's signature first line—a heresy for critics and an odd decision from a pedagogical standpoint.[35] One notable abridgment was in The Masterpiece Library's Penny Novels series, published by the *Review of Reviews* and its editor William T. Stead (1849–1912). These titles were promoted for use in schools. Stead was in favor of compulsory primary and secondary school education and universal male and female suffrage, and his publishing ventures align with those goals.[36] Stead's 90 Penny Novels included two titles by Austen: *Pride and Prejudice* (1896) and *Sense and Sensibility* (1897). The former was reduced to eight chapters and the latter to twenty-eight "very brief" chapters.[37] These titles were also advertised as "The Cheapest Library in the World," at a pound, sold in "a neat bookcase with folding-doors."[38] Stead might be seen as a one-man educational marching band and Austen as one of his many instruments.

The reach of his library was impressive. Stead claims to have sold enormous numbers of his Penny Novels and Penny Poets: "I have at present issued about 5,276,000 of the Poets and about 9,000,000 of the novels, making a total of 14,000,000 in all."[39] He notes that some novels of intrinsic worth did not sell as well as "those which only by a stretch of courtesy could be regarded as Masterpieces," but that "no person can now complain that the treasures of our literature are denied to them owing to inability to pay." As he concludes, there are now very few books "not accessible to any one who can command the price of a cigarette." For Stead, this is not just sales but educational proselytizing. He proposes to send bulk copies parcel free to regions "where people read nothing, or next to nothing," and to "clubs, schools, and local centres of reading unions" "where no newsagent or bookseller exists" (390).

Seeing Austen read in such contexts, we can better understand how her novels built a massive readership among those seeking an education. By Stead's own (unquestionably self-interested) calculations, each text in his Masterpiece Library series sold an average of one hundred thousand copies. Illustrated novels by Hugh Thomson were a hit with a certain class of readers, but the abridged Penny Novels furthered Austen's reach to places and people that a full-length, gilt-covered edition never could have. Working-class readers may have been getting Austen Lite, or Partial Austen, but there was also exposure to her, especially as Stead attempted to sell to far-flung locations and schools.

What appears to have been the first shortened version of *Pride and Prejudice* marketed specifically for schools came from a tonier publisher: Cambridge University Press. It appeared in their English Literature for Schools series in 1910, abridged and edited by Mrs. Frederick (Henrietta O'Brien) Boas (1863–1953). She straightforwardly explained why she undertook her task, describing it in direct contrast to literary excerpts or selections. Its benefit was that it was still short enough to be in a form suitable for school reading. As she wrote, "It is in this form only about half of its original size, and the chapters have been necessarily re-divided."[40] Boas made a practice of abridging works for schools, having undertaken Gaskell's *Cranford* and Goldsmith's *Vicar of Wakefield*. Boas wrote original works of her own, too, and later edited a complete Austen novel, *Northanger Abbey*.[41] About one of Boas's other original works, a reviewer concludes, "Mrs. Boas knows how to win attention and excite interest."[42]

Most reviewers were less than enthusiastic about her *Pride and Prejudice* abridged. The *Saturday Review* found it an abomination, in an unsigned review by R. A. Austen-Leigh (1872–1961), an Austen descendant we saw in part 2 on dramatization (Gilson, *Bibliography* 290). R. A. Austen-Leigh describes being appalled by Boas herself, as well as by the abridgment: "What are we to say of this book? What can we think of a lady who hopes to present 'Pride and Prejudice' in a form suitable for school-reading . . . by the omission of short passages, the curtailment of conversations, and the shortening of descriptions? Boys and girls at school have little use for Austen at any time, and it is hardly likely that they will find her any more attractive when most of the best passages in her novels have been excised."[43] Austen-Leigh is right that there are some egregious errors in Boas's abridgment, described in excruciating detail in his review, but he was wrong about her edition being an unappealing text for schools. Boas's edition was advertised as part of "a new series of reading books for the upper and middle forms of secondary schools," "particularly suitable for rapid reading"; it still was for sale two decades later.[44] By then other abridgments had joined it, such as Stead's the same year (as we saw, 1910), H. A. Treble's in 1917 (advertised as "abridged for schools") and David Salmon's in 1924 (Gilson, *Bibliography* 290, 293, 300). Boas herself created a second Austen abridgement, *Sense and Sensibility*, in 1926 (301).

For a time in the early twentieth century, the bulk of the new Austen editions were designed for students and schools. It may be difficult to see the big picture from these brief descriptions. But to tell it by the numbers, between the years 1908 (the year that Heermans published her bestselling Macmillan pocket school edition) and 1931 (when Elizabeth D'Oyley published an edition of Austen's connected extracts), there were fifty-seven new editions of Austen's novels, according to Gilson (*Bibliography*, 285–306). Of these, fourteen specifically identified themselves as delivered in abridged, excerpted, or student-marketed formats. That adds up to one-quarter of all new Austen editions published, a remarkable dominance for a just-created type. A third of those abridged titles were completed by editors identifiable as female. This is a smaller number of females than we saw with Austen dramatizations in part 2, but it's a significant number nonetheless.

In the dozen years leading up to the publication of R. W. Chapman's famed scholarly edition, the first so-called standard edition of Austen in 1923, these numbers are similar. More than a quarter of the new Austen editions published in the 1910s were specifically packaged or described as for school use. This gives further meaning to the information Kathryn Sutherland has provided from Chapman's papers about his having considered a "school edition (abortive) of *Emma* (written on a troop train)" (qtd. in Sutherland 32). As Sutherland shows, Chapman's editorial work on Austen was inspired by that of his Austen scholar-editor wife, Katharine M. Metcalfe, who after marriage became his Austen editor-collaborator, and on whose work "his" later Austen edition was based. Few have realized that Chapman's (or rather, the Chapmans') scholarly, standard edition was born out of the first moment— and out of the first sustained era—of textual dominance for Austen school editions. It was also a time when women (including the woman who would become his wife) first made up a substantial minority of Austen editors. Yet today Chapman's is the only Austen edition from this era that we talk about, as if it and he emerged out of thin air. Chapman's Austen would come to eclipse, and outlast, all textual work that came before it. The degree to which his/their scholarly standard edition of Austen was influenced (negatively and positively) by school editions is clearly more extensive than we've previously understood.

As Austen's fiction was repurposed into new media—especially drama, radio, and film—those new media were also reconfigured as pedagogical opportunities. We saw in part 2 how schools and community theaters mounted Austen dramatizations. Teaching Austen through radio and film also became common. Most tellingly, MGM's *Pride and Prejudice* (1940) was classed early on as an "educational motion picture," a designation that got it included in catalogs circulated to schools, community groups, libraries, and museums. Essays like "Using Films for Teaching" (1946) mention *Pride and Prejudice* specifically as "creditable material," among films that "fit admirably into the curriculum of public schools and literally bring the world into the classroom."[45] MGM understood this market well. It produced a forty-one-minute "condensed version" of its film to market for educational sale and rental, starting in 1949.[46]

MGM mounted an even more ambitious rerelease of *Pride and Prejudice* in 1962, setting out to capture a new generation of young readers and film-goers, as well as to recapture their parents' nostalgia for the films and books of their youth. The rerelease was marketed to community cinemas and schools. MGM partnered with *Scholastic Magazine* in what it ambitiously called its World Heritage Film and Book Program. *Pride and Prejudice* was among the eight film-book pairings sold to communities as providing the op-portunity to see the dramatization (on film) of some of literature's greatest works. As one commentator has recognized, this was "big business," with theaters in 230 cities in the United States booking the series. Such bookings involved showing one film per month over eight months. It went well. As that commentator notes, "The success of this 'Read-the-book, See-the-picture' project has already decided the sponsors to repeat it" in 1963–64.[47]

Little has been written about this film-classroom Austen venture. One recent blogger notes about the film side of the equation that MGM "went after the school kids"; busloads of them would be taken to the cinema to see black and white movies, like *Pride and Prejudice*, that had been playing free on TV for years. This was a cash cow for MGM. There was even a National Advisory Committee of Educators that served to endorse the project. The blogger notes, "It was an unholy alliance between schools and movie houses."[48] Not all educators were skeptical of the unholy alliance. Some, such as Marion Sheridan, chair of that National Advisory Committee, and an early champion of using film in the English curriculum, saw it as a way to help students fur-ther appreciate literature.[49] In the late nineteenth and early twentieth cen-turies, Austen's place in schools had been cemented through fashionable educational exercises in elocution and dramatization, abridgments and ex-cerpts, as well as the reading of her texts in their entirety in school editions and other formats. By the mid-twentieth century, Austen's fiction was being sold to students through the *Pride and Prejudice* on screen, with the hope that whetting their appetites for the story and fame of the author in the cinema would lead to their reading the novel in its entirety.

This movement may also help us read a famous essay on teaching Austen through a different lens. In "Why We Read Jane Austen," literary critic and professor Lionel Trilling (1905–75) reports on his recent experience running an Austen course at Columbia University. (Trilling's essay was published in 1976 in the *Times Literary Supplement*, having originated as a version of a lecture he did not get a chance to deliver before he died.) Trilling had envisioned his course as enrolling a maximum of 20 to 30 students. He was amazed and distressed when 150 of them showed up the first day. Because he wanted to stick to the original enrollment, he conducted interviews to determine which students would be allowed in. These experiences led Trilling to consider Austen's reputation, especially among the young and as a result of "the contemporary demand for female figures," in the wake of the second wave of the women's movement.[50]

His experiences with Austen also led him to despair, as he received appeals and expressions of bitterness from some of the more than one hundred students that he rejected for enrollment in the course. As he writes, "There was something [students] wanted, not from me, as was soon apparent, but from Jane Austen, something that was making for them an intensity in their application for the course such as I had no preparation for in all my teaching career." Teaching Austen, Trilling finds, is sui generis. Why, Trilling asks, did this course mean so much, did Austen mean so much? One of the reasons he considers is that students flocked to Austen to "in some way transcend our sad contemporary existence" (250). It would seem that for Trilling all of Austen's college-age readers had become Winston Churchill, seeking out Austen's fiction as escapism.

But this may just be another moment in which a member of the literati provides us with a high-culture reason for Austen's renewed fashionability that doesn't explain quite enough. Popular reasons might be explored just as well. Trilling was facing a generation of students who had been bused to local cinemas and had been raised on school film showings and TV reruns of *Pride and Prejudice* (1940). This was a generation of students whose parents may have seen *Pride and Prejudice* on stage or, during its first release, who were sold cigarettes with advertisements featuring Jane Austen quotations. Perhaps even more worthy of our consideration, however, is the fact that Jane Austen had made it to the October 1971 Back-to-School Issue of *National Lampoon Magazine*. Its circulation was then in the ballpark of a quarter to half a million predominantly college-aged readers.[51] That October issue included a one-page, black-and-white mock Jane Austen advertisement, encouraging students to take college courses in English literature.

The *National Lampoon* mock ad features a 1950s-looking perky blonde in a gingham dress and white heels, who is gesticulating in front of her filled shopping cart. (A box of Wheaties cereal peeks out of the grocery bag.) She points to the white box that's being held by a bow-tied and white-aproned grocery boy. The box, in dark script, reads, "Jane Austen." Surely this is meant to remind readers of Dolly Madison, then a well-known American snack food company, named after a real person, the early nineteenth-century president James Madison's wife, Dolley Madison (1768–1849). The real Dolley Madison was known for her social graces; the cupcake company sold its prepackaged baked goods in flimsy boxes. The *National Lampoon* mock ad's headline reads, "Jane Austen. Isn't that the kind of cupcake they used to sell at the A&P?"

Below the photo of the woman and boy, the joke continues, "Sorry, cupcake, but Jane's nobody's food. She's the English novelist who wrote *Pride and Prejudice*, *Emma*, and many other classics satirizing provincial life. If

Figure 11.1. Jane Austen / English literature poster, School of Hard Sell series, *National Lampoon Magazine*, October 1971, 19.

you had taken English Literature, you'd know who Jane was. And Emily. And Geoffrey. And Oliver and Rudyard. And even Percy." The punch line next to this admonishing minilecture is, "English Literature. A course to remember." *National Lampoon* not only ran this as a mock advertisement; it also sold the design in a poster-size version, presumably available to decorate a bedroom or a dorm room, or even, for a teacher with a sense of humor, an office or a classroom.[52]

The ad is part of a series in the issue called The School of Hard Sell, by George W. S. (William Swift) Trow (1943–2006) and Michael O'Donoghue (1940–94). A recent writer describes the two men as the National Lampoon's "house blue bloods" (Stein 157). Trow was a *Harvard Lampoon* editor who joined *National Lampoon* and would go on to a career with the *New Yorker*. O'Donoghue, after a stint as writer and editor of *National Lampoon*, became the first head writer of the television sketch-comedy show, *Saturday Night Live*. Their School of Hard Sell series was said to be an attempt to combat "college students signing up in droves" for courses such as "*Sioux Studies, Basic Tantric Buddhism, Understanding Laing,* [and] *A Brief History of the Geodesic Dome.*" Trow and O'Donoghue ask, "But what of the traditional subjects such as *Latin, Geography, Mathematics, Sciences, History,* and *English*? Nobody cares about them anymore. To combat flagging interest, it may become necessary to do something more than just list these courses in the college catalogue. It may become necessary to advertise … School of Hard Sell."[53] A series of advertisements was created for philosophy, classics, geography, English literature, and calculus. The ads are both satirical and serious, simultaneously making fun of the trendy, ephemeral desires of college students and colleges and the crass manipulations of advertisers.

Jane Austen was no doubt chosen for this purpose because of her "satirizing provincial life," as Trow and O'Donoghue put it. In that she shared an element in common with *National Lampoon*. That magazine had made satirical youth culture popular again. Jane Austen was, literally, in this case, its poster author for satire. The ad works by insulting the reader as the "cupcake" who doesn't know Jane Austen. The point—and there does also seem to be a serious point being made—is that Jane Austen is not a cupcake. The mock ad suggests that once you take a course in English literature, you are neither in the place of the plastic-looking housewife nor the naïve grocery boy. You are not a cupcake, and Jane Austen's not the frosting. She's not dessert. She's a classic. She's the main course. She allows you to join those in the know, those who know better.

In *National Lampoon* in 1971—and there was little that was more cool among students then than *National Lampoon*—Jane Austen and her novels are made to stand rhetorically in league with other humor writers. The mock ad suggests, between the lines, "If you, college student, do not take a Jane Austen course, instead electing to take the Brief History of the Geodesic Dome, then you may be as ignorant and old-fashioned as someone who shops or works at the A&P. You are stuck in the naive 1950s." In this mock ad, "Jane's nobody's food," and if you read her, you're nobody's fool. Humor writer-illustrators of the early 1970s set out to make Jane Austen, the Satirist, hip again. It's their popular work, too, not just the musings of educational elites and old-guard culture makers like Trilling, that led us to the Jane Austens who are still schooling us today.

Coda

Twenty-First-Century
Jane Austen

While I rejoice in some ways in the Austenizing of modern culture,
I have to say I worry, sometimes.

— Marjorie Garber, *Quotation Marks* (2003)

There has been a spate of recent popular essays we might simply retitle "Why Jane Austen Is Not Relevant." These pieces regularly engender snarky ripostes that could be titled, "Why Jane Austen Is Still Relevant, or If She Isn't in Your World, She Probably Should Be, and P.S. You Might Have a Higher Respect for My Nerves." It could serve as the sarcastic subtitle of this book. But really, there's no need to get defensive. What this book's chapters collectively show is that, whatever we've thrown at "Jane Austen" by way of slaying her over the course of the past two centuries, it hasn't worked. She has adapted, or, rather, many of us have adapted her, finding in her what best suits us. Her reputation has shifted with the times and with the needs and desires of her multiple audiences. If there is any takeaway message that this book seeks to leave us with, it's that it's ridiculous to wring our hands with worry that zombie movies, female-student-dominated college courses, or Etsy products are ruining Austen's status in the literary canon in the present and for posterity.

I don't mean to discount the understandable feeling that some may have now and again that Jane Austen could stand to be around just *a little bit* less. Any person in her or his right mind experiences occasional fatigue at Mrs. Elton's dialogue being quoted as a nugget of Austenian wisdom or at the umpteenth homage to *Pride and Prejudice* in the form of mommy porn. Please recognize, however, that such moments of fatigue do not signal that Jane Austen's good name is dying. To believe that whatever happens to Austen this year could snuff her out for good ignores the twists-and-turns history of her long-term canonical status and popularity. The next time someone tries to argue as much, reply that Austen's critical and popular legacies have traveled quite well together, thank you very much, for a very long time. To

declare that Jane Austen is on her last legs in the twenty-first century involves investing our own moment with far too much weight and the past
with far too little.

Yet that's exactly what a 2015 article that fluttered around social media
from Australia, ultimately landing in *Newsweek*, would have us believe.
Camilla Nelson's "Is Popularity Killing Jane Austen?" worries that the man
who wrote in *Slate* in 2013 that Austen was "overhyped" might be right.[1] She
suspects that her female creative writing student who is anxious that others
will judge her harshly for loving "rom-com corny" Austen could be onto something. Finally, Nelson suggests that the "gender agenda" working on Austen's
image is really to blame, because to have a huge popular following (especially
with women, or, God forbid, feminists!) and to be considered a great writer is
"something of a paradox" in literary history (n.p.). We saw how that paradox worked out for the suffragists using Jane Austen in the early twentieth
century. One can't credit Austen, of course, but women did win the vote.

Austen's literary legacy proves that you can't be both a popular and a
highbrow author in the way that Ronald Reagan proves that an actor can't
become president. Holding the attention of scholarly and popular audiences
alike is precisely what Austen has done through two centuries of images,
stages, screens, schools, and soapboxes. I suspect many of us have remained
in the dark about these details because the story of Austen's afterlife has thus
far been much better told as a literary-critical, rather than a popular culture,
story, especially before 1995. It's probably because those of us who are scholars, who care a great deal about such things, have been the ones packaging
her story for wider consumption. We've been too focused on repeating and
engaging with the words and ideas of our own academic networks—our heroes and nemeses—or on quoting the ideas espoused by our mentors or our
mentors' mentors. We've been too little focused on how the specifics of the
Austen popular and commercial have intertwined with the Austen critical
and scholarly, whether in conflict with each other, oblivious to each other,
or in tandem. If attention to her and her writings dies down or dies out over
the course of the next generation, it's not likely to be because of those things.
It's more likely to be because, in whatever form their successor phenomena
take, popular-culture makers decide not to take her there with them.

Each medium considered in this book has an Austenian afterlife that
builds on past patterns and practices, extending the histories told in this book
up to the present day. In illustrated Austen, for example, the current craze
for adult coloring books means that visualizing her and her characters in

drawings is newly hot again. (I say "again" because the *Greer Garson Coloring Book* includes four oversized pages devoted to *Pride and Prejudice* [1940]. In that girls' coloring book, the emphasis in image and caption is entirely on the dresses.[2]) In the spate of new adult coloring books, it's not just the Austen films or manga versions that are inspiring the images. The 1890s Austen illustration craze images are also duplicated, sometimes literally. Their popularity may rest on the fact that they are out of copyright, but it means they are attracting new looks. Jane Austen's *Pride and Prejudice: A Coloring Classic* (2016) puts peacock feathers on its title page, in imitation of the 1894 Peacock edition.[3] *Jane Austen's Pride and Prejudice Colouring & Activity Book: Featuring Illustrations from 1895* (2015) reprints the Brock brothers' Austen images of that year.[4] *Persuasion: The Coloring Book* (2016) and *Jane Austen's Pride and Prejudice: The Adult Coloring Book* (2015) both reprint Hugh Thomson's illustrations of the 1890s.[5] *Color and Colorability: An Adult Coloring Book Celebrating the Work of Jane Austen* (2016) takes its images from a smattering of both the Brocks and Thomson.[6] Other coloring books consist of an abundance of Austen quotations, accompanied by floral motifs, echoing what seems to be the current trends in tattoo design. It's intriguing to consider what kinds of effects these images will have on Austen's visual lexicon going forward. It's particularly interesting to consider what it means and will mean to resurrect the Brocks, Thomson, and peacocks from the 1890s into this 2010s format.

The fad for illustrated Austen on the coloring book page is more than matched by the renewal of interest in dramatized Austen. Both amateur and professional stage versions of Austen are experiencing a big comeback. Jane Austen on the stage became hot in the 2010s, with new dramatic adaptations of almost all of her titles, in one form or another. Austen plays were professionally mounted and well received. A *Pride and Prejudice* by writer-producer Simon Reade debuted at the Theatre Royal Bath in 2009 and had a successful run at Regent's Park Open Air Theatre in London in 2013, followed by a US production at the Minneapolis Guthrie Theatre. It was headed back to Regent's Park in 2016, touring into 2017. Reade offers a greater focus on the Bennet parents, ending with Mr. Bennet's whisking Mrs. Bennet off to dance, after she voices the novel's famous first line for the play's last.[7] (It's almost as if the ending of that unrealized 1974 screenplay finally had its day.) *Austen's Pride: A New Musical of Pride and Prejudice* by Lindsay Warren Baker and Amanda Jacobs did well in 2015, racking up accolades, awards, and scheduling future productions. In 2014–15, a *Sense and Sensibility* by playwright-actor Kate Hamill (starring as Marianne Dashwood) had a successful New York run, attracting positive notice and heading for further stages at this writing.

These are just two of the most visible of the new professionally staged Austens. If you include theater of all kinds, the global prevalence of performed Austen is enormous, with hundreds of separate community and school productions per year. We're seeing a rebirth of the tradition that Rosina Filippi set in motion in the 1890s. The theatrical licensing company Samuel French reports handling an astonishing 332 Austen-inspired school and community theater productions from 2012 to 2017, most as full-length plays. The vast majority were for *Pride and Prejudice*. Samuel French also still licenses Helen Jerome's 1935 play, which makes up some unknown number of those performances. According to Samuel French's data, then, it received fees for 2,000 licensed separate performances of dramatized Austen over the course of a nearly five-year period.[8] One playwright, Jon Jory, has completed an edition of dramatized Austen, "the complete works of Jane Austen for the stage" for 2017 publication.[9] When you consider the numbers of actors and audience members who were part of Austen on stages of all kinds in the past several years, the dramatic reach is extensive. What new Austen-inspired messages or patterns might be emerging in these dramatizations, actors, and performances is yet to be determined.

Austen also continues to be a powerhouse figure in schools and curricula. The Open Syllabus Project, using data from a million syllabi worldwide, offers a sense of Austen's popularity in college classrooms from 2005 on: *Pride and Prejudice* is the thirty-eighth-most popular text assigned in English courses.[10] That number might seem low, when you consider that Aphra Behn's *Oroonoko* ranks thirty-sixth and Mary Shelley's *Frankenstein* is second. But when you add to that the fact that Jane Austen now has a new college named after her, her educational clout seems formidable. (In America, we'd understand a college of this kind to be an upper-grades high school.) A group of students will now be identifying themselves on applications and resumes of all kinds as graduates of Jane Austen College.

Jane Austen College chose its name with care. Claire Heald, executive principal of the school, reports that it's part of a family of schools in Norwich: Sir Isaac Newton Sixth Form, Jane Austen College, and Charles Darwin Primary. Their names indicate each school's different disciplinary specialism. As Principal Heald reports, "Jane Austen . . . was chosen to be an inspirational role model for our students. In addition, the school's pastoral houses follow a literary theme: Thackeray, Brontë, Chaucer, Eliot, and Shakespeare. The intention is to inspire, motivate, and instill a love of literature and great writers in our students. It was also important to me that our namesake was a woman, in the interests of equality and diversity. Our core values are independence, scholarship, aspiration, and resilience, and I think Jane Austen embodies those values."[11] Independence, scholarship, and aspiration seem a far cry from the late nineteenth-century study guides' and textbooks' quiet and placid clergyman's daughter version of Austen. It does, however, seem quite close to the suffragists' vision of her. That may suggest that Austen's reputation in schools and among educators is the arena in which she has most changed since the early twentieth century.

If Austen's educational credibility remains high, so does her political clout. She continues to be a lightning rod for debate, quoted and repurposed by people who may otherwise have few opinions in common. To name only the most notable of the recent past: When Austen's face was chosen for the British ten-pound note in 2013, it prompted Austen-related rape and death threats on Twitter, aimed at a feminist activist.[12] The US Supreme Court had what is believed to be its first-ever mention of Jane Austen in its proceedings, when *Pride and Prejudice* was cited in an opinion by the late justice Antonin Scalia, a Ronald Reagan appointee.[13] (Scalia's interest in Austen seems to have been linguistic.) In the summer of 2016, Hillary Clinton's daughter, Chelsea, delivered a speech at the Democratic National Convention in which she revealed that she had fond memories of watching *Pride and Prejudice* with her mother on movie nights.[14] Although the default political option now seems to be to imagine Austen as a liberal or a feminist, Tories and conservatives continue to question those who would claim the author for progressive causes, seeing Austen instead as one of their own.

As a result, I don't worry overmuch about Jane Austen's good reputation going forward. As to its going forward at all, all signs point to yes. I worry more about our ability to study it with the historical nuance and cultural scope it deserves. I worry about our ability to see her beyond the established critical voices and author-celebrities that we've so long cited and repeated. It's incredibly important that we not keep intoning the limiting stories about Austen, her fiction, and her cultural legacy ("She was hesitant to publish!" "Darcy became sexy in 1995!"). It's important that we stop quoting only the most expected, recycled supporting evidence ("Little bit [two-inches wide] of ivory," "Big bow-wow strain," etc.). Doing so means handing down flawed, partial stories to the next generation. Loving Jane Austen didn't once belong to the privileged few, only to be ruined by having been wrested away by partisan interests or the hoi polloi. The recognition of her greatness didn't begin or "surge" in 1870. There was an awful lot going on for Jane Austen and popular culture prior to the 1990s Austen boom, some of which even made that boom possible. It's only by considering more and better information, whether printed, visual, rare, or archival, that we recognize that Austen's mass popularity, political divisiveness, and high literary reputation aren't on some new collision course. If it is a collision course, it's a very old collision course.

As we've seen, Austen was so oft-staged and illustrated that Henry James worried that commercializing Austen had run amok by 1905. Suffragists marched through the streets of London with an Austen banner in 1908, witnessed by large crowds, in the same period that elite men in nearby private clubs were claiming an Austen who had no connection to politics. Today's Jane Austen societies have not stained her good character by introducing cosplay. People have been dressing up as Austen, on the stage and at society parties, for more than a century. None of these things destroyed her upmarket status. Every previous blow that Jane Austen's reputation has supposedly endured at the hands of popular audiences who would sully her has failed to rub her out. Reports of Jane Austen's posthumous death have been recurrently exaggerated.

But let's suppose I'm wrong, and history proves we're living in the very moment when Jane Austen jumps the shark. I'd have to count myself as part of the problem. As an Austen scholar who team-teaches a Jane Austen course at Arizona State University (with my Austen-scholar husband, a man I met over a conversation on Austen), and as a skater who's played roller derby under the name of Stone Cold Jane Austen, I'm one of those who contributes in my own little way to making her ridiculous.[15] This combination of experiences is preposterous, and I freely acknowledge it. It's absurd that one literary figure could enable and structure so many parts of an adult life, from work, to love, to hobby. It's also very unusual to end a book of argument and information with revelations about oneself. But doing so seems only honest and fair to readers who have come this far with me; I've spent much of this book marshalling literary, historical, and biographical evidence to make sense of Austen's legacy and little-known legacy makers—how their lives and choices may have shaped their productions and our visions of her. Jane Austen, in myriad ways, has made me, too. My sense of that no doubt shapes the questions I've brought to this study and the conclusions I've drawn and speculations I've made. As Austen's narrator in *Northanger Abbey* (1818) might say, let us not desert one another; we are an injured body. As common sense might say, physician, heal thyself.

But this isn't only personal. It's collective and historical. If past is prologue, no matter what questionable, odd, or innovative things any of us do in her name, Jane Austen's fiction will continue to be noticed, read, and valued beyond, or even because of, outliers and oddballs. What the history of Austen's legacy shows us is that, as long as her fiction morphs in meaningful ways from one fresh popular medium to the next—those very transformations that have been so repeatedly fretted over or decried by the guardians of high culture—she'll probably stick around. As long as cultural innovators and risk takers want to play with her novels and characters, that should breathe new life into her legacy. But rather than end this book with any truth universally acknowledged, I'll riff with this: I leave it to be settled by whomsoever it may concern, whether the tendency of this work be altogether to recommend haughty, highbrow exclusivity or celebrate uncritical adulation.

Afterword

The year 2017 was alive with Austen. To claim that all eyes turned to her on the two-hundredth anniversary of her death—July 18, 2017—is an exaggeration, sure, but it's not an outrageous one. Noticing her became a global phenomenon. *The Making of Jane Austen* was published just before the hoopla, although the final manuscript had been completed a gestationally appropriate nine months earlier. How lucky it now seems to me that the book's arrival coincided with her bicentenary and could play a part in reshaping understandings of her rise to cultural importance. It feels just as fortunate to have a chance, with the book's publication in paperback, to add a few words about Austen's legacy going forward.

It's useful to glance back before looking ahead. That's especially true in this case because we might actually follow Elizabeth Bennet's advice to Darcy in *Pride and Prejudice* and think only of the past as its remembrance gives us pleasure. The commemorations of Austen's two-hundredth were more joyful than somber. It was de rigueur to call her "Jane," especially while irreverently joining her name to verbs or rhyming adjectives. Gone were the once-popular familial nicknames (Aunt Jane) and massive honorifics (St. Jane, England's Jane, etc.). Her name was regularly invoked with a question mark or with the suggestion that she's a cipher. When celebrating her, money sometimes seemed no object. At other times, it *was* the object.

New Austen-inspired products launched, as commercial interests saw an opportunity, but there was also copious public art. What's believed to be the first life-sized statue of Austen was unveiled in Basingstoke in July 2017—a bronze, bonneted likeness with an estimated cost of £100,000. In Hampshire, artists designed twenty-four benches, in a public sculpture series called *Sitting with Jane*. There was *Rain Jane*, a trail of twelve Austen quotations in thirty-six locations around Winchester, created with paint that becomes visible on a wet surface. It was as if Austen had taken to the streets—or so I put it in an essay for the independent magazine *Big Issue North*. The magazine's cover featured Austen's portrait alongside Mary J. Blige, who was positioned with her head resting on the novelist's shoulder, under the headline "The Strength of Women." This, too, was a new version of the author, getting cozy with a hip-hop star. Austen's image on the cover of *The Big Issue*, which is sold by people who have limited other ways of earning an income, adds a further layer to the still-developing story of her affiliations and impact.[1]

She found indoor perches as well, with libraries on at least three continents mounting exhibitions, from the Bodleian Library's *Which Jane Austen?* in Oxford, to Winchester's *The Mysterious Jane Austen*, to a multimedia design and virtual reality exhibition, *Jane Austen: By a Lady*, at Monash University in Melbourne. The Chawton House Library presented its Austen alongside Germaine de Staël, the famous French-Swiss contemporary she would later eclipse, in the exhibition *Fickle Fortunes*. In the United States, the Folger Shakespeare Library had already shuttered its stunning *Will & Jane* exhibit from 2016, which co-commemorated Shakespeare and Austen. Timed more closely to his milestone moment than hers—the four-hundredth anniversary of his death—it served as a striking precursor for her bicentenary. Such a high-profile pairing with the mighty Shakespeare, more than anything, cast Austen's literary stature as beyond question.

Surely the pinnacle was when two versions of her face appeared on the Bank of England's £10 note and £2 coin. It was the culmination of a successful feminist campaign for the inclusion of a woman's face, other than the queen's, on English currency. The choice to feature Austen catapulted her into a new realm. Not only did she become the first woman writer featured on English money; she's now a daily face for millions, whether or not they've ever read, or seen, her stories. This was, and is, cultural saturation at an unprecedented level.

Once again, many wondered, "What does it all mean?" In trying to parse it out, we often returned to old fault lines, using new terms. The most visible debates were over Austen's politics and political implications today. As in the past, divergent claims emerged and clashed. Austen was outed as a doyenne of the alt-right *and* discovered to be a secret radical.[2] How are both views possible? Are we even reading the same books? Yet this stark contrast shouldn't surprise, because we've already seen how Austen has been claimed for diametrically opposed causes. Her popular appeal and critical acclaim make her well worth drafting onto any team. What we must ask of those who would enlist her on their side, then, is not only their motives but their evidence.

Even that is unlikely to settle things for good, however, because Austen's fiction is almost anti-dogmatic. Her novels, by design, open up complex questions, far more often than they provide pat answers. We could lament this difficult slipperiness, or seek to close it down by setting out to crack some imagined code, but we might instead see these ambiguities as an opportunity. Austen once quipped, in a private letter to her sister, "I do not write for such dull Elves / As have not a great deal of ingenuity themselves."[3] Many have read that line as her humorous condescension. They perceive in it the proud declaration that she writes only for a chosen few, whether out of discerning selectivity or gross snobbery.

But what if, instead, we see that line as her sign of confidence in us? We could envision it as Austen's putting her trust in readers to approach her writings using their own ingenuity. I much prefer that interpretation, which is why I also trust you to read this book with ingenuity. Problem-posing criticism presents solid information and invites tough questions; it seeks further discoveries. It doesn't have one preset conclusion that it's advancing. That's fitting, because there's so much more to ask, argue, and investigate where Austen is concerned. Many questions remain unsettled. Reading, making, and remaking Jane Austen may or may not support an individual's attempts to build a meaningful life in a world that's often deeply unfair. What attending to her words, and all they've inspired, absolutely does is serve as an antidote to becoming a dull elf.

Happily, this doesn't have to be the end of the road. Today's books need not be finite objects. We extend them with podcast conversations, book trailer videos, and web image galleries. This book has all of them. It's easy to overlook the notice about *The Making of Jane Austen*'s web-based gallery, because it's in small print on the copyright page, so I want to highlight it here. The website makingjaneausten.com includes many more images to illuminate each chapter and may serve to deepen your reading. There are also ways to share your thoughts and stay in touch. (Please do!) I continue to add to the gallery, while I'm completing a new book on Austen's once-famous, now-forgotten contemporaries, the sister-novelists Jane and Anna Maria Porter. For all of these reasons, I'd rather not close with a *"Finis."* As we reread Austen and continue to chronicle her spectacular afterlife, especially in the years leading up to 2025 and the 250th anniversary of her birth, surely the more suitable sign-off is *"To be continued."*

Portions of this book were revised from essays published previously. An earlier version of the Ferdinand Pickering material in chapter 1 appeared in "Jane Austen, Illustrated," in the *London Magazine: A Review of Literature and the Arts*, October/November 2015, 92–112. Parts of chapters 5 and 7 appeared in "Mr. Darcy through the Ages: In Early Portrayals of Jane Austen's Hero, He Wasn't Always Quite So Hot," in the *Independent* (London), 13 October 2015. Chapter 9 includes information previously published in "Jane Austen, Feminist Icon," *Los Angeles Review of Books*, 20 January 2014, and in "The Cult of *Pride and Prejudice* and Its Author," *Cambridge Companion to "Pride and Prejudice,"* ed. Janet Todd (Cambridge: Cambridge University Press, 2013), 174–85. I am grateful to the publishers for permission to include this work here in revised and expanded form.

This book could not have been written without the help of many libraries and generous librarians. First and foremost, I must thank Arizona State University Libraries, who informed me that I qualify as a "heavy user" of their services. They bore those heavy labors lightly, for which I am excessively grateful. This book also benefited from the materials and assistance of librarians at the Bodleian Library, Oxford; the British Library; Cambridge University Special Collections; Goucher College; Harry Ransom Center, University of Texas; Heinz Library, National Portrait Gallery; Huntington Library (especially Gayle Richardson); King's College, Cambridge Special Collections; Library of Congress, Manuscript Division, Margaret Herrick Library, Academy of the Motion Picture Arts; Morgan Library; New York Public Library; UCLA Special Collections; University of London Senate House Library; Victoria & Albert Theatre and Performance Archive; Syracuse University Special Collections; the University of Michigan; University of Virginia Special Collections;

Westminster Abbey Archives; and the Women's Library at the London School of Economics.

There are many people and organizations who made the research and writing of this book possible. The National Endowment of the Humanities supported my direction of a 2012 Summer Seminar for College and University Teachers at the University of Missouri (my former employer). Its sixteen seminar participants and the coordinator, Caitlin Kelly, as well as NEH program officer Barbara Ashbrook, encouraged new thinking about Austen at every turn. These colleagues energized and sustained me then and, what is even more amazing, continue to do so.

I had the pleasure of delivering some chapters in draft as invited lectures. I'm grateful to the organizers of these lectures and the perceptive comments and questions I received from audiences at the North American Society for the Study of Romanticism (Nick Mason and Andy Franta); Cardiff University and the British Association of Romantic Studies (Anthony Mandal and Jane Moore); Chawton House Library (Gillian Dow); the International Conference on Romanticism (Jared Richman and William Davis); California State University–Northridge (Danielle Spratt and Nazanin Keynejad); Lucy Cavendish College, Cambridge University (Janet Todd); Northern Arizona University (Donelle Ruwe; with thanks to James Leve for introducing me to the *First Impressions* soundtrack); Pomona College (Kevin Dettmar, Sarah Raff); Rice University (Judith Roof); Southern Methodist University (Rajani Sudan and Tom DiPiero); Tulane University (Ed White); University of Colorado–Boulder (Conny Cassity, Kurtis Hessel, Deven Parker, Grace Rexroth, and Rebecca Scheider); University of Indianapolis (Kyoko Amano and Jen Camden); University of Tennessee–Knoxville (Misty Anderson and Hilary Havens); Virginia Commonwealth University (Richard Godbeer and Catherine Ingrassia); and Wright State University (Crystal Lake, Hank Dahlman).

No writer can do her or his work without skilled, enthusiastic editors. I'm fortunate to have worked on Austen writing with some of the best, including Linda Bree, Greg Britton, Logan Browning, Tim Bullamore, Michael Caines, Lenika Cruz, Sarah Emsley, Emily Firetog, Sayre Greenfield, Claudia L. Johnson, Bob Markley, Stephen O'Brien, Thea Lenarduzzi, Tom Lutz, Kate Singer, Janet Todd, Linda Troost, and Clara Tuite. I am grateful to the two anonymous readers of the manuscript for helping to significantly reshape the book during revision. My greatest thanks must go to Matt McAdam of Johns Hopkins University Press, whose vision guided the direction of the book, crucially allowing for a more expansive project than I'd first conceived.

My affiliation with the Jane Austen Society of North America and its regional chapters has spanned two decades, and the friendships I have made through it are an incredible social sustenance and intellectual resource. I'm particularly grateful for Diana Birchall, Sheryl Craig, Lynda Hall, Liz Philosophos-Cooper, Kerri Spennicchia, Freydis Welland, and especially Deborah Yaffe. She helped me think about Janeites past and present in new ways. JAS UK's Maggie Lane and Chris Viveash provided invaluable assistance. Others whom I haven't even met gave generously of their time. Film critic Kenneth Turan answered queries about Harpo Marx and *Pride and Prejudice*. Hunt Stromberg Jr. scholar and biographer Sam Irvin did, too. Phalguni Shah helped generously with a translation.

Colleagues who offered support, resources, and feedback include Paula Backscheider, Annika Bautz, Antoinette Burton, Katharine Cockin, Jeffrey Cox, Alistair Duckworth, Margaret Ezell, Lisa Freeman, Michael Gamer, Anne Goldgar, Jocelyn Harris, Sonia Hofkosh, Terry Kelley, Tom Keymer, Nora Nachumi, Mary Ann O'Farrell, Claude Rawson, Al Rivero, Joe Roach, Peter Sabor, Clifford Siskin, Kristina Straub, Kathryn Sutherland, and Juliette Wells. An extra shout-out to Janine Barchas, who has been an inspiration and an enabler of this book and all things Jane. I will never tire of telling the story about that night she prevented me from going to a Regency Ball with my dress on inside out.

Colleagues and former graduate students at the University of Missouri—too many to name—are in these pages in ways large and small. You were there at the beginning of this work and helped me get it off the ground. A few had a direct impact that deserves mention: Karen Laird fostered, through her own fine work, an interest in dramatization, and Leigh Dillard and Stephanie Lotven did so for book illustration. Ruth Knezevich and Grace McNamee never fail to keep my Austen enthusiasm at a high pitch. More recently, I've benefited from the wisdom of Arizona State University colleagues, including Ron Broglio, Kalissa Hendrickson, Tara Ison, Mark Lussier, Kevin Sandler, Jacque Wernimont, and Eric Wertheimer. I thank the talented graduate students in the fall '13 Austen seminar and the amazing undergraduates in the hybrid Jane Austen course. I'm inspired and energized by the ASU Derby Devils. I regret not skating with you more often.

This book would not have made it to the finish line without the expert editorial advice, coaching, and friendship of Alexander Regier. When I try to reciprocate the gift that his labor has given me, it doesn't feel adequate, but it also doesn't feel like work.

Many people helped us with the raising of our sons during the writing of this book, especially the community of All Saints' Episcopal Day School. I made Jane Austen friends there, too, including the incomparable Teri Barnwell and JoAn Chun. Among others who gave so generously were Katinka Kersten and the Cheek family, the Cisneros-Wertheimers, Karen Feltz, Anna Gellert, my in-laws, Jack and Judy Justice, and my parents, Sharon and LeRoy Looser. You were our closest thing to three or four families in a country village, and we can't thank you enough.

I wrote parts of this book in my husband's hospital room at the Mayo Clinic. If readers are unable to tell which parts were written there, that's because of the incredible care he, and I, received from uniformly talented doctors and nurses. I consider our affiliation with the Mayo to be one of the most incredibly fortunate things to arise out of deep misfortune.

Our sons, Carl and Lowell Justice, tough critics both, consistently move me forward, despite their well-earned and burning hatred for all things Austen.

'Tis never easy to thank properly George Justice, my Jane Austen cosmic traveling partner, but fortunately, I'm already doing it.

Suggested Further Reading

One book cannot possibly do justice to describing Jane Austen's rise to celebrity, as all who have tried to tell it would join me to testify. We've had the benefit of wonderful books on Austen's textual lives, her cults and cultures, her readers, and her uses, on Jane's fame, everybody's Jane, Janeites, and why Jane Austen? We've seen ongoing contentious debates in scholarly venues and in the popular press over her letters, editions, and portraits and their provenance. The present book could not have been written without this accomplished body of scholarship, making sense of how Austen's life and works have been received (hence "reception studies") in the years since the 1810s.

No scholars or serious students of Austen could complete our research without the equivalent of our "bibles." For Austen's texts themselves, we quote from the most reliable, edited versions, the standard edition, now widely considered to be the *Cambridge Edition of the Works of Jane Austen*, under the general editorship of Janet Todd. There isn't an easily agreed upon standard biography, but my vote would be for Claire Tomalin's *Jane Austen: A Life* (1997). For a valuable account of Austen's life with a focus on her career as an author, Jan Fergus's *Jane Austen: A Literary Life* (1991) has not yet been surpassed. For the whole shebang of undigested biographical facts, we use Deirdre Le Faye's *A Chronology of Jane Austen and Her Family* (rev. ed., 2013) and *Jane Austen's Letters* (4th ed., 2011).

Personally, I also cannot live without concordances to Jane Austen—print and digital—to look up particular words and phrases across most (but unfortunately not all) of her writings. We would benefit from updated versions of these tools, combining the best print-born texts with the freely available digitized manuscripts at the *Jane Austen's Fiction Manuscripts* site. At the moment, most of us sift through combinations of jumbled results from multiple print and electronic sources, in order to search and consult the six published novels, juvenilia and early or unfinished fiction, miscellaneous writings, and surviving letters. I hope the future holds a freely available online resource that would include the ability to search the contents of all of her writings and letters at once. (An electronic version of the *Letters* is available by prohibitively expensive library subscription through Oxford Scholarly Editions.)

For the study of Austen's history as an author beyond the family, David Gilson's *A Bibliography of Jane Austen* (1997, rev. ed.) remains the gold standard. Gilson's decades of painstaking work, locating and describing thousands of print sources, is, for my money, every bit as important a contribution to Austen scholarship as the far more often lauded efforts of her famed twentieth-century textual editor, R. W. Chapman (1881–1960). Chapman is credited with creating the first standard edition of Austen's novels—sometimes described as the first standard edition of *any* English novelist—based on his collations of and annotations to the earliest texts. What Chapman was to establishing standards for presenting Austen's original writings to modern audiences, Gilson was to documenting republications of her work and writings about her. Chapman had himself published a 62-page critical bibliography of Austen (2nd ed., 1955), but Gilson's bibliography, at 877 pages, dwarfs it. He examines and catalogues seemingly every Austen-related object published up until 1975 or so. He describes with care the original editions, American editions, translations, later editions, minor works, letters, dramatizations (published), continuations and completions, books owned by Jane Austen, and biography and criticism on her. For digging into the critical history, Barry Roth's three volumes of annotated bibliographies of Jane Austen have one drawback—they cover only the period 1952–94. (Roth's work has been continued sporadically by others in *Persuasions On-line*.[1])

Early formative sources in laying the groundwork for our conversations about Austen's reception and legacy were edited collections of historical documents. These books offer direct evidence (usually in the form of excerpts) that allow us glimpses into the unfolding and establishment of her reputation. None of these collections looms larger than B. C. Southam's *Jane Austen: The Critical Heritage*, published in two volumes. Volume 1 compiles materials from 1811 to 1870 and volume 2 from 1870 to 1940. The influence of these books on Austen scholarship has been immense. The forty-five excerpts (more than three hundred pages) from Southam's volume 1 serve as urtexts for decades of critical arguments that followed. These excerpts are drawn largely from essays published in well-known magazines or from once-private commentary about Austen made by well-recognized literary figures. Southam's volume 2 includes forty-one later selections from similar types of material.

Southam's introduction to volume 2, at 158 pages, is like a book all its own. It has extensive documentation of Austen's reputation in that period, despite some inevitable blind spots and limitations. One is his focus on selecting excerpts from book-length works and prominent periodical essays. As a result, the *Critical Heritage* documents tend to showcase Austen from a high-culture vantage point. The Austen heritage that Southam assembles is most certainly a Heritage with a capital H. He deftly documents the origin and the flowering of Austen *criticism*, but he (intentionally) leaves aside most of the popular angles of Austen's reception. They come in for brief mention in his introduction, but they are implicitly made to sound ancillary, if not inconsequential.

The *Critical Heritage* volumes must be given their due. They helped establish reception studies, as Kathryn Sutherland points out in her obituary notice of

Southam: "Before digitisation of early newspapers and periodicals, such materials were inaccessible without good scholarly guides and anthologies. In providing these, [Southam's] Critical Heritage volumes helped to stimulate the fashion for reception studies and histories of reading still powerful today."[2] That's unquestionable true. But it's also true that we've come far beyond them and ought rightly to be further beyond them still. There's no longer a need to limit ourselves to quoting from the Austen excerpts and documents that Southam assembled. In fact, we now know that doing so constricts our picture of her complicated reception.

Primary source documents on Austen's reception continued to be published after Southam's *Critical Heritage* volumes. These collections further his work, although most of them hew rather close to what he provides, in offering an overwhelmingly critical scope. The most extensive collection is Ian Littlewood's *Jane Austen: Critical Assessments* (1998) in four volumes, with 187 excerpts organized by subject (e.g., biographical background, social background, intellectual background), by chronology (e.g., nineteenth-century response, twentieth-century response), and by single Austen text (*Pride and Prejudice, Lady Susan, Letters*, etc.). Littlewood made exceptionally good choices, and the volumes remain valuable.

Joan Klingel Ray's *Jane Austen's Popular and Critical Reception: A Documentary Volume* (vol. 365 of the *Dictionary of Literary Biography*, 2012) uses its contents to tell a story, with subheads declaring what the critical excerpts set out to narrate: "Jane Austen's Slow Rise in Popularity," "Answering the Demand for a Growing Interest in Jane Austen," and "Jane Austen Enters the Academy." The volume is heavily illustrated and includes "sidebar" discussions of the feature texts by the editor. The volume's main drawbacks are its prohibitive expense ($315) and the brevity of its excerpts, although offering a taste of many more sources is obviously the best editorial choice during an era when getting access to complete works, especially those out of copyright protection, has become more widely possible.

Books about Austen's reception have also helpfully paved the way to understanding the contours and scope of her posthumous fame. Lawrence W. Mazzeno's *Jane Austen: Two Centuries of Criticism* (2011) considers the documents in the sources above and more. He crafts a book about their meanings, describing how critical trends have shifted and how they might be grouped, in a way that is spot on. He calls his study one "intended to gaze at the gazers" of Austen. It helps readers grasp what he calls the "Great Austen Controversy," whether she's "a conservative or a radical."[3] If you want to understand the big-tent history of Jane Austen criticism, this is the book for you.

Claire Harman's *Jane's Fame* (2009) remains the best one-stop shopping for a chronological concatenation of Austen-afterlife details that includes some popular culture. Its drawbacks are that its story is told on a surface level, with little analysis to sink your teeth into. At 342 pages, its ostensible charge was to summarize two hundred years of "changing public tastes and critical practices."[4] It's a tall order, and the book delivers a breezy romp. Harman's thesis throughout is that there were two "big surges" of "Austen mania," the first in 1870, with the publication of her nephew's *Memoir of Jane Austen*, and the 1990s, with its film and

TV adaptations (7). It makes for a neatly packaged story, but it accords more with previous scholarship than with the facts. Harman does have a knack for an apt turn of phrase; her description of Austen as "an infinitely exploitable global brand" hits the nail on the head (3).

There have also been volumes devoted to Austen's reception through the lens of the history of the book—looking at the practices of publishers, editors, authors, and readers. These studies ask us to resituate Austen, not as a sui generis exception, above the fray, in a class by herself, whether in her own day and thereafter, but as an author working in a literary marketplace with many moving parts, on which she and her reputation depended. Such work, especially books by Annika Bautz (on Austen's reception in comparison with Scott's), Katie Halsey and Olivia Murphy (each with a book on Austen, reading, and readers), Anthony Mandal (on Austen's publishers and authorial practices), Kathryn Sutherland (on Austen's textual legacy), and the essay collection by Anthony Mandal and B. C. Southam (on Austen's reception in Europe), compel us to re-see the author in a widened textual and literary historical framework.

Kathryn Sutherland's *Jane Austen's Textual Lives* (2005) breaks new ground in its brilliant, careful attention to the construction and afterlife of Austen's texts, especially helping us understand the impact of R. W. Chapman's 1923 edition of Austen's novels. She also turns her careful eye to the formation of the Austen biography industry, to Austen descendants' role in forming her image, and to the print and film Austen adaptations, among other subjects. As the prime mover of the *Jane Austen's Fiction Manuscripts* website, Sutherland has also changed the face of Austen studies for the digital generation.

Single-volume treatments on Austen's legacy with distinct emphases have appeared. These include Juliette Wells's *Everybody's Jane* (2011), valuable for its work on Austen collectors, tourists, and print adaptations. In *Why Jane Austen?* (2011), Rachel Brownstein offers a multilayered teaching memoir, a study of the sexing-up of recent Austen adaptations, and a consideration of academic approaches to Austen. Her reprinting of a 1949 *New York Times* cartoon by Carl Rose, "The Two Camps of Jane Austen Devotees"—featuring a statue of Austen at its center, with a marching band on her left and a high-society receiving line on her right—is a terrific visual microcosm of Brownstein's revelations on the history of Austen's later celebrity.[5]

Emily Auerbach's *Searching for Jane Austen* (2004) was an early entrant to the field but made possible many of the studies above and remains valuable. Her introductory chapter comparing the images and portraits of Jane Austen with those of Emily Dickinson is superb. Auerbach considers Austen's writings and her legacy, asking us to "break free of dear Aunt Jane—and of two centuries of putdowns and touchups."[6] I hope that my own book's wallowing in such putdowns and touchups in more kinds of popular media gives us another way to "break free," in grasping more clearly what we've inherited and in clarifying how we might choose to re-see the present as a result.

The most recent major study of Austen's legacy, Claudia Johnson's *Jane Austen's Cults and Cultures* (2012), propels forward our re-seeing. Her book reorients us to consider anew many subjects, including Austen's portraits, the literal and metaphorical positioning of her as a ghost, the meanings of her writings in a posthumous tradition of fairy tales, her centrality to the reading practices of men in the World Wars, and the history of Austen worship and monuments. Johnson, more than anyone, has been a foundational force in the renewed study of what she calls "the deathlessly divine Austen," pondering "what loving her has meant to readers from the nineteenth century to the present."[7] No work on Austen's legacy would be possible without the benefit of her discoveries and analysis. I know mine certainly couldn't have proceeded, as Johnson's ideas influence in some way nearly every page of this book.

Essay collections, too, offer many scholars the chance to have a brief say on an aspect of Austen's legacy. Deidre Lynch's *Janeites* (2000), its fine introduction, and its many contributors give us ways to tease out "tension between alternative Austens" and to turn to the past, not in order to wallow in nostalgia but to "reactivate the past in ways that empower us to revise the future"—a goal my book shares.[8] Gillian Dow and Clare Hanson's *The Uses of Austen: Jane's Afterlives* (2012) describes Austen as a "crossover author, bridging high and low culture," noticing the pattern that "while male critics may be the first to publish 'appreciations' of Austen, it is women writers who publish creative responses and reworkings in their own fiction."[9] This is especially in the case of dramatic reworkings, as I show in chapters 4 and 5 of this book. If you want more information on Austen and dramatic adaptation before 1975, Andrew Wright's "Austen Adapted" remains the most complete source.[10]

Drama has been largely passed over in Austen studies, but text, film, and TV adaptation have not. Scholarship on Austen print adaptations, sequels, and continuations is featured in many of the collections named above, as well as in stand-alone essays. Readers may be surprised to learn that the first full-length, Austen-inspired mash-up novel, or fan fiction, is said to be Sybil G. Brinton's *Old Friends and New Fancies: An Imaginary Sequel to the Novels of Jane Austen*, believed first published in 1912–13.[11] Austen scholars have devoted more concerted attention to Austen's afterlife on screen, particularly after 1995. This scholarship includes Linda Troost and Sayre Greenfield's edited collection *Jane Austen in Hollywood* (1998), John Wiltshire's *Recreating Jane Austen* (2001), Sue Parrill's *Jane Austen on Film and Television* (2002), Gina and Andrew Macdonald's *Jane Austen on Screen* (2003), Suzanne Pucci and James Thompson's *Jane Austen and Co.: Remaking the Past in Contemporary Culture* (2003), Lisa Hopkins's *Relocating Shakespeare and Austen on Screen* (2009), David Monaghan's *The Cinematic Jane Austen* (2009), and many others. An impressive body of work on the subject of Austen adaptation has been published or edited by Deborah Cartmell and Imelda Whelehan.[12] Cartmell's *Screen Adaptations: Jane Austen's Pride and Prejudice: The Relationship between Text and Film* (2010) is an ideal first stop for the Austen-and-film curious.[13]

The most recent Austen legacy work moves into the realm of the web video and digital text adaptation, including Kylie Mirmohamadi's *The Digital Afterlives of Jane Austen: Janeites at the Keyboard* (2014), Gabrielle Malcolm's *Fan Phenomena:*

Jane Austen (2015), Hanne Birk and Marion Gymnich's *Pride and Prejudice 2.0: Interpretations, Adaptations and Transformations of Jane Austen's Classic* (2015), as well as a spate of essays on the Emmy-award winning online web series content of Pemberley Digital.

Individual essays on Austen's legacy are too numerous to name, but readers will find their influence and trace their contributions in the notes to the book. One important recent essay is that on the Folger Shakespeare Library's 2016 *Will & Jane* exhibit, by Janine Barchas and Kristina Straub. Their work situates William Shakespeare and Jane Austen's popular legacy in comparison and contrast.[14] For excellent critical content, some freely available, readers will want to consult the Jane Austen Society of North America's print and online journals, *Persuasions* and *Persuasions On-Line*. The *Jane Austen Society Report*, published annually since 1949, is not digitally available or free but is equally excellent and includes important essays on Austen's legacy. Scholarly websites and popular blogs devoted to Jane Austen deliver content that varies greatly in quality but that forwards our collective work on her reputation and legacy. Each of us will have a favorite site, but I'm grateful for *What Jane Saw, Republic of Pemberley, AustenProse, AustenBlog,* and *Molland's*.

This book appears in 2017, the two-hundredth anniversary of Jane Austen's death. That bicentenary year will no doubt produce a spate of new work, assessing her past, describing her present, and predicting her future. I look forward to documenting more of each in future research, as well as to providing images that enhance the reading of this book and the greater understanding of Austen's knotty legacy at www.makingjaneausten.com.

Introduction: Jane Austen Matters

1. Simone de Beauvoir, *The Second Sex*, trans. H. M. Parshley (New York: Knopf, 1953), 267. Subsequent references cited parenthetically in the text.

2. On celebrity, its emergence, and its history, see Joseph Roach, *It* (Ann Arbor: University of Michigan Press, 2007). A century after her death, Austen became a literary "It" girl.

3. I mention Austen's global resonances cursorily throughout this book, from the first illustrations of her fiction appearing in France in the 1820s, to the time, circa 1909, that a woman actor dressed as Jane Austen on a stage in South Africa and when a director sought to have one do so in Hungary. But the book's focus is principally on the British, one-time Commonwealth, and American receptions of Austen. It was in those places that Austen's legacy was most forcefully forged during her middle years. For further work on Austen's global reception, see Laurence Raw and Robert G. Dryden, eds., *Global Jane Austen: Pleasure, Passion, and Possessiveness in the Jane Austen Community* (New York: Palgrave Macmillan, 2013); Anthony Mandal and Brian Southam, eds. *The Reception of Jane Austen in Europe* (New York: Continuum, 2007); Gillian Dow, "Uses of Translation: The Global Jane Austen," in *Uses of Austen: Jane's Afterlives* (New York: Palgrave Macmillan, 2012), 154–74; and Susannah Fullerton, "Pride and Prejudice Goes Overseas: The Translations," in *Happily Ever After: Celebrating Jane Austen's Pride and Prejudice* (London: Frances Lincoln, 2013), 131–39. Future scholarly work on global Austen is needed and promises to shift conversations in further fruitful directions.

4. For the history of that familiarity and intimacy with authors, see Deidre Shauna Lynch, *Loving Literature* (Chicago: University of Chicago Press, 2015). As she puts it, the "logic of affect" among readers, literature, and its authors is "often perverse, aligning individuals and their desires in unexpected ways, or casting love as something that can collapse time and connect the living and the dead" (13).

5. Rudyard Kipling would later dub her "England's Jane" in his poem "Jane's Marriage." Rudyard Kipling, *Debits and Credits* (London: Macmillan, 1926), 170–71.

6. Jane Austen to James Edward Austen, 16–17 December 1816, in *Jane Austen's Letters*, ed. Deirdre Le Faye, 4th ed. (Oxford: Oxford University Press, 2011), 337. The tone is clearly playful in context: "By the bye, my dear Edward, I am quite concerned

for the loss your Mother mentions in her Letter; two Chapters & a half to be missing is monstrous! It is well that *I* have not been at Steventon lately, & therefore cannot be suspected of purloining them;—two strong twigs & a half towards a Nest of my own, would have been something.—I do not think however that any theft of that sort would be really very useful to me. What should I do with your strong, manly, spirited Sketches, full of variety & Glow?—How could I possibly join them on to the little bit (two Inches wide) of Ivory on which I work with so fine a Brush, as produces little effect after much labour?" (337).

7. Tony Tanner, *Jane Austen* (Cambridge, MA: Harvard University Press, 1986), 1.

8. David Cecil, foreword to *Jane Austen's Sir Charles Grandison*, ed. Brian Southam (Oxford: Clarendon, 1980), ix.

9. The author attributes the origin of the phrase for a Shakespearean Austen to Thomas Babington Macaulay. Albert Romer Frye, *Sobriquets and Nicknames* (Boston: Houghton, Mifflin, 1887), 319. Subsequent references cited parenthetically in the text. On Austen's relationship to Shakespeare, see John Wiltshire, *Recreating Jane Austen* (Cambridge: Cambridge University Press, 2001), 58–76. On Austen's uses of Shakespeare, see Jocelyn Harris, *Jane Austen's Art of Memory* (Cambridge: Cambridge University Press, 1989).

10. Fiona Ritchie, "Joanna Baillie: The Female Shakespeare," in *Women Making Shakespeare: Text, Reception and Performance*, ed. Gordon McMullan, Lena Cowen Orlin, and Virginia Mason Vaughan (London: Bloomsbury, 2014), 143.

11. J. J. English, "In Shakespeare's County," *Victorian Review* 4 (October 1881): 652. G. H. Lewes, partner of Eliot, suggested Austen was a female Shakespeare.

12. One critic—who found Shakespeare gross and wrongly proud of it—worried that a female Shakespeare might one day emerge to "defy decency" thanks to "emancipation." George Parsons Lathrop, "Audacity in Women Novelists," *North American Review* 150 (May 1890): 616. This phenomenon could also be traced through the "female Scotts," although that designation was significantly less often discussed.

13. On Richardson, see E. Cobham Brewer, *The Reader's Handbook of Allusions, References, Plots and Stories* (Philadelphia: J. P. Lippincott, 1880), 899. On Fielding, see Frye 319.

14. Goldwin Smith, *Lectures and Essays* (New York: Macmillan, 1881), 71. On Austen and Shakespeare, see Janine Barchas and Kristina Straub, "Curating *Will & Jane*," *Eighteenth-Century Life* 40, no. 2 (April 2016): 1–35.

15. James Edward Austen-Leigh was Jane Austen's nephew by her eldest brother, James Austen. Edward Knatchbull-Hugessen, Lord Brabourne, was the son of Jane Austen's favorite niece, Fanny Knight. Several other book-length works on Austen had joined these two titles by the end of the century, including Sarah Tytler's [Henrietta Keddie], *Jane Austen and Her Works* (1880), designed for young readers, Sarah Fanny Malden's *Jane Austen* (1889), Goldwin Smith's *Life of Jane Austen* (1890), and Oscar Fay Adams's *The Story of Jane Austen's Life* (1890), a precursor to the Hills' pilgrimage to Austen-Land. See J. E. Austen-Leigh, *A Memoir of Jane Austen and Other Family Recollections*, ed. Kathryn Sutherland (Oxford: Oxford University Press, 2002). Subsequent references cited parenthetically in the text.

16. Emily Auerbach, *Searching for Jane Austen* (Madison: University of Wisconsin Press, 2004), 7.

17. S. M. [Menella Bute Smedley], *The Maiden Aunt* (New York: D. Appleton, 1849), 1. The novel was first serialized in *Sharpe's Magazine* and then published in book form in London.

18. The author of the latter, Mrs. T. D. Crewdson, was indeed named Jane, but the point here is that the figure Aunt Jane circulated in popular culture. Elizabeth Warren, *Aunt Jane's Grammar: Question and Answer, for the Use of Schools and Families* (London: Charles Adeney, 1850). Mrs. T. D. [Jane] Crewdson, *Aunt Jane's Verses for Children*, 2nd ed. (London: Grant & Griffith, 1855). Prior to these books, there was also Christian Isobel Johnstone's collections of moral tales for children, *Nights of the Round Table; or, Stories of Aunt Jane and Her Friends*, 2 vols. (Edinburgh: John Johnstone, 1832).

19. The use of Jane Doe and Jane Roe as terms to describe an everywoman date back to the eighteenth century, although "Aunt" has a more indelicate slang history, as a euphemism either for bawd or madam or for going to the toilet.

20. Margaret Oliphant, "Miss Austen and Miss Mitford," *Blackwood's Edinburgh Magazine* 105 (1870): 41. For an excellent discussion of Oliphant's views on Austen and her review of Austen-Leigh's memoir, see Katie Halsey, *Jane Austen and Her Readers, 1786–1945* (London: Anthem, 2012), 176.

21. [Richard Simpson], review of *Memoir of Jane Austen*, by James Edward Austen-Leigh, *North British Review* 52 (April 1870): 152.

22. Reports had it that they were "engaged a long time" in completing the work, said to be "mainly" by Constance. "A Life of Jane Austen," *Walsall Advertiser*, 28 September 1901, 3.

23. Kathryn Sutherland, *Jane Austen's Textual Lives: From Aeschylus to Bollywood* (Oxford: Oxford University Press, 2005), 10.

24. Constance Hill, *Jane Austen: Her Homes and Her Friends* (London: John Lane, 1902), v. Subsequent references cited parenthetically in the text.

25. Chapter 1, titled "An Arrival in Austen-Land," closes with Ellen Hill's drawing of a road sign pointing to Austen-Land. The sketch and photograph showing the signpost are reproduced in Claudia L. Johnson's *Jane Austen: Cults and Cultures* (Chicago: University of Chicago Press, 2012), 74–75. Johnson's discussion of the Hills' text is groundbreaking. She argues that Austen is presented as magical and that Austen-Land may take its inspiration from *Alice in Wonderland*. It's a compelling reading. In this section, I'm taking the analysis of the text in a more historical, familial direction that I hope is compelling as well. From surviving sketches and photographic evidence, the Austen-Land sign appears to be based on an actual signpost that was there in Chawton, at the fork in the road, across from Austen's late-life home, at the turn of the century (Johnson 74).

26. There may be no wooden signpost today that reads "To Austen-Land," but there are now road signs near Chawton, England, directing motorists to Jane Austen's House Museum. There are markers for pedestrians, leading through what's now called the Jane Austen Heritage Trail. The Hill sisters themselves later played a determining part in establishing Austen signage. Constance Hill planned, fundraised, and memorialized the author with a plaque, designed by Ellen, in Chawton in 1917, the centenary of Austen's death.

27. As Claudia Johnson notes, the Hills' book was "sustained," "elaborate," and "influential" (69).

28. Those editions were published in 1904 and 1923. See David Gilson, *A Bibliography of Jane Austen*, rev. ed. (New Castle, DE: Oak Knoll Press, 1997), 512.

29. The Hills used their established narrative mix to produce books about places associated with other women authors including Frances Burney (*Juniper Hall: Rendezvous of Certain Illustrious Personages During the French Revolution, Including Alexander D'Arblay and Fanny Burney* [1904] and two other Burney-related titles), Mary Russell Mitford (*Mary Russell Mitford and Her Surroundings* [1920]), and Maria Edgeworth (*Maria Edgeworth and Her Circle: In the Days of Buonaparte and Bourbon* [1910]).

30. At the time, readers would have known that Jane wrote and Cassandra drew, although they would not yet have known their collaboratively authored and illustrated juvenile work, *The History of England*. Ellen, the artist, may even have been the first Austen-inspired sister. She depicted Austen's fictional characters in watercolor paintings exhibited in the 1880s. Ellen Hill exhibited a watercolor scene from *Emma*, "Going into Supper at the Crown." See "The Water Colour Institute," *Era*, 30 April 1887, 7. Three years earlier, she had exhibited "Catherine Morland at the Ball." See "The Dudley Gallery Art Society," *Standard*, 26 February 1884, 3.

31. Their book repeats the phrase "Aunt Jane" twenty times in the body of the text; the word "aunt" (not always to refer to Jane) appears some sixty times in the course of its 279 pages. By comparison, Austen-Leigh used the phrase "Aunt Jane" only seven times and "my aunt" seventeen times. Austen-Leigh seems to extend Austen's aunt-ness to a wider group (of relatives or perhaps of the public), referring once to "our own dear 'Aunt Jane' " (141).

32. The Hills removed this line from their book's second edition, for reasons unknown.

33. *Cornwall Artists Index Online*, n.d., s.v. "Ellen Gertrude Hill." When (Mary) Constance Hill died, she left an estate of £8,000. See Ancestry.com, *England & Wales, National Probate Calendar (Index of Wills and Administrations), 1858–1966* (database on-line) (Provo, UT: Ancestry.com Operations, 2010), s.v. "Mary Constance Hill," probate date 5 March 1929. Original data: Principal Probate Registry, *Calendar of the Grants of Probate and Letters of Administration made in the Probate Registries of the High Court of Justice in England* (London).

34. "Art. II: In Memoriam: Mrs. Frederic Hill," *Englishwoman's Review* 173 (5 October 1887): 437.

35. The Hills' family of origin mattered a great deal to how they presented Aunt Jane to readers as a relative and public servant. Their father was penal reformer, Frederic Hill (1803–95), whose autobiography Constance edited in 1893. He was inspector of prisons and general secretary of the General Post Office. See Frederic Hill, *Frederic Hill: An Autobiography of Fifty Years in Times of Reform*, ed. Constance Hill (London: Richard Bentley, 1893). Uncle Rowland Hill (1795–1879) invented the penny postage system. Previous critics have noted these connections. The Hills' unexplored female ancestors prove more crucial to understanding the sisters' attraction to and repackaging of "Aunt Jane" Austen. Their mother, Martha Cowper (Hill) (1803–91), published children's books that date almost back to Austen's era ("Art. II" 437).

Constance and Ellen Hill's paternal aunts were also involved in reform work in prisons, education, female emigration, and temperance. Rosamond Davenport Hill

(1825–1902) and Florence Davenport Hill (1828/29–1919) were joint author-memoirists and editors of *their* parents' lives and writings. See Deborah Sara Gorham, "Hill, Rosamond Davenport (1825–1902)," in *Oxford Dictionary of National Biography Online* (Oxford: Oxford University Press, 2004; online ed., May 2007). In the Hill family, "maiden aunts" *were* family writer-activists.

36. This book more often scrutinizes Austen's legacy for its impact on issues of gender difference. We would benefit from Austen legacy studies that focused principally on class, looking at the ways that her novels have been used to underwrite (and write underground) class difference. As James Thompson puts it, with cutting accuracy, representations and especially adaptations of Austen often "[turn] on the transcoding of class from brute exclusionary practice to class as elegance and grace, to class in a commodity culture." James Thompson, "How to Do Things with Jane Austen," in *Jane Austen and Co.: Remaking the Past on Contemporary Culture*, ed. Suzanne R. Pucci and James Thompson (Albany: State University of New York Press, 2003), 23.

The same might be said for the subject of Austen, race, and ethnicity—that her reputation rests on but doesn't highlight racial and ethnic exclusion. Not every one of Austen's characters is white, although her critically much-vaunted mixed-race ("half-mulatto") heiress, briefly featured in her unfinished last novel, *Sanditon* (1817), is little known among popular audiences. Jane Austen, *Later Manuscripts*, ed. Janet Todd and Linda Bree (Cambridge: Cambridge University Press, 2008), 202. The whiteness of Jane Austen's fiction has informed her scholarly and popular stature over two centuries. Although I touch on these implicit exclusions, they deserve more extended analysis in the growing Austen legacy studies corpus in a multiethnic and multinational framework.

Part 1 • *Jane Austen, Illustrated*

1. Only a dozen essays—some very brief—on Austen and book illustration make up what we've had to go on to make sense of the subject, with much of that work focusing on the 1890s heyday. See Annika Bautz, "'In Perfect Volume Form,' Price Sixpence': Illustrating *Pride and Prejudice* for a Late Victorian Mass-Market," in *Romantic Adaptations: Essays in Mediation and Remediation*, ed. Cian Duffy, Peter Howell, and Caroline Ruddell (Burlington, VT: Ashgate, 2013), 101–24; Laura Carroll and John Wiltshire, "Jane Austen, Illustrated," in *A Companion to Jane Austen*, ed. Claudia L. Johnson and Clara Tuite (Oxford: Wiley-Blackwell, 2009), 62–78; Maggie Hunt Cohn, "Illustrations for Jane Austen," in *The Jane Austen Companion*, ed. J. David Grey (New York: Macmillan, 1986), 219–22; David Gilson, "Later Publishing History, with Illustrations," in *Jane Austen in Context*, ed. Janet Todd (Cambridge: Cambridge University Press, 2005), 121–59; Katie Halsey, *Jane Austen and Her Readers, 1786–1945* (London: Anthem Press, 2012); Claire Harman, *Jane's Fame: How Jane Austen Conquered the World* (Edinburgh: Canongate, 2009); Joan Hassall, "Illustrating Jane Austen," in *The Jane Austen Companion*, ed. J. David Grey (New York: Macmillan, 1986), 215–18; Sarah M. Horowitz, "Picturing *Pride and Prejudice*: Reading Two Illustrations of the 1890s," *Persuasions On-Line* 34, no. 1 (2013): n.p., Web; Andrew Maunder, "Making Heritage and History: The 1894 Illustrated *Pride and Prejudice*," *Nineteenth-Century Studies* 20 (2006): 147–69; Emily L. Newman, "Illustrating Elizabeth Bennet and Mr Darcy: Jane Austen's Pride and Prejudice,"

Journal of Illustration 1, no. 2 (2014): 233–56. Jeffrey Nigro, "Visualizing Jane Austen and Jane Austen Visualizing," *Persuasions On-Line* 29, no. 1 (Winter 2008): n.p., Web; Keiko Parker, "Illustrating Jane Austen," *Persuasions* 11 (1989): 22–27; Nadežda Rumjanceva, "'And She Beheld a Striking Resemblance to Mr. Darcy': Nineteenth-Century Illustrations of Jane Austen's Pride and Prejudice," in *Pride and Prejudice 2.0: Interpretations, Adaptations and Transformations of Jane Austen's Classic*, ed. Hanne Birk and Marion Gymnich (Göttingen: Bonn University Press, 2015), 51–76; B. C. Southam, introduction to *Jane Austen: The Critical Heritage*, vol. 2, *1870–1940* (London: Routledge & Kegan Paul, 1987), 1–158; Kathryn Sutherland, *Jane Austen's Textual Lives: From Aeschylus to Bollywood* (Oxford: Oxford University Press, 2005); Chris Viveash, "Jane Austen—as You Desire Her," *Jane Austen Society Report for 2015* (2015): 44–49.

2. The relative lack of information on the history of Austen and book illustration is not mirrored in studies of other authors. Sir Walter Scott's pictorial legacy has enjoyed book-length treatment. See Richard Hill, *Picturing Scotland through the Waverley Novels: Walter Scott and the Origins of the Victorian Illustrated Novel* (Burlington, VT: Ashgate, 2010). Shakespeare studies benefit from several period-specific books of the subject. See, for instance, Stuart Sillars, *The Illustrated Shakespeare, 1709–1875* (Cambridge: Cambridge University Press, 2008). There is work considering Jane Austen and book *covers*. See Margaret C. Sullivan, *Jane Austen from Cover to Cover: 200 Years of Classic Covers* (Philadelphia: Quirk Books, 2014).

3. Sheila Kaye-Smith and G. B. Stern, *Talking of Jane Austen* (London: Cassell, 1943), 1. Subsequent references cited parenthetically in the text.

4. As J. Hillis Miller puts it, studying illustration is valuable because we look at "not just pictures and words separately, but the meanings and forces generated by their adjacency." J. Hillis Miller, *Illustration* (Cambridge, MA: Harvard University Press, 1992), 9. Hillis Miller points out that this kind of investigation might begin by taking seriously the captions that accompany images and the interplay of text and image in illustrated books, newspapers, and magazines.

5. David Gilson, *A Bibliography of Jane Austen*, rev. ed. (New Castle, DE: Oak Knoll Press, 1997). The illustrations that David Gilson's *Bibliography* catalogues appeared between 1823 and 1975, in at least 150 different editions, some of which were multivolume editions divided into as many as twelve separate books.

6. The *Database of Printed Illustrations to the Waverley Novels* contains just over 1,500 entries for British illustrations to Scott's prose fiction. See Peter Garside and Ruth M. McAdams, *Illustrating Scott: A Database of Printed Illustrations to the Waverley Novels, 1814–1901* (Edinburgh: University of Edinburgh, 2008–9), Web.

7. Most novels were believed destined for the circulating library, in volumes devoured once and returned. Books were expensive. For the few who could afford to buy them, works of fiction were rarely coveted as permanent additions to private libraries. On production, authorship, and circulation, see Peter Garside and Karen O'Brien, eds., *The Oxford History of the Novel in English*, vol. 2, *English and British Fiction 1750–1820* (Oxford: Oxford University Press, 2015), 3–69. See also Annika Bautz, *The Reception of Jane Austen and Sir Walter Scott* (London: Continuum, 2007), 89–91.

8. See Terri Doerksen, "Framing the Narrative: Illustration and Pictorial Prose in Burney and Radcliffe," in *Book Illustration in the Long Eighteenth Century: Reconfiguring the Visual Periphery of the Text*, ed. Christina Ionescu (Cambridge: Cambridge

Scholars Press, 2011), 466. A publisher making the work more appealing to buyers with an illustration didn't even necessarily provide any benefit to the author. The artists involved in illustrating *Evelina*'s fourth edition received more money for their work than Burney did for writing the novel itself, yet her publisher wrote to tell her that the engravings had been done as a compliment to the lady-author. George Justice, "Burney and the Literary Marketplace," in *The Cambridge Companion to Frances Burney*, ed. Peter Sabor (Cambridge: Cambridge University Press, 2007), 151.

9. For information on how much each novel made or lost, for each publisher or for Austen herself, see Jan Fergus, *Jane Austen: A Literary Life* (New York: St. Martin's, 1991); and Anthony Mandal, *Jane Austen and the Popular Novel: The Determined Author* (Basingstoke, UK: Palgrave Macmillan, 2007). Austen's literary earnings amounted to at least £1,625, but a great deal of that was paid out posthumously to her family-member executors (Mandal 184).

10. Richard Bentley was the copyright holder in Britain from 1833 onward. Bautz, *The Reception of Jane Austen and Walter Scott*, 79. On Continental illustrations of Austen, see Anthony Mandal and Brian Southam, *The Reception of Jane Austen in Europe* (London: Bloomsbury, 2007). A publisher might acquire the copyright to a work in exchange for a flat fee or under a number of potential financial terms, or the author might retain copyright and take on the financial risk of publication. (Austen published both ways.) Newly illustrated editions of a previously published title—legal ones, at any rate—were feasible with the copyright holder's initiative or support.

11. P., "Reputations Reconsidered: Jane Austen," *Academy* 53 (5 March 1898): 264.

12. Previous critics have often erroneously dated an explosion of interest in Austen's fiction to the publication of her nephew's biography of her, the first of its kind: James Edward Austen-Leigh's *Memoir of Jane Austen* (1870). But this claim simply doesn't hold up, as a recent critic points out, once we look at the history of Austen's singly published titles, in concert with the collected editions. According to Annika Bautz, "The evidence of single editions also suggests that the *Memoir* did not cause an instant upsurge of interest in Austen's novels . . . Editions . . . indicate that her popularity develops gradually, rather than being marked by turning points, so that the *Memoir* comes as part of an upward trend" (*The Reception of Jane Austen and Sir Walter Scott*, 81). Her recently collected data shows that a better indicator of Austen's gradually growing popularity might be (1) each title's release from copyright, (2) the period when all titles were finally available for reissue in collected editions, and (3) innovations in book production resulting in cheaper and better-quality books being printed and sold in new formats by century's end. The potential for illustration was determined by these factors, too.

13. Gilson, "Later Publishing" 123. On Chasselat, see Michael Bryan, *Dictionary of Painters and Engravers, Biographical and Critical*, ed. Robert Graves (London: George Bell, 1886), 1: 266. Gilson's essay discusses and reproduces a few of these Austen images in foreign editions in his chapter.

Chapter 1 • *Austen's First English Illustrator*

1. Anthony Mandal, *Jane Austen and the Popular Novel: The Determined Author* (Basingstoke: Palgrave Macmillan, 2007), 207. Subsequent references cited parenthetically in the text.

2. Mandal (208) records their succession as *Emma* (February), *Mansfield Park* (April), *Northanger Abbey and Persuasion* (May), and *Pride and Prejudice* (July).

3. B. C. Southam, *Jane Austen: The Critical Heritage* (London: Routledge, 1968), 1:21.

4. See David Gilson, "D. Editions Published by Richard Bentley," in *A Bibliography of Jane Austen*, rev. ed. (New Castle, DE: Oak Knoll Press, 1997), 209–34. Subsequent references cited parenthetically in the text.

5. Greatbatch is sometimes mistakenly rendered "Greatbach." See F. M. O'Donoghue, "Salter, William (bap. 1804, d. 1875)," rev. Morna O'Neill, in *Oxford Dictionary of National Biography Online Edition* (Oxford: Oxford University Press, 2004), Web.

6. Llewellynn Frederick William Jewitt, *The Ceramic Art of Great Britain* (London: J. S. Virtue, 1883), 396.

7. "Mr. Salter's Picture of the Waterloo Banquet," *Polytechnic Journal* 4 (June 1841): 387.

8. Maggie Hunt Cohn attributes them to "One 'Pickering'" in "Illustrations for Jane Austen," in *The Jane Austen Companion*, ed. J. David Grey (New York: Macmillan, 1986), 219. Subsequent references cited parenthetically in the text. The attributions to "probably George" Pickering originated with Gilson ("D. Editions" 213). David Gilson also refers to Bentley's Standard Novels Austen illustrations as by Greatbatch, "after, probably, George Pickering," in "Later Publishing History, with Illustrations," in *Jane Austen in Context*, ed. Janet Todd (Cambridge: Cambridge University Press, 2005), 121–59.

9. Albert Nicholson, "Pickering, George (1794–1857)," rev. Anne Pimlott Baker, in *Oxford Dictionary of National Biography Online Edition* (Oxford: Oxford University Press, 2004; online ed., May 2008), Web.

10. Laura Carroll and John Wiltshire mistakenly attribute the images outright to "George Pickering" in "Jane Austen, Illustrated," in *A Companion to Jane Austen*, ed. Claudia L. Johnson and Clara Tuite (Oxford: Wiley-Blackwell, 2009), 63. Subsequent references cited parenthetically in the text. So, too, does Emily L. Newman, noting that "not much is known" about him. Emily L. Newman, "Illustrating Elizabeth Bennet and Mr. Darcy," *Journal of Illustration* 1, no. 2 (2014): 236. Despite this received error, her essay is an excellent one.

11. My essay in the *London Magazine* first provided the information for the new attribution. See Devoney Looser, "Jane Austen, Illustrated," *London Magazine: A Review of Literature and the Arts*, October/November 2015, 92–112.

12. Records indicate Ferdinand's birth was November 21, 1810, and that he was baptized January 13, 1811. See London Metropolitan Archives, St Pancras Old Church, Camden, register of baptisms, including index, Jan 1810–Dec 1812, P90/PAN1/010.

13. To date, the only repository to make the correct attribution is the British Museum's *Collection Online*, for sixteen digitized frontispieces and vignettes attributed "After Ferdinand Pickering," including those for two of Bentley's Jane Austen novels. See British Museum, *Collection Online*, Web.

14. Cohn rightly points out that Cassandra Austen was Jane Austen's first illustrator (219), but here I refer to Pickering as Austen's first professional British illustrator in a print publication.

15. David Gilson, "Later Publishing History, with Illustrations," in *Jane Austen in Context*, ed. Janet Todd (Cambridge: Cambridge University Press, 2005), 127, 128.

16. Robert L. Patten, "Bentley, Richard (1794–1871)," in *Oxford Dictionary of National Biography Online Edition* (Oxford: Oxford University Press, 2004).

17. Royal A. Gettmann, *A Victorian Publisher: A Study of the Bentley Papers* (Cambridge: Cambridge University Press, 1960), 52–53.

18. For derivative American editions using Pickering, see Gilson, *Bibliography*, entries E21, E24 (246–47).

19. Kathryn Sutherland suggests that the Cranfordization phenomenon of the 1890s may have played a role in MGM's Victorian-costumed *Pride and Prejudice* (1940), another plausible origin story, in *Jane Austen's Textual Lives: From Aeschylus to Bollywood* (Oxford: Oxford University Press, 2005), 344. For an explanation of Cranfordization, see chapter 3 on the 1890s Austen illustration boom.

20. [Thomas Babington Macaulay], review of *Diary and Letters of Madame D'Arblay*, *Edinburgh Review* 76 (1 January 1843): 561.

21. Thomas Babington Macaulay, *The Letters of Thomas Babington Macaulay*, ed. Thomas Pinney, 3 vols. (Cambridge: Cambridge University Press, 1974), 2:253.

22. Christopher Wood, *The Dictionary of Victorian Painters*, 2nd ed. (Woodbridge, UK: Antique Collectors Club), 369. See also Algernon Graves, *The Royal Academy of Arts: A Complete Dictionary of Contributors and Their Work from Its Foundation in 1769 to 1904* (London: Henry Graves, 1906), 6:137.

23. Angus Easson and Margaret Brown, "The Letters of Charles Dickens: Supplement VII," *Dickensian* 103, no. 1 (2007): 38. Pickering's name and address were noted in Dickens's diary on March 10, 1838, leading some scholars to suspect that is when Pickering may have begun the portrait. As Easson and Brown write, "No portrait of CD by [Pickering] is known to exist" (39n3).

24. Charles Dickens to John Forster, 4 January 1839, in Madeline House, Graham Storey, and Kathleen Tillotson, eds., *The Letters of Charles Dickens*, vol. 1, *1820–1870*, 1st release, electronic ed. (Charlottesville, VA: InteLex Corp, 2001), n.p.

25. Richard Ormond, "Art Students through a Teacher's Eyes: The Royal Academy Schools in the 1860s," *Country Life*, 23 May 1968, 1348. Subsequent references cited parenthetically in the text.

26. On fifty years, see "The Registration Courts," *Morning Post*, 24 September 1885, 3.

27. David Robertson, "Cope, Charles West (1811–1890)," in *Oxford Dictionary of National Biography Online Edition* (Oxford: Oxford University Press, 2004).

28. "Bigamy," *Hampshire Chronicle*, 15 June 1867, 7.

29. "Charge of Bigamy," *London Standard*, 27 May 1867, 7.

30. William de Morgan, *Alice-for-Short: A Dichronism* (London: Heinemann, 1907), 118. Subsequent references cited parenthetically in the text.

31. J. Hillis Miller, *Illustration* (Cambridge, MA: Harvard University Press, 1992), 61.

Chapter 2 • *Visual Austen Experiments*

1. This situation is changing as emerging scholarship on Austen and her illustrations—and generous Janeites in their blog postings—share digital images. See also Margaret C. Sullivan, *Jane Austen from Cover to Cover: 200 Years of Classic Covers* (Philadelphia: Quirk Books, 2014).

2. David Gilson, "Later Publishing History, with Illustrations," in *Jane Austen in Context*, ed. Janet Todd (Cambridge: Cambridge University Press, 2005), 130. Subsequent references cited parenthetically in the text.

3. Katie Halsey, *Jane Austen and Her Readers, 1786–1945* (London: Anthem Press, 2012), 111. David Gilson, *A Bibliography of Jane Austen*, rev. ed. (New Castle, DE: Oak Knoll Press, 1997), 241. Subsequent references cited parenthetically in the text.

4. Michael Sadleir, "Yellow-Backs," in *New Paths in Book Collecting: Essays by Various Hands*, ed. John Carter (London: Constable, 1934), 133.

5. On noted, see Gilson, *Bibliography* 244. On Shakespeare, see Paul Goldman, "John Gilbert as a Book Illustrator: Master of Historical Romance," in *Sir John Gilbert: Art and Imagination in the Victorian Age*, ed. Spike Bucklow and Sally Woodcock (Farnham, UK: Lund Humphries, 2011), 92.

6. Gilbert became president of the Old Watercolour Society. See Lisa Small, "Gilbert, Sir John (1817–1897)," in *Oxford Dictionary of National Biography Online* (Oxford: Oxford University Press, 2004), Web. Stuart Sillars includes discussion of Gilbert in his *The Illustrated Shakespeare, 1709–1875* (Cambridge: Cambridge University Press, 2008), 289–91. Sillars suggests Gilbert brought "immediacy" and "vigor" to Shakespeare through his illustrations, descriptors that it is difficult to apply to his Austen image (323).

7. It was in a poem dedicated to a rival Austen illustrator. See Austin Dobson, "To Hugh Thomson (with a Copy of Sir John Gilbert's Shakespeare)," in *The Complete Poetical Works of Austin Dobson* (London: Oxford University Press, 1923), 442.

8. Paul Goldman, "John Gilbert as a Book Illustrator: Master of Historical Romance," in *Sir John Gilbert: Art and Imagination in the Victorian Age*, ed. Spike Bucklow and Sally Woodcock (Farnham, UK: Lund Humphries, 2011), 95.

9. Timothy Wilcox, "'He Kinged It There among the Nigglers': Sir John Gilbert and the Royal Watercolour Society," in Bucklow and Woodcock, *Sir John Gilbert*, 129.

10. Sullivan includes this image, along with other Austen yellowback covers, in *Jane Austen: Cover to Cover* (24).

11. Deirdre Gilbert, "From Cover to Cover: Packaging Jane Austen from Egerton to Kindle," *Persuasions On-Line* 29, no. 1 (2008): n.p., Web. Subsequent references cited parenthetically in the text.

12. Lydon, although less renowned than his mentor Fawcett, comes down to us with a reputation for being "a man of great industry, skill and sterling high character," whose talents are credited with establishing the "house style" for which Fawcett's engravings became known. Lydon had "joined Fawcett as an apprentice wood-engraver" in 1854, but he would move fully into drawing, completing work on which Fawcett's famed engravings are based. Qtd. in Ruari McLean and Antonia McLean, *Benjamin Fawcett: Engraver and Colour Printer* (Aldershot, UK: Scolar Press, 1988), 58; 36.

13. [Anna Cabot Lowell Quincy], "Jane Austen," *Atlantic Monthly* 11 (February 1863): 236. Quincy's essay was reprinted, among other places, in Goldwin Smith, *Life of Jane Austen* (London: Walter Scott, 1890), 140. The anecdote she describes is said to have included among its participating men Thomas Babington Macaulay and Arthur Hallam. The story was still circulating in the 1920s.

14. Logan Pearsall Smith, *Reperusals and Recollections* (London: Constable, 1936), 366.

15. *Northanger Abbey* is a novel title that Austen may not have had a hand in choosing, as it was published posthumously. We know that an earlier version of the work was initially sold to a publisher (who then did not publish it after all) as *Susan* in 1803.

16. "Presentation to Mr. A. F. Lydon at Driffield," *Driffield Times*, 25 August 1883, 2.

17. "New Books," *Driffield Times*, 21 January 1871, 2.

18. A.F.L. [Lydon], *Fairy Mary's Dream* (London: Groombridge and Sons, 1870), n.p.

19. Qtd. in McLean and McLean 22.

20. See Annika Bautz, "'In Perfect Volume Form, Price Sixpence': Illustrating *Pride and Prejudice* for a Late Victorian Mass-Market," in *Romantic Adaptations: Essays in Mediation and Remediation*, ed. Cian Duffy, Peter Howell, and Caroline Ruddell (Burlington, VT: Ashgate, 2013), 101–24. Subsequent references cited parenthetically in the text. See also Emily L. Newman, "Illustrating Elizabeth Bennet and Mr. Darcy," *Journal of Illustration* 1, no. 2 (2014): 243.

21. Bautz 111. In the United States, *Harper's Franklin Square Library* (although unillustrated), functioned similarly to *Dick's* and included two of Austen's novels (*Pride and Prejudice* and *Sense and Sensibility*) in its cheap reprint series, starting in 1880. These novels were sold in paper covers, unbound, at a price of fifteen cents.

22. Janine Barchas, "Sense, Sensibility, and Soap: An Unexpected Case Study in Digital Resources for Book History," *Book History* 16 (2013): 185–214.

Chapter 3 • *A Golden Age for Illustrated Austen*

1. Susannah Fullerton, "Illustrating and Covering *Pride and Prejudice*," in *Happily Ever After: Celebrating Jane Austen's Pride and Prejudice* (London: Frances Lincoln, 2013), 143.

2. Illustrators of Austen-inspired graphic novels must have surpassed Thomson, which is why the word "traditional" is invoked here.

3. On first and second golden age, see Lorraine Janzen Kooistra, *Christina Rossetti and Illustration: A Publishing History* (Athens: Ohio University Press, 2002), 56.

4. It is difficult to tell whether Austen's illustrators were leading the charge or reflecting and repeating others' gradually changing conceptions of her and her fiction. Regardless, their illustrations had the potential to reach and potentially influence many more reader-viewers.

5. Olivia Fitzpatrick and Debby Shorley, *Illustrated by Hugh Thomson, 1860–1920: A Library Exhibition* (Belfast: University of Ulster at Belfast, 1989), n.p. Subsequent references cited parenthetically in the text.

6. "For girls we can conceive of no better gift than the new edition of Jane Austen's *Pride and Prejudice*." "The Gift Books of the Year: A Brief Survey," *Review of Reviews*, 14 December 1895, 558.

7. "Messrs. Dent's Christmas List: A Selection," *Athenaeum* 3868 (14 December 1901): 821.

8. Henry James, *The Question of Our Speech: The Lesson of Balzac; Two Lectures* (Boston: Houghton, Mifflin, 1905), 61–62. James's essay was first published in the *Atlantic Monthly*.

9. David Gilson, "Later Publishing History, with Illustrations," in *Jane Austen in Context*, ed. Janet Todd (Cambridge: Cambridge University Press, 2005), 138. Subsequent references cited parenthetically in the text.

10. Claudia L. Johnson, "Austen Cults and Cultures," in *The Cambridge Companion to Jane Austen*, ed. Edward Copeland and Juliet McMaster, 2nd ed. (Cambridge: Cambridge University Press, 2011), 232.

11. Hairstyles proved difficult for illustrators to render with historical accuracy. See Joan Hassall, "Illustrating Jane Austen," in *The Jane Austen Companion*, ed. J. David Grey (New York: Macmillan, 1986), 215–18. Hassall was the Austen illustrator daughter of another Austen illustrator, John Hassall, discussed in chapter 8.

12. "The New Books: Recent American and English Publications," *Review of Reviews* 10 (December 1894): 697.

13. Olivia Fitzpatrick, "Thomson, Hugh (1860–1920)," in *Oxford Dictionary of National Biography Online* (Oxford: Oxford University Press, 2004), Web.

14. Harry G. Aldis, rev. John Carter and E. A. Crutchley, "Book Illustration," in *Reader in the History of Books and Printing*, ed. Paul A. Winckler (Englewood, CO: Indian Head, 1978), 122.

15. Patrick Spedding counts sixteen titles in Macmillan's New Cranford Series and forty in its Illustrated Standard Novels in "Macmillan's New Cranford Series and Illustrated Standard Novels," *Research Notes / Informal Writing* (blog), 7 July 2011.

16. Jane Austen, *Pride and Prejudice* (London: George Allen, 1894), 89. Subsequent references cited parenthetically in the text.

17. Fitzpatrick and Shorley n.p.

18. Kathryn Sutherland, *Jane Austen's Textual Lives: From Aeschylus to Bollywood* (Oxford: Oxford University Press, 2005), 9. Subsequent references cited parenthetically in the text as *Jane Austen*.

19. Michael Felmingham, *The Illustrated Gift Book 1880–1930* (Aldershot, UK: Scolar Press, 1988), 40.

20. M. H. Spielmann and Walter Jerrold, *Hugh Thomson: His Art, His Letters, His Humour, and His Charm* (London: A. C. Black, 1931), 86. Subsequent references cited parenthetically in the text.

21. Hugh Thomson to Macmillan & Co., 28 March 1891, British Library Western Manuscripts, Add MS 55231, f. 120.

22. Hugh Thomson to Macmillan & Co., 18 December 1891, British Library Western Manuscripts, Add MS 55231, f. 122.

23. Memorandum of agreement between Hugh Thomson to Macmillan & Co., 1 December 1893, British Library Western Manuscripts, Add MS 55231, f. 125. Macmillan agreed to give him three pence per copy for every one sold over ten thousand in British dominions and one penny per copy in America. There is a letter, too, suggesting that Macmillan may have wanted to purchase Thomson's *Pride and Prejudice* illustrations from George Allen but that there was no willingness to sell. See Hugh Thomson to Macmillan & Co., 8 March 1894, British Library Western Manuscripts, Add MS 55231, f. 126. In 1903, Thomson agreed to lower his royalty rate to two from three pence, due to a lowering of prices in the Illustrated Standard Novels Series. Hugh Thomson to Macmillan & Co., 1 October 1903, British Library Western Manuscripts, Add MS 55231, f. 141.

24. Hugh Thomson to Macmillan & Co., 15 August 1912, British Library Western Manuscripts, Add MS 55231, f. 179.

25. Hugh Thomson to Macmillan & Co., 24 March 1915, British Library Western Manuscripts, Add MS 55231, f. 195.

26. For Macmillan's gift to Thomson of an unspecified large sum of money, see Hugh Thomson to Macmillan & Co., 18 December 1917, British Library Western Manuscripts, Add MS 55231, f. 198. On the letter about the publisher's supporting his receiving a pension, see Hugh Thomson to Macmillan & Co., 15 May 1918, British Library Western Manuscripts, Add MS 55231, f. 200.

27. This fact is revealed in a letter from Thomson's wife. Jessie Thomson to Macmillan & Co., 12 July 1920, British Library Western Manuscripts, Add MS 55231, f. 243. His biographers mentions the death but not the debt. Spielmann and Jerrold 85–86.

28. E. M. Forster, "Jane, How Shall We Ever Recollect?" *New Republic* (30 January 1924): n.p., Web. Subsequent references cited parenthetically in the text.

29. Kathryn Sutherland, "Jane Austen on Screen," in Copeland and McMaster, *Cambridge Companion*, 219. She notes his illustrations were "visually influential far into the twentieth century." They remain influential today.

30. Johnson 232. In her book *Jane Austen: Cults and Cultures* (Chicago: University of Chicago Press, 2012), she revises her assessment down to "lavishly" and omits "inane" (68).

31. Claire Harman, *Jane's Fame: How Jane Austen Conquered the World* (Edinburgh: Canongate, 2009), 160.

32. For a precise accounting of these Brock illustrations and Austen editions, using Gilson's bibliography, see Cinthia García Soria, "Austen Illustrators Henry and Charles Brock," *Mollands Circulating Library*, accessed 21 April 2016, http://www.mollands.net/etexts/other/brocks.html.

33. C. M. Kelly, *The Brocks: A Family of Cambridge Artists and Illustrators* (London: Charles Skilton, 1975), 52–57. Subsequent references cited parenthetically in the text.

34. Sarah M. Horowitz, "Picturing *Pride and Prejudice*: Reading Two Illustrations of the 1890s," *Persuasions On-Line* 34, no. 1 (2013), n.p., Web.

35. On "Hammond, Christopher," see Harman 334. On Hammond as influenced by the Brocks, see Simon Houfe, *The Dictionary of 19th Century Book Illustrators and Caricaturists* (Suffolk: Antiques Collectors Club, 1996), 166.

36. Alfred Forman, "Chris Hammond: In Memoriam," *Argosy*, July 1900, 346. Subsequent references cited parenthetically in the text as "Chris."

37. Alfred Forman, "The Late Chris. Hammond," *Sketch*, 23 May 1900, 194. Subsequent references cited in the text as "The Late."

38. Jane Austen, *Emma*, with an introduction by Joseph Jacobs and illustrations by Chris Hammond (London: George Allen, 1898), 138.

39. Jane Austen, *Sense and Sensibility*, with an introduction by Joseph Jacobs and illustrations by Chris Hammond (London: George Allen, 1899), 65.

40. Jane Austen, *Persuasion*, ed. Janet Todd and Antje Blank (Cambridge: Cambridge University Press, 2006), 73.

41. [H. C. Beeching], *Pages from a Private Diary* (London: Smith, Elder, 1898), 110. Subsequent references cited parenthetically in the text. Beeching envisions Austen's receiving illustrated treatment in the periodicals of the 1860s, where many Victorian fiction greats were first serialized.

42. As Gilson notes, this edition was republished in 1925 by George Harrap, "identical with the original issue." David Gilson, *A Bibliography of Jane Austen*, rev.

ed. (New Castle, DE: Oak Knoll Press, 1997), 285. Subsequent references cited parenthetically in the text. What constituted "complete" in this era had also become subject to debate, as Austen's letters, some recently released juvenilia pieces, and the unfinished novels were sometimes touted as necessary for "completeness."

43. "Noteworthy Fall Books," *Dial* 45 (1908): 99. The ad also suggests the Chatto & Windus edition is the only "complete set" with "colored illustrations" in a "convenient size."

44. Jane Austen, *The Novels of Jane Austen in Ten Volumes*, vol. 9, *Mansfield Park* (London: Chatto & Windus, 1909), 212.

45. Skrenda's little fame at the time rested on his editions of *Minute Stories of the Bible* (1932) and *Minute Wonders of the World* (1933), also published by Grosset and Dunlap. Skrenda was an American, based in New York for much of his life, having served in both world wars, in World War I as a seaman and as a painter. In his 1942 World War II enlistment record, he declared himself single and without dependents, listing his profession as commercial artist. See National Archives and Records Administration, *U.S. World War II Army Enlistment Records, 1938–1946* (database online), s.v. "Alfred G. Skrenda," 6 August 1942 (Provo, UT: Ancestry.com Operations, 2005).

46. F. Maurice Speed, *Movie Cavalcade: The Story of the Cinema—Its Stars, Studios, and Producers* (London: Raven Books, 1944). Paul Monaco, *A History of American Movies: A Film-by-Film Look at the Art, Craft, and Business of Cinema* (Lanham, MD: Scarecrow Press, 2010), 141.

47. Deirdre Gilbert, "From Cover to Cover: Packaging Jane Austen from Egerton to Kindle," *Persuasions On-Line* 29, no. 1 (Winter 2008): n.p., Web.

48. Arnie Davis, *Photoplay Editions and Other Movie Tie-In Books: The Golden Years; 1912–1969* (East Waterboro, ME: Mainely Books, 2002), 182–83.

49. Emily L. Newman, "Illustrating Elizabeth Bennet and Mr. Darcy," *Journal of Illustration* 1, no. 2 (2014): 236.

50. Jane Austen, *Pride and Prejudice*, shortened version prepared by H. Oldfield Box (London: Hodder and Stoughton, 1951). Box made a radio version for the BBC Home Service, which aired in parts from May 28 to August 13, 1950 (Gilson, *Bibliography* 328). Box prepared many classic novels in this format, including titles by Charlotte Brontë and Anthony Trollope, and also produced a 1948 radio dramatization of *Emma*.

Part 2 • Jane Austen, Dramatized

1. A. B. Walkley, "The Drama: *The Bennets*," *Literature*, 6 April 1901, 261.

2. Claire Harman devotes one page to dramatization in *Jane's Fame: How Jane Austen Conquered the World* (Edinburgh: Canongate, 2009), 214. B. C. Southam's *Jane Austen: The Critical Heritage*, vol. 2, *1870–1940* (London: Routledge & Kegan Paul, 1987) doesn't mention them. Juliette Wells considers them briefly through collector Alberta Burke's scrapbooks of Austeniana on radio, stage, and film in *Everybody's Jane: Austen in the Popular Imagination* (London: Continuum, 2011), 47–51. The most extensive discussions are Chris Viveash on Rosina Filippi in "The Bennets on Stage," in *Jane Austen Society: Collected Reports, 2001–2005* (2003): 243–48; and Andrew Wright, "Jane Austen Adapted," *Nineteenth-Century Fiction* 30, no. 3 (December 1975): 421–53. Wright published this material in slightly different, shortened form in "Dramatizations of the Novel," in *The Jane Austen Companion*, ed. J. David Grey (New

York: Macmillan, 1986), 120–30. More typical is Marc DiPaolo's *Emma Adapted: Jane Austen's Heroine from Book to Film* (New York: Peter Lang, 2007), which leaves dramatization (but not television) out of its equation of "from book to film."

3. At first, it was not a happy financial event. MGM's *Pride and Prejudice* proved a moderate success with audiences but, because of its high production costs, incurred an initial loss of $241,000. See H. Mark Glancy, *When Hollywood Loved Britain: The Hollywood "British" Film 1939–45* (Manchester: Manchester University Press, 1999), 89.

4. Sue Birtwistle and Susie Conklin, *The Making of Pride and Prejudice* (London: Penguin, 1995), 98.

5. A few previous critics have recognized the play's influence, even if they haven't approved its plot choices. Emily Auerbach argues, for instance, that Jerome's "distorted approach to Austen," through Huxley and Murfin's screenplay, "reached an enormous audience." Emily Auerbach, *Searching for Jane Austen* (Madison: University of Wisconsin Press, 2004), 278.

6. Robert Grey, "The Scotch and the Drama," *Green Book Album* 3 (1910): 1260.

7. Ann Rigney, *The Afterlives of Walter Scott: Memory on the Move* (Oxford: Oxford University Press, 2012), 95.

8. H. Philip Bolton, *Women Writers Dramatized: A Calendar of Performances from Narrative Works Published in English to 1900* (London: Mansell, 2000), 75. Subsequent references cited parenthetically in the text.

9. Bolton used data from the United States and the UK only. See also Karen E. Laird, *The Art of Adapting Victorian Literature: Dramatizing "Jane Eyre," "David Copperfield," and "The Woman in White"* (New York: Routledge, 2015).

10. Catherine Hamilton, *Women Writers: Their Works and Ways*, 1st ser. (London: Ward, Lock, Bowden, 1892), 194–95. On Hamilton, see Brian Corman, *Women Novelists before Jane Austen: The Critics and Their Canons* (Toronto: University of Toronto Press, 2008).

11. George Saintsbury, preface to *Pride and Prejudice*, by Jane Austen (Mineola, NY: Dover, 2005), xi–xii.

12. David Gilson, *A Bibliography of Jane Austen*, rev. ed. (New Castle, DE: Oak Knoll, 1997), 403–18. Subsequent references cited parenthetically in the text. With so much material to work with, you'd think that there would be a significant body of scholarship on the subject. Yet, despite their popularity with audiences, stage versions of Austen have not always been considered a welcome innovation by critics. The plays are usually declared disappointments in studies of Austen.

13. The few who have approached the subject of Austen dramatization have set out to summarize the plays in order to measure their fidelity to the original novels. Most decide, with David Gilson, that "the texts read uniformly badly" (*Bibliography*, 405). As the foremost scholar of Austen dramatization, Andrew Wright, put it in a 1975 essay, these dramatizations prove "the all too easily demonstrable fact that no one writes Jane Austen as well as Jane Austen." Andrew Wright, "Jane Austen Adapted," *Nineteenth-Century Fiction* 30, no. 3 (1975): 423. Wright acknowledges, however, that "dramatization can make her novels more widely known" (420).

14. B. C. Southam, introduction to *Jane Austen's Sir Charles Grandison*, ed. B. C. Southam (Oxford: Clarendon, 1980), 8. Subsequent reference cited parenthetically in the text.

15. Joseph Roach, "Bodies of Doctrine: Headshots, Jane Austen, and the Black Indians of Mardi Gras," *Choreographing History*. Ed. Susan Leigh Foster (Bloomington: Indiana University Press, 1995), 150.

16. Rosina Filippi, *Duologues and Scenes from the Novels of Jane Austen: Arranged and Adapted for Drawing-Room Performance* (London: J. M. Dent, 1895), viii. Subsequent references cited parenthetically in the text to this edition.

Chapter 4 • Austen's First Dramatist

1. Reading novels aloud also has a long history apart from the stage. See Patricia Michaelson, *Speaking Volumes: Women, Reading, and Speech in the Age of Austen* (Palo Alto, CA: Stanford University Press, 2002).

2. Some bibliographies list an American version of *Pride and Prejudice* published in 1895. Davis Risdon's *Pride and Prejudice* (1895) was a Western melodrama set in Louisville that owes nothing to Austen's story. If Risdon's title is making a sly reference to Austen, it is doing so without any connection to the novel's contents. See Davis Risdon, *Pride and Prejudice: An Original Drama in Prologue and Four Acts* (Gallup, NM: Gleaner, 1895).

3. Laurence Irving, *The Successors* (London: Rupert Hart-Davis, 1967), 69.

4. "Literary Topics in Boston: Boston, December 20, 1894," *Book Buyer* 11 (January 1895): 737. Subsequent references cited parenthetically in the text.

5. See, for instance, W. Eliot Fette, *Dialogues from Dickens for School and Home Amusement*, 3rd ed. (Boston: Lee and Shepard, 1874; originally published in 1869). See also H. Philip Bolton, *Dickens Dramatized* (London: Mansell, 1987).

6. Rosina Filippi, *Duologues and Scenes from the Novels of Jane Austen: Arranged and Adapted for Drawing-Room Performance* (London: J. M. Dent, 1895), vii. Subsequent references cited parenthetically in the text.

7. "Jane Austen Dramatized," *Times* (London), 24 May 1895, 13.

8. Mary Jane Phillips-Matz, *Puccini: A Biography* (Boston: Northeastern University Press, 2002), 31, 32. On Verdi and Wagner, see Gundula Kreuzer, *Verdi and the Germans: From Unification to the Third Reich* (Cambridge: Cambridge University Press, 2010), 112.

9. Per Ahlander, "Madame Pauline Vaneri Filippi—an Anglo-Scottish-French-Italian Revolutionary?," unpublished paper, *Academia.edu*. On the Filippis, see G. Gasparella, "Un critico d'arte e musica: Filippo Filippi," *La Rassegna Nationale* 120 (1901): 300–34.

10. "Jane Austen for the Stage," *Sketch* 9 (1895): 709. Madame Colmache was the avowed editor of her late husband's papers, published by Henry Colburn. It's possible she was more than an editor. See M. Colmache, *Revelations of the Life of Prince Talleyrand*, edited from the papers of the late M. Colmache, private secretary to the prince, 2nd ed. (London: Henry Colburn, 1850).

11. Obituary, Madame Colmache, *Times* (London), 26 January 1904, 6. Anne Thackeray Ritchie (William Thackeray's daughter) mentions visiting the Colmache daughters, Pauline and Laura, in Paris. Their grandmothers were friends. See John Aplin, *The Inheritance of Genius: A Thackeray Family Biography, 1798–1875* (Cambridge: Lutterworth Press, 2010), 51.

12. Obituary, Rosina Filippi, *Times* (London), 28 February 1930, 9.

13. Ancestry.com, *1881 England Census* (database online) (Provo, UT: Ancestry .com Operations, 2011), s.v. "Georgina Colmache." Ancestry.com, *1911 England Census* (database online) (Provo, UT: Ancestry.com Operations, 2011). A later record describes her daughter, Laura Colmache as a single professor of music, and another record finds Rosina as a niece in a London household with Laura and one servant. See Ancestry .com, *1891 England Census* (database online) (Provo, UT: Ancestry.com Operations, 2005), s.v. "Sanna [Laura] Colmache." That record reports Rosina as having been born in Italy.

14. "A School for the Drama," *Bow Bells*, 8 May 1896, 480.

15. Richard Findlater, *Lilian Baylis: The Lady of the Old Vic* (London: Allen Lane, 1975), 106.

16. Harcourt Williams, *Old Vic Saga* (London: Winchester, 1949), 25.

17. The production was canceled because of high costs, although Filippi went on to play Lady Britomart in Shaw's *Lady Barbara*. See Ann L. Ferguson, *The Instinct of an Artist: Shaw and the Theater; An Exhibition from the Bernard F. Burgunder Collection of George Bernard Shaw* (Ithaca, NY: Cornell University Library, 1997), 13–14.

18. Rosina Filippi to George Bernard Shaw, n.d., British Library Western Manuscripts, Add MS 50515, vol. VII, f. 100.

19. Steve Turner, *The Band That Played On: The Extraordinary Story of the 8 Musicians Who Went Down with the Titanic* (Nashville: Thomas Nelson, 2011), 77. One of the musicians that Dowson played with in Oxford went down with the Titanic.

20. On Filippi's work establishing a low-cost people's repertory theater, see Susie Gilbert, *Opera for Everybody: The Story of English National Opera* (London: Faber and Faber, 2009), 22. As Gilbert notes, "From April 1914, Filippi started, on a shoestring, to present two Shakespeare plays a week. Her season was, however, short-lived and ill-attended" (22). It's an interesting fact of Janeite history that the most famous British and American proponents of a repertory theater for the poor were visionary, progressive women who wrote, directed, or acted in Austen plays. For the American-based innovator of repertory theater and of Austen, see chapter 6 on Eva Le Gallienne and *Dear Jane* (1932).

21. Review of *Duologues and Scenes from the Novels of Jane Austen: Arranged and Adapted for Drawing-Room Performance*, by Rosina Filippi, *Bookman* 8 (July 1895): 120.

22. Review of *Duologues and Scenes from the Novels of Jane Austen: Arranged and Adapted for Drawing-Room Performance*, by Rosina Filippi, *Cambridge Review* 16 (6 June 1895): 382–83.

23. Richard Arthur Austen-Leigh was the grandson of James Edward Austen-Leigh, Austen's nephew and author of the *Memoir*.

24. Robin Myers, "Leigh, Richard Arthur Austen (1872–1961)," in *Oxford Dictionary of National Biography Online* (Oxford: Oxford University Press, 2004; online ed., May 2009), Web.

25. Review of *Duologues*, *Cambridge Review*, 383.

26. As one reviewer notes, "We believe that most of them have been several times performed in Oxford 'with great applause.' " Review of *Duologues and Scenes from the Novels of Jane Austen*, by Rosina Filippi, *Athenaeum* 3536 (3 August 1895): 171.

27. "Notes and Comments," *Oxford University Extension Gazette*, September 1895, 120.

28. Margaret Fletcher, *Christian Feminism: A Charter of Rights and Duties* (London: P. S. King and Sons, 1915).

29. Jane Austen, *Pride and Prejudice*, ed. Pat Rogers (Cambridge: Cambridge University Press, 2006), 391. The novel having Elizabeth think to herself, "How could I ever think her like her nephew?" seems a more reflective and less angry rendering than Filippi's interpretation.

30. Ernest Pertwee, ed., *The Reciter's Treasury of Prose and Drama* (London: George Routledge, 1904), 433–45. Pertwee includes "Lady Catherine's Visit" and "Literary Tastes" (from *Northanger Abbey*).

31. In an 1895 interview, Filippi identifies herself as an actor, a writer, and a teacher, with teacher the most prized role among them. "Madame Vinard: A Chat with Miss Rosina Filippi," supplement, *Sketch*, 25 December 1895, 6.

32. H. Philip Bolton, *Women Writers Dramatized: A Calendar of Performances from Narrative Works Published in England to 1900* (London: Mansell, 2000), 15. Bolton catalogues two Filippi-derived Austen radio plays from 1924 and 1925.

33. Fanny Johnson, "School Plays," *School World: A Monthly Magazine of Educational Work and Progress* 11 (March 1909): 100. Subsequent references cited parenthetically in the text.

34. David Gilson, *A Bibliography of Jane Austen*, rev. ed. (New Castle, DE: Oak Knoll, 1997), 405–17. Subsequent references cited parenthetically in the text.

35. See the card index of Lord Chamberlain's Plays Correspondence files, arranged alphabetically by title, at the British Library, for further information. It includes early *Pride and Prejudice* playscripts by Dorinda Hartley, Christine Longford, A. Watson (for a play performed at a girls' school), Edith Hoare, and Mary Whelan.

36. Sybil Thorndike to Miss Booth, 7 November 1933, collection of the author. Thorndike suggests that she's returned Booth's script to Mr. Mudd, who sent it on to Dame May Whitty. Thorndike's brother Russell was Filippi's son-in-law. Dame May Whitty had previously played Mrs. Bennet in a 1922 production of *Pride and Prejudice*.

37. Fanny Johnson, *Dramatic Scenes from English Literature, Selected and Adapted by Fanny Johnson* (London: Edward Arnold, n.d.). Gilson estimates a publication of 1909 (*Bibliography* 416). Johnson adapted a scene from *Northanger Abbey*. On Johnson, see Victoria Millington, *Fanny Eliza Johnson: A Thoroughly Modern Victorian Headmistress, Bolton High School for Girls 1888–1893* (West Yorkshire, Royd Press, 2008). The biography records Johnson's having acted scenes from Shakespeare as a girl and from Dickens when headmistress of the school (58). By 1912, she was press secretary for the Cambridge women's suffrage association (132), keeping the issue alive during the war and working directly counter to Jane Austen's descendant and antisuffrage activist Florence Austen-Leigh, as we'll see in chapter 11. Fanny Johnson was the sister of Reginald Brimley Johnson, the Austen critic and first editor of the J. M. Dent Austen, illustrated by William Cooke, as described in chapter 2 (Millington 132). Her younger sister Alice was a member of the Society for Psychical Research and worked with Richard Hodgson (described in chapter 12). Alice devoted considerable time to the study of automatic writing (141). The Johnsons seem to have had their hand in every form of popular Austen.

38. Review of *Duologues*, *Bookman*, 120.

39. See "Ohio," *Public Libraries: A Monthly Review of Library Matters and Methods* 20 (1915): 504.

40. "The Story of the Helen Hunt Club," in *Memoirs of the Miami Valley*, ed. John C. Hover et al., 3 vols. (Chicago: Robert O. Law, 1919), 2:219.

41. Mary Keith (Medbery) MacKaye, [Mrs. Steele], *Pride and Prejudice: A Play, Founded on Jane Austen's Novel* (New York: Duffield, 1906).

42. On Scott, see also H. Philip Bolton, *Scott Dramatized* (London: Mansell, 1992).

43. Rosina Filippi, *Duologues and Scenes from the Novels of Jane Austen: Arranged and Adapted for Drawing-Room Performance*, 2nd ed. (London: J. M. Dent, 1904), n.p.

44. Sophie M. Trasel and Elizabeth D. Williams, "Mr. Collins in Search of a Wife: Being Scenes from Jane Austen's Novel 'Pride and Prejudice'" (Unpublished script, 1903).

45. Phosphor Mallam, *Mr. Collins Proposes: From "Pride and Prejudice" by Jane Austen*, arranged as a dialogue or scene (London: J. Curwen & Sons, 1912); Phosphor Mallam, *Lady Catherine Is Annoyed with Elizabeth Bennet: From "Pride and Prejudice" by Jane Austen*, arranged as a dialogue or scene (London: J. Curwen & Sons, 1912). These pamphlets appeared in the series Sketches from Classical Authors.

46. Margaret Macnamara, *Elizabeth Refuses: A Miniature Comedy from Jane Austen's "Pride and Prejudice"* (London: Joseph Williams, 1926). Subsequent references cited parenthetically in the text. Macnamara added new material in her revised edition of 1947. On Macnamara, see Patricia Lufkin, "An Analysis of the Plays of Margaret Macnamara" (PhD diss., Louisiana State University, 2002). Lufkin says the Austen plays earned Macnamara enough for a lifetime annuity of £200 (215, 4).

Chapter 5 • Playing Mr. Darcy before Laurence Olivier

1. Sue Birtwistle and Susie Conklin, *The Making of Pride and Prejudice* (London: Penguin, 1995), 98.

2. Laurence Olivier, *On Acting* (London: Weidenfeld and Nicolson, 1986), 183.

3. There was one moving-image Darcy before Olivier, in a 1938 BBC TV version, which does not survive. See Deborah Cartmell, *Screen Adaptations: Jane Austen's Pride and Prejudice: The Relationship between Text and Film* (London: Methuen, 2010). She notes that it was broadcast from Alexandra Palace (London) with a transmission range of twenty-five miles. Its Darcy was Andrew Osborn (1910–85).

4. Nicholas Barber, "*Pride and Prejudice* at 20: The Scene That Changed Everything," *BBC Culture*, 22 September 2015, n.p., Web. On Firth's Darcy and the problem of Darcy on film, see Roger Sales, *Jane Austen and Representations of Regency England* (London: Routledge, 1996), 234–36.

5. Deborah Cartmell and Imelda Whelehan, "A Practical Understanding of Literature on Screen: Two Conversations with Andrew Davies," in *The Cambridge Companion to Literature on Screen*, ed. Deborah Cartmell and Imelda Whelehan (Cambridge: Cambridge University Press, 2007), 244.

6. P.C., "The Theatre: Some Trial Matinees; The German Theatre," *Speaker*, 6 April 1901, 17, 18. On the cultural interpenetration of fiction, book illustration, and dramatization, see Martin Meisel, *Realizations: Narrative, Pictorial, and Theatrical Arts in Nineteenth-Century England* (Princeton: Princeton, 1983). Much of Meisel's argument has interesting resonances with Austen, but he mentions her just once, in passing.

7. The program for *The Bennets* survives in the Victoria & Albert Theatre and Performance Archive. The playscript is missing from the Lord Chamberlain's Plays at the British Library.

8. Williams directed *Pot and Kettle* in 1909. See *The Methuen Drama Book of Suffrage Plays*, ed. Naomi Paxton (London: Methuen, 2013), 50.

9. "Drama: The Week," *Athenaeum*, no. 3832 (6 April 1901): 443. Subsequent references cited parenthetically in the text.

10. "Heard in the Green Room," *Sketch*, 5 February 1908, 118.

11. Johnson Briscoe, "March 30: E. Harcourt Williams," in *The Actor's Birthday Book* (New York: Moffat, Yard, 1907), 82.

12. A. B. Walkley, "The Drama: *The Bennets*," *Literature*, 6 April 1901, 262. One of Harcourt Williams's contemporaries, writing later, suggested this was a pattern of regular, "unconscious imitation" on Williams's part, as a young actor of "tremendous ambition" who had "admiration for Martin Harvey." Constance Benson, *Mainly Players: Bensonian Memories* (London: Thornton Butterworth, 1926), 155.

13. Walkley 262.

14. "Sir John Martin-Harvey (1863–1944), Actor and Theatre Manager," in *Collections* (London: National Portrait Gallery, n.d.).

15. Max, "Mr. Lyall Swete in Two Plays," *Saturday Review*, 6 April 1901, 438.

16. Ibid. 437–38.

17. "Court Theatre," *Times* (London), 30 March 1901, 14.

18. "Dramatics: The Zeta Alpha Play," *Wellesley Magazine* 7, no. 9 (June 1899): 475–76. This was an era in which women playing men's parts on the stage was fashionable. Edmond Rostand wrote his play *L'Aiglon* (1900), about Napoleon's son, with Sarah Bernhardt in mind. She played the part in Paris and London, and it became one of her signature roles.

19. Spencer Ogden, "Drama at the Women's Colleges," *Puritan* 8, no. 2 (May 1900): 155. Miss Willis appears, from class notes, to have been Clara Lucretia Willis (b. 1872–?). Although there is no scholarship yet on cross-dress Austen performances, there is a robust body of work on women playing Shakespearean male parts. See Tony Howard, *Women as Hamlet: Performance and Interpretation in Theatre, Film and Fiction* (Cambridge: Cambridge University Press, 2007).

20. "Biography & History: Family History," in *MacKaye Family Papers, 1751–1998*, Rauner Special Collections Library, Hanover, NH, Dartmouth College, n.d.

21. The MacKayes are usually associated with Shakespeare performance, as Steele MacKaye was the first American to play Hamlet in London, but two generations of MacKaye women published Austen adaptations. Mary MacKaye's daughter-in-law, wife of her son Percy MacKaye, was Marion MacKaye, author of an *Emma* dramatization. Marion Morse MacKaye, *Emma: A Play* (New York: Macmillan, 1941).

22. Mrs. Steel MacKaye, *Pride and Prejudice: A Play, Founded on Jane Austen's Novel* (New York: Duffield, 1906), 18. Subsequent references cited parenthetically in the text.

23. "Comment on Current Books," *New Outlook*, 13 October 1906, 385.

24. Critics complained that Joe Wright's film *Pride and Prejudice* (2005) brought too much Brontë to the adaptation and especially to its hero, Matthew Macfayden's Darcy.

25. A. M. Drummond, "Plays for the Country Theater," *Cornell Extension Bulletin* 53 (June 1922): 295.

26. "The Senior Girls' Play," *Michigan Alumnus* 13 (July 1907): 450.

27. David Gilson, *A Bibliography of Jane Austen* (New Castle, DE: Oak Knoll, 1997), 150. *Vikar-vilasita* [Tragedy of thought] (Pune: Venus Prakashan, 1883) was the title of a *Hamlet* translation by Gopal Ganesh Agarkar. There is no record of any text with either title also being an Austen-derived text, although perhaps the particular work Gilson refers to awaits future discovery. Many Austen scholars, including me, have repeated Gilson's description of *Vichar-vilasit* as an Austen dramatization in our scholarship, but that identification now seems worth our skepticism.

28. Kṛshṇājīr Keśava Gokhale's *Ājapāsūna pannāsa varshānnī Āṅgla kādambarīkartrī "Jena Ôṣṭina" yāñcyā "Prāiḍa êṇḍa prejuḍisa" yā kādambarīcē rūpāntara* (Mumbai: Manoranjaka Granthaprasaraka Mandali, 1913). For biographical information on Gokhale, see Govind Chimnaji Bhate, *A History of Modern Marathi Literature, 1800–1938* (Mahad: Author, 1939), 444. This Marathi-language Austen text by Gokhale is mentioned in Nalini Natarajan, "Reluctant Janeites: Daughterly Value in Jane Austen and Sarat Chandra Chatterjee's *Swami*," in *The Postcolonial Jane Austen*, ed. You-me Park and Rajeswari Sunder Rajan (London: Routledge, 2000), 161. Natarajan identifies Gokhale's Austen text once as an adaptation (151) and once as a translation (160). Adaptation seems more accurate to what Gokhale published in 1913, in that he changed characters' names and omitted, it would seem, Kitty Bennet.

29. I am grateful to Phalguni Shah for this translation of the title, which is hers. She offers further information for Austen scholars: "The word *rupantara* literally means 'conversion' or 'variation,' so I would guess it is not an exact translation of the novel. The preface of said book is available on the Internet archives in audio form, and the following points may be useful to you: Chapter 3 in this book serves mostly as an extended preface to put the book in context. The contents of chapters 2 to 5 in the original book are contained in chapters 2, 4 and 5. Other than that, all the chapters are kept untouched in the conversion. The fifth girl, Lydia, is made into the fourth girl, Sundari, in the conversion, none of the other characters have undergone much change. I have modified some content or added some of my own to appeal to the Marathi sensibilities, without much affecting the original gist. The social scenario in England at the end of the 18th century has still not reached Indian society after a century of western education. I offer you this title, hoping that it will reach here at least in 50 years from now." Phalguni Shah, e-mail message to the author, 3 October 2016.

30. Gyles Brandreth, *Oxford Dictionary of Humorous Quotations*, 5th ed. (Oxford: Oxford University Press, 2013), 98.

31. Eileen H. A. Squire and J. C. Squire, *Pride and Prejudice: A Play in Four Acts* (London: William Heinemann, 1929). Subsequent references cited parenthetically in the text.

32. May Whitty served on the Executive Committee of the Actresses Franchise League with Winifred Mayo. See *The Suffrage Annual and Women's Who's Who* (London: Stanley Paul, 1913), 10.

33. Andrew Wright, "Jane Austen Adapted," *Nineteenth-Century Fiction* 30, no. 3 (December 1975): 430.

34. Broadway League, "Pride and Prejudice," *Internet Broadway Database* (2015).

35. Maggie Gale, *West End Women: Women and the London Stage, 1918–1962* (London: Routledge, 1996), 221.

36. Burns Mantle, ed., *The Best Plays of 1935–36 and the Year Book of Drama in America* (New York: Dodd, Mead, 1936), 356.

37. "New Reputations," *Vogue* 87 (15 May 1936): 86.

38. *Aust Lit: The Australian Literature Resource*, n.d., s.v. "Armand Jerome," n.p., Web.

39. Ibid. n.p.

40. *Aust Lit: The Australian Literature Resource*, n.d., s.v. "Helen Jerome," n.p., Web.

41. Their daughter married three times. Her last brief marriage was to a viscount.

42. "All Sorts of People," *Free Lance* 15, no. 732 (11 July 1914): 4.

43. "Men and Women," *Advocate*, 8 August 1924, 2.

44. "New Reputations," *Vogue* 87 (15 May 1936): 86. Helen Jerome's second marriage to Ali (d. 1942) may produce confusion, as there was another entertainment-industry Helen Jerome married to a different George Ali. The Jane Austen dramatizer Jerome was *not* married to the animal impersonator Ali. Jerome's Ali was in business, an oil company executive. Obituary of George D. Ali, *New York Times*, 24 March 1942, 10.

45. Helen Jerome, *Pride and Prejudice: A Sentimental Comedy* (Garden City, NY: Doubleday, Doran, 1935); subsequent references cited parenthetically in the text. Her next play was Helen Jerome, *Jane Eyre: A Drama of Passion in Three Acts*, dramatized from Charlotte Brontë's novel (Garden City, NY: Doubleday, Doran, 1937).

46. Helen Jerome, *Pride and Prejudice: A Sentimental Comedy in Three Acts* (New York: Samuel French, 1935). Subsequent references cited parenthetically in the text.

47. The few critics who have written about the play in recent years find much to despise in it. Joseph Wiesenfarth describes it as a "dumbing down" of the novel, concluding that it "turns a novel of manners that sparkles with wit into a melodrama that drips with sentiment." Joseph Wiesenfarth, "The Garson-Olivier Pride and Prejudice: A Hollywood Story," in *Text und Ton im Film*, ed. Paul Goetsch and Dietrich Scheunemann (Tubingen: Narr, 1997), 85.

48. The radio show based on Jerome's play, featuring Joan Fontaine, did not keep the passionate kiss at the end. The MGM version interrupts the viewer's appreciation of the Darcy-Elizabeth kiss immediately by showing a spying Mrs. Bennet's giddy response to it.

49. "'Pride and Prejudice' as a Play," *Times* (London), 4 February 1936, 10, *The Times Digital Archive*, Web.

50. The line "as willingly without Pemberley as with it" is from critic George Saintsbury. See his preface to Jane Austen, *Pride and Prejudice* (London: George Allen, 1894), xxiii.

51. "The Week's Theatres: 'Pride and Prejudice.'" *Observer* (London), 1 March 1936, 15.

52. "Pride, Prejudice, and Free Wit," *Literary Digest* 120, no. 20 (16 November 1935): 20.

Chapter 6 • Dear Jane

1. D. H. Lawrence, "A Propos of Lady Chatterley's Lover," in *Sex, Literature, and Censorship: Essays*, ed. Harry T. Moore (New York: Twayne, 1953), 119.

2. B. C. Southam, *Jane Austen: The Critical Heritage* (London: Routledge & Kegan Paul, 1968), 128.

3. Claudia L. Johnson, "The Divine Miss Jane: Jane Austen, Janeites, and the Discipline of Novel Studies," *boundary 2* 23, no. 3 (1996): 148–49. Reprinted in Deidre Lynch, ed., *Janeites: Austen's Disciples and Devotees* (Princeton: Princeton University Press, 2000), 25–44.

4. Terry Castle, "Sister, Sister," *London Review of Books*, 3 August 1995, 3.

5. "Terry Castle Stands By Jane Austen Review," Stanford University Archived News Release, 16 August 1995.

6. It wasn't the first appearance of Jane Austen as a character on a professional stage. That happened in the suffrage play, *A Pageant of Great Women* (1909), as described in part 3.

7. See "Eva Le Gallienne," *Time: The Weekly Newsmagazine*, 25 November 1929, 32+. Le Gallienne's father was the English poet Richard Le Gallienne, and her mother was a Danish journalist Julie Norregard. When Norregard (Le Gallienne's second wife) left him, she took their daughter Eva to Paris. Richard Le Gallienne went on to live in the United States and France, and Eva Le Gallienne was raised in Britain and France. Eva later immigrated to the United States to pursue a career on Broadway.

8. Hutchinson's recorded birthdates vary from 1898 to 1904. Obituary, Josephine Hutchinson, *Independent*, 12 June 1998, n.p., Web.

9. Helen Sheehy, *Eva Le Gallienne: A Biography* (New York: Alfred A Knopf, 1996), 155. Subsequent references cited parenthetically in the text.

10. "Bell Divorces Actress, Eva Le Gallienne's Shadow," *New York Daily News*, 8 July 1930, n.p.

11. Later in her life, Eva Le Gallienne would deny that the label lesbian applied to her, something one biographer saw as part and parcel of an artist's rejections of categories of all kinds (Sheehy 198–99). She lived her life with a series of female lovers in what has been described as "a closet with transparent walls" (198).

12. Qtd. in Kaier Curtin, *"We Can Always Call Them Bulgarians": The Emergence of Lesbians and Gay Men on the American Stage* (Boston: Alyson, 1987), 205.

13. The play had its last performance on January 28, 1933, according to *The Billboard Index of the New York Legitimate Stage* (Season 1932–33), (New York: Billboard, 1933), 23. According to Le Gallienne biographer Robert Schanke, "Most criticism of the production centered upon the writing; it lacked a conflict. Eva had been attracted by Austen's dilemma, but she had again misjudged the value of a script." Robert Schanke, *Shattered Applause: The Lives of Eva Le Gallienne* (Carbondale: Southern Illinois University Press, 1992), 101. Subsequent references cited parenthetically in the text. *Dear Jane* was outshone by the far more successful *Alice in Wonderland* production, which opened on December 12, 1932, and made Hutchinson (its Alice) a star (Sheehy 219). Because of the theater's economic difficulties in the Depression era, some brought on by costs of the extravagant *Alice* production, the Civic Rep would end up closing its doors and transferring *Alice* to a commercial stage. By touring its most successful shows, it sought to shore up its damaged finances. *Dear Jane* was a casualty of this period, as well as of what seems a relative lack of audience enthusiasm. See Eva Le Gallienne, *With a Quiet Heart: An Autobiography* (New York: Viking Press, 1953), 58–60. Subsequent references cited parenthetically in the text.

14. Russell Clark and William Phillips, "Eleanor Holmes Hinkley's 'Lost' Play, *Dear Jane*: Jane Austen in the Theatre," *Sensibilities* 45 (2012): 91–109.

15. Two copies are held at the Library of Congress and one at the Beinecke Library.

16. Lyndall Gordon, *T. S. Eliot: An Imperfect Life* (New York: Norton), 78–79.

17. Eliot married elsewhere, although he and Hale continued to be romantically entangled. She bequeathed his letters to her to Princeton University, under seal until January 1, 2020. See Michelle Dean, "Saturday History Lessons: On Emily Hale and T. S. Eliot," *Rumpus*, 7 April 2012, n.p., Web.

18. "Miss Hinkley: Local Playwright," *Boston Globe*, 26 January 1971, 37.

19. E. H. Hinkley, *Dear Jane* (10 July 1919); Class D: Dramatic Compositions, *Catalog of Copyright Entries*, 16.1 (Washington, DC: Government Printing Office, 1919), 19487.

20. "Local Playwright Launches Success," *Cambridge Tribune*, 25 March 1922, 3.

21. Eva Le Gallienne to Julia Norregaard Le Gallienne, 18 April 1932, box 12, folder 8, Eva Le Gallienne Papers, Manuscript Division, Library of Congress, Washington, DC, MSS 84002.

22. Paul Reuben Cooper, "Eva Le Gallienne's Civic Repertory Theatre" (PhD diss., University of Illinois, 1967), 20. Subsequent references cited parenthetically in the text.

23. Josephine Hutchinson to Julia Norregaard Le Gallienne, 4 June 1932, box 10, folder 2, Eva Le Gallienne Papers, Manuscript Division, Library of Congress, Washington, DC, MSS 84002.

24. *Dear Jane*, Eva Le Gallienne Papers, box 29, folder 1, Manuscript Division, Library of Congress, Washington, DC, 1–6. The script is numbered by scene, followed by page number within that scene. Subsequent references will be cited, in this format, parenthetically in the text.

25. Le Gallienne's friend Constance Collier helped with the direction of *Dear Jane*. See Schanke 101.

26. "*Dear Jane*: Jane Austen Is Heroine of Play at Civic," *Brooklyn Daily Eagle*, 15 November 1932, 6.

27. Arthur Ruhl, "'Dear Jane': Civic Repertory Theatre Offers Play about Jane Austen," *New York Herald Tribune*, 15 November 1932.

28. Eleanor Holmes Hinkley to Eva Le Gallienne, 10 June 1932, box 19, folder 7, Eva Le Gallienne Papers, Manuscript Division, Library of Congress, Washington, DC, MSS 84002.

Chapter 7 • *Stage to Screen* Pride and Prejudice

1. Kenneth Turan, "*Pride and Prejudice*: An Informal History of the Garson-Olivier Motion Picture," *Persuasions* 11 (1989): 140–43. Subsequent references cited parenthetically in the text. This sum is the equivalent of $900,000 in 2016 dollars.

2. "Pride and Prejudice (1940)," *Turner Classic Movies*, Time Warner, accessed 26 July 2016, http://www.tcm.com/tcmdb/title/2153/Pride-and-Prejudice/articles.html.

3. "Program," *Showplace: The Magazine of Radio City Music Hall; "Showplace of the Nation"* 4, no. 32 (8 August 1940): 4–5. This issue of the magazine claimed a circulation of fifty thousand copies.

4. Deborah Cartmell, *Adaptations in the Sound Era, 1927–37* (London: Bloomsbury, 2015), 58. Subsequent references cited parenthetically in the text.

5. Lisa Hopkins, *Relocating Shakespeare and Austen on Screen* (New York: Palgrave Macmillan, 2009), 8.

6. H. Philip Bolton, *Women Writers Dramatized: A Calendar of Performances from Narrative Works Published in English to 1900* (London: Mansell, 2000), 85–88.

7. Among the best essays on MGM's *Pride and Prejudice* (1940) is Deborah Cartmell, *Jane Austen's Pride and Prejudice: The Relationship between Text and Film* (London: Methuen, 2010).

8. The film's production was hardly economical. Its budget was $1,437,000. Despite good domestic and foreign box office receipts—described as "moderately successful"—the film was initially counted as a loss of $241,000 for the studio. (As we'll see in chapter 11, it was likely a long-term financial gain, as a result of the education market and its 1962 rerelease.) On the film's costs and losses, see H. Mark Glancy, *When Hollywood Loved Britain: The Hollywood "British" Film 1939–45* (New York: St. Martin's, 1999), 70.

9. Harriet Margolis, "What Does the Name 'Jane Austen' Authorize?," in *Jane Austen on Screen*, ed. Gina Macdonald and Andrew F. Macdonald (Cambridge: Cambridge University Press, 2003), 26.

10. On Marx and *Pride and Prejudice*, see Turan 140.

11. Kenneth Turan, e-mail message to author, 1 September 2015.

12. Hepburn had just starred in George Cukor's film *Little Women* (1933), and Cukor was floated as a possible *Pride and Prejudice* film director. Again, Louisa May Alcott's *Little Women* and its road to film was a significant progenitor of Jerome's stage hit and MGM's Austen film project.

13. Burns Mantle, ed., *The Best Plays of 1935–36 and the Year Book of Drama in America* (New York: Dodd, Mead, 1936), 356.

14. Willard Keefe, "New Austen Hit Is Aloof from Lure of Films," *Washington Post*, 10 November 1935, M2.

15. Edward Hogan, synopsis of *Pride and Prejudice*, 25 February 1933, box 2321, *Pride and Prejudice* Scripts, Turner MGM Scripts, P-936, Margaret Herrick Library, Beverly Hills, CA. After her *Pride and Prejudice*, Helen Jerome would write a stage adaptation of *Jane Eyre*. It did star Katharine Hepburn, the actor originally sought for the stage *Pride and Prejudice*. (*Jane Eyre* would not, however, prove a similar stage success for Jerome.)

16. Michael Schlossheimer, *Gunmen and Gangsters: Profiles of Nine Actors Who Portrayed Memorable Screen Tough Guys* (Jefferson, NC: McFarland, 2002), 259.

17. "Hays Sees an Era of Literary Films," *New York Times*, 27 March 1934, 24. I became aware of this source from Greg M. Colón Semenza and Bob Hasenfratz, *The History of British Literature in Film, 1895–2015* (London: Bloomsbury, 2015), 175.

18. On the film's shift forward in time, see Linda A. Robinson, "Crinolines and Pantalettes: What MGM's Switch in Time Did to *Pride and Prejudice* (1940)," *Adaptation* 6, no. 3 (2013): 283–304.

19. MPAA PCA Files, Academy of Motion Picture Arts and Sciences, 30 January 1940, Margaret Herrick Library, Beverly Hills, CA. A memo from Joseph Breen declares that Mr. Collins was in violation of the production code: "As you know, the Production Code states specifically 'Ministers of religion in their character as ministers of religion should not be used as comic characters or as villains.'"

20. H. Mark Glancy, "Hollywood and Britain: MGM and the British 'Quota' Legislation," in *The Unknown 1930s: An Alternative History of the British Cinema, 1929–1939*, ed. Jeffrey Richards (London: I. B. Tauris), 67.

21. Joseph Wiesenfarth, "The Garson-Olivier Pride and Prejudice: A Hollywood Story," in *Text und Ton im Film*, ed. Paul Goetsch and Dietrich Scheunemann (Tubingen: Narr, 1997), 91. Wiesenfarth's essay is one of the few published essays that considers MGM's unpublished scripts.

22. "Script of Play to Be Produced by Max Gordon," MPAA PCA Files, Academy of Motion Picture Arts and Sciences, 5 Sept 1935, Margaret Herrick Library, Beverly Hills, CA.

23. Screenplay by Sarah Y. Mason and Victor Heermans, 11 May 1936, box 2321, *Pride and Prejudice* Scripts, Turner MGM Scripts, P-939, 10, Margaret Herrick Library, Beverly Hills, CA.

24. Victor Heermans Papers, Collection 96, "Sequence Survey," *Pride and Prejudice*, MGM 1940, 8 February 1936, Margaret Herrick Library, Beverly Hills, CA.

25. "Seq. 1: Establishes a period; the Hugh Thomson illustration of Bingley's chaise launches our picture well," in "Sequence Survey," Victor Heermans Papers, Collection 96, *Pride and Prejudice*, MGM 1940, 14 April 1936, Margaret Herrick Library, Beverly Hills, CA.

26. John Wiltshire, afterword to *The Cinematic Jane Austen: Essays on the Filmic Sensibility of the Novels*, ed. David Monaghan, Ariane Hudelet, and John Wiltshire (Jefferson, NC: Macfarland, 2009), 163.

27. Dialogue continuity from Tess Slesinger, 22 June 1936, box 2321, *Pride and Prejudice* Scripts, Turner MGM Scripts, P-941, Margaret Herrick Library, Beverly Hills, CA.

28. Henry Grace, "Set Decoration in the Golden Era of Metro Goldwyn Mayer," Henry Grace Collection, scrapbook #1, U-419, Margaret Herrick Library, Beverly Hills, CA. Writes Grace, "On the village street, for the bookstore, I had some old engravings enlarged for display in the book store. Greer Garson, starring, asked where I got them. I said they were copies of Cruikshank—'You know, the man who illustrated Dickens.' She was British, she put me in my place nicely, smiling, she said, 'Don't you think Rowlandson would be better for the period?'"

29. Virginia Clark describes another version of this scene. There were several Akins scripts. Virginia M. Clark, *Aldous Huxley and Film* (Metuchen, NJ: Scarecrow Press, 1987), 43.

30. Zoe Akins, screenplay for *Pride and Prejudice*, 11 June 1937, box 2321, *Pride and Prejudice* Scripts, Turner MGM Scripts, P-948, Margaret Herrick Library, Beverly Hills, CA.

31. Ibid.

32. Jacco (not Jacko) Maccaco was an actual celebrated fighting monkey in London's Westminster Pits in the 1820s. Ibid. Akins may have taken inspiration for these connected male-bonding scenes from Pierce Egan's *Life in London* (1821), the book that indirectly spawned Tom and Jerry.

33. Jane Murfin, screenplay for *Pride and Prejudice*, 26 September 1939, box 2321, Pride and Prejudice Scripts, Turner MGM Scripts, P-948, Margaret Herrick Library, Beverly Hills, CA.

34. Ibid. In 954, "Darcy crawls out of a mud hole and is very annoyed at a stupid dairy-maid." In P-955 (dated September 28, 1939), Elizabeth is covered in mud, and Darcy throws a shilling at her.

35. Clark 39.

36. Leonard Huxley, introduction to *Jane Austen: Her Life and Art*, by David Rhydderch (London: Jonathan Cape, 1932), 11–12.

37. Aldous Huxley, *Letters of Aldous Huxley* (London: Chatto & Windus, 1969), 450, 448. Using the money to help those suffering in the war was apparently the suggestion of Anita Loos. See Clark 39.

38. *Pride and Prejudice* Complete OK Screenplay, by Jane Murfin and Aldous Huxley, January 11, 1940, through March 26, 1940, box 2324, Turner MGM Scripts, P-967, 27, Margaret Herrick Library, Beverly Hills, CA. Subsequent references cited parenthetically in the text. On Byronic heroes in women's writing and on screen, see Sarah Wootton, *Byronic Heroes in Nineteenth-Century Women's Writing and Screen Adaptation* (Basingstoke, UK: Palgrave Macmillan, 2016), 86–92, connecting Austen, Byron, and more recent film Darcys.

39. Qtd. in Jerry Vermilye, *The Complete Films of Laurence Olivier* (New York: Citadel Press, 1992), 101.

40. One recent critic, Sue Parrill, declares that although Darcy's film role is "underwritten" and reactive, "Olivier may be the most expressive of those who have played Darcy on film and television." Olivier's "Darcy goes in minutes from being disdainful of Elizabeth to being intrigued by and attracted to her," as Parrill also rightly notes. Sue Parrill, *Jane Austen on Film and Television: A Critical Study of the Adaptations* (Jefferson, NC: McFarland, 2002), 51, 53.

41. Abe Burrows, *Honest, Abe: Is There Really No Business Like Show Business?* (Boston: Little, Brown, 1980), 348.

42. Abe Burrows, *First Impressions: A Musical Comedy* (New York: Samuel French, 1962), 15. Subsequent references cited parenthetically in the text.

43. Christopher Isherwood, *Liberation: Diaries*, vol. 3, *1970–1983*, ed. Katherine Bucknell (New York: Harper Collins, 2012), 211. Subsequent reference cited parenthetically in the text. I'm grateful to Sam Irvin for bringing this material to my attention.

44. A woman driving a carriage was not customary in Austen's day, but there are hints of it as a possible skill. See Mrs. Croft's "coolly giving the reins a better direction herself" in *Persuasion*. Jane Austen, *Persuasion*, ed. Janet Todd and Antje Blank (Cambridge: Cambridge University Press, 2006), 99.

45. *Pride and Prejudice* screenplay, Unrealized Scripts Collection, box 10, folder 65, 23 September 1974 to 12 December 1974, Margaret Herrick Library, Beverly Hills, CA.

46. Jerome Lawrence and Robert Edwin Lee to Hunt Stromberg Jr., 16 September 1974, Unrealized Scripts Collection, box 10, folder 65, Margaret Herrick Library, Beverly Hills, CA.

Part 3 • Jane Austen, Politicized

1. The Women's Disabilities Removal Bill, which had a long, complicated history in Parliament in the 1870s, was ultimately stopped short by Prime Minister W. E. Gladstone, acting on behalf of the government. It took two decades for another women's

suffrage bill to go as far as that bill had. See Sophia A. Van Wingerden, *The Women's Suffrage Movement in Britain, 1866–1928* (Basingstoke: Palgrave Macmillan, 1999), 28.

2. See "Women's Disabilities Removal Bill," *Hansard's Parliamentary Debates*, 211 (1 May 1872), 38. Subsequent references cited parenthetically in the text.

3. G. K. Chesterton, *Come to Think of It* (Freeport, NY: Books for Libraries Press, 1971), 195. Subsequent references cited parenthetically in the text. The essay "Jane Austen and the General Election" was also republished in G. K. Chesterton, *The Collected Works of G. K. Chesterton*, vol. 35, *The Illustrated London News, 1929–1931*, ed. Lawrence J. Clipper (San Francisco: Ignatius Press, 1991).

4. On men's club Janeites, see Devoney Looser, "The Cult of *Pride and Prejudice* and Its Author," in *Cambridge Companion to "Pride and Prejudice,"* ed. Janet Todd (Cambridge: Cambridge University Press, 2013), 174–85.

5. There is a robust body of work on political Austen, although far less published on Austen's legacy as it's been used politically. Much of that work confines itself to her critical, rather than her popular, legacy. For work on her popular political legacy, see Mary Ann O'Farrell, "'Bin Laden a Huge Jane Austen Fan': Jane Austen in Contemporary Political Discourse," in *Uses of Austen: Jane's Afterlives*, ed. Gillian Dow and Clare Harman (New York: Palgrave Macmillan, 2012), 192–207.

6. On the history of and the illustrations accompanying "The Janeites," see Janine Barchas, "G.I. Jane: Austen Goes to War," *JHU Press Blog*, 3 October 2014.

7. Winston Churchill, *Closing the Ring* (Boston: Houghton Mifflin, 1951), 5:425.

Chapter 8 • The Night of the Divine Jane

1. As Claudia L. Johnson puts it in her groundbreaking essay, "The Divine Miss Jane: Jane Austen, Janeites, and the Discipline of Novel Studies," *boundary 2* 23, no. 3 (1996): 143–63, "Male admirers of Jane Austen have had much to endure in a world that frowns upon their love" (149). Johnson's is a tour de force essay. But in the course of making an argument about the queerness of Austen, she also claims that, in the early twentieth century, to be a Janeite was "principally a male enthusiasm shared among an elite corps of publishers, professors, and literati" (150). My research on Austen's legacy, in this chapter and the next, suggests otherwise.

2. John Glassco, *Memoirs of Montparnasse*, 2nd ed. (New York: Oxford University Press, 1995), 80. Subsequent references cited parenthetically in the text.

3. H. Lawrenny, review of J. E. Austen-Leigh's *A Memoir of Jane Austen* and Jane Austen's *Sense and Sensibility*, *Academy*, 12 February 1870, 118.

4. Susanne Stark, "Simcox, Edith Jemima (1844–1901)," in *Oxford Dictionary of National Biography Online* (Oxford: Oxford University Press, 2004), n.p., Web.

5. An important exception is *The History of England*. See Jane Austen, *Juvenilia*, ed. Peter Sabor (Cambridge: Cambridge University Press, 2006).

6. B. C. Southam, *Jane Austen: The Critical Heritage, 1870–1940* (London: Routledge & Kegan Paul, 1987), 2:ix. Subsequent references cited parenthetically in the text.

7. Arnold Bennett, *Arnold Bennett: The "Evening Standard" Years; "Books and Persons" 1926–1931*, ed. Andrew Mylett (Hamden, CT: Archon, 1974), 68.

8. Ibid. 68.

9. The *OED* credits Saintsbury with the first usage of the word, which he preferred to spell Janite, in 1896. But before there were Janeites, there were Austen-

ites and even Anti-Austenites described in the periodical press. See [Richard Holt Hutton], "The Charm of Miss Austen," *Bookmart*, June 1890, 9.

10. In the same sentence, he declares Scott the father of nineteenth-century romance. See George Saintsbury, *A History of Nineteenth Century Literature* (New York: Macmillan, 1896), 128–29.

11. William Dean Howells, *Criticism and Fiction* (New York: Harper and Brothers, 1891), 73.

12. On Howells, see Southam 2:202; on Bradley, see Southam 2:233.

13. Chesterton could also be critical of men's clubs. The social history of such clubs is far more complex than this chapter describes. I use the term "men's club Janeite" as a shorthand to signal elite men imagining themselves in conversation with other elite men about Austen in single-sex rhetorical (and actual) spaces.

14. G. K. Chesterton, "June 1, 1929: Jane Austen and the General Election," in *The Collected Works of G. K. Chesterton*, vol. 35, *The Illustrated London News, 1929–1931*, ed. Lawrence J. Clipper (San Francisco: Ignatius Press, 1991), 100.

15. "Chesterton Thinks Women Will Tire of New Freedom," *Pittsburgh Post Gazette*, 14 October 1930, 26.

16. G. K. Chesterton, *A Gleaming Cohort* (London: Methuen, 1926), 159.

17. "Chesterton as a Champion of Women Novelists," *Current Opinion*, June 1913, 494–95. The essay points out the odd juxtaposition of Chesterton's backward views on women to his reverence for Victorian women novelists.

18. See Barbara Rogers, *Men Only: An Investigation into Men's Organisations* (London: Pandora, 1988). The phrase "Very Important Men's Clubs" is hers. There were and are men's clubs with members from many kinds of professions and class backgrounds. In this chapter, I am referring to the most exclusive and elite of the type.

19. George Saintsbury, introduction to *Pride and Prejudice*, by Jane Austen (London: George Allen, 1894), xxiii.

20. "The New Pride and Prejudice," supplement, *Sketch*, 5 December 1894, 9.

21. Goldwin Smith, *Life of Jane Austen* (London: Walter Scott, 1890), 45–48.

22. R. Brimley Johnson, "Jane Austen," in *Sense and Sensibility*, by Jane Austen (London: J. M. Dent, 1892), 1:xxv.

23. C. Johnson, "Divine" 145.

24. Ibid. 150.

25. Henry Gilbert, ed., *The Literary Year-Book and Bookman's Directory 1903*, s.v. "Sette of Odd Volumes, The. 1878" (London: George Allen), 370–71. For recent work on the Sette, see Ellen Crowell, "The Necromancer and the Seer: Bibliophilia at the Fin de Siècle," *Times Literary Supplement*, 18 December 2015, 15–17.

26. David Cuppleditch, *The London Sketch Club* (Dover, NH: Alan Sutton, 1994), 78. Subsequent references cited parenthetically in the text as *London*.

27. *The Year-Boke of the Sette of Odd Volumes: An Annual Record of the Transactions of the Sette; Twenty-Fifth Year, 1902–03* (London: Sette of Odd Volumes, 1910), 121, 123. Subsequent references cited parenthetically in the text.

28. On fourth Tuesday and motto, see *Literary Year-Book*, "Sette" 370.

29. John Hassall, "The Divine Jane: Domine" (cartoon), *The 236th Meeting of the Sette of Odd Volumes: 27 May 1902* (London: Sette of Odd Volumes, 1902), menu.

30. This was an image created a decade before Austen's likeness was actually made into a bust by Percy Fitzgerald, in a controversial piece of art ultimately removed from the Pump Room at Bath, as Claudia L. Johnson describes in *Jane Austen: Cults and Cultures* (Chicago: University of Chicago Press), 55–58.

31. David Cuppleditch, *The John Hassall Lifestyle* (Essex: Dilke Press, 1979), 8. Subsequent references cited parenthetically in the text as *John*.

32. *Literary Year-Book*, "Sette" 370.

33. Obituary, Mr. W. F. Lord, *Times* (London), 27 April 1927, 19.

34. Walter Frewen Lord, *Mirror of the Century* (London: John Lane, 1906), vi. Subsequent references cited parenthetically in the text.

35. Walter Frewen Lord, "Jane Austen's Novels," *Nineteenth Century and After* 52 (October 1902): 665. Subsequent references cited parenthetically in the text as "Jane."

36. Its circulation during the period rose as high as twenty thousand. Priscilla Metcalf, *James Knowles: Victorian Editor and Architect* (Oxford: Clarendon, 1980), 285. Subsequent references cited parenthetically in the text.

37. In 1888, Lord had married Knowles's daughter, Millicent Knowles. See "Marriages," *Times* (London), 12 January 1888, 1.

38. Annie Gladstone, "Another View of Jane Austen's Novels," *Nineteenth Century and After* 311 (January 1903): 113–21. Subsequent references cited parenthetically in the text.

39. "Alice's Looking Glass," *Academy* 1774 (5 May 1906): 424.

40. Later critic Ida Beatrice O'Malley puts the case of Austen's feminism even more clearly: Jane Austen's "importance to the women's movement is two-fold. She described the cage, and in doing so she showed qualities which were not expected in the canary." Ida Beatrice O'Malley, *Women in Subjection: A Study of the Lives of Englishwomen before 1832* (London: Duckworth, 1933), 243.

41. Although four-time prime minister W. E. Gladstone had, in fact, published often in the pages of the same periodical, the *Nineteenth Century*, Miss Annie Gladstone did not have a connection to *that* Gladstone family.

42. Annie Gladstone, class RG13, piece 559, folio 10, page 12, *Census Returns of England and Wales, 1901*, Kew, Surrey, England, The National Archives, 1901, data imaged from the National Archives, London, Ancestry.com, *1901 England Census* (database online) (Provo, UT: Ancestry.com Operations, 2005).

43. For a time, Gladstone used her father's first and middle names as a pseudonym: "James Nairn." Under the name James Nairn, Gladstone's most enduring published essay was on Ralph Waldo Emerson, a piece that generously mentions Louisa May Alcott and Margaret Fuller. See James Nairn [Annie Gladstone], "Emerson's Home in Concord," *Temple Bar* 115 (October 1898): 290–97. Gladstone would, in 1904, use her real name as a byline once again for an essay. That one decried the state of literature, politics, and society. Annie Gladstone, "The Decay of Conviction," *Westminster Review* 161 (June 1904): 683–90.

44. Charles Stevenson, "A Voice for All Times: Annie Martha (Gladstone) Wilton, 1857–1932," *Journal of the Historical Society of South Australia* 30 (2002): 84. Subsequent references cited parenthetically in the text.

45. In an echo of Walter Frewen Lord, Annie Gladstone Wilton would publish her writing in the paper for which her new father-in-law served as literary editor, the *Advertiser*. Stevenson 85.

46. Rebecca West (1892–1983) found ridiculous those critics who saw Austen's writings as "little" or limited. West argued, "Really, it is time this comic patronage of Jane Austen ceased." Rebecca West, *The Strange Necessity: Essays by Rebecca West* (Garden City, NY: Doubleday, 1928), 289. West believed that "the feminism of Jane Austen . . . was very marked" and "quite conscious." Rebecca West, preface to *Northanger Abbey*, by Jane Austen (London: Jonathan Cape, 1940), viii, v–xi.

47. For "clever criticism," see "Literary Notes," *Medical Sentinel* 11, no. 5 (May 1903): 318. On "clever analysis," see *Literary Year-Book*, "Sette" 370.

48. "Jane Austen and Her Biographers," *Church Quarterly Review* 112 (July 1903): 358.

49. "Miscellaneous: Notes on Books & c." *Notes and Queries*, 9th ser., 11 (10 January 1903): 39. The reviewer takes issue with Gladstone's assertions about Shakespeare.

50. W. D. Howells, *Heroines of Fiction* (New York: Harper & Brothers, 1903), 48. Subsequent references cited parenthetically in the text.

51. She shows how three Victorian women's magazines embraced Austen for different political ends, struggling with how to represent her as "worldly and domestic, professional and unambitious." Marina Cano-López, "The Outlandish Jane: Austen and Female Identity in Victorian Women's Magazine," *Victorian Periodicals Review* 47, no. 2 (Summer 2014): 255.

52. Jane Austen, *Northanger Abbey*, ed. Barbara M. Benedict and Deirdre Le Faye, in *The Cambridge Edition of the Works of Jane Austen* (Cambridge: Cambridge University Press, 2006), 113.

Chapter 9 • *Stone-Throwing Jane Austen*

1. Elizabeth Crawford, "Suffrage Stories: An Army of Banners—Designed for the NUWSS Suffrage Procession 13 June 1908," *Woman and Her Sphere* (blog), 26 November 2014, n.p., Web. The NUWSS was founded in 1896. The first British suffrage society originated in 1866.

2. Millicent Fawcett, "The Woman Suffrage Procession," *Times* (London), 13 June 1908, 9, *Times Digital Archive*, 14 February 2016. Subsequent references cited parenthetically in the text as "Woman."

3. For an exception to this neglect, see Diana Birchall, "'The Use of the Pen': Women Writers, Banners, and Cat Tails," *Light, Bright, and Sparkling* (blog), 29 September 2010, n.p., Web; and Elizabeth Crawford, "Suffrage Stories" (blog), 26 November 2014, n.p., Web.

4. It's an investigation needed for many other nineteenth-century novelists, including Brontë, Burney, Edgeworth, Eliot, Gaskell, and others. All had their place in the women's suffrage movement.

5. Lisa Tickner, *The Spectacle of Women: Imagery of the Suffrage Campaign, 1907–14* (Chicago: University of Chicago Press, 1988), 84. Subsequent references cited parenthetically in the text.

6. Katharine Cockin et al., eds., *Women's Suffrage Literature*, 4 vols. (New York: Routledge, 2007), 3:ix.

7. "Woman Suffragist Demonstration: An Impression," *Dunstan Times*, 17 August 1908, 5.

8. Irene Cockroft and Susan Croft, *Art, Theatre and Women's Suffrage* (Twickenham: Aurora Metro Press, 2010), 34.

9. Ella Hepworth Dixon, *"As I Knew Them": Sketches of the People I Have Met on the Way* (London: Hutchinson, 1930), 124.

10. "Life and Letters," *Academy*, 11 July 1908, 27.

11. James Douglas's prosuffrage report was reprinted as "Woman Suffragist Demonstration: An Impression," *Dunstan Times*, 17 August 1908, 5.

12. *Souvenir and Programme: Women's Suffrage March and Mass Meeting at the Albert Hall, on Saturday, June 13: Grand Procession of Ten Thousand Women! Seventy Banners English & International* (London, 1908), n.p.

13. Cockin et al 1:xv.

14. Ibid.

15. Caroline Gordon, "To the Editor of the Times," *Times* (London), 13 June 1908, 9, *Times Digital Archive*, 14 February 2016.

16. Frances Hooper, "To the Editor of the Times," *Times* (London), 13 June 1908, 9, *Times Digital Archive*, 14 February 2016.

17. Millicent Fawcett, "To the Editor of the Times," *Times* (London), 15 June 1908, 9, *Times Digital Archive*, 14 February 2016. Subsequent references cited parenthetically in the text as "To the Editor."

18. *Programme of Banners Designed by the Artists' League for Women's Suffrage and Carried in the Procession Organized by The National Union of Women's Suffrage Societies, Saturday, June 13th, 1908* (London, 1908), 1. Subsequent references cited parenthetically in the text.

19. See "Women's Suffrage: A Reply," *Fortnightly Review* 46 (1889): 132.

20. See "Opposing Woman Suffrage," *Cambridge Magazine* 3 (1913): 246. On Augustus Austen-Leigh, see M. C. Curthoys, "Leigh, Augustus Austen (1840–1905)," in *Oxford Dictionary of National Biography* (Oxford: Oxford University Press, 2004), n.p., Web.

21. Florence E. Austen-Leigh and Mary A. P. Seeley, "Woman Suffrage," *Times* (London), 29 January 1917, 9. *Times Digital Archive.*

22. Quoted in Kathryn Sutherland, *Jane Austen's Textual Lives: From Aeschylus to Bollywood* (Oxford: Oxford University Press, 2005), 171.

23. "Votes for Women," *Manchester Guardian*, 22 June 1910, 9.

24. Crawford, "Suffrage Stories" n.p.

25. Lis Whitelaw, *The Life and Rebellious Times of Cicely Hamilton: Actress, Writer, Suffragist* (London: Women's Press, 1990), 88. Subsequent references cited parenthetically in the text.

26. On "most celebrated play of the Suffrage movement," see Roberta Gandolfi, "Edy Craig and Suffrage Theatre," *Open Page* 3 (1998): 54. On the count of one hundred plays, see Gandolfi 55. Subsequent references cited parenthetically in the text.

27. Cicely Hamilton, *A Pageant of Great Women* (London: Suffrage Shop, 1910). Subsequent references cited parenthetically in the text.

28. Sheila Stowell, *A Stage of Their Own: Feminist Playwrights of the Suffrage Era* (Ann Arbor: University of Michigan Press, 1992), 44.

29. Jefferson Hunter, *English Filming, English Writing* (Bloomington: Indiana University Press, 2010), 55.

30. Shelley Cobb, "What Would Jane Do? Postfeminist Media Uses of Austen and the Austen Reader," in *Uses of Austen: Jane's Afterlives*, ed. Gillian Dow and Clare Hanson (New York: Palgrave Macmillan, 2012), 215.

31. Katharine Cockin, introduction to Cockin et al., *Women's Suffrage Literature* 3:x. Katharine Cockin, "Cicely Hamilton's Warriors: Dramatic Reinventions of Militancy in the British Women's Suffrage Movement," *Women's History Review* 14, nos. 3–4 (2005): 527–42. Subsequent references cited parenthetically in the text as introduction and "Cicely."

32. See Cicely Hamilton, *Souvenir: "A Pageant of Great Women" and the One-Act Play "How the Vote Was Won"* (Johannesburg, South Africa: Women's Reform, 1911).

33. "Satire and Art in Suffragist Plays," *Washington Times*, 21 May 1913, 11.

34. Joy Melville, *Ellen and Edy: A Biography of Ellen Terry and Her Daughter, Edith Craig, 1847–1947* (London: Pandora, 1987), 211.

35. Review of *The Bennets*, by Rosina Filippi ["The Court Theatre"], *Times* (London), 30 March 1901, 14.

36. Her father was Thomas Monck Mason (1803–89). On her birth in India, see *The Suffrage Annual and Women's Who's Who* (London: Paul Stanley, 1913), 300.

37. Elizabeth Crawford, "Mayo, Winifred," *Women's Suffrage Movement: A Reference Guide, 1866–1928* (London: UCL Press, 1999), 394.

38. "Miss W. Monck-Mason: Suffragette and Actress," *Times* (London), 2 March 1967, 14, *Times Digital Archive.*

39. Crawford, "Mayo, Winifred," 393; "Miss W. Monck-Mason" 14.

40. Winifred Mayo, "Prison Experiences of a Suffragette," *Idler: An Illustrated Monthly Magazine*, April 1908, 85–99.

41. "Winifred Mayo: A Smashing Time in Pall Mall," BBC Radio Broadcast (originally aired 13 July 1958), in *Suffragettes: Women Recall Their Struggle to Win the Vote*, BBC Archive, 2014. Web. Subsequent references cited parenthetically in the text as BBC.

42. "Miss W. Monck-Mason" 14.

43. "A Pageant of Famous Men and Women: Costume Dinner of Suffragists," *Votes for Women*, 3 July 1914, 618.

44. Ibid.

45. Advertisement for May Sinclair's novels, *Bookman Advertiser* 24, no. 1, September 1906, n.p.

46. Suzanne Raitt, *May Sinclair: A Modern Victorian* (Oxford: Clarendon, 2000), 109.

47. Bertha Brewster, "The Feminism of Jane Austen," *Votes for Women* IX, no. 430 (1917): 282. Subsequent references cited parenthetically in the text as "Feminism."

48. Brewster's letter appeared in the *Daily Telegraph* on February 26, 1913, reprinted in Shaun Usher, ed., *More Letters of Note: Correspondence Worthy of a Wider Audience* (London: Canongate, 2015).

49. E. Sylvia Pankhurst, *The Suffragette: The History of the Women's Militant Suffrage Movement 1905–1910* (Boston: Woman's Journal, 1911), 479.

50. Janine Barchas and Kristina Straub used this Carreras Austen image in their Folger Shakespeare Library exhibition *Will and Jane* in fall 2016. "Curating *Will &*

Jane," Eighteenth-Century Life 40, no. 2 (April 2016): 1–35. Austen's connections to tobacco products continued with scenes from the first Hollywood Austen film adaptation, MGM's *Pride and Prejudice* (1940). "A. & M. Wix Cinema Cavalcade, Volume 2," Moviecard.com, n.d., Web.

51. Benson & Hedges advertisement, *New Yorker*, 12 January 1957, 15.

52. Lloyd W. Brown, "Jane Austen and the Feminist Tradition," *Nineteenth-Century Fiction* 28 (1973–74): 321–38.

53. Sandra M. Gilbert and Susan Gubar, *Madwoman in the Attic: The Woman Writer and the Nineteenth-Century Literary Imagination* (New Haven: Yale University Press, 1979); Mary Poovey, *The Proper Lady and the Woman Writer: Ideology as Style in the Works of Mary Wollstonecraft, Mary Shelley, and Jane Austen* (Chicago: University of Chicago Press, 1984). See also Margaret Kirkham, "Jane Austen and Contemporary Feminism," in *The Jane Austen Companion*, ed. J. David Grey (New York: Macmillan, 1986), 157; as well as her *Jane Austen, Feminism and Fiction* (Totowa, NJ: Barnes & Noble, 1983).

54. On the Twitter trolls and the Austen tenner, see Alexandra Topping, "Jane Austen Twitter Row: Two Plead Guilty to Abusive Tweets," *Guardian*, 7 January 2014, n.p., Web.

Part 4 • Jane Austen, Schooled

1. Thomson's images are used to accompany the *Mentor*'s entries on Gaskell and Eliot in the magazine, too, and a male-dominated Gaskell image is chosen for her printed plate. See Hamilton Wright Mabie, *The Mentor: Famous Women Writers of England* 3, no. 8 (1 June 1915): n.p. Subsequent references cited parenthetically in the text.

2. The *Mentor* had an advisory board of leading educators, as well as academic departments and an inquiry department. The association provided outlines and plans for its curriculum, along with lists of supplementary reading. The *Mentor* ran weekly, then biweekly, and then monthly from 1913 to the early 1930s. Its circulation ranged between fifty and eighty-five thousand over the course of those years. On its publication history and publishers, see Deanna Dahlsad, "The *Mentor* Magazine," *Inherited Values* (blog), 10 January 2011, n.p. Web.

3. The included loose plates are listed as featuring "Jane Austen, George Eliot, Charlotte Brontë, Elizabeth Barrett Browning, Mrs. Gaskell, and Jean Inglow" (Mabie 1).

4. In his *Journal*, Scott compares himself to Austen, writing of his own powers, "The Big Bow-wow strain I can do myself like any now going." He goes on to acknowledge that Austen was among those who wrote as he could not, with the "exquisite touch, which renders ordinary commonplace things and characters interesting." Sir Walter Scott, *The Journal of Walter Scott: From the Original Manuscript at Abbotsford*, vol. 1, ed. David Douglas (Cambridge: Cambridge University Press, 2013), 155.

5. Mabie wrongly suggests that Austen made her "two inches of ivory" statement in response to being asked to write a historical romance, conflating two stories of her alleged authorial modesty (3).

6. "Mr. Darcy and Sir William Lucas," in *Jane Austen*, Monograph Number One in the *Mentor* Reading Course (New York: Mentor Association, 1915), n.p. Subsequent references cited parenthetically in the text.

7. "A Centenary: Jane Austen," *Saturday Review* 124 (14 July 1917): 25–26.

8. On Austen, Chapman's editing, and the influence of schoolroom texts, see Kathryn Sutherland, *Jane Austen's Textual Lives: From Aeschylus to Bollywood* (Oxford: Oxford University Press, 205), 32.

Chapter 10 • The First Jane Austen Dissertation

1. David Lodge, *Changing Places: A Tale of Two Campuses* (New York: Penguin, 1975), 44.

2. George Pellew, *Jane Austen's Novels* (Boston: Cupples, Upham, 1883). Subsequent references cited parenthetically in the text.

3. Henry James, *Henry James Letters*, ed. Leon Edel, 4 vols. (Cambridge, MA: Harvard University Press, 1975), 2:422.

4. The most complete account is Michael G. Kenny, "The Return of George Pellew," in *The Passion of Ansel Bourne: Multiple Personality in American Culture* (Washington, DC: Smithsonian Institution Press, 1986), 97–128. Subsequent references cited parenthetically in the text.

5. Richard Cary, "William Dean Howells to Thomas Sergeant Perry," *Colby Library Quarterly* 8 (December 1968): 3, 5. On Franklin, see James Munves, "Richard Hodgson, Mrs. Piper and 'George Pelham': A Centennial Reassessment," *Journal of the Society for Psychical Research* 62, no. 849 (October 1997): 142. Subsequent references cited parenthetically in the text.

6. Pellew ultimately gave a Harvard lecture, "A Critical Estimate of Miss Austen's Novels," reportedly complaining in it that Austen's fiction didn't have enough poetry in it. This would differ from his book, which argues that under the spell of her humor we do not feel the absence of poetry (*Novels* 50). On the lecture, see "Fact and Rumor," *Harvard Crimson*, 17 April 1883, n.p.

7. Anne-Marie Scholz, *"An Orgy of Propriety": Jane Austen and the Emergence and Legacy of the Female Author in America, 1826–1926* (Trier: Wissenschaftllicher Verlag, 1999), 97.

8. It would remain so until the Dead Wife Sister's Marriage Act of 1907. Men, including Jane Austen's brother, Charles, married their sisters-in-law prior to its being outlawed in 1835.

9. W. D. Howells, introduction to *The Poems of George Pellew* (Boston: W. B. Clarke, 1892), vi. Subsequent references cited parenthetically in the text.

10. "Prize Descriptions," Harvard University Prize Office (2014), n.p., Web.

11. Claire Harman calls it "the first time the author had been studied in the academy"—true in a sense—but given that Pellew presumably learned Austen from Perry, the origin is more difficult to pin down. Claire Harman, *Jane's Fame: How Jane Austen Conquered the World* (Edinburgh: Canongate, 2009), 124.

12. "George Pellew Found Dead," *New York Times*, 19 February 1892, 9.

13. Thomas Sergeant Perry, *Selections from the Letters of Thomas Sergeant Perry*, ed. Edwin Arlington Robinson (New York: Macmillan, 1929), 7.

14. Perry gives "hearty thanks" to "my friend, Mr. George Pellew" in *English Literature of the Eighteenth Century* (New York: Harper & Brothers, 1883), x.

15. Eric Haralson and Kendall Johnson, *Critical Companion to Henry James: A Literary Reference to His Life and Work* (New York: Facts on File, 2009), 429. Subsequent reference cited parenthetically in the text.

16. Meredith Martindale, *Lilla Cabot Perry: An American Impressionist* (Washington, DC: National Museum of Women in the Arts, 1990), 126.

17. Munves 144–45. Munves, a member of the Society for Psychical Research, which had conducted a long-term investigation of Mrs. Piper's powers, uses archival sources and unpublished letters to show the SPR's shoddy approach to documenting the Pellew case. He is the one who makes the questionable supposition about Mrs. Perry and Pellew in love.

18. Henry James, *Letters, Fictions, Lives: Henry James and William Dean Howells*, ed. Michael Anesko (New York: Oxford University Press, 1997), 260.

19. Letter from William Dean Howells to George W. Curtis, 3 March 1888, *W. D. Howells: Selected Letters, Volume 3: 1882–1891*, ed. Robert C. Leitz III with Richard H. Ballinger and Christoph K. Lohmann (Boston: Twayne, 1980), 219.

20. Deborah Blum, *Ghost Hunters: William James and the Search for Scientific Proof of Life after Death* (New York: Penguin, 2006), 185.

21. "George Pellew Found Dead" 9.

22. Letter from William Dean Howells to George W. Curtis, 3 March 1888, 220. It is suggested in an editors' note on this letter that Pellew learned his own views on women's suffrage from serving as the legal assistant to Josiah Quincy (1859–1919) (220).

23. Lucy Stone to George Pellew, 18 January 1889, Lucy Stone Letters, box 8, folder SC 41, Syracuse University Special Collections, Syracuse, NY. On Pellew as secretary, see "New York Suffrage Work," *Woman's Journal*, 16 August 1890, 263. On Pellew addressing a suffrage meeting, see "In Memoriam," *Woman's Journal*, 27 February 1892, 71.

24. [William Dean Howells], "On the Immortality of Jane Austen," *Harper's Magazine* 127 (1913): 958–61.

25. William James, *Report on Mrs. Piper's Hodgson-Control* (London: 1909), 36. Subsequent references cited parenthetically in the text.

26. "Mrs. Piper a Human Telephone to the Spirit World," *New York Herald*, 18 June 1899, sixth section, 1. On "most famous," see Martin Gardner, *The Night Is Large: Collected Essays 1938–1995* (New York: St. Martin's Press, 1996), 214. Subsequent references cited parenthetically in the text.

27. W. James 6.

28. Murray T. Bloom, "America's Most Famous Medium," *American Mercury*, May 1950, 580.

29. Anne Manning Robbins, *Past and Present with Mrs. Piper* (New York: Henry Holt, 1922), 4. On Sir Walter Scott, see Joseph McCabe, *Is Spiritualism Based on Fraud? The Evidence Given by Sir A. C. Doyle and Others Drastically Examined* (London: Watts, 1920), 104. Subsequent references cited parenthetically in the text.

30. M. Sage, *Mrs. Piper and the Society of Psychical Research*, trans. Noralie Robertson (New York: Scott-Thaw, 1904), 68.

31. Richard Hodgson, "A Further Record of Observations of Certain Phenomena of Trance," *Proceedings of the Society for Psychical Research* 13 (1897–98): 284–582. Subsequent references cited parenthetically in the text.

32. Murray Teigh Bloom, "The Housewife Who Confounded Two Countries," *Reader's Digest*, May 1950, 53. Subsequent references cited parenthetically in the text.

33. Mrs. Henry Sidgwick offers a different reading of Hodgson's account of Norton, Pellew, and Austen in "Discussion of the Trance Phenomena of Mrs. Piper," *Proceedings of the Society for Psychical Research*, vol. 16, part 36 (1901), 31. That volume mentioning Austen also notes that one of the current members and associates of the SPR is "Leigh, W. Austen, MA" in Roehampton (498). This was Austen descendant William Austen-Leigh, who with his nephew Richard Arthur Austen-Leigh, published *Jane Austen: Her Life and Letters: A Family Record* (London: Smith, Elder, 1913). William Austen-Leigh is listed in SPR records spanning from 1884 to 1907, suggesting decades-long affiliation, as well as small donations.

34. Andrew Lang, *The Making of Religion*, 3rd ed. (London: Longmans, Green, 1909), 139.

35. Arthur Conan Doyle, *The History of Spiritualism*, 2 vols. (New York: Arno Press, 1975), 1:80.

36. Claudia L. Johnson's *Jane Austen: Cults and Cultures* (Chicago: University of Chicago Press, 2012) has an extended, learned exploration on imagining Jane Austen as a ghost. See, too, Paul Westover, *Necromanticism: Travelling to Meet the Dead, 1750–1860* (New York: Palgrave Macmillan, 2012).

37. Andrew Lang, "At the Sign of St. Paul's: Andrew Lang on a Case of Spiritualism," *Illustrated London News*, no. 644 (6 November 1909): 14.

Chapter 11 • Textbook Austens

1. H. A. [Austin] Dobson, *The Civil Service Handbook of English Literature: For the Use of Candidates for Examinations, Public Schools, and Students Generally* (London: Lockwood, 1874), 1. Subsequent references cited parenthetically in the text.

2. B. C. Southam, introduction to *Jane Austen: The Critical Heritage*, vol. 2, *1870–1940* (London: Routledge & Kegan Paul, 1987), 5.

3. Benjamin Brawley, *A New Survey of English Literature: A Text Book for Colleges* (New York: Alfred A. Knopf, 1925), 252–53. His Austen is quiet, narrow, and retiring (rather than placid), and unsurpassed.

4. A 1988 national survey of US high schools found Austen was one of three women authors most taught among 30 percent of Catholic schools, along with Harper Lee and Emily Brontë. In 1963, Austen and Eliot were the top two. Public schools were less likely to teach Austen, preferring Harper Lee and Anne Frank as its representative women authors. See Arthur W. Applebee, *A Study of Book-Length Works Taught in High School English Courses*, Report Series 1.2 (Albany, NY: Center for the Learning and Teaching of Literature, 1989).

5. *UK RED: Reading Experience Database* (Milton Keynes: Open University, 2016), Web; *Book Traces* (Charlottesville: University of Virginia, 2016), n.p., Web.

6. In the United States, some states published very specific recommended curricula for public high schools, with Austen's name included on reading lists. In the United Kingdom and the Commonwealth, one might trace the ways Austen has been

used in A-level exams, established in 1951, or their predecessor, the Higher School Certificate Examination, from 1918. Systematic study of Austen's place in them would undoubtedly yield new insights.

7. "Dr. Wines Dead: His Valuable Services in Behalf of Prison Reform—the Books He Wrote," *New York Times*, 11 December 1879, 5.

8. E. C. Wines, *Hints on a System of Popular Education* (Philadelphia: Hogan and Thompson, 1838). The first American edition of all six of Austen's novels was published by Carey and Lea in 1832–33. In 1816, Carey published *Emma* as a stand-alone title in Philadelphia.

9. J. Cordy Jeaffreson, *Novels and Novelists from Elizabeth to Victoria*, 2 vols. (London: Hurst and Blackett, 1858), 2:84. Subsequent references cited parenthetically in the text.

10. Lawrence Mazzeno, "Austen's Status in Surveys of Literature," in *Jane Austen: Two Centuries of Criticism* (Rochester, NY: Camden House, 2011), 27–30.

11. Joseph Angus, *The Handbook of English Literature* (London: Religious Tract Society, 1865), 618–19.

12. William Baker, "Janeites," in *Critical Companion to Jane Austen: A Literary Reference to Her Life and Work*" (New York: Facts on File, 2008), 547.

13. H. J. Jackson, *Those Who Write for Immortality: Romantic Reputations and the Dream of Lasting Fame* (New Haven: Yale University Press, 2015), 100. Jackson's excellent section on Austen considers in brief many issues given extended attention in this book.

14. "A Novel Course for Teachers: Jane Austen," *Southern Educational Journal* 12 (February 1899): 135.

15. M. and C. Lee, "Parallel Lives: Charlotte Younge and Jane Austen," *Journal of Education* 24 (1902): 212–13.

16. Arlo Bates, *Talks on the Study of Literature* (Boston: Houghton Mifflin, 1897), 189. Subsequent references cited parenthetically in the text.

17. Jane Austen, *Pride and Prejudice*, ed. Josephine Woodbury Heermans (New York: Macmillan, 1908). The edition was reprinted in 1911, 1912, 1914, 1915, 1916, and beyond. Subsequent references cited parenthetically in the text.

18. Sarah Nyman, "SC86-2 Josephine Woodbury Heermans Greenwood Papers Finding Aid," Kansas City Public Library, Missouri Valley Special Collections, 2002, Web.

19. Review of *Pride and Prejudice*, by Jane Austen, edited by Josephine Woodbury Heermans, *Journal of Education* 68 (November 1908): 577.

20. "The Jackson County Institute," *Missouri School Journal* 14 (September 1897): 532, 533.

21. Jane Austen and Elizabeth Gaskell, *The Austen-Gaskell Book: Scenes from the Works of Jane Austen and Mrs. Gaskell*, ed. J. Compton (London: G. Bell and Sons, 1926), iii. Subsequent references cited parenthetically in the text.

22. David Gilson, *A Bibliography of Jane Austen*, rev. ed. (New Castle, DE: Oak Knoll Press, 1997), 291.

23. William Peacock, preface to *English Prose*, 5 vols. (London: Oxford University Press, 1921), 1:v.

24. Donald E. Stahl, *A History of the English Curriculum in American High Schools* (Chicago: Lyceum Press, 1965), 81.

25. Victor Neuberg, "Cheap Reprints of Literary Classics," in *The Popular Press Companion to Popular Literature* (Bowling Green, OH: Bowling Green State University Popular Press, 1983), 57–58.

26. Fred Hunter, "Morley, Henry (1822–1894)," in *Oxford Dictionary of National Biography Online* (Oxford: Oxford University Press, 2004; online ed., October 2009), n.p., Web.

27. H. Morley, ed., *Sketches of Longer Works of English Verse and Prose*, Cassell's Library of English Literature (London: Cassell, Petter, Galpin, 1876), 385.

28. *McGuffey's High School Reader*, rev. ed. (Cincinnati: Eclectic Press; Van Antwerp, Bragg, 1889), 134–39. Subsequent references cited parenthetically in the text. Out of eighty-six writers in the volume, Austen is the first woman to appear, with a total of eleven females included. Two-thirds of the writers would today be classified as British.

29. John H. Westerhoff III, *McGuffey and His Readers: Piety, Morality, and Education in Nineteenth-Century America* (Nashville: Abingdon, 1978), 14.

30. George Saintsbury, *Specimens of English Prose Style from Malory to Macaulay* (London: Kegan, Paul, Trench, 1886), 299.

31. Henry Craik, ed., *English Prose Selections*, vol. 5, *Nineteenth Century* (New York: Macmillan, 1900), 53. Subsequent references cited parenthetically in the text.

32. Anna Vaninskaya, "The Novel, Its Critics, and the University: A New Beginning?," in *The Oxford Handbook of the Victorian Novel*, ed. Lisa Rodensky (Oxford: Oxford University Press, 2013), 709.

33. Leah Price, *The Anthology and the Rise of the Novel: From Richardson to George Eliot* (Cambridge: Cambridge University Press, 2000), 92.

34. Andrew Wright, "Jane Austen Adapted," *Nineteenth-Century Fiction* 30, no. 3 (1975): 441–42.

35. Jane Austen, *Pride and Prejudice*, abridged from the story by Jane Austen, Laurel & Gold Series (London: Collins, 1942). This version begins, "'My dear Mr. Bennet,' said his lady to him one day" (5). Wright declares many of the omissions "startling" (427).

36. Joseph O. Baylen, "Stead, William Thomas (1849–1912)," in *Oxford Dictionary of National Biography Online* (Oxford: Oxford University Press, 2004; online ed., September 2010), n.p., Web. Stead, an investigative journalist, advocate for the poor, for liberal causes, for women's rights, and for peace, as well as for the paranormal/spiritualism, died aboard the Titanic.

37. Gilson, *Bibliography* 270–71.

38. "Christmas Presents: From a Penny to Five Pounds," *Review of Reviews* 16 (1897): 502.

39. "The Best Christmas Present: A Library for a Pound," *Review of Reviews* 16 (1897): 390. Subsequent references cited parenthetically in the text.

40. Jane Austen, *Pride and Prejudice*, abridged and edited by Mrs. Frederick Boas (Cambridge: Cambridge University Press, 1910), n.p.

41. Jane Austen, *Northanger Abbey*, ed. Mrs. Frederick Boas, illus. Hugh Thomson (London: Macmillan, 1934). Boas includes her own original introduction, copious notes, and a final section, "Essay Questions," showing that this, too, was intended as a

school edition. My personal favorite is "Describe John Thorpe driving a car instead of a horse" (225).

42. "The World of Books: Nature and Art," *London Quarterly Review* 101 (January 1904): 181.

43. Review of *Pride and Prejudice*, by Jane Austen, abridged and edited by Mrs. Frederick Boas, *Saturday Review of Politics, Literature, Science, and Art* 110 (12 November 1910): 613.

44. "English Literature for Schools," *Journal of Education and the School World* 50 (April 1928): 241.

45. Ford L. Lemler, "Using Films for Teaching," *Michigan Alumnus*, 9 November 1946, 97.

46. "Pride and Prejudice," MGM (1949), *Educational Films: 1973* (Ann Arbor: University of Michigan Audio-Visual Education Center, 1973), 417.

47. Stewart Beach, "Good Books Make Good Movies," *Spokesman-Review*, 2 February 1963, 17.

48. John McElwee, "MGM's Perpetual Product Plan," *John McElwee's Greenbrier Picture Shows* (blog), 10 May 2006, n.p. Web.

49. Sharon Hamilton-Wieler, "Marion C. Sheridan," in *Missing Chapters: Ten Pioneering Women in NCTE and English Education*, ed. Jeanne Marcum Gerlach and Virginia R. Monseau (Urbana, IL: National Council of Teachers of English, 1991), 116–38.

50. Lionel Trilling, "Why We Read Jane Austen," *Times Literary Supplement*, 5 March 1976, 250–52. Subsequent references cited parenthetically in the text.

51. Ellin Stein, *That's Not Funny, That's Sick: The National Lampoon and the Comedy Insurgents Who Captured the Mainstream* (London: W. W. Norton, 2013), 94. Subsequent references cited parenthetically in the text.

52. National Lampoon poster by Michael O'Donoghue and George W. S. Trow, box 6, Jeanne Tupper Collection about Jane Austen (Collection 1514), Department of Special Collections, Charles E. Young Research Library, University of California, Los Angeles.

53. George W. S. Trow and Michael O'Donoghue, School of Hard Sell, *National Lampoon: The Humor Magazine*, October 1971, 19.

Coda

1. Camilla Nelson, "Is Popularity Killing Jane Austen?," *Newsweek*, 10 March 2015, accessed 22 May 2016, http://www.newsweek.com/popularity-killing-jane-austen-311974. Subsequent references cited parenthetically in the text. Ron Rosenbaum, "Is Jane Austen Overhyped?," *Slate*, 13 February 2013, Web.

2. *Greer Garson Coloring Book* (Chicago: Merrill, 1944), 10–13. The coloring book indicates it is produced "Courtesy of Metro-Goldwyn-Mayer."

3. Chellie Carroll, *Pride and Prejudice: A Coloring Classic* (New York: Doubleday Books for Young Readers, 2016), 1.

4. Eva Maria Hamilton, *Jane Austen's Pride and Prejudice Colouring & Activity Book: Featuring Illustrations from 1895* (n.p.: Lilac Lane, 2015).

5. M. C. Frank, *Persuasion: The Coloring Book* (San Bernardino, CA: n.p., 2016); Katrina King, *Jane Austen's Pride and Prejudice: The Adult Coloring Book* (San Bernardino, CA: n.p., 2015).

6. Michael Allford and Dianne Allford, *Color and Colorability: An Adult Coloring Book Celebrating the Work of Jane Austen* (San Bernardino, CA: n.p., 2016).

7. Simon Reade, *Pride and Prejudice: A Romantic Comedy* (London: Oberon Books, 2009).

8. Ryan Haddad (licensing representative, Samuel French, Inc.), "Jane Austen Data," e-mail communication with the author, 10 June 2016.

9. Jon Jory, *Austen on Stage: The Complete Works of Jane Austen Adapted for the Stage* (New York: Playscripts, 2017). The complete dramatic works are listed as four hundred pages long.

10. See Joe Karaganis and David McClure, "What a Million Syllabuses Can Teach Us," *New York Times*, 22 January 2016, SR9. Austen is not the most–highly ranked woman author. The most often assigned college English text, according to the Online Syllabus Project, is Diana Hacker's *The Bedford Handbook*, a composition textbook.

11. Claire Heald (executive principal, Jane Austen College), "Jane Austen College," e-mail communication with the author, 22 June 2016.

12. On the Twitter trolls and the Austen tenner, see Alexandra Topping, "Jane Austen Twitter Row: Two Plead Guilty to Abusive Tweets," *Guardian*, 7 January 2014, Web.

13. Eugene Volokh, "*Pride and Prejudice* Gets Its First U.S. Supreme Court Citation," *Washington Post*, 13 January 2015, Web.

14. Lauren Gambino and Paul Owen, "Chelsea Clinton, in Spotlight She Once Shunned, Speaks of Hillary the Mother," *Guardian*, 28 July 2016, Web.

15. Our story is further described in Deborah Yaffe's book, *Among the Janeites: A Journey through the World of Jane Austen Fandom* (Boston: Mariner Books, 2013).

Afterword

1. On the Basingstoke statue, see "Jane Austen Statue Unveiled in Basingstoke," *BBC News*, 18 July 2017, https://www.bbc.com/news/uk-england-hampshire-40642894. On the benches, see *Sitting with Jane*, 2017, http://www.sittingwithjane.com. On *Rain Jane*, see "Winchester 'Rain Jane' Trail Makes a Splash for Jane Austen Bicentenary," *Jane Austen: A Life in Hampshire*, 26 October 2016, http://janeausten200.co.uk/winchester -%E2%80%98rain-jane%E2%80%99-trail-makes-splash-jane-austen-bicentenary. On Jane Austen taking to the streets, see Devoney Looser, "Adapt and Adaptability," *Big Issue North*, 24 July 2017, https://www.bigissuenorth.com/features/2017/07/adapt-and -adaptability/.

2. Nicole M. Wright, "Alt-Right Jane Austen," *Chronicle Review*, 12 March 2017, https://www.chronicle.com/article/Alt-Right-Jane-Austen/239435; Helena Kelly, *Jane Austen, the Secret Radical* (New York: Knopf, 2017).

3. Austen's line is a paraphrase from Sir Walter Scott's poem *Marmion* (1808): "I do not rhyme to that dull elf, / Who cannot image to himself" (canto 6, stanza 38). See Jane Austen to Cassandra Austen, 29 January 1813, *Jane Austen's Letters*, ed. Deirdre Le Faye, 4th ed. (Oxford: Oxford University Press, 2011), 210.

Appendix: Suggested Further Reading

1. See Barry Roth and Joel Weinsheimer, *An Annotated Bibliography of Jane Austen Studies, 1952–1972* (Charlottesville: University Press of Virginia, 1973); Barry Roth, *An Annotated Bibliography of Jane Austen Studies, 1973–1983* (Charlottesville:

University Press of Virginia, 1985); Barry Roth, *An Annotated Bibliography of Jane Austen Studies, 1984–1994* (Athens: Ohio University Press, 1985).

2. Kathryn Sutherland, "Brian Southam: Scholar and Critic Who Altered the Landscape of Jane Austen Studies," *Guardian*, 5 November 2010, 47.

3. Laurence W. Mazzeno, *Jane Austen: Two Centuries of Criticism* (Rochester, NY: Camden House, 2011), 2.

4. Claire Harman, *Jane's Fame: How Jane Austen Conquered the World* (Edinburgh: Canongate, 2009), 6. Subsequent references cited parenthetically in the text.

5. Rachel Brownstein, *Why Jane Austen?* (New York: Columbia University Press, 2011), 1.

6. Emily Auerbach, *Searching for Jane Austen* (Madison: University of Wisconsin Press, 2004), 40.

7. Claudia Johnson, *Jane Austen's Cults and Cultures* (Chicago: University of Chicago Press, 2012), 13, 14.

8. Deidre Lynch, introduction to *Janeites: Austen's Disciples and Devotees* (Princeton: Princeton University Press, 2000), 6.

9. Gillian Dow and Clare Harman, eds., *Uses of Austen: Jane's Afterlives* (New York: Palgrave Macmillan, 2012), 1, 5.

10. Andrew Wright, "Jane Austen Adapted," *Nineteenth-Century Fiction* 30, no. 3 (1975): 423.

11. Sybil G. Brinton, *Old Friends and New Fancies: An Imaginary Sequel to the Novels of Jane Austen* (London: Holden & Hardingham, 1913).

12. Linda Troost and Sayre Greenfield, eds., *Jane Austen in Hollywood* (Lexington: University Press of Kentucky, 1998); Sue Parrill, *Jane Austen on Film and Television: A Critical Study of the Adaptations* (Jefferson, NC: McFarland, 2002); Suzanne R. Pucci and James Thompson, eds., *Jane Austen and Co.: Remaking the Past in Contemporary Culture* (Albany: State University of New York Press, 2003); Lisa Hopkins, *Relocating Shakespeare and Austen on Screen* (New York: Palgrave, 2009); Deborah Cartmell and Imelda Whelehan, eds., *Adaptations: From Text to Screen, Screen to Text* (New York: Routledge, 1999).

13. Deborah Cartmell, *Screen Adaptations: Jane Austen's "Pride and Prejudice"; The Relationship between Text and Film* (London: Methuen, 2010).

14. Janine Barchas and Kristina Straub, "Curating *Will & Jane*," *Eighteenth-Century Life* 40, no. 2 (April 2016): 1–35.

Jane Austen's Writings

Emma. Edited by Richard Cronin and Dorothy McMillan. Cambridge: Cambridge University Press, 2005.

Jane Austen's Letters. Edited by Deirdre Le Faye. 4th ed. Oxford: Oxford University Press, 2011.

Juvenilia. Edited by Peter Sabor. Cambridge: Cambridge University Press, 2006.

Later Manuscripts. Edited by Janet Todd and Linda Bree. Cambridge: Cambridge University Press, 2008.

Mansfield Park. Edited by John Wiltshire. Cambridge: Cambridge University Press, 2005.

Northanger Abbey. Edited by Barbara Benedict and Deirdre Le Faye. Cambridge: Cambridge University Press, 2006.

Persuasion. Edited by Janet Todd and Antje Blank. Cambridge: Cambridge University Press, 2006.

Pride and Prejudice. Edited by Pat Rogers. Cambridge: Cambridge University Press, 2006.

Sense and Sensibility. Edited by Edward Copeland. Cambridge: Cambridge University Press, 2006.

Selected Bibliography on Jane Austen's Legacy

Auerbach, Emily. *Searching for Jane Austen*. Madison: University of Wisconsin Press, 2004.

Austen-Leigh, J. E. *A Memoir of Jane Austen and Other Family Recollections*. Edited by Kathryn Sutherland. Oxford: Oxford University Press, 2002.

Baker, William. *Critical Companion to Jane Austen: A Literary Reference to Her Life and Work*. New York: Facts on File, 2008.

Barchas, Janine. "Sense, Sensibility, and Soap: An Unexpected Case Study in Digital Resources for Book History." *Book History* 16 (2013): 185–214.

Barchas, Janine, and Kristina Straub. "Curating *Will & Jane*." *Eighteenth-Century Life* 40, no. 2 (April 2016): 1–35.

Bautz, Annika. "'In Perfect Volume Form, Price Sixpence': Illustrating *Pride and Prejudice* for a Late Victorian Mass-Market." In *Romantic Adaptations: Essays in*

Mediation and Remediation, edited by Cian Duffy, Peter Howell, and Caroline Ruddell, 101–24. Burlington, VT: Ashgate, 2013.

———. *The Reception of Jane Austen and Walter Scott: A Comparative Longitudinal Study*. London: Continuum, 2007.

Birchall, Diana. "'The Use of the Pen': Women Writers, Banners, and Cat Tails." *Light, Bright, and Sparkling* (blog). 29 September 2010. http://lightbrightandsparkling .blogspot.com/2010/09/use-of-pen-women-writers-and-their.html.

Birtwistle, Sue, and Susie Conklin. *The Making of Pride and Prejudice*. London: Penguin, 1995.

Bolton, H. Philip. *Women Writers Dramatized: A Calendar of Performances from Narrative Works Published in English to 1900*. London: Mansell, 2000.

Brewster, Bertha. "The Feminism of Jane Austen." *Votes for Women* IX, no. 430 (1917): 282.

Brown, Lloyd W. "Jane Austen and the Feminist Tradition." *Nineteenth-Century Fiction* 28, no. 3 (1973): 321–38.

Brownstein, Rachel. *Why Jane Austen?* New York: Columbia University Press, 2011.

Byrne, Paula. *Jane Austen and the Theatre*. London: Hambledon, 2002.

Cano-López, Marina. "The Outlandish Jane: Austen and Female Identity in Victorian Women's Magazine." *Victorian Periodicals Review* 47, no. 2 (Summer 2014): 255–73.

Carroll, Laura, and John Wiltshire. "Jane Austen, Illustrated." In *A Companion to Jane Austen*, edited by Claudia L. Johnson and Clara Tuite, 62–78. Oxford: Wiley-Blackwell, 2009.

Cartmell, Deborah. *Jane Austen's "Pride and Prejudice": The Relationship between Text and Film*. London: Methuen, 2010.

Cartmell, Deborah, and Imelda Whelehan, eds. *Adaptations: From Text to Screen, Screen to Text*. New York: Routledge, 1999.

———. "A Practical Understanding of Literature on Screen: Two Conversations with Andrew Davies." In *The Cambridge Companion to Literature on Screen*, edited by Deborah Cartmell and Imelda Whelehan, 239–51. Cambridge: Cambridge University Press, 2007.

Castle, Terry. "Sister, Sister." *London Review of Books*, 3 August 1995, 3–6.

Chaney, Jen. *As If! The Oral History of "Clueless" as Told by Amy Heckerling, the Cast, and the Crew*. New York: Touchstone, 2015.

Chapman, R. W. *Jane Austen: A Critical Bibliography*. 2nd ed. Oxford: Clarendon Press, 1969.

Chesterton, G. K. *The Collected Works of G. K. Chesterton*. Vol. 35, *The Illustrated London News, 1929–1931*. Edited by Lawrence J. Clipper. San Francisco: Ignatius Press, 1991.

Clark, Russell, and William Phillips. "Eleanor Holmes Hinkley's 'Lost' Play, *Dear Jane*: Jane Austen in the Theatre." *Sensibilities* 45 (2012): 91–109.

Cohn, Maggie Hunt. "Illustrations for Jane Austen." In *The Jane Austen Companion*, edited by J. David Grey, 219–22. New York: Macmillan, 1986.

Di Paolo, Marc. *Emma Adapted: Jane Austen's Heroine from Book to Film*. New York: Peter Lang, 2007.

Dow, Gillian, and Clare Hanson, eds. *Uses of Austen: Jane's Afterlives*. New York: Palgrave Macmillan, 2012.

Favret, Mary. "Free and Happy: Jane Austen in America." In *Janeites: Austen's Disciples and Devotees*, edited by Deidre Lynch, 166–87. Princeton: Princeton University Press, 2000.

Fergus, Jan. *Jane Austen: A Literary Life*. New York: St. Martin's, 1991.

Filippi, Rosina. *Duologues and Scenes from the Novels of Jane Austen: Arranged and Adapted for Drawing-Room Performance*. London: J. M. Dent, 1895.

Fullerton, Susannah. *Happily Ever After: Celebrating Jane Austen's Pride and Prejudice*. London: Frances Lincoln, 2013.

Garside, Peter, and Karen O'Brien, eds. *The Oxford History of the Novel in English*. Vol. 2, *English and British Fiction 1750–1820*. Oxford: Oxford University Press, 2015.

Gay, Penny. *Jane Austen and the Theatre*. Cambridge: Cambridge University Press, 2002.

Gilbert, Deirdre. "From Cover to Cover: Packaging Jane Austen from Egerton to Kindle." *Persuasions On-Line* 29, no. 1 (Winter 2008). http://www.jasna.org /persuasions/on-line/vol29no1/gilbert.html.

Gilson, David. *A Bibliography of Jane Austen*. Rev. ed. New Castle, DE: Oak Knoll Press, 1997.

———. "Later Publishing History, with Illustrations," In *Jane Austen in Context*, edited by Janet Todd, 121–59. Cambridge: Cambridge University Press, 2005.

Gladstone, Annie. "Another View of Jane Austen's Novels." *Nineteenth Century and After* 311 (January 1903): 113–21.

Halsey, Katie. *Jane Austen and Her Readers, 1786–1945*. London: Anthem Press, 2012.

Hamilton, Cicely. *A Pageant of Great Women*. London: Suffrage Shop, 1910.

Harman, Claire. *Jane's Fame: How Jane Austen Conquered the World*. Edinburgh: Canongate, 2009.

Hassall, Joan. "Illustrating Jane Austen." In *The Jane Austen Companion*, edited by J. David Grey, 215–18. New York: Macmillan, 1986.

Hopkins, Lisa. *Relocating Shakespeare and Austen on Screen*. New York: Palgrave, 2009.

Horowitz, Sarah M. "Picturing *Pride and Prejudice*: Reading Two Illustrations of the 1890s." *Persuasions On-Line* 34, no. 1 (2013). Web.

Howells. W. D. *Heroines of Fiction*. New York: Harper & Brothers, 1901.

———. "On the Immortality of Jane Austen." *Harper's Magazine* 127 (1913): 958–61.

Jackson, H. J. *Those Who Write for Immortality: Romantic Reputations and the Dream of Lasting Fame*. New Haven: Yale University Press, 2015.

James, Henry. *The Question of Our Speech: The Lesson of Balzac; Two Lectures*. Boston: Houghton, Mifflin, 1905.

Jane Austen's Fiction Manuscripts Digital Edition. University of Oxford and King's College London, 2012. Web.

Johnson, Claudia L. "Austen Cults and Cultures." In *Cambridge Companion to Jane Austen*. 2nd ed., edited by Edward Copeland and Juliet McMaster, 232–47. Cambridge: Cambridge University Press, 2011.

———. "The Divine Miss Jane: Jane Austen, Janeites, and the Discipline of Novel Studies." *boundary 2* 23, no. 3 (1996): 143–63.

———. *Jane Austen's Cults and Cultures*. Chicago: University of Chicago Press, 2012.

Kirkham, Margaret. *Jane Austen, Feminism and Fiction*. New ed. London: Athlone, 1997.

———. "Jane Austen and Contemporary Feminism." In *The Jane Austen Companion*, edited by J. David Grey, 154–59. New York: Macmillan, 1986.

Lane, Maggie, and David Selwyn. *Jane Austen: A Celebration*. Manchester: Fyfield Books, 2000.

Lauritzen, Monica. *Jane Austen's Emma on Television: A Study of a BBC Classic Serial* Göteborg, Sweden: Acta Universitatis Gothoburgensis, 1981.

Le Faye, Deirdre. *A Chronology of Jane Austen and Her Family, 1600–2000*. 2nd ed. Cambridge: Cambridge University Press, 2013.

——. "Imaginary Portraits of Jane Austen." *Jane Austen Society Report* (2007): 42–52.

Littlewood, Ian, ed. *Jane Austen: Critical Assessments*. 4 vols. Mountfield: Helm Information, 1998.

Lodge, David. *Changing Places: A Tale of Two Campuses*. New York: Penguin, 1975.

Looser, Devoney. "Jane Austen, Illustrated." *London Magazine: A Review of Literature and the Arts*, October/November 2015, 92–112.

Lord, Walter Frewen. "Jane Austen's Novels." *Nineteenth Century and After* (October 1902): 665–75.

Lynch, Deidre, ed. *Janeites: Austen's Disciples and Devotees*. Princeton, NJ: Princeton University Press, 2000.

MacKaye, Mary Keith (Medbery) [Mrs. Steele]. *Pride and Prejudice: A Play, Founded on Jane Austen's Novel*. New York: Duffield, 1906.

Macnamara, Margaret. *Elizabeth Refuses: A Miniature Comedy from Jane Austen's Pride and Prejudice*. London: Joseph Williams, 1926.

Malcolm, Gabrielle. *Fan Phenomena: Jane Austen*. Bristol: Intellect Books, 2015.

Mandal, Anthony. *Jane Austen and the Popular Novel: The Determined Author*. Basingstoke, UK: Palgrave Macmillan, 2007.

Mandal, Anthony, and Brian Southam, eds. *The Reception of Jane Austen in Europe*. New York: Continuum, 2007.

Margolis, Harriet. "What Does the Name 'Jane Austen' Authorize?" In *Jane Austen on Screen*, edited by Gina Macdonald and Andrew F. Macdonald, 22–43. Cambridge: Cambridge University Press, 2003.

Maunder, Andrew. "Making Heritage and History: The 1894 Illustrated *Pride and Prejudice*." *Nineteenth-Century Studies* 20 (2006): 147–69.

Mazzeno, Laurence W. *Jane Austen: Two Centuries of Criticism*. Rochester, NY: Camden House, 2011.

Mirmohamadi, Kylie. *The Digital Afterlives of Jane Austen: Janeites at the Keyboard*. New York: Palgrave Macmillan, 2014.

Monaghan, David, Ariane Hudelet, and John Wiltshire, eds. *The Cinematic Jane Austen: Essays on the Filmic Sensibility of the Novels*. Jefferson, NC: Macfarland, 2009.

Nelson, Camilla. "Is Popularity Killing Jane Austen?" *Newsweek*, 10 March 2015. http://www.newsweek.com/popularity-killing-jane-austen-311974.

Newman, Emily L. "Illustrating Elizabeth Bennet and Mr. Darcy." *Journal of Illustration* 1, no. 2 (2014): 233–56.

Nigro, Jeffrey. "Visualizing Jane Austen and Jane Austen Visualizing." *Persuasions On-Line*. 29, no. 1 (Winter 2008). Web.

O'Farrell, Mary Ann. "'Bin Laden a Huge Jane Austen Fan': Jane Austen in Contemporary Political Discourse." In *Uses of Austen: Jane's Afterlives*, edited by Gillian Dow and Clare Harman, 192–207. New York: Palgrave Macmillan, 2012.

O'Malley, Ida Beatrice. *Women in Subjection: A Study of the Lives of Englishwomen before 1832*. London: Duckworth, 1933.

Parker, Keiko. "Illustrating Jane Austen," *Persuasions* 11 (1989): 22–27.

Parrill, Sue. *Jane Austen on Film and Television: A Critical Study of the Adaptations*. Jefferson, NC: McFarland, 2002.

Pellew, George. *Jane Austen's Novels*. Boston: Cupples, Upham, 1883.

Pucci, Suzanne R., and James Thompson, eds. *Jane Austen and Co.: Remaking the Past in Contemporary Culture*. Albany: State University of New York Press, 2003.

Raw, Laurence, and Robert G. Dryden, eds. *Global Jane Austen: Pleasure, Passion, and Possessiveness in the Jane Austen Community*. New York: Palgrave Macmillan, 2013.

Ray, Joan Klingel, ed. *Jane Austen's Popular and Critical Reputation: A Documentary Volume*. Vol. 365 of *Dictionary of Literary Biography*. Detroit: Gale Cengage, 2012.

Roach, Joseph. *It*. Ann Arbor: University of Michigan Press, 2007.

Robinson, Linda A. "Crinolines and Pantalettes: What MGM's Switch in Time Did to *Pride and Prejudice* (1940)." *Adaptation* 6, no. 3 (2013): 283–304.

Roth, Barry. *An Annotated Bibliography of Jane Austen Studies, 1952–72*. Charlottesville: University Press of Virginia, 1973.

———. *An Annotated Bibliography of Jane Austen Studies, 1973–83*. Charlottesville: University Press of Virginia, 1985.

———. *An Annotated Bibliography of Jane Austen Studies, 1984–94*. Athens: Ohio University Press, 1996.

Rumjanceva, Nadežda. "'And She Beheld a Striking Resemblance to Mr. Darcy': Nineteenth-Century Illustrations of Jane Austen's Pride and Prejudice." In *Pride and Prejudice 2.0: Interpretations, Adaptations and Transformations of Jane Austen's Classic*, edited by Hanne Birk and Marion Gymnich, 51–76. Göttingen: Bonn University Press, 2015.

Sales, Roger. *Jane Austen and Representations of Regency England*. London: Routledge, 1996.

Scholz, Anne-Marie. *An Orgy of Propriety: Jane Austen and the Emergence and Legacy of the Female Author in America, 1826–1926*. Trier: Wissenschaftllicher Verlag, 1999.

Scott, Jennifer. *After Jane: A Review of the Continuations and Completions of Jane Austen's Novels*. Bourne, Lincolnshire: Privately published, 1998.

Sørbø, Marie N. *Irony and Idyll: Jane Austen's "Pride and Prejudice" and "Mansfield Park" on Screen*. Amsterdam: Rodopi, 2014.

Soria, Cinthia García. "Austen Illustrators Henry and Charles Brock." *Mollands Circulating Library*. Web.

Southam, B. C. *Jane Austen: The Critical Heritage*. London: Routledge & Kegan Paul, 1968.

———. *Jane Austen: The Critical Heritage, 1870–1940*. Vol. 2. London: Routledge & Kegan Paul, 1987.

———. "Janeites and Anti-Janeites." In *The Jane Austen Handbook*, edited by J. David Grey, 237–43. London: Athlone Press, 1986.

Sullivan, Margaret C. *Jane Austen from Cover to Cover: 200 Years of Classic Covers*. Philadelphia: Quirk Books, 2014.

Sutherland, Kathryn. "Jane Austen on Screen." In *The Cambridge Companion to Jane Austen*. 2nd ed., edited by Edward Copeland and Juliet McMaster, 215–31. Cambridge: Cambridge University Press, 2011.

——. *Jane Austen's Textual Lives: From Aeschylus to Bollywood*. Oxford: Oxford University Press, 2005.

Todd, Janet, ed. *The Cambridge Companion to "Pride and Prejudice."* Cambridge: Cambridge University Press, 2013.

——. *Jane Austen in Context*. Cambridge: Cambridge University Press, 2005.

Trilling, Lionel. "Why We Read Jane Austen." *Times Literary Supplement*, 5 March 1976, 250–52.

Troost, Linda, and Sayre Greenfield, eds. *Jane Austen in Hollywood*. Lexington: University Press of Kentucky, 1998.

Turan, Kenneth. "*Pride and Prejudice*: An Informal History of the Garson-Olivier Motion Picture." *Persuasions* 11 (1989): 140–43.

Tytler, Sarah [Henrietta Keddie]. *Jane Austen and Her Works*. London: Cassell, Petter, Galpin, 1880.

Viveash, Chris. "The Bennets on Stage." *Jane Austen Society: Collected Reports, 2001–2005* (2003): 243–48.

——. "Jane Austen—as You Desire Her." *Jane Austen Society Report for 2015* (2015): 44–49.

Waller, P. J. *Writers, Readers, and Reputations: Literary Life in Britain, 1870–1918*. Oxford: Oxford University Press, 2006.

Weber, Brenda R. "For the Love of Jane: Austen, Adaptation, and Celebrity." *Adaptation in Contemporary Culture: Textual Infidelities*, edited by Rachel Carroll, 186–96. London: Continuum, 2009.

Wells, Juliette. *Everybody's Jane: Austen in the Popular Imagination*. London: Continuum, 2011.

West, Rebecca. *The Strange Necessity: Essays by Rebecca West*. Garden City, NY: Doubleday, 1928.

What Jane Saw. University of Texas-Austin. http://www.whatjanesaw.org.

Wiesenfarth, Joseph. "The Garson-Olivier Pride and Prejudice: A Hollywood Story." In *Text und Ton im Film*, edited by Paul Goetsch and Dietrich Scheunemann, 80–93. Tubingen: Narr, 1997.

Wilkes, Joanne. *Women Reviewing Women in Nineteenth-Century Britain: The Critical Reception of Jane Austen, Charlotte Brontë, and George Eliot*. Burlington, VT: Ashgate, 2010.

Wiltshire, John. *Recreating Jane Austen*. Cambridge: Cambridge University Press, 2001.

Wootton, Sarah. *Byronic Heroes in Nineteenth-Century Women's Writing and Screen Adaptation*. Basingstoke, UK: Palgrave Macmillan, 2016.

Wright, Andrew. "Dramatizations of the Novel." In *The Jane Austen Companion*, edited by J. David Grey, 120–30. New York: Macmillan, 1986.

——. "Jane Austen Adapted." *Nineteenth-Century Fiction* 30, no. 3 (December 1975): 421–53.

Yaffe, Deborah. *Among the Janeites: A Journey through the World of Jane Austen Fandom*. Boston: Mariner Books, 2013.